FIRST MEN, AMERICA'S PRESIDENTS

JOHN F. KENNEDY: THE NEW FRONTIER PRESIDENT

(A VOLUME IN FIRST MEN, AMERICA'S PRESIDENTS SERIES)

OTHER BOOKS IN THE FIRST MEN, AMERICA'S PRESIDENTS SERIES

Barbara Bennett Peterson, Series Editor

Citizen Lincoln
Ward M. Mcafee
2004. ISBN 1-59454-112-4
2008. ISBN 978-1-60456-628-4
(Softcover)

Theodore Roosevelt: A Political Life
Thomas Lansford
2004. ISBN 1-59033-990-8

George Washington, America's Moral Exemplar
Barbara Bennett Peterson
2005. ISBN 1-59454-230-9
2011. ISBN 978-1-61761-678-5
(Softcover)

John Quincy Adams: Yankee Nationalist
Paul E. Teed
2005. ISBN 1-59454-797-1
2010. ISBN 978-1-60876-914-8
(Softcover)
2001. ISBN 978-1-61761-172-8
(E-book)

President James K. Polk
Louise Mayo
2006. ISBN 1-59454-718-1

Franklin Delano Roosevelt, Preserver of Spirit and Hope
Barbara Bennett Peterson
2006. ISBN 1-60021-117-8
2008. ISBN 978-1-60456-496-9
(Softcover)

Benjamin Harrison: Centennial President
Anne Chieko Moore and Hester Anne Hale
2006. ISBN 1-60021-606-X
2009. ISBN 978-1-60456-330-6
(Softcover)
2009. ISBN 978-1-61728-668-1
(E-book)

President Zachary Taylor: The Hero President
Elbert B. Smith
2007 ISBN 1-60021-602-1
2010. ISBN 978-1-60876-912-4
(Softcover)
2010. ISBN 978-1-61761-173-5
(E-book)

Chester Alan Arthur: The Life of a Gilded Age Politician and President
Gregory J. Dehler
2007. ISBN 1-60021-079-1
2010. ISBN 978-1-60876-913-1
(Softcover)

In the Shadow of the Great Rebellion: The Life of Andrew Johnson, Seventeenth President of the United States (1808-1875)
G.L. Donhardt
2007. ISBN 1-60021-086-4
2007. ISBN 978-1-60456-944-5 (Softcover)

William Henry Harrison: General and President
Mary Jane Child Queen
2007. ISBN 1-600-21407-X

President Herbert Hoover
Donald W. Whisenhunt
2007. ISBN 1-60021-476-2
2008. ISBN 978-1-60456-382-5 (Softcover)

Woodrow Wilson: The Last Romantic
Mary Stockwell
2008. ISBN 1-60021-815-6

John Tyler: A Rare Career
Lyle Nelson
2008. ISBN 1-60021-961-6
2011. ISBN 978-1-61761-668-6 (Softcover)

Thomas Jefferson: A Public Life, A Private Life
David Kiracofe
2008. ISBN 978-1-60456-061-9
2011. ISBN 978-1-61761-679-2 (Softcover)

Martin Van Buren: The Little Magician
Pierre-Marie Loizeau
2008. ISBN 978-1-60456-773-1
2011. ISBN 978-1-61761-781-2 (Softcover)
2008. ISBN 978-1-61668-054-1 (E-book)

James Madison: Defender of the American Republic
Donald Dewey
2009. ISBN 978-1-60456-858-5
2011 ISBN 978-1-61761-669-3 (Softcover)

John F. Kennedy: The New Frontier President
David L. Snead
2010. ISBN 978-1-61668-925-4
2010. ISBN 978-1-61728-777-0 (E-book)

Andrew Jackson in Context
Matthew Warshauer
2009. ISBN 978-1-60741-709-5

William H. Taft
Richard G. Frederick
2010. ISBN 978-1-60876-917-9
2010. ISBN 978-1-61668-821-9 (E-book)

The Presidency of Grover Cleveland
Joel D. Benson
2010. ISBN 978-1-60876-974-2

FIRST MEN, AMERICA'S PRESIDENTS

JOHN F. KENNEDY: THE NEW FRONTIER PRESIDENT

(A VOLUME IN FIRST MEN, AMERICA'S PRESIDENTS SERIES)

DAVID L. SNEAD

Nova Science Publishers, Inc.
New York

LIBRARY OF CONGRESS CATALOGING-IN-PUBLICATION DATA

Snead, David L. (David Lindsey)
John F. Kennedy : the new frontier president / David L. Snead ; editor, Barbara Bennett Peterson.
p. cm.
Includes bibliographical references and index.
ISBN 978-1-61668-925-4 (hardcover : alk. paper)
1. Kennedy, John F. (John Fitzgerald), 1917-1963. 2. United States--Politics and government--1961-1963. 3. United States--Economic policy--1961-1971. 4. United States--Social policy. I. Peterson, Barbara Bennett, 1942- II. Title.
E841.S58 2010
973.922092--dc22
[B]

2010026077

Published by Nova Science Publishers, Inc. ✝ New York

CONTENTS

PREFACE

President of the United States of America is an official title sought by many and won by only a few individuals. Most American Presidents are of high merit and political acumen and reflected wisdom, leadership, and integrity. This series titled *First Men, America's Presidents* published by NOVA Science Publishers contains a book length biography of each President of the United States of America. Every book contains information on the President's early education, professional career, military service or political service prior to the presidency, interpretative discussion of both domestic and foreign policies during each presidency, and the conclusion of their political lives in public service. Every presidential biography in the NOVA series has been written by a professional historian or political scientist well versed in the field of presidential scholarship. The two major themes of this series are the character traits marking success in the presidency, and the changes in the office of the presidency through America's history. Character matters in all walks of life, but perhaps matters most within the character of the President of the United States.

The duties of the President of the United States are delegated through Article II of the Constitution of the United States of America, and from the successive laws passed by Congress over time. Each president takes the Oath of Affirmation:--"I do solemnly swear (or affirm) that I will faithfully execute the Office of the President of the United States, and will to the best of my Ability, preserve, protect and defend the Constitution of the United States." The president's duties and responsibilities under the Constitution are to serve as "Commander in Chief of the Army and Navy of the United States, and the Militia of the several States, when called into actual Service of the United States." The president may invite the counsel and opinions of his various department heads upon any subject related to the execution of the duties of their offices, either in writing or orally as has become the custom within the president's Cabinet. The president "shall have the power to grant Reprieves and Pardons for Offenses against the United States, except in Cases of Impeachment." Every president has realized that each must administer through constitutional principles, as each was elected by the voting majority of the people to be their chief executive through the Electoral College. Each president of the United States "shall have Power, by and with the Advice and Consent of the Senate, to make Treaties, provided two thirds of the Senators present concur." As the president directs both the domestic and foreign activities of the government, he has the power to "nominate and by and with the Advice and Consent of the Senate....appoint Ambassadors, other public Ministers and Consuls, Judges of the Supreme Court, and all other Officers of the United States, whose Appointments are not herein otherwise provided for, and which shall be established by law." The president also receives foreign ambassadors and officials on behalf of the American people. The president "shall have the Power to fill up all Vacancies that may happen during the Recess of the Senate, by granting Commissions which shall expire at the End of their next Session." The president under the Constitution shall give Congress a State of the Union address every year to acquaint them with his policy agenda and plans for the future. Usually in this address to Congress he recommends "to their Consideration such Measures as he shall judge necessary and expedient." Above all, the president of the United States "shall take Care that the Laws be faithfully executed, and shall Commission all the Officers of the United States." A strong role for the President had been envisioned by the Founding Fathers who rejected the obsolete Articles of Confederation and replaced the framework of government with the Constitution of the United States. Article II of the Constitution outlining the powers of the presidency provided that the office of the President would be held by one individual. It provided the President with enumerated powers including the power of the veto. And stipulated that the president's election would be above the control of the Congress to ensure the separation of powers and the system of checks and balances. It stipulated that the president, vice president, and all civil officers of the United States *must govern in the name of the American people* lest they "be removed from Office on Impeachment for, and Conviction of Treason, Bribery, or other high Crimes and Misdemeanors."

From Presidents George Washington through John Quincy Adams candidates for the presidency were selected in caucuses of senators and congressmen and then the state legislatures indirectly chose the president through the selection of Electors to the Electoral College. This system had worked for Washington, Adams, Jefferson, Madison and Monroe—they were statesmen who held wide appeal within Congress and the state legislatures and claimed to represent the people. But as demands for greater democracy in the election process were heard, the process was changed. In the outcome of the election of 1824, John Quincy Adams was chosen president by the Congressional House of Representatives under constitutional law after no candidate had received a majority of the electoral ballots in the Electoral College. Jackson, the candidate who had received the most popular votes was not chosen president and his supporters called for more direct popular participation and worked to introduce changes. Hence, the voting process was altered in the name of democracy. In the election of 1828 President Andrew Jackson triumphed after voting had been given directly to the people and removed from the state legislatures. Democracy further triumphed by the elimination of the congressional caucuses in naming presidential candidates and the holding of national political party conventions to name them instead, allowing greater voice and participation of the people. The institution of the party convention to nominate presidential candidates remains, although winners in various state primaries command party delegates to vote the choice of the people. The Presidency, molded by the character and designs of each president, oversees command, administration, diplomacy, ceremony, legislation, and public opinion. The modern strength of the Presidency is a reflection of the mighty power of the United States within a global world.

The majority of America's presidents have served for one four-year term or less as some died in office. Four presidents served out part of their predecessor's term and won subsequent re-election in their own right: Theodore Roosevelt, Calvin Coolidge, Harry S. Truman, and Lyndon Baines Johnson. Only one president, Grover Cleveland, was elected to two discontinuous terms of office and thus was both the twenty-second and the twenty-fourth president of the United States. Several outstanding presidents have been elected to two four-year terms or more. They were: George Washington, Thomas Jefferson, James Madison, James Monroe, Andrew Jackson, Abraham Lincoln, Ulysses S. Grant, Grover Cleveland, William McKinley, Woodrow Wilson, Franklin D. Roosevelt, Dwight D. Eisenhower, Richard Nixon, Ronald Reagan, William Jefferson ("Bill") Clinton, and George W. Bush. Only one president, Franklin D. Roosevelt, was elected for a third and fourth term. Eight presidents have achieved their office as a result of being the vice-president of a preceding president who died in office or resigned: John Tyler, Millard Fillmore, Andrew Johnson, Chester Arthur,

Theodore Roosevelt, Calvin Coolidge, Harry S. Truman, Lyndon Baines Johnson, and Gerald R. Ford. Additionally, John Adams, Thomas Jefferson, Martin Van Buren, Richard M. Nixon and George H.W. Bush also rose from the office of vice-president to president. Besides the vice-presidency as a stepping stone to the presidency, two thirds of the presidents elected had held congressional office earlier in their political careers such as Barack Obama, America's 44th President elected in 2008 who had served as a Senator from Illinois. Twenty presidents had served as Governors of states or territories before being elected. They were: Thomas Jefferson (Virginia), James Monroe (Virginia), Andrew Jackson (Florida), Martin Van Buren (New York), William Henry Harrison (Indiana), John Tyler (Virginia), James K. Polk (Tennessee), Andrew Johnson (Tennessee), Rutherford B. Hayes (Ohio), Grover Cleveland (New York), William McKinley (Ohio), Theodore Roosevelt (New York), William Howard Taft (The Philippines), Woodrow Wilson (New Jersey), Calvin Coolidge (Massachusetts), Franklin D. Roosevelt (New York), Jimmy Carter (Georgia), Ronald Reagan (California), William Jefferson Clinton (Arkansas), and George W. Bush (Texas). Some states with larger voting populations and hence more electoral votes have seen their native sons rise to the presidency of the United States. The American Presidents have come from both coasts, east and west, and from both the upper tier and the lower tier of states geographically, north and south. When elected, the president becomes the president of 'all the people', not just those of his political party. Since the president acts as America's commander in chief, the majority of the presidents of the United States have served in the U.S. military. George Washington, Andrew Jackson, William Henry Harrison, Zachary Taylor, Franklin Pierce, Ulysses S. Grant, Rutherford B. Hayes, James Garfield, Chester Arthur, Benjamin Harrison, and Dwight David Eisenhower served in the capacity of generals. James Monroe, John Tyler, Abraham Lincoln, William McKinley, Theodore Roosevelt, Harry Truman, John F. Kennedy, Lyndon Baines Johnson, Richard Nixon, Gerald R. Ford, Jimmy Carter, Ronald Reagan, George Herbert Walker Bush, and George W. Bush also served their country in military service at various ranks, and always with dedication. The youngest elected president was John F. Kennedy (1960) at forty-three. The youngest man to ever serve as president was Theodore Roosevelt who at forty-two assumed the office following William McKinley's assassination. The average age for an elected president was fifty-four. The oldest elected president was Ronald Reagan at sixty-nine (1980) and seventy-three (1984).[1]

---

[1] David C. Whitney and Robin Vaughn Whitney, *The American Presidents,* Garden City, New

One of the major features of American constitutional development has been the growth of the presidency both in power and prestige as well as in new Cabinet positions, departments and agencies under the control of the president. The Federal government has grown mightily in comparison with the States' governments since the inception of the Constitution. Increases in presidential powers have been occasioned by wars, depressions, foreign relations, and the agenda of the presidents themselves. Henry F. Graff, Emeritus Professor at Columbia University, described the office of the president as "the most powerful office in the world" in *The Presidents.* The Executive Office of the President (EOP) was created during the administration of President Franklin D. Roosevelt upon passage by Congress of the Reorganization Act of 1939. The EOP originally included the White House Office (WHO), the Bureau of the Budget, the Office of Government Reports, the National Resources Planning Board, and the Liaison Office for Personnel Management. In addition, wrote Henry F. Graff, the 1939 Act provided that an "office for emergency management" may be formed "in the event of a national emergency, or threat of a national emergency." [2] Today the White House Office has become "the political as well as policy arm of the chief executive." The larger, all encompassing Executive Office of the President has expanded through time to include a myriad number of departments in addition to the first five listed above and the president is advised by nearly 60 active boards, committees and commissions. During and immediately after World War II the following additional departments within the purview of the EOP were organized: Committee for Congested Production Areas, 1943-1944, War Refugee Board, 1944-1945, Council of Economic Advisers, 1946-, National Security Council, 1947-, and National Security Resources Board, 1947-1953. During the Cold War, additions to the EOP were made adding the following departments: Telecommunications Adviser to the President, 1951-1953, Office of the Director for Mutual Security, 1951-1954, Office of Defense Mobilization, 1952-1958, President's Advisory Committee on Government Organization, 1953-1961, Operations Coordinating Board, 1953-1961, President's Board of Consultants on Foreign Intelligence Activities, 1956-1961, Office of Civil and Defense Mobilization, 1958-1962, and National Aeronautics and Space Council, 1958-1993. By the Sixties, some of the earlier departments organized in the 1939 to 1960 decades were allowed to close, with newer agencies with a new focus and expanded technology taking their

York: Doubleday, 1993, pp. v-ix.

[2] Henry F. Graff, Editor, *The Presidents,* New York: Charles Scribner's Sons, Simon & Schuster Macmillan, 2nd edition, 1996, Appendix C pp. 743-745.

place. These newer agencies included: President's Foreign Intelligence Advisory Board, 1961-1977, Office of Emergency Planning, 1962-1969, Office of Science and Technology, 1962-1973, Office of Economic Opportunity, 1964-1975, Office of Emergency Preparedness, 1965-1973, National Council on Marine Resources and Engineering Development, 1966-1971, Council on Environmental Quality, 1969-, Council for Urban Affairs, 1969-1970, and Office of Intergovernmental Relations, 1969-1973. By the mid-Seventies, once again there was a general reorganization with some of the earlier departments and offices being swept away and replaced by newer agencies reflecting new presidential agendas. Many of the new agencies reflected the urgencies in domestic policies and included: the Domestic Council, 1970-1978, Office of Management and Budget, 1970-, Office of Telecommunications Policy, 1970-1977, Council on International Economic Policy, 1971-1977, Office of Consumer Affairs, 1971-1973, Special Action Office for Drug Abuse Prevention, 1971-1975, Federal Property Council, 1973-1977, Council on Economic Policy, 1973-1974, Energy Policy Office, 1973-1974, Council on Wage and Price Stability, 1974-1981, Energy Resource Council, 1974-1977, Office of Special Representative for Trade Negotiations, 1974-, Presidential Clemency Board, 1974-1975, Office of Science and Technology Policy, 1976-, Office of Administration, 1977-, and Domestic Policy Staff, 1978-1981. Many of the departments, councils and agencies organized as part of the Executive Office of the President by the late Seventies and early Eighties included: Office of Policy Development, 1981-, Office of the U.S. Trade Representative, 1981-, National Critical Materials Council, 1984-, Office of National Drug Control Policy, 1988-, National Economic Council, 1993-. By the 21st Century the EOP continued several effective agencies started earlier: Council of Economic Advisers 1946-, National Security Council 1947-, Council on Environmental Quality 1964-, Office of Management and Budget 1970-, Office of Science and Technology Policy 1976-, Office of Administration 1977-, Office of the U.S. Trade Representative 1981-, Office of Policy Development 1981-, and the Office of National Drug Control Policy 1988-. In addition to the White House Office of the president, the Office of the Vice President functions and is administered as part of the EOP.[3] At the turn of the millennium the department of Homeland Security 2001- was established by presidential Executive Order and

[3] Henry F. Graff, Editor, *The Presidents,* New York: Charles Scribner's Sons, Simon & Schuster Macmillan, 3rd edition, 2002, Appendix C pp. 743-747.

administered by the Executive Office of the President that continues to be evolutionary in response to new issues, demands, and events.

Capable presidents have responded to America's changing needs and responsibilities by retooling their administrations to meet new crises, opportunities, and challenges. This series *First Men, America's Presidents* published by NOVA explains the personal and public life of each President of the United States. Their qualities of character and leadership are aptly interpreted and offer strong role models for all citizens. Presidential successes are recorded for posterity, as are the pitfalls that should be guarded against in the future. This series also explains the domestic reasons and world backdrop for the expansion of the Executive Office of the President. The President of the United States is perhaps the most coveted position in the world and this series reveals the lives of all those successfully elected, how each performed as president, and how each is to be measured in history. The collective life stories of the presidents reveal the greatness that America represents in the world.

Dr. Barbara Bennett Peterson
First Men, America's Presidents NOVA Series Editor
Professor of History, Oregon State University (retired)
Emeritus Professor University of Hawaii
Former Adjunct Fellow East-West Center
Professor of History, California State University San Bernardino, Palm Desert

ACKNOWLEDGMENTS

While authors ultimately get credit for writing books, no author has written a book where he or she did not receive significant assistance from people at every stage of the publishing process. This book is no exception. I began this project in 2004 with plans on completing it in a few years. However, as so often happens with best made plans, I was delayed on numerous occasions. Without the help of many people, I would not have been able to finish it when I did.

I must first thank Barbara Bennett Peterson, the editor of the *First Men, America's Presidents* series, for asking me to do this study and then showing unbelievable patience as I slowly finished it. She has supported me throughout and shown considerable skill in editing my work. I also want to thank the editors and staff at Nova Science Publishers for deciding to publish the series and providing the necessary support to get it done.

As with any project, I have relied heavily on colleagues for support and guidance. The project began while I was teaching at Texas Tech University. My history department chair, Bruce Daniels, provided the assistance I needed to make my first trip to the John F. Kennedy Library. Jorge Iber and Gretchen Adams encouraged me to accept the challenge of writing a book on the Kennedy administration. I will forever cherish my friendships with them.

My visits to the Kennedy Library to gather materials for the book were intellectually challenging and rewarding. The Kennedy Library awarded me a travel grant in 2005 that facilitated my research. I am particularly indebted to the library's grant coordinator, Sharon Kelly, for working with me through the grant process. I also must express my appreciation to the archivists at the library who answered my many questions and directed me to documents that were very helpful in my research.

I moved to Liberty University in 2004 and have had the opportunity to work with a wonderful History Department. I cannot imagine a more collegial or helpful group of scholars. Over the years, many of them have read parts of the manuscript, discussed events from the Kennedy years, and been constant fountains of support. I want to particularly thank Michael Davis, Doug Mann, Bill Matheny, Roger Schultz, and Sam Smith for the many hours they have spent with me discussing Kennedy and history in general. Last, but not least, I have to thank Kris Burdeaux, the History Department secretary, for her dedication and assistance in bringing this project to completion.

As anybody who knows me realizes, I truly cherish my family. I have dedicated this book to my mom, Marilyn Snead, who has supported me for over four decades. The words "Thank You" do not begin to express my appreciation for all she has done for me. My in-laws, D.C. and Carolyn Hughes, have treated me like their own son. They have provided love and support, and made themselves available whenever my family needed their assistance. They have earned my deepest respect and gratitude. My children, Reagan, Delaney, and Darel, have brought more joy to my life than they will ever know. They have been incredibly patient and supportive of their daddy as he worked on a project that they had no way of understanding. Their love is amazing. Without them, I would not have been able to get through the bumps and grinds of life.

My final thank you goes to my wife, Lori Snead. She has been and will forever be the love of my life. When I was ready to give up on this project on several occasions, she was always there to encourage me. On my many research trips, she had to manage the house and raise our children by herself, and she did so without complaint. When I finished drafts of chapters, I knew I could always rely on her for providing a careful review. The manuscript is better because of her efforts. While I will never be able to express by love and appreciation to her sufficiently, I will never stop telling her "Thank You" and "I Love You."

Chapter 1

IN TRAINING FOR THE WHITE HOUSE

In the early afternoon on November 22, 1963, America's activity came to a crashing halt. The unthinkable happened—President John F. Kennedy was dead, a victim of an assassin's bullet as he rode through the streets of Dallas, Texas. As millions of Americans uttered questions like "How?" and "Why?", pundits were already debating the deceased president's legacy.[1] Even now, decades after his assassination, college students ask me for more information about this "great" president than for any other American leader. Who was this man who served less than one full term in office but has been both revered and jeered every since? Kennedy's background before he became president gives some hints to the man who would lead the country through some of its most difficult times.

John Kennedy, who was called Jack from birth by his family and close friends, was only 46 years old at the time of his death. Next to Teddy Roosevelt, Kennedy had been America's youngest president. He had a young, beautiful wife and two little children. His life showed so much promise but now it was over. Who was this man and why does he remain such an influential figure in America history?

His story begins in Brookline, Massachusetts where on May 29, 1917 Rose Fitzgerald Kennedy gave birth to her second son, John Fitzgerald Kennedy. John's older brother, Joe, Jr. had been born in July 1915, and Rose would go on to have seven more children by 1932. John's father, Joe, Sr. was

---

[1] See "Editorial Reaction to Kennedy's Death," November 24, 1963, *New York Times*, p. 10. For an early scholarly attempt at assessing the Kennedy presidency, see Richard E. Neustadt, "Kennedy in the Presidency: A Premature Appraisal," *Political Science Quarterly*, 79:3 (September 1964), pp. 321-334.

a Boston businessman who built on his parents' fortunes.[2] John grew up in a privileged environment, wanted for little, and never faced any significant material hardship.

John's ancestors originated in Ireland and immigrated to the United States during the 1840s and 1850s because of the Irish Potato Famines. His grandfathers, Patrick Joseph "P.J." Kennedy and John F. "Fitz" Fitzgerald, were born in Boston in the late 1850s and early 1860s. P.J. was born in 1858 and while his family was not rich, he managed to earn a scholarship to Boston College. After graduating, he made his living in the liquor business and became very active in local politics. He was elected to the Massachusetts legislature in 1884 and served there for over a decade. In 1888 his wife, Mary Augusta Hickey, gave birth to Joseph Patrick Kennedy—John's father. John Fitzgerald's parents, although also recent immigrants, had prospered more than P.J.'s. "Fitz" attended an elite public school before enrolling at Boston College. While a banker by trade, he, like P.J., was very interested in local politics. In 1892 he was elected to the Massachusetts Senate; later served in the U.S. Congress; and in 1906, became the first Irish-Catholic mayor of Boston. He married Mary Josephine Hannon in 1889, and she eventually gave birth to six children, the oldest being Rose Elizabeth—Kennedy's mother. By the early 20th century, the Kennedys and the Fitzgeralds were two of the most prominent families in Boston.[3]

Joe Kennedy grew up with a great deal of wealth but always felt discriminated against because he was Irish-Catholic. He admired the great capitalist of his day—John Rockefeller, Andrew Carnegie, and J.P. Morgan—and dreamed one day of being one himself. He had an eye for business, and he made his first small fortune during the summer between his junior and senior years at Harvard University when he operated a small tour bus company. From an investment of $600, he made $10,000. After graduating from Harvard, he began a career best described as him being an entrepreneur. His first job was a bank examiner, and by age 25, he was the president of Columbia Trust. During World War I he supervised a major shipyard in Massachusetts and met then

[2] The best single volume on Kennedy's life and presidency is Robert Dallek, *An Unfinished Life: John F. Kennedy, 1917-1963* (Boston: Little, Brown and Company, 2003). I have relied heavily on his descriptions of Kennedy's family life in this chapter.

[3] Thomas C. Reeves, *A Question of Character: A Life of John F. Kennedy* (New York: The Free Press, 1991), pp. 19-20. For more detailed studies of Joe Kennedy, see also David Talbot, *Brothers: The Hidden History of the Kennedy Years* (New York: Free Press, 2007); Richard J. Whalen, *Founding Father: The Story of Joseph P. Kennedy* (New York: New American Library, 1964); and Laurence Leamer, *The Kennedy Men: 1901-1963* (New York: William Morrow, 2001).

Assistant Secretary of the Navy Franklin Delano Roosevelt for the first time. After the war he began to work as a stock broker, and by the early 1920s he had reportedly made nearly $2 million. He also owned a company during Prohibition that had a license to import alcohol for medicinal purposes legally. He managed to make several million dollars in profit by stockpiling alcohol before the end of Prohibition and selling it as soon as it ended. Beyond these investments and businesses, he bought and sold several Hollywood movie studios in the 1920s, bringing him even more wealth.[4]

Rose Fitzgerald was her father's favorite and grew up amidst great wealth. She was very intelligent and graduated from high school at age 15. She was also quite pretty. Rose met Joe Kennedy when they were children and had fallen in love in the summer of 1906.[5] Since her father did not believe the Kennedys were social equals, he decided it would be best if he kept the two teenagers apart. While he was able to do so for eight years, he ultimately relented in 1914, and they married.

Rose and Joe had a challenging marriage, as he traveled extensively and was a widely known womanizer. Rose's devout Catholicism also caused some difficulties as she tried to conform to the church's teachings when Joe was not as interested. Rose was also the disciplinarian in the family. She later asserted that "I often used a ruler [for spankings]—and sometimes a coat hanger which was often more convenient because in any room there would be a closet and the hangers in them would be right at hand."[6] On the other hand, Joe was anything but a disciplinarian. He liked to buck convention and really enjoyed the company of other women. He was so brazen that he even brought some of his mistresses to the family house. To make the marriage work, Rose and Joe developed a working arrangement where she put up with his womanizing, and he supported her travels, especially to Europe. Without question, John Kennedy's own womanizing was little more than following in his own father's footsteps.[7]

All of the Kennedy children grew up in a very privileged environment. John Kennedy was closest to his older brother Joe, Jr. while growing up. They very much had a love-hate relationship. His brother always pushed John to do more whether it meant running faster or swimming further. They once played a game of chicken on their bicycles where Joe rode his bike down one hill and

[4] Reeves, *A Question of Character*, pp. 23-25.

[5] Ibid., p. 25.

[6] Quoted in "Writing Reveal Mother at Heart of Kennedy Dynasty," September 29, 2006, found at www.cnn.com, accessed on October 2, 2006.

[7] For Kennedy's family history, see Dallek, *An Unfinished Life*, pp. 7-35.

John rode his down another towards each other. Both brothers refused to turn and collided in the street. While Joe emerged from the collision only a little shaken, John had to get twenty-eight stitches.[8] Despite hating not being able to always keep up with his brother, John admired his brother more than anyone.

One of the things that slowed John down was his poor health. He suffered bouts of bronchitis, chicken pox, German measles, measles, mumps, scarlet fever (which left him in the hospital for over two months just before he turned three), and whooping cough. As he grew up, his health remained a constant worry. At no time was John completely healthy.[9] One of his family's jokes was that any mosquito biting John would face a grave risk of death because it had ingested some of the future president's blood.[10]

John showed irreverence for authority figures from an early age and was not very concerned about others around him. The Kennedy family employed numerous domestic servants, and John quickly recognized that they were at his beck and call. He generally did not pick up after himself as he could always depend on servants to come after him. He was almost never on time but never suffered any negative consequences. Historian Robert Dallek argues that John "did not feel he had to live by the ordinary rules governing everyone else. He was always arriving late for meals and classes, setting his own pace, taking the less traveled path."[11] His lackadaisical attitude towards those around him extended to his mother's great love—the Roman Catholic Church. Similar to his father, he saw little need for religion.[12] He even considered renouncing his family's Catholicism in the early 1940s. By the time he was a teenager, John had a reputation for being competitive, smart when he wanted to be, and challenging to those who were around him.

John went to a series of private schools in the 1920s and 1930s and suffered no depravations from the Great Depression. His grades reveal a

[8] Ibid., p. 28.

[9] A brief, but good biographical sketch of Kennedy's life can be found at http://www.jfklibrary.org/Historical+Resources/Biographies+and+Profiles/Biographies/John+F.+Kennedy+The+35th+President+of+the+United+States.htm, accessed on August 4, 2006.

[10] Ibid.

[11] Dallek, *An Unfinished Life*, pp. 32.

[12] Richard Goodwin, one of Kennedy's speech writers during the 1960 campaign and an adviser to him during his presidency later claimed, "John Kennedy was among the most secular of men, his values derived not from his catechism, but from the mainstream of Western thought, Christian and pagan." Richard N. Goodwin, *Remembering America: A Voice from the Sixties* (Boston: Little, Brown and Company, 1988), p. 110. James Wolfe argues that "Kennedy's own religion was composed of Catholicism, humanism, and patriotism" and Catholicism was "the weakest strand." James S. Wolfe, "The Religion of and about John F. Kennedy," in Paul Harper and Joann P. Krieg, eds., *John F. Kennedy: The Promise Revisited* (New York: Greenwood Press, 1988), p. 288.

general lack of interest in schoolwork. His report card from the Canterbury School in the late fall 1930 showed John's fairly typical range of grades. He earned a failing grade in Latin, average grades in history, science and religion, a good grade in English, and an excellent grade in math.[13] As far as the Depression, John later claimed, "I have no first-hand knowledge of the depression…. I really did not learn about the depression until I read about it at Harvard."[14] From 1931 to 1935 he went to Choate, an elite boarding school for the well-to-do. He remained very active there between major bouts of undiagnosed illnesses. Sports and having fun, not education, were his main desires. Simply getting by was key to him. At one point, he even organized the so-called "Muckers" Club whose only purpose was to defy rules. While he only graduated 65th out of the 110 students in his class, he still "earned" admission to Princeton and eventually, Harvard. He stayed at Princeton for less than a year before enrolling in Harvard in 1936.[15]

While at Harvard, John remained an average student but did develop a special interest in contemporary politics, especially the rising crisis in Europe in the late 1930s. Since his father was the U.S. ambassador to Great Britain from 1937 to 1940, John was able to pursue his interest while watching the deteriorating conditions in Europe. He traveled throughout much of Europe, and because of his father's connections, he gained audiences with many European leaders. Interestingly, despite his father's well-known anti-Semitism and pro-Germany views, John came to see Germany as a great threat and considered the decision by Great Britain and France to appease Hitler at the September 1938 Munich Conference a colossal mistake. For his senior thesis, John pursued his interest in the coming of World War II and utilized his father's connections to gather research materials on the Munich Conference. He used the information to evaluate how Great Britain, in particular, had developed its policies as Adolf Hitler rose to power. While his thesis committee found his work solid, no one envisioned his ideas as path-breaking.[16] However, his father called upon his friend, *N.Y. Times'* columnist Arthur Krock, to help John with revisions and later to get the study published with the title of *Why England Slept*.

---

[13] See his report card at http://www.jfklibrary.org/Historical+Resources/Biographies+and+Profiles/Biographies/John+F.+Kennedy+The+35th+President+of+the+United+States.htm , accessed on August 4, 2006.

[14] Quoted in Dallek, *An Unfinished Life*, p. 31.

[15] Ibid., pp. 37-41.

[16] Ibid., pp. 49-65.

Kennedy argued in his book that Great Britain's policies were shortsighted because it had been unwilling to rearm in the face of the growing crisis in Europe. With the help of his father's friends, the book received a great deal of attention and became a bestseller. The editor of *Time* magazine, Henry Luce, asserted "For all Americans who are wide awake enough to read—and that, thank God, would seem to include most of us now—this book is invaluable." Joe Kennedy's friend Arthur Krock called the book, "An unmistakable lesson for the people of the United States."[17]

While John was proud of his first book, his academic performance did not reflect the same interest. Beyond his love of history and contemporary politics, John was mostly concerned about sports and women. The competition he had enjoyed with his older brother carried over into his college years. He played football at Harvard until he ruptured a disk in his back and also swam on the swim team. He only surpassed his athletic prowess with his pursuit of women. Without question, John viewed women as opportunities for conquest and considered it a major accomplishment to have sex with any woman he saw as desirable. He bragged to a friend in the late 1930s, "I can now get my tail as often and as free as I want which is a step in the right direction."[18] John's desires and actions in this area did not recede as his career unfolded. Unfortunately, his affairs complicated both his private and public life in the years to come.

John graduated cum laude from Harvard in 1940 with a degree in government. While John listed his intended career as in law in the 1940 Harvard yearbook; upon his graduation, he really had no set plans.[19]

One dominant feature of the remainder of John's life was his struggles with health problems. He never fully recovered from his college back injury and continued to struggle with other illnesses, in particular stomach problems. His father helped him get some of the best medical care available at the time. Unfortunately, some of the care involved experimental medications, including steroids, that probably did more harm than good. His health problems left him

---

17 "Out Today!," August 1, 1940, *New York Times*, p. 19.

18 Quoted in Dallek, *An Unfinished Life*, p. 46. See also Christopher Andersen, *John and Jackie: Portrait of an American Marriage* (New York: William Morrow and Company, Inc.), pp. 38-9.

19 See Kennedy's 1940 Harvard Yearbook Entry at http://www.jfklibrary.org/Historical+Resources/Biographies+and+Profiles/Biographies/John+F.+Kennedy+The+35th+President+of+the+United+States.htm, accessed on August 4, 2006. See also "List of Candidates for Degrees at Today's Harvard Commencement," June 20, 1940, *New York Times*, p. 27.

with the belief that his life would be short, and he should live it to the fullest.[20] They also hampered his efforts to join the American military after the fall of France and the beginning of the Battle of Britain in the summer of 1940.

No doubt influenced by his brother's decision to join the navy and become a pilot, and his own sense of patriotism, John wanted to join the military. His desire grew even more after Congress passed the Selective Service Act in September 1940 initiating the first peacetime draft in American history. John did not want to miss out on the big adventure, but his back injury and other health problems seemed to preclude military service. Both the army and the navy rejected his initial efforts to enlist. It was only after his father intervened and found a navy doctor who was willing to overlook John's medical history and approve his fitness for military duty that the navy finally accepted him. He began training as a Seaman Second Class in July 1941 and was commissioned as an ensign in October 1941.[21]

John's naval career got off to an inauspicious start during his first assignment in the U.S. Navy's Office of Intelligence in Washington, D.C. He began a relationship with Inga Arvad, a beautiful blonde Danish reporter working for the *New York Times*. Unfortunately, Arvad, or as John called her "Inga-Binga", also had connections to key leaders in Nazi Germany. The acting director of the Federal Bureau of Investigation (FBI) J. Edgar Hoover believed she was a spy. Hoover went as far as to place wiretaps in the hotel rooms where John and Arvad rendezvoused. John's romance also bothered Joe Kennedy. He did not like that Arvad was divorced and not a Catholic. While he did not hold to most of the church's teachings, he did not want to damage the Kennedy reputation amongst fellow Catholics. Furthermore, he also heard rumors of her Nazi connections, and he became worried that a disloyal tag might become attached to the Kennedy name. To avert this possible disaster, Joe got John transferred from Washington to a desk job in Charleston, S.C. While Arvad and John tried to continue their relationship from a distance for a short time, it eventually fizzled out.[22]

John's desire to serve in a combat zone led him to look continually for opportunities to transfer to a front-line assignment. In 1942, he entered Officer's Training School at Northwestern University where he graduated as a

---

[20] For an interesting examination of the influence of various ailments and medications on Kennedy's life, especially as president, see History News Network Staff, "Dallek and Kennedy: The Media Reaction," found at http://hnn.us/articles/1113.html, accessed on October 2, 2006.

[21] Dallek, *An Unfinished Life*, pp. 73-81.

[22] See James N. Giglio, *The Presidency of John F. Kennedy* (Lawrence: University of Kansas Press, 1991), pp. 19-20; and Dallek, *An Unfinished Life*, pp. 83-85.

lieutenant. Through his father's connections, John was then able to obtain an assignment to train as a PT-boat commander. Out of over 1,000 applicants, Kennedy was one of only fifty who got this assignment. After completing this training, he headed for his duty station in the Solomon Islands in March 1943. From all indications, John enjoyed his duties in the South Pacific and earned the respect of his crew. The one thing he came to dislike was higher ranking officers. He saw little use for what he considered the petty discipline that many officers demanded.[23]

John's career took a sudden change while commanding PT-109 in the Solomons. On a night patrol on August 2, 1943 in the Blackett's Straits near the Solomon Island of New Georgia, a Japanese destroyer appeared on a collision course with John's PT-boat. John had been idling his boat in the water in anticipation of the approach of the Japanese ships, but unfortunately, he and his men failed to detect the approaching Japanese destroyer in time. Before he could react, the destroyer sliced the PT-boat in half. Two members of John's crew died instantly, while the others were scattered in the water. The boat's stern sank quickly, and the oil and gas on the surface caught fire. Although he had re-injured his back in the collision, John was able to get the survivors together. They clung to the boat's bow for hours until they eventually decided that they needed to swim to a nearby atoll because they feared that the bow might sink and that the Japanese might return. Despite wrenching back pain, John clinched the strap from the life vest of his most severely wounded crewmember in his teeth and dragged him several hours to the atoll. The next night, John swam out in the straits in hopes of signaling a passing PT-boat but without success. The other PT boats reported Kennedy's boat lost, and aerial searches failed to locate the survivors.

Since he and his crew were hungry and dehydrated, John decided they had to leave their small atoll on August 4 to reach a larger island nearby. After a three-hour swim, the crew arrived and found a plentiful supply of coconuts. On August 5, John swam to another nearby island and made his first contact with some native scouts who worked for a local Australian coast watcher, A. R. Evans. After overcoming their initial fears, John carved a message in a coconut, "NAURO ISL/NATIVE KNOWS POSIT/HE CAN PILOT/11 ALIVE/NEED SMALL BOAT/KENNEDY" and sent it with the natives to Evans. On the night of August 7, a PT-boat picked up John and the rest of his crew.[24]

---

[23] Dallek, *An Unfinished Life*, pp. 87-88.

[24] The best account of the circumstances surrounding PT-109 and the one I relied on for this summary is Robert J. Donovan, *PT 109: John F. Kennedy in World War II* (New York:

John's actions during the first week of August made him a national celebrity almost over night. While the Kennedy name was widely known because of the exploits of Joe Sr., John's heroics drew widespread attention. The *New York Times* claimed, "Kennedy's Son Is Hero in Pacific,"[25] and the *Christian Science Monitor* described how Kennedy's "Crew 'Came Through' Sea of Flames."[26] Kennedy's story became legendary with the publication of articles in *The New Yorker* and *Reader's Digest*, and the release of Robert Donovan's book, *PT 109: John F. Kennedy in World War II*, in 1961.[27]

While some people have questioned why his PT-boat was caught in such a vulnerable position, no one can challenge Kennedy's bravery or commitment to his crew. He easily could have avoided military service altogether, and once in the navy, he deliberately sought combat duty. He risked his life on several occasions in the Solomons to save his crew from further suffering and the real possibility of Japanese captivity. Unfortunately for John, the collision with the Japanese destroyer aggravated his back injury. Furthermore, he experienced a reoccurrence of some of the stomach problems that had plagued him earlier in life and was no longer able to serve in the navy. He received his honorable discharge in 1945.

The war's impact on the Kennedy family did not end with John's harrowing experience in the South Pacific. Joe, Jr. had become a B-24 pilot and flew missions from Great Britain against German targets in occupied Europe. Perhaps influenced by the attention John received, Joe volunteered to fly a very risky mission in August 1944. He agreed to pilot an old B-24 packed with explosives towards a target in Europe. The plan was for Joe and his co-pilot to bail out of the plane over the English Channel and then have radio control operators guide the plane to its final target. Unfortunately, an inadvertent radio signal detonated the explosives killing Joe and his co-pilot instantly. The Kennedy family was devastated. Soon after the war, John's sister, Kathleen, married a British veteran. Unfortunately, both of them died in a tragic plane crash in 1948. Joe's death and even more so Kathleen's, who John had grown closer to than any of his other siblings, left a deep void in his

---

McGraw-Hill, 1961). See also Stephen Plotkin, "Sixty Years Later, the Story of PT-109 Still Captivates," *Prologue* 35:2 (Summer 2003) at http://www.archives.gov/publications/prologue/2003/summer/pt109.html, accessed on August 4, 2006.

25 "Kennedy's Son Is Hero in Pacific As Destroyer Splits His PT Boat," August 20, 1943, *New York Times*, p. 1.

26 "PT-Boat Crew 'Came Through' Sea of Flames," August 19, 1943, *Christian Science Monitor*, p. 1.

27 See Dallek, *An Unfinished Life*, pp. 95-98. A copy of *The New Yorker* article can be found at http://www.orwelltoday.com/jfkpt109.shtml, accessed on August 4, 2006.

life and further encouraged him to recognize the frailty of his own life and to live it for the moment.[28]

After his discharge from the navy, John still did not know exactly what he wanted to do. His older brother's death left him as the likely successor to his father's dream of having a Kennedy as president. However, John did not instantly take to this idea. Instead, he initially dabbled in journalism for the *Chicago Herald-American* and covered the 1945 UN Conference in San Francisco in the late spring. In July, he reported on major European events, including Winston Churchill's defeat as prime minister and the Potsdam Conference. After Japan's surrendered in September, Joe Kennedy arranged for John to travel as a guest of U.S. Navy Secretary James Forrestal on a tour of Europe. While traveling, John met President Harry Truman, General Dwight Eisenhower, new British Prime Minister Clement Attlee, British Foreign Secretary Ernest Bevin, Soviet Foreign Minister Vyachelav Molotov, and Soviet Ambassador Andrey Gromyko. While none these men remembered the young Kennedy, they all made an impression on him.[29]

In 1946, John faced some difficult decisions. He was almost 30 years old, yet he had not truly pursued a career. While interested in journalism, he did not see that as his vocation. Joe, Sr. did have plans, however. Joe wanted John to run for the 11th Massachusetts Congressional District seat in the House of Representatives. Although not overly enamored about a political career, John saw no better alternative and viewed the campaign as a challenge. John struggled initially in public speaking, but soon became a great campaigner. He typically campaigned from 7 am until well after dark and frequently visited popular establishments, including saloons, restaurants, and barber shops. Even before he officially declared himself as a candidate, he began to speak to organizations about his views of the future.[30] In March 1946 he laid out two themes. He stressed the importance of Americans valuing their democratic freedoms and asserted that Americans who did not do this would "wake up some day and find their freedom gone." He also suggested that the transition for veterans from war to peace was more difficult than many of them imagined. He encouraged veterans by claiming, "It is my belief that if we work together in peace as we did in war, we will meet that challenge [of

[28] Dallek, *An Unfinished Life*, p. 108.
[29] Ibid., pp. 95-98.
[30] Ibid., pp. 121-28. See also Kenneth P. O'Donnell and David F. Power, *"Johnny, We Hardly Knew Ye": Memories of John Fitzgerald Kennedy* (Boston: Little, Brown and Company, 1970), pp. 59-79.

peace] successfully."[31] His energetic campaigning, his father's financial support, and the Kennedy family's reputation led to John's victory in the Democratic Party primaries.[32]

The general campaign against Lester Bowen, his Republican opponent, was actually easier.[33] Bowen simply could not compete with John's energy and Joe's financial resources. By Election Day, Joe had provided between $250-300,000 to the campaign. At age 29, John won in a landslide with over 70% of the vote.[34]

John stayed in the House of Representatives for three terms and never faced any serious challenges to his seat. Joe continued to have aspirations for his son, and John began to have some of his own. John's main goal after making it to the House was to get elected to the Senate. He did not find the lower house very challenging and believed that most of the other representatives were simply too old and set in their ways. Joe worked behind the scenes to expand John's name recognition and helped get his son named as one of the Ten Outstanding Young Men in 1946 by the Junior Chamber of Commerce. Further, he assisted in getting John appointed to the House Education and Labor Committee—a prized position for a young congressman. However, John never found his work very interesting or rewarding.[35]

John did like foreign policy and viewed communism as a real threat both at home and abroad. He was virulently anti-communist and believed the United States needed to develop more assertive national security policies. In a speech to a Massachusetts labor organization in 1947, he described how organized labor had lost the public's support because of perceptions that communists had obtained leadership positions in unions. He told the group, "It is of primary importance not only for the purpose of gaining back public opinion, but for our own national security, that labor itself continue its unrelenting fight to remove Communists from positions of control."[36] Additionally, he saw no problems when Senator Joseph McCarthy made his initial claims in the early 1950s that there were communists working in the government.[37]

---

31 "Kennedy Urges U.S. Work For Own Democratic Beliefs," March 14, 1945, *Christian Science Monitor*, p. 4.

32 O'Donnell and Power, *"Johnny, We Hardly Knew Ye"*, p. 79.

33 "Kennedy Wins Over Rivals In 11th District," June 19, 1946, *Christian Science Monitor*, p. 1.

34 Dallek, *An Unfinished Life*, pp. 130-33.

35 Ibid., pp. 139-142

36 "Kennedy Urges Labor to Oust Communists," July 31, 1947, *Christian Science Monitor*, p. 2.

37 Dallek, *An Unfinished Life*, p. 162.

The one perk he did like was the social opportunities that came with his position. He very much enjoyed the socializing, especially with women. Ted Sorensen explained that Kennedy was "unfailing flirtatious with all young women, particularly pretty, single women."[38] A congressman, who was one of John's closest friends, claimed that the Massachusetts congressman "came by it naturally. His daddy liked girls…. John liked girls and girls liked him."[39] *The Washington Post* reported in 1949 that the "Current emotional heat wave on Capitol Hill is attributed to bachelor Representative John F. Kennedy of Massachusetts. Seems as if all the unmarried Hill secretaries and other women employees peek their heads around corridors and have heart palpitations when word spreads that the young lawmaker is approaching."[40] Another newspaper story in 1952 under the title, "Surely He'll Need a First Lady—If!", looked at unmarried politicians with presidential ambitions and claimed that John was "personable, brainy and brave" and possessed "youthful charm".[41]

As John began serving his third term in 1951, he started to consider running for the Senate. He traveled throughout Massachusetts delivering speeches, and according to at least one political correspondent, "made a strong impression."[42] He announced on NBC's "Meet the Press" in December that he would "like to go to the Senate."[43] While popular in his district, this was a major leap for the young Kennedy, as he was only 34 years old. Furthermore, he would be challenging Henry Cabot Lodge, an entrenched and popular incumbent Republican senator. Lodge came from a very active political family as his father had served in the Senate for over thirty years. Henry Cabot had first been elected to the Senate in 1936 and served there until 1944 when he resigned to begin active duty in the army. He was re-elected in 1946 and was quite popular in Massachusetts.

John's election campaign involved the entire Kennedy clan. His younger brother, Bobby, served as his campaign manager and created a true political

---

38 See Ted Sorensen, *Counselor: A Life at the Edge of History* (New York: Harper, 2008), p.116.

39 Quoted in ibid., p.152.

40 Genevieve Reynolds, "Capitol Has Own Heat Wave, Attributed to John Kennedy," May 22, 1949, *The Washington Post and Times Herald*, p. S7.

41 Elizabeth Maguire, "Surely He'll Need a First Lady—If!," March 2, 1952, ibid., p. S5. For Kennedy's sexual escapades during this period, see Dallek, *An Unfinished Life*, pp. 151-152. See also Giglio, *The Presidency of John F. Kennedy*, p. 10; and Nellie Bly, *The Kennedy Men: Three Generations of Sex, Scandal and Secrets* (New York: Kensington Books, 1996).

42 Edgar M. Mills, "Kennedy Due to Announce Senate Candidacy in April," March 18, 1952, *Christian Science Monitor*, p. 1.

43 "Rep. Kennedy May Run Against Sen. Lodge," December 3, 1951, *The Washington Post and Times Herald*, p. 3.

machine.[44] His other siblings went door to door and hosted gatherings of potential voters to win their support. As with the 1946 House race, Joe influenced the campaign significantly by contributing several million dollars. An example of his influence was his efforts to get the *Boston Globe* to endorse John. The owner of the paper was facing a financial crisis, and Joe loaned him $500,000. Two weeks before the election, the paper endorsed John.[45] His family's efforts should not take away from John's own campaigning. He was continually on the go and effectively reached out to the average voter. His dashing good looks were especially popular with women voters, and his ability to show the Kennedy family's immigrant roots appealed to Massachusetts' large immigrant population. His opponent's approach to campaigning also helped Kennedy's cause. Lodge traveled the country supporting the Republican nominee for president, Dwight Eisenhower, and in the process offended some Massachusetts Republicans who wanted Robert Taft to be the party's presidential nominee.[46] All of these factors led to a narrow victory for Kennedy in which he won 51.5% of the vote and had a margin of victory of only 70,000 votes.[47]

John's years as a senator from 1953 to 1961 were quite eventful, although not always for professional reasons. In the senate, he came to view most of his colleagues in the same light as congressmen—old, boring, and of little substance.[48] He primarily occupied himself with local Massachusetts' issues and national security topics. Locally, he focused on landing more defense contracts, protecting the fishing industry, and labor issues. For instance, he criticized the Navy for awarding the construction of a new aircraft carrier to Newport News, VA rather than to Quincy, Massachusetts. He claimed the deal was "a heavy blow to the hopes of New England."[49]

Kennedy spoke on many occasions about economic issues, particularly ones related to labor unions. One of his most frequent targets was the minimum wage. In 1953, he called for raising the minimum wage from 75 cents to $1.00 per hour.[50] Congress eventually passed legislation in 1956 to do this. In 1958, he unsuccessfully proposed expanding the coverage of the

---

44 O'Donnell and Power, *"Johnny, We Hardly Knew Ye"*, pp. 94-98.
45 Giglio, *The Presidency of John F. Kennedy*, p. 9.
46 Edgar M. Mills, "Lodge Looms as Cabinet Choice—Defeat Analyzed," November 6, 1952, *Christian Science Monitor*, p. 8.
47 The best summary of the 1952 Senate campaign is in Dallek, *An Unfinished Life*, pp. 170-75.
48 For an overall assessment of Kennedy's senate career, see ibid., pp. 177-226.
49 "Kennedy in Protest," February 4, 1954, *New York Times*, p. 7.
50 "$1 Minimum Wage Urged by Kennedy," May 20, 1953, *Christian Science Monitor*, p. 1.

federal minimum wage law to an additional 6 million people.[51] In 1959, he recommended increasing the minimum wage to $1.31, again without success.[52] During the 1958 recession, he pushed for changes in the unemployment compensation program "so that it will provide adequate benefits for a sufficient length of time so as to be of really effective help to those who, through no fault of their own, are jobless."[53] Despite his efforts for increasing the minimum wage and expanding unemployment compensation, he achieved relatively little in these areas. Additionally, his relationship with labor unions was not always the best. While he supported certain issues that most union members supported like the minimum wage, he also called for the end of racketeering in unions and for putting Jimmy Hoffa, the president of the International Brotherhood of Teamsters, "and his ilk" out of business.[54] Little came from Kennedy's efforts and his support of a particular labor bill in 1959 led to some unionists claiming that he "double-crossed labor".[55]

Kennedy did occasionally take positions that were not supported by many of his constituents as when he threw his support behind creating an international waterway with Canada—the St. Lawrence Waterway. This was a very controversial issue in Massachusetts and the rest of New England as many feared the waterway would take business away from Boston and other ports. John showed a pragmatic side in this dispute. Kennedy explained to his constituents that he believed the affect of the seaway on New England would be minor and that Canada was going to build the seaway with or without American support. Rather than having no say-so in the project, he cautioned that New England needed to put aside some of its sectional concerns and "participate in the construction, operation and administration" of the seaway.[56]

51 "Wider Coverage Asked," January 26, 1958, *New York Times*, p. 22.

52 "Program for U.S. Given By Kennedy," June 7, 1959, ibid., p. 51.

53 Memorandum, April 22, 1958, John F. Kennedy Presidential Library and Museum [hereafter JFKL], Papers of President Kennedy [hereafter Kennedy Papers], Pre-Presidential Papers, Senate Files, Legislation, Legislation Files, 1953-1960, 1958 Defense-Education: General, Box 689, Folder – Economy, 4/22/58-4/22/58, p. 1. For his actual program recommendation, see "Statement of Senator John F. Kennedy (Dem. - Mass.) Upon Introducing the Unemployment Compensation Amendments of 1958, February 6, 1958, ibid., Holburn, Subject 1957-1959, Press, Radio, Television-Urban Renewal, Box 565, Folder – Unemployment Compensation, pp. 1-3.

54 "Kennedy Offers Labor Bill Aimed at Hoffa 'and His Ilk'," January 21, 1959, *New York Times*, p. 1.

55 "Unionists Say Kennedy Double-Crossed Labor," September 23, 1959, *The Washington Post and Times Herald*, p. A17.

56 "Kennedy Quits Opposition in Seaway Fight," January 15, 1954, *The Washington Post and Times Herald*, p. 10.

John's support for the Eisenhower administration's proposal to work with Canada on the waterway helped lead to its completion in 1959.

Kennedy did not venture much into other issues unless the political winds led him to as in the case of civil rights for black Americans. The 1950s civil rights' struggle created deep divisions in the country and made it almost impossible for any politician to make a stand on an issue without offending someone. The Democratic Party was clearly split into northern and southern factions. Kennedy attempted to portray himself as a moderate on civil rights issues who was willing to reach out to both sides. He wanted to see steps to black equality, but he was not willing to push for the immediate end of discrimination. The 1957 Civil Rights Act is a prime example of how senators like Kennedy approached civil rights. Congress passed the first civil rights act since the 19th century, but it had significant limitations. Kennedy supported the act with its limitations hoping that blacks would recognize his efforts in favor of their rights, while southerners would see he supported only minimal change.

Kennedy supported an amendment to the act that required a jury trial for those accused of a crime under this legislation. This amendment stoked fires of controversy, as it would allow southern juries to decide whether the act had been violated or not. Since only whites sat on most southern juries, there was a good chance that people who violated the law would be found not guilty. Kennedy claimed he voted for the amendment because he was "confident that Southern juries, presented with convincing evidence of restriction and ever mindful of the watching eyes of the nation—and indeed the world—will convict those who dare interfere with orderly legal processes."[57] This position pleased neither black Americans nor most southerners. Mississippi College President D. M. Nelson chastised the senator for attempting "to force a distasteful order and a repulsive way of life upon the section [of the country] that has long been the stronghold of the Democratic party."[58] Roy Wilkins, the Executive Secretary of the NAACP, took a different position. In a letter to one of Kennedy's friends, he explained that the senator "had been taken in by the popular wave of [southern] propaganda about the 'injustice of convicting a man without a jury trial' when that really was not the issue at all. He added, "we believe that on an issue as crucial as this one to millions of Negro American citizens who have been systematically deprived of their right to

---

[57] Statement of John F. Kennedy (D-Mass.) on the Floor of the Senate – Pending Amendment to Civil Rights Act 1957, JFKL, Kennedy Papers, Pre-Presidential Papers, Senate Files, Legislation, Legislation Files, 1953-1960, 1956-1957 Civil Rights-Constitution, Box 664, Folder – Civil Rights, 7/22/57-8/9/57, p. 2.

[58] D.M. Nelson to John F. Kennedy, August 2, 1957, ibid., p. 1.

vote, United States senators have a duty to pass up glib talking points and to ascertain the truth for themselves."[59]

The criticism did not end with this legislation. After the worst of the Little Rock crisis was over in the fall of 1957, Kennedy proclaimed that he had "accepted the Supreme Court's decision on desegregation as the law of the land. I know we do not all agree on that issue—but I think most of us do agree on the necessity of upholding law and order in every part of the land."[60] However, many black Americans looked beyond his statements and focused on his actual actions. In an effort to win over black Americans Kennedy lunched with civil rights leaders like Thurgood Marshall, and to appease southerners, he met with the likes of Alabama Governor John Patterson, Alabama State Senator Sam Englehardt, and Georgia Governor Marvin Griffin, several of the South's staunchest defenders of segregation. This approach did not always go over well. Wilkins explained that "we must be pardoned for exhibiting some alarm at the apparent wooing of Southern support three years before the nominating convention."[61] In 1960, baseball great Johnie Robinson announced his opposition to the Massachusetts senator's candidacy for president. He claimed, "it is quite clear to me by now that Sen. Kennedy—or any other candidate—cannot expect any self-respecting Negro to support him with the image of Patterson, Englehardt, and their ilk sitting across his breakfast table. … As long as he continues to play politics at the expense of 18,000,000 Negro Americans, then I repeat: Sen. Kennedy is not fit to be President of the U.S."[62] Wilkins and Robinson's views did not necessarily reflect the opinions of most black Americans, but they do show that Kennedy's efforts to be a moderate did produce some controversy.

While Kennedy's stance on civil rights was controversial and drew some attention, Kennedy spoke much more often and forcefully about national security issues. This focus reflected the political realities of the time as the dangers of the Cold War resonated through the American population. It also revealed Kennedy's real interests. He was much more concerned about

---

[59] Roy Wilkins to Peter Arlos, May 16, 1958, JFKL, Kennedy Papers, Pre-Presidential Papers, Senate Files, Legislation, Legislation Files, 1953-1960, 1958 Banking-Civil Service, Box 687, Folder – Civil Rights, 10/30/57-5/27/58, p. 2.

[60] Carroll Kilpatrick, "Kennedy, the Moderate," October 24, 1957, *The Washington Post and Times Herald*, p. A13.

[61] Wilkins to Arlos, May 16, 1958, JFKL, Kennedy Papers, Pre-Presidential Papers, Senate Files, Legislation, Legislation Files, 1953-1960, 1958 Banking-Civil Service, Box 687, Folder – Civil Rights, 10/30/57-5/27/58, p. 3.

[62] Jackie Robinson, *New York Post Sports*, June 3, 1960, found at JFKL, Kennedy Papers, Pre-Presidential Papers, Senate Files, Legislation, Legislation Files, 1953-1960, 1960 Civil Rights-Defense: General, Box 732, Folder – Civil Rights, 6/22/60-7/7/60.

national security questions and became a leading critic of the Eisenhower administration.

After his inauguration in January 1953, Eisenhower made significant changes to the national security programs he inherited from President Harry Truman. He believed the country could not afford to continue spending so much on defense programs and devised the "so-called" New Look program. While the New Look called for continuing the basic strategy of containment as articulated in the Truman administration, it also supported reductions in defense spending by cutting conventional forces and placing greater reliance on nuclear weapons as a deterrent.[63] Critics, including Kennedy, quickly challenged the program as sacrificing America's capability to wage war. The Massachusetts politician claimed in late 1953 that the United States needed a national security program "more in keeping with the perils of the time than the one that is at present our national policy." He particularly argued that that the Air Force's strategic capability was insufficient.[64]

Kennedy and the other Eisenhower critics made little headway before the Soviet Union launched *Sputnik*, the world's first artificial satellite, in October 1957. This technological marvel seemed to indicate that the Soviet Union was ahead of the United States and gave rise to the likes of Kennedy, Lyndon Johnson, and Stuart Symington claiming there was a missile gap. Kennedy told a group of Democrats that "The people of America are no longer willing to be lulled by paternalistic reassurances, spoon-fed science-fiction predictions or by pious platitudes of faith and hope."[65] Others even claimed that the launch of Soviet satellite was "another Pearl Harbor."[66] For the remainder of the Eisenhower administration, Kennedy was one of the president's most vocal critics. He argued that the United States needed to spend much more on national security programs and to close the gap with the Soviet Union.[67]

Kennedy did not let up on his criticism for the remainder of the Eisenhower administration. He asserted in January 1958 that "the national interest is in greater peril than it has been at any time in the 20th century."[68]

---

63 Richard H. Immerman and Robert R. Bowie, *Waging Peace: How Eisenhower Shaped an Enduring Cold War Strategy* (New York: Oxford University Press, 1998), pp. 178-201.

64 "Kennedy Asks U.S. Air Power Second to None," October 17, 1953, *The Washington Post and Times Herald*, p. 6.

65 "Kennedy Assails U.S. Missile Lag," November 7, 1957, *New York Times*, p. 16.

66 Quoted in David L. Snead, *The Gaither Committee, Eisenhower, and the Cold War* (Columbus: Ohio State University Press, 1999), p. 80.

67 The most extensive study of Kennedy and the missile gap claims is Christopher A. Preble, *John F. Kennedy and the Missile Gap* (DeKalb: Northern Illinois University Press, 2004).

68 "Kennedy Sees Defense Lag," January 13, 1958, *Christian Science Monitor*, p. 2.

Later that year he criticized the Eisenhower administration for "drift and indecision in foreign affairs."[69] One of Kennedy's most common claims was that there was a missile gap in favor of the Soviet Union. In a particularly contentious speech in August 1958, he presented his clearest critique of Eisenhower's national security programs and explained how he thought the United States should attempt to deal with the crisis. He quoted General James Gavin, a World War II hero and Eisenhower critic, who claimed that the United States was fast approaching a situation "in which our own offensive and defensive missile capabilities will lag so far behind those of the Soviets as to place us in a position of great peril." Kennedy then explained that the most critical years of the missile gap were going to be from 1960 to 1964.[70]

Kennedy went on to argue that "Our peril is not simply because Russian striking power during the years of the gap will have a slight edge over us in missile power—they will have several times as many." He did not discount American retaliatory capabilities completely but argued that the ability to destroy part of the Soviet Union "might not deter the leaders of a totalitarian state—particularly in a moment of recklessness, panic, irrationality, or even cool miscalculation." To minimize the dangers, he advocated expanding American military strategic retaliatory capabilities and air defense systems, as well as spending more money to better equip the military to fight limited wars.

Kennedy laid blame for America falling behind the Soviet Union squarely at the feet of the Eisenhower administration. In particular, he asserted that "The fact of the matter is that during that period when emphasis was laid upon our economic strength instead of our military strength, we were losing the decisive years when we could have maintained a lead against the Soviet Union in our missile capacity." He then asked that since "the coming years of the gap present us with a peril more deadly than any wartime danger we have ever known," should not the nation's security override "budgetary considerations"?[71] Kennedy's speech was so critical of U.S. policies that it led to a heated exchange with Senate Homer Capehart, a Republican from Indiana, who said that comments like those made by Kennedy, invite "Russia to attack

[69] "Kennedy Condemns U.S. Policy 'Drift'," June 28, 1958, *New York Times*, p. 3.

[70] John F. Kennedy, "United States Military and Diplomatic Policies—Preparing for the Gap," August 14, 1958, *Congressional Record: Proceedings and Debates of the 85th Congress, Second Session*, found at JFKL, Kennedy Papers, Pre-Presidential Papers, 1960 Campaign Press and Publicity Speeches, Statements, and Sections, 1958-1960, Defense and Disarmament: Missile Gap-Education, p. 2.

[71] Ibid., pp. 2-7.

us because we will be saying that we have nothing" with which to defend the country.[72]

Kennedy's withering critique continued in 1959 as he prepared for his presidential run. He obviously believed that the United States was in danger, but it is equally clear that he saw an opportunity to capitalize on the growing fear in the United States. Kennedy invoked Abraham Lincoln's fight for democracy in the Civil War to explain how seriously he took America's conflict with the Soviet Union. He later explained, "this is a battle for survival."[73] In October, he received a letter from "a Republican" citizen expressing dismay at the Eisenhower and Nixon approach to the struggle with the Soviet Union and implicitly offered Kennedy his vote if he adopted a more assertive policy.[74] Kennedy quickly responded to the letter by stating that the United States was behind the Soviet Union by up to six years in some areas and "that if anything, we should err … by spending a little too much rather than too little."[75] This would be Kennedy's common theme throughout his upcoming presidential campaign.

Beyond his critique of Eisenhower's national security programs, Kennedy was clearly a staunch anti-communist who got along well with Senator Joseph McCarthy in the early 1950s. While he did not support some of McCarthy's antics, he did not question the need to fight communism at home. When the senate voted to censure McCarthy in 1954, Kennedy was the only Senate Democrat to not do so. His excuse was that he was in the hospital at the time of the vote. However, he could have made arrangements to get his vote counted.[76]

There was only one issue that seemed to interest Kennedy as much as his contempt for Eisenhower's national security policies and that was the growing unrest in less developed areas, especially those tied to European colonialism. Kennedy spoke out on many occasions against colonialism and the lack of understanding that America's leaders had for other parts of the world. He recognized that the French struggle in Indochina would only end when

[72] "Kennedy Speech Brings Threat of Star Session," August 15, 1958, *The Washington Post and Times Herald*, pp. A1 and A8.

[73] "Can Democracy Meet the Space Age Challenge," CBS Television Network, March 22, 1959, found at JFKL, Kennedy Papers, Pre-Presidential Papers, Senate Files, Holburn, Research Materials, Agriculture-Defense, Box 568, Folder – Defense-Disarmament-Space, pp. 2-11.

[74] Bruce L. Pickering to J.F. Kennedy, October 17, 1959, JFKL, Kennedy Papers, Pre-Presidential Papers, Senate Files, Legislation, Legislation Files, 1953-1960, 1959 Small Business-Thank You's, Box 726, Folder – Space, 1.

[75] John F. Kennedy to Bruce L. Pickering, October 23, 1959, ibid., 1.

[76] Dallek, *An Unfinished Life*, pp. 189-91.

Western countries recognized that the Vietnamese simply wanted their independence.[77] He asserted that "to pour money, material, and men into the jungles of Indochina without at least a remote prospect of victory would be dangerous, futile, and self-destructive." To obtain victory, the United States and its allies had to make clear that their efforts in Indochina were focused on resisting communism and not restoring French colonial control.[78] He later added, "An essential element in Western policy must be the granting of independence to all areas which are prepared for self-government and which are now held under Western colonial domination."[79] Kennedy elaborated, "We would have better served France itself, and the cause of the whole free world, had we insisted firmly at the beginning upon the complete Vietnamese independence which was essential to rally native and other Asiatic forces."[80]

His criticisms were not just directed at the situation in Indochina. He spoke out against American polices in other areas of the world like Algeria. He expressed his exasperation when he told an audience that "We fight to keep the world free from Communist imperialism—but in doing so we hamper our efforts and bring suspicion upon our motives by being closely linked with western imperialism."[81] France's efforts to maintain control of Algeria were of particular interest to Kennedy. He claimed that "The imperatives of Western unity and the need to sustain Western influence in the uncommitted areas of the world make the Algerian question one of the pivotal issues in world politics and in the balance of world power."[82] He pressured the Eisenhower administration to help shape a course towards Algerian independence and to quit its "head-in-the-sands policy" of trying to ignore the colonial conflict.[83] "The longer legitimate Algerian aspirations are suppressed," Kennedy concluded, "the greater becomes the danger of a reactionary or Communist takeover in all of Africa."[84]

Kennedy's critique did not stop with the crisis in Algeria but involved American policies towards the rest of Africa, India, and Latin America. Kennedy mused, "I do not think we have always recognized the equality and

---

[77] "Kennedy Says Reds May Get Indochina," March 13, 1954, *Christian Science Monitor*, p. 19.

[78] "Kennedy Links Liberty to Victory in Indochina," April 7, 1954, ibid., p. 7.

[79] "Kennedy Says U.S. Lags," May 12, 1954, *New York Times*, p. 28.

[80] Partial Remarks before the Executives' Club, Chicago, Illinois, May 28, 1954, JFKL, Kennedy Papers, Pre-Presidential Files, Senate Files, Legislation, Legislation Files, 1953-1960, 1953-1955, Immigration-Indo-China, Box 647, Folder – Indo-China, 5/6/54-8/4/54, p. 5.

[81] "Sen. Kennedy Urges End to U.S. 'Please All' Policy," April 14, 1956, *Los Angeles Times*, p. 9.

[82] John F. Kennedy, "The Algerian Crisis: A New Phase?," October 5, 1957, *America*, p. 15.

[83] "Kennedy Prods U.S. to Seek Free Algeria," July 2, 1957, *Christian Science Monitor*, p. 2.

[84] Kennedy, "The Algerian Crisis," p. 17.

dignity of every nation, large or small, as we pursue a course that too often ignores their fears and aspirations."[85] To help countries like India and other developing nations, Kennedy called for "a substantial, long-term program of productive loans to under-developed areas from a fully capitalized central fund, capable of working with either independent nations or regional groupings."[86] He feared that until the United States rejected colonialism outright, communism would continue to be viewed as a viable alternative in the developing world.

While Kennedy was outspoken on a few issues, his senatorial career was not particularly distinguished. Part of his problem was that he came to view his senate seat as a stepping stone to the presidency with maybe an intermediate stop as vice president. Although he did not necessarily enjoy the senate's slow pace, he knew his service there was necessary to achieve his ambitions. In 1956, he decided to seek the vice presidential nomination even though he was a first-term senator and not even 40-years old. Those who favored his nomination liked his youthful good looks and his political moderation.[87] In the end, Adlai Stevenson, the Democratic Party's unsuccessful candidate in 1952, won the nomination again in 1956 and maneuvered his party to select Estes Kefauver as his running mate. While Kennedy was deeply disappointed, he still managed to deliver one of the best speeches at the Democratic Party National Convention in support of his party's presidential ticket. This speech and his cross country campaigning for the Stevenson/Kefauver ticket placed him in good stead with his party and set him on the path to the party's 1960 presidential nomination.[88]

The 1950s proved adventurous for Kennedy even beyond his political career. During the decade he got married, almost died, and won a Pulitzer Prize. Kennedy's appetite for women had not decreased as he matured, and he was even considered one of the country's most eligible bachelors. In 1951 he met Jacqueline Bouvier, and they dated for two years before announcing their engagement in June 1953.[89] They married in an elegant and star-studded

85 "U.S. Policy Misses Issues, Kennedy Says," November 24, 1958, *The Washington Post and Times Herald*, p. A24.

86 "The Economic Gap," February 19, 1959, JFKL, Kennedy Papers, Pre-Presidential Papers, Senate Files, Holburn, Subject 1957-1958, Europe-Germany, Box 561, Folder – Foreign Aid, p. 7.

87 Edgar M. Mills, "Second Spot Stock Rises for Kennedy," May 29, 1956, *Christian Science Monitor*, p. 1.

88 See Giglio, *The Presidency of John F. Kennedy*, pp. 12-13; and Dallek, *An Unfinished Life*, pp. 203-8.

89 "Kennedy-Bouvier Nuptials Scheduled for September," June 25, 1953, *Christian Science Monitor*, p. 2.

service in September. Archbishop Richard Cushing performed the service at St. Mary's Catholic Church in Newport, Rhode Island. 800 guests attended the wedding, and 1,200 people went to the private reception.[90]

While they unquestionably loved each other, their marriage had rough patches almost from the beginning. Kennedy thought Jackie spent too much money, while she thought he focused too much time on work. Even more troublesome, Kennedy remained very promiscuous. An informal survey by the "Bachelorettes", a group of fifty Hollywood actresses and models, placed Kennedy in their top ten of most desired dates.[91] Kennedy loved this type of attention. One of his friends later claimed that Jackie was not "prepared for the humiliation she would suffer when she found herself stranded at parties while John would suddenly disappear with some pretty young girl." Even when Jackie was pregnant, Kennedy frequently visited other women. In the late stages of her pregnancy in 1956, he went on a cruise in the Mediterranean where he enjoyed different women at every port. He even delayed returning home after Jackie had a miscarriage. If that was not insulting enough, while attending his brother Ted Kennedy's wedding in 1958, Kennedy was caught on tape claiming, "that being married didn't really mean that you had to be faithful to your wife." Jackie never got used to her husband's promiscuous behavior but rationalized, "I don't think there are any men who are faithful to their wives. Men are such a combination of good and evil."[92]

Kennedy's brush with death came in 1954 when he underwent back surgery.[93] As he had done most of his life, he continued to struggle with various illnesses and injuries. Although not known to the general public, in 1947 John had been diagnosed with Addison's disease and placed on medication. His back gave him even more trouble, and he finally decided to let his doctors insert a metal plate in his back to stabilize his spine. While recovering, he developed a urinary tract infection and lapsed into a coma. It was touch and go for a short time, and he actually received last rites from a priest. However, he again escaped death and recovered.[94]

The last great event of this time period of Kennedy's life was his publication of *Profiles in Courage* in 1956. Kennedy was very interested in history and, in particular, great leaders. With the help of his close aide, Ted

[90] "Notables Attend Senator's Wedding," September 13, 1953, *New York Times*, pp. 1 and 25.
[91] "Bachelorettes Name 10 Dates Most Desired," May 23, 1953, *The Los Angeles Times*, p. B1.
[92] Quoted in Dallek, *An Unfinished Life*, pp. 194-95.
[93] Robert A. Hart, "Failed Spine Surgery Syndrome in the Life and Career of John Fitzgerald Kennedy," *The Journal of Bone and Joint Surgery* 88A:5 (May 2006), pp. 1141-45.
[94] Dallek, *An Unfinished Life*, pp. 195-97.

Sorensen, and Georgetown University historian Jules David, he explored the careers of eight U.S. senators— John Quincy Adams, Daniel Webster, Thomas Hart Benton, Sam Houston, Lucius Quintus Cincinnatus Lamar, Edmund G. Ross, George Norris, and Robert Taft. The book became an instant best seller, and with the assistance of his father, won numerous awards, including the 1957 Pulitzer Prize, the 1956 American Library Association Notable Book Award, and the Christopher Book Award. Although Sorensen and David wrote most of the book, Kennedy's name on the cover raised his stature even more and continued to place him in the limelight.[95]

Kennedy's family background, health issues, wartime experience, and legislative career profoundly affected his personal and professional development. His privileged background and philandering father allowed him little room for empathy towards the average American or respect for women. This does not mean that he could not on occasion show concerns for different groups, but he had few common experiences with those who were below his economic status, and he did not show a commitment to their problems unless it served his own ends. Like his father, he enjoyed the company of women and took personal and political risks to fulfill his desires. Even after he was married and later into his presidency, his affairs would become legendary. His wartime experience colored his opinion of authority and enhanced his confidence in his own abilities. It, without question, also furthered his image as an energetic and potentially strong leader. His legislative record was mixed, especially while he was a member of the House of Representatives. In part, this can be explained by the difficulties all new representatives and senators face in their first couple of terms in office. However, Kennedy also had little respect for the other representatives and senators and often found the work tedious and unchallenging. Furthermore, while he reluctantly entered the political arena after World War II, his ambitions quickly led him to focus on one day being president.

As 1960 approached, Kennedy was ready to announce his candidacy. He was still quite young, but he did have a range of experience, name recognition throughout most of the country, and extensive family resources. He believed that he was the only one of the potential Democratic candidates who had the necessary skills to end eight years of Republican governance. He also hoped to capitalize on the country's fears of the Soviet Union and the perceived lethargy of the Eisenhower administration to propel him into the presidency.

---

[95] Ibid., pp. 198-99. See also John F. Kennedy, *Profiles in Courage* (New York: Harper & Row, 1956). Sorensen admitted that he "did a first draft of most chapters" but gave credit to Kennedy for "setting the tone and philosophy of the book". See Sorensen, *Counselor*, p. 146.

Chapter 2

Transition from Candidate to President

John Kennedy began to eye the presidency seriously after the 1956 presidential election when he was 39 years old. While Kennedy was still quite young, most political analysts placed him near the top of potential democratic candidates for the 1960 election. His main opponents for his party's nomination were Democratic stalwart Adlai Stevenson and Senators Hubert Humphrey, Lyndon Johnson, and Stuart Symington, all more senior and respected politicians. His path to the victory in the 1960 election was a difficult one and tested him in many ways. However, he emerged triumphant. Kennedy showed his evolving skills as a campaigner and overcame every challenge that came before him.

While his father had long envisioned one of his sons becoming president, John Kennedy did not give it that much attention until 1955. President Eisenhower had a heart attack that year, and there was some question whether he would run for re-election. Prior to Eisenhower's heart attack, his popularity made it very unlikely that any Democratic Party nominee could win. However, his heart attack changed the equation. If he did not run, the field would be quite open as Eisenhower's vice president, Richard Nixon, did not have the same support and was not nearly as well-known. After doing some political calculations about Kennedy's age, relative inexperience, and limited standing within his own party, the Kennedy family decided he should first seek the Democratic Party vice-president nomination and then follow that with a presidential run in four, or more likely, eight years. After Eisenhower recovered and announced his intention to run again, Kennedy's father expressed reservations about his son running for the nomination as vice president when the Democratic ticket had little chance of winning. The young Kennedy insisted, however, that there would really be no better time to run for the nomination.[1]

The Kennedys viewed Lyndon Johnson as the most viable Democratic option in 1955. The presumed leader of the Democratic Party, Adlai Stevenson, had already lost once and they believed he simply did not have the popularity to compete with Eisenhower. Johnson, on the other hand, was an emerging star in the Democratic Party. While nine years older than Kennedy, his political experience was not much more extensive. He had been elected to the House of Representatives in 1937 to a vacant seat and served there until 1949 with the exception of a two-year period during World War II when he served in the navy. In 1948 he won one of Texas' two senatorial seats by 87 votes. However, unlike Kennedy, Johnson loved the give-and-take of Washington, D.C. politics and had earned the respect of his peers. He quickly assumed leadership roles among Democratic senators and in 1953 became the youngest Senate Minority leader in history. When the Democratic Party won back control of the Senate the following year, he became the Senate Majority leader. Considering his relative youth—only 47 in 1955—Johnson was a rising star in American politics who was well-respected on both sides of the aisle and had the potential to be a strong candidate.[2]

Joe Kennedy decided in 1955 to encourage Johnson to challenge Eisenhower. He even offered to bankroll the Texan's presidential bid if he promised to make his son his vice presidential running mate. To the elder Kennedy's surprise, the Texas senator turned him down. Johnson was not willing to commit to a campaign with Eisenhower's status unknown.[3] The elder Kennedy was furious and decided to turn his attention to Adlai Stevenson who ultimately won the Democratic nomination for the second time. While it is unclear just how much John knew about his father's behind the scenes activities, he probably wanted the vice presidential nomination as much as his father did. Unfortunately, he had several strikes going against him. He was still very young, hailed from the northeast, and was not that well-known around the country. Stevenson was from the Midwest and wanted a

[1] Dallek, *An Unfinished Life*, pp. 204-6.

[2] For a summary of Johnson's career, see "President Lyndon B. Johnson's Biography" at the Lyndon Baines Johnson Library and Museum, Austin, Texas, http://www.lbjlib.utexas.edu/johnson/archives.hom/biographys.hom/lbj_bio.asp#1950, accessed on March 21, 2008. See also, Robert A. Caro, *Master of the Senate: The Years of Lyndon Johnson* (New York: Alfred A. Knopf, 2002).

[3] Caro, *Master of the Senate*, pp. 646-47.

southerner or someone from a border state on the ticket. After winning his party's nomination, Stevenson left it up to the delegates to the Democratic National Convention to select his running mate, knowing full well that they would select Tennessee Senator Estes Kefauver. Although angry and disappointed, Kennedy did not sulk.[4] Instead, he used the ensuing campaign to gain more national recognition. He gave a brilliant nomination speech for Stevenson and then campaigned nationally in support of the Democratic ticket.[5] While Stevenson lost a second time to Eisenhower in a landslide, the election campaign boosted Kennedy's image around the country. Kennedy's energy and enthusiasm captivated audiences, and commentators began to mark him as a rising star in the Democratic Party.[6]

The conclusion of the 1956 election campaign in reality marked the beginning of Kennedy's run for the presidency in 1960.[7] While he did not officially announce his candidacy until January 1960, almost every one of his actions over the next three years pointed to this objective. He became more outspoken within his own party by arguing that Democrats had become stagnant and needed a new agenda. In March 1957 he challenged fellow Democrats to develop new ideas and to rely less on the past. He chided his party for living in the past when their most likely Republican nominee in 1960, Richard Nixon, would be a "tough, skillful, shrewd opponent" who would focus on the future. To meet such a potentially strong challenger, Democrats needed "new ideas, new policies and new faces." He also called for unity within the party as it developed and presented a distinct program for the future.[8]

One of the first steps he had to make was to convince his fellow Democrats that he was a viable candidate. He had shown in 1956 that he was an able campaigner, but he was still young—only turning 40 in 1957—and faced stiff opposition. Besides Kennedy, four other Democrats—Humphrey, Johnson, Symington, and Stevenson—wanted the nomination. Despite his defeats in the last two presidential campaigns, Stevenson was still quite popular with the more liberal wing of the party and was open to running

4 O'Donnell and Power, *"Johnny, We Hardly Knew Ye"*, pp. 136-43.

5 "Here's the Speech Placing Adlai in Nomination," *Chicago Daily Tribune*, Aug. 17, 1956, p. 2.

6 James Reston, "Race Is Left Open," *New York Times*, Aug. 17, 1956, p. 1.

7 See Theodore C. Sorensen, "Election of 1960," in *History of American Presidential Elections, 1789-1968*, vol. IV, ed. Arthur M. Schlesinger, Jr. (New York: Chelsea House Publishers, 1971), p. 3450. See also O'Donnell and Power, *"Johnny, We Hardly Knew Ye"*, p. 142; and Goodwin, *Remembering America*, p. 78.

8 "Kennedy Warns His Party on '60," *New York Times*, March 7, 1957, p. 20.

again.[9] All the other candidates knew that even if Stevenson decided not to run, they would have to at least have him on their side. Johnson and Symington, however, were the more likely candidates to receive this support. Having struck out twice, Stevenson remained influential but had little chance for a third campaign. Assuming he did not run, Johnson and Symington both had more experience than Kennedy and were more respected as senators.[10]

Johnson was not a favorite of the Kennedy family as his rejection of Joe Kennedy's offer in 1955 had left a bad taste in their mouths. However, they recognized his political skill as Senate majority leader, his strength within the Democratic Party, and his position as a southerner, but not "too" southern an elected official. Hailing from Texas, Johnson would have an advantage in a presidential campaign of having as his home state one of the largest ones in the country. Furthermore, while being from Texas would help Johnson in the South, it would not hurt him as much in the North as a candidate from a deep south state like Alabama, Georgia, Mississippi, or Georgia. aAdditionally, Johnson had been very successful in the Senate. His quick rise to the leadership of the Democratic Party and his ability to work effectively with Republicans to pass many important pieces of legislation made him a national figure. Finally, while Johnson was older than Kennedy, he was young enough to carry the mantle of a new generation of leaders when compared to Eisenhower who would be 70 in 1960. To prevail in the 1960 general election, Kennedy was going to have to unseat Johnson as the leading candidate for the Democratic nomination.[11]

Symington was Kennedy's most significant challenger besides Johnson. Symington had been a career businessman before joining the Truman administration in 1945 as the chairman of the Surplus Property Board. He served in several different positions under President Truman before becoming the first Secretary of the Air Force in 1947 where he became well-known for his outspoken support of air power. Even after he resigned as the secretary in 1950, he remained one of the leading advocates of the Air Force for the next twenty-five years. In 1952 he ran successfully for a Senate seat in Missouri and was reelected in 1958. Symington, in many ways, was Kennedy's most difficult challenger in the late 1950s as they shared many of the same ideas. Kennedy's problem, but also potentially an advantage, was that Symington was sixteen years older and had the look of an elder statesman. His fellow senators and many Americans particularly respected him for his expertise on

[9] Dallek, *An Unfinished Life*, p. 231.
[10] Sorensen, "Election of 1960," p. 3452. See also Goodwin, *Remembering America*, p. 78.
[11] See Caro, *Master of the Senate*.

national security issues. While Symington did not have Kennedy's looks or financial backing, Joe and John still recognized him as a strong challenger.[12]

Kennedy's final significant opponent and the only one who decided to run in the 1960 Democratic primaries was Minnesota Senator Hubert Humphrey. Next to Stevenson, Humphrey was the darling of the liberal wing of the Democratic Party.[13] He championed the causes of the disenfranchised and the poor, and supported reductions in defense spending. Furthermore, he was known as a tireless campaigner for liberal candidates nationwide. While supported by liberals, his positions alienated most Americans in the center and on the right. He did not have the wide appeal necessary to win a general election, but he had the potential to become the compromise candidate for liberals if Stevenson did not run.[14]

Kennedy's problems did not end with his main challengers. While his father was an asset on many occasions, he could also be a liability. Some critics, including former First Lady Eleanor Roosevelt, claimed that Kennedy was tied too closely to his father and had gotten to his current position because of his father's influence more than his own ability. Kennedy was indeed close to his father, but he went to great lengths on occasion to stake out different positions on many issues. For instance, Kennedy was much more of an internationalist in foreign affairs than his father. When his father had adopted an America first position during the period of American neutrality before World War II, Kennedy openly questioned whether the United States should have been doing more to help Great Britain.[15] This internationalist outlook continued after the war as Kennedy focused on issues such as national security and decolonization.

The claim that the elder Kennedy's influence had helped his son advance was much more difficult to refute. Clearly, Joe had used his immense resources to help his son previously. In 1957, one source estimated Joe Kennedy's net worth at between $200 and $400 million.[16] He had helped get

---

12 For brief biographical information on Symington, see the "Biographical Dictionary of the United States Congress, 1774-Present," http://bioguide.congress.gov/scripts/biodisplay.pl?index=S001136, accessed on March 21, 2008. See also, James C. Olson, *Stuart Symington: A Life* (Columbia: University of Missouri Press, 2003).

13 See for example, "Mrs. Roosevelt Lauds Humphrey," *New York Times*, Dec. 8, 1958, p. 34.

14 Sorensen, "Election of 1960," pp. 3452-53. See also a brief biography at the Minnesota Historical Society, http://www.mnhs.org/library/tips/history_topics/42humphrey.html, accessed on March 21, 2008.

15 See John F. Kennedy, *While England Slept* (New York: Wilfred Funk, Inc., 1940).

16 Roger Creene, "Not Too Reluctant Is the Coy Kennedy," *The Washington Post and Times Herald*, Nov. 10, 1957, p. E3. See also Drew Pearson, "Kennedy Wealth Tops Rockefellers'," ibid., July 6, 1960, p. B9.

John's senior thesis published, pulled strings to get him into the navy and assigned to specific duties, financed his election campaigns for the House and Senate, and used his influence to persuade the Pulitzer Prize awards committee to award his son's *Profiles in Courage* the 1957 Pulitzer Prize. That being said, the younger Kennedy had proven himself to be no lightweight. He was an effective campaigner and had gained polish as a politician. Kennedy appreciated his father's support but believed he was where he was because of his own hard work.

Kennedy's dilemma concerning his relationship with his father is best seen in the position taken by Eleanor Roosevelt. In late 1958, Mrs. Roosevelt wrote a newspaper column and lavished praise on Senator Humphrey and two-time Democratic nominee Adlai Stevenson. While she still favored the latter, his two defeats made her assume that he would not be able to win the nomination. With this in mind, she claimed Humphrey was the best of the potential Democratic nominee for the 1960 presidential campaign. She further claimed that Humphrey had a "spark of greatness" that Eisenhower's successor would need. She did not have the same regards for John Kennedy. She asserted, "I would hesitate to place the difficult decisions that the next President will have to make with someone who understands what courage is and admires it, but has not quite the independence to have it." She went on to assert that Joe Kennedy had spent "oodles of money all over the country" for his son and that he "probably has paid representatives in every state by now."[17]

Kennedy reacted swiftly and negatively to her claims. In December 1958 and January 1959, Kennedy and Mrs. Roosevelt exchanged several letters and telegrams. He wrote her, "Because I know of your long fight against the injudicious use of false statements, rumors or innuendo as a means of injuring the reputation of an individual, I am certain that you are the victim of misinformation." He then went on to ask her to reveal the names of any of his father's "representatives."[18] A week later, the former first lady replied, "If my comment is not true, I will gladly so state. I was told that your father said openly he would spend any money to make his son the first Catholic President of this country, and many people … tell me of money spent by him on your

[17] "Mrs. Roosevelt Lauds Humphrey," *New York Times*, Dec. 8, 1958, p. 34.

[18] John F. Kennedy to Mrs. Franklin D. Roosevelt, December 11, 1958, JFKL, Kennedy Papers, President's Office Files, Special Collections, Box 32, Folder – Roosevelt, Eleanor 6/2/58-11/24/60, p. 1. This letter and the ones that are cited in the next footnotes can also be found at http://www.nps.gov/elro/teach-er-vk/lesson-plans/er-and-jfk.htm. Accessed on August 9, 2006.

behalf. This seems commonly accepted as fact."[19] Kennedy still was not satisfied and persisted in his next letter to ask that she "correct the record in a fair and gracious manner."[20] In early January, Roosevelt wrote a newspaper column where she published Kennedy's denial and stated, "That is the fairest way I know of dealing with a situation of this kind."[21]

Kennedy still was not ready to let the issue rest. He sent her another letter asking her to explicitly repudiate her earlier statements since she was unable to provide the "evidence to justify the rumors." He added that while it might seem that he was being "overly sensitive," he was concerned that the readers of Mrs. Roosevelt's column could still interpret her statement as meaning that she still supported the charges.[22] The former first lady replied one more time that her information came from casual conversations and that she would state in the future that she had the senator's "assurance that the rumors are not true." She even offered to write another column if he requested.[23] It was only at this point that Kennedy dropped the issue without requesting a new column.[24] What is interesting is that Mrs. Roosevelt offered a parting shot in a telegram: "My dear boy I only say these things for your own good. I have found in [a] lifetime of adversity that when blows are rained on one, it is advisable to turn the other profile."[25]

The question of Joe Kennedy's influence on his son was not the only one raised in the years leading up to the 1960 campaign. Of even greater concern to the Kennedy family was whether Americans were willing to elect the first Catholic president of the United States. For example, Georgia Baptists voted in 1958 on a resolution that called for only supporting candidates who defended the "God-given right to worship God according to the dictates of our own consciences." The sponsor of the resolution claimed that "By voting for a Roman Catholic, we would be voting to close every Baptist church in

[19] Eleanor Roosevelt to Senator Kennedy, December 18, 1958, JFKL, Kennedy Papers, President's Office Files, Special Collections, Box 32, Folder – Roosevelt, Eleanor 6/2/58-11/24/60, p. 1.

[20] John F. Kennedy to Mrs. Franklin D. Roosevelt, December 11, 1958, ibid., p. 1.

[21] Eleanor Roosevelt to Senator Kennedy, January 6, 1959, ibid., p. 1. An excerpt from the column was attached to the letter.

[22] John F. Kennedy to Mrs. Franklin D. Roosevelt, January 10, 1959, ibid., p. 1.

[23] Eleanor Roosevelt to Senator Kennedy, January 20, 1959, ibid., p. 1.

[24] John F. Kennedy to Mrs. Franklin D. Roosevelt, January 22, 1959, ibid., p. 1.

[25] Telegram from Eleanor Roosevelt to Honorable John F. Kennedy, January 29, 1959, ibid., p. 1. When using the term "profile", Mrs. Roosevelt was obviously playing on the title of Kennedy's Pulitzer Prize winning book, *Profiles in Courage*.

America."[26] While the resolution did not pass, this type of effort was what scared the Kennedys. Senator Kennedy had begun to address this issue a year earlier by trying to assure Americans that he believed in a clear separation between the church and state. In a November 1957 television interview, he claimed, "What Church I go to on Sunday, or the dogmas of the Catholic Church I believe in, is a personal matter.... There's no reason why that personal obligation of faith in any way limits your obligation to perform your constitutional duties."[27] He continued to wage this battle in 1959 when he argued, "I believe as a senator that the separation of church and state is fundamental to our American concept and heritage and should remain so."[28]

Questions about Kennedy's faith and whether it would influence his decision-making waxed and waned in late 1959 and through the 1960 presidential campaign.[29] A controversy arose in December 1959 when Reverend Daniel Poling, a leading Protestant clergyman, claimed in a new book that then Representative Kennedy agreed to speak at an interfaith banquet in 1947, but pulled out two days before the event.[30] According to Reverend Poling, who arranged the banquet, Kennedy called him and said he could not appear because Dennis Cardinal Dougherty told him not to participate, and "as a loyal son of the church, he had no alternative but not to come."[31] Kennedy admitted in January that he did pull out from speaking, but denied that it was because he had been told to do so by Cardinal Dougherty. He claimed that he withdrew when he came to understand that he was to be the representative of Catholicism at the interfaith event and he did not believe he should do this "without any credentials."[32]

---

[26] "Georgia Baptists Defeat Anti-Kennedy Resolution," *The Washington Post and Times Herald*, Nov. 14, 1958, p. A2. See also, "Kennedy Faith Is Issue: Lutheran Demands Statement on Political Implications," *New York Times*, May 9, 1959, p. 9.

[27] "Kennedy Tells Church-Constitution Stand," *The Christian Science Monitor*, Nov. 25, 1957, p. 13.

[28] "Kennedy Backs State and Church Separation," *Los Angeles Times*, Feb. 17, 1959, p. 7.

[29] The best study of Kennedy, Catholicism, and the 1960 presidential election is Thomas J. Carty, *A Catholic in the White House: Religion, Politics, and John F. Kennedy's Presidential Campaign* (New York: Palgrave MacMillan, 2008). See also T. Davis Lisle, "Southern Baptists and the Issue of Catholic Autonomy in the 1960 Presidential Campaign," in Harper and Krieg, *John F. Kennedy*, pp. 273-85.

[30] Poling initially claimed the banquet was in 1950, but later corrected the date to 1947. For the correction to the date, see John F. Kennedy, Greater Houston Ministerial Association Q & A, Sept. 12, 1960, found at http://www.americanrhetoric.com/speeches/jfkhoustonministerialQ&A.htm, accessed on December 19, 2007.

[31] "Kennedy Bow to Church Cited," *The Washington Post and Times Herald*, Dec. 6, 1959, p. A23.

[32] "Kennedy Recalls Poling Conversation," *Christian Science Monitor*, Jan. 15, 1960, p. 4.

Concerns about whether Kennedy's Catholicism would hinder his candidacy continued through the summer of 1960. In July, Clark Clifford, one of Kennedy's advisers, asked him to enlist former President Harry Truman's support in part because he was a Baptist.[33] The possibility that Protestants might not vote for Kennedy because he was Catholic was quite real. Billy Graham, the leading Christian evangelist of the last half of the twentieth century, had serious reservations about the United States electing a Catholic and worked behind the scenes to support Richard Nixon.[34] In a recent study of Graham's role as an advisor to many different presidents, Graham revealed that he "was strongly for Nixon" and admitted "I did give political advice [to Nixon], and I shouldn't have."[35] While Graham did not openly campaign for Nixon, he went as far as to encourage Eisenhower to become more actively involved in the Nixon election campaign. He wrote Eisenhower, "I know this would mean two months of hard work, but I believe the rewards to the Nation would be as great as when you led the armies at Normandy."[36]

In response to Clifford's warning, Kennedy sent one of his representatives to meet with Truman about joining the campaign more actively as the former president "could be very helpful in the Baptist country where our problem is greatest."[37] A month later, John Kenneth Galbraith wrote Kennedy that he needed to urgently address the "problem of religion in the farm belt." Galbraith argued that "Religion in the rural corn belt, Great Plains and down into rural Texas has become an issue greater than either income or peace." He went on to explain that to average Midwest farmer, Kennedy was "a distant figure from the East" with whom they could not relate. The problem, according to Galbraith, was that because they could not relate to Kennedy, they focused on the fact that he was a Catholic. He encouraged Kennedy to tackle the religious issue head-on, preferably through a television interview.[38]

Kennedy forcefully and directly addressed his faith and his strong support for the separation of church and state in September 1960 when he participated

---

33 Clark M. Clifford to John F. Kennedy, July 19,1960, JFKL, Kennedy Papers, President's Office Files, Special Correspondence, Box #29, Folder – Clifford, Clark M., p. 1.

34 Carty, *A Catholic in the White House*, pp. 56-57.

35 Nancy Gibbs and Michael Duffy, *The Preacher and the President: Billy Graham in the White House* (New York: Center Street, 2007), p. 78.

36 Quoted in ibid., p. 85, and in Richard Peirard, "Billy Graham and the U.S. Presidency," *Journal of Church and State* 22 (Winter 1980), p. 120.

37 John F. Kennedy to Clark M. Clifford, July 29, 1960, JFKL, Kennedy Papers, President's Office Files, Special Correspondence, Box #29, Folder – Clifford, Clark M., p. 1.

38 J. K. Galbraith to John F. Kennedy, Aug. 25,1960, ibid., '60 Campaign Issues, Position and Briefing Papers, 1960, Nuclear Testing – Briefing Papers, Box #993, Folder – Religious Issues, pp. 1-3.

in a meeting with leading Protestant clergymen in Houston, Texas.[39] He, in many ways, was going into the lions' den of Protestant America. He delivered an opening address where he boldly laid out his views:

> "I believe in an America where the separation of church and state is absolute--where no Catholic prelate would tell the President (should he be Catholic) how to act, and no Protestant minister would tell his parishoners [*sic*] for whom to vote--where no church or church school is granted any public funds or political preference--and where no man is denied public office merely because his religion differs from the President who might appoint him or the people who might elect him."[40]

After his speech, he answered numerous pointed questions from the audience and reiterated that in making decisions he would follow the guidelines of the Constitution. When asked again about why he withdrew from speaking at the Rev. Poling's interfaith banquet in 1947, he reiterated that he withdrew on his own accord because he did not believe he had the qualifications to speak as a representative of the Catholic Church. After being asked if he would follow the dictates of Cardinal Richard Cushing or other Catholic officials in the Vatican, he exclaimed, "I do not accept the right of any … ecclesiastical official, to tell me what I shall do in the sphere of my public responsibility as an elected official."[41] While the issue did not go away completely after this address, it went a long way in relieving the concerns of those who were reluctant to vote for a Catholic but had not ruled it out completely.[42]

The questions of Joe Kennedy's influence and Kennedy's Catholic faith mixed with many other issues during the Democratic nomination process and the general campaign. Senator Kennedy deliberately waited until 1960 to begin his formal candidacy. On January 2, he announced his candidacy for the Democratic nomination for president and proclaimed that throughout his career he had "developed an image of America as fulfilling a noble and

[39] Randall Balmer, *God in the White House: How Faith Shaped the Presidency from John F. Kennedy to George W. Bush* (New York: HarperOne, 2008), pp. 7-8.

[40] "Address of Senator John F. Kennedy to the Greater Houston Ministerial Association," September 12, 1960, found at http://www.jfklibrary.org/Historical+Resources/Archives/Reference+Desk/Speeches/JFK/JFK+Pre-Pres/Address+of+Senator+John+F.+Kennedy+to+the+Greater+Houston+Ministerial+Association.htm, accessed on Dec. 19, 2007.

[41] John F. Kennedy, Greater Houston Ministerial Association Q & A, Sept. 12, 1960, found at http://www.americanrhetoric.com/speeches/jfkhoustonministerialQ&A.htm, accessed on Dec. 19, 2007.

historic role as the defender of freedom in a time of maximum peril—and of the American people as confident, courageous, and persevering."[43] His only declared opponent for the Democratic nomination was Senator Humphrey. While Humphrey was popular with liberals, Kennedy did not see him as great of a threat as Johnson, Stevenson, and Symington. Those three deliberately chose not to declare early in the Democratic nomination process.[44]

Kennedy entered the campaign with resources and the political organization that his opponents, both declared and undeclared, lacked. Kennedy's father had been eyeing his son's presidential campaign for years and had been laying the foundation for his son's run by supporting Democrats financially in key battleground states. Kennedy selected his brother, Robert Kennedy, as campaign manager and he could not have found anyone better suited for the position. He was ruthlessly effective.[45] Further, Kennedy could count on the support of his entire family to campaign for him. Finally, his wife, Jackie, proved incredibly popular. While Kennedy had to overcome many disadvantages, he was better positioned at the start of the campaign than most recognized.[46]

Kennedy devoted considerable energy to the Democratic primaries, not so much to win the backing of each state's delegates, as important as this support was, but to gain national name recognition. While not well understood by the other candidates, Kennedy recognized that political campaigning had entered a new era where television coverage would be vitally important. By running in the primaries, Kennedy knew he would gain exposure and become a better known national figure. As Gary Donaldson asserts, Kennedy "seemed to chew up the camera, and America quickly fell in love with him and his family."[47] Since Stevenson and Johnson did not declare that they were running for the nomination, and Symington did not join the campaign until the spring, Kennedy only had one major opponent, Humphrey, in the early state

---

[42] For a good summary of the role of religion in the 1960 campaign, see Balmer, *God in the White House*, pp. 16-46.

[43] "The Kennedy Statement," January 3, 1960, *New York Times*, p. 44.

[44] This was not unusual. The 1960 election marked a transition in presidential campaigns where state primaries gained a lot more importance. Before then, the political parties' national conventions were most important.

[45] Dallek, *An Unfinished Life*, pp. 242-3.

[46] For a description of the role of the Kennedy family, see Robert A. Divine, *Foreign Policy and U.S. Presidential Election: 1952 1960* (New York: New Viewpoints, 1974), pp. 197-98; Gary A. Donaldson, *The First Modern Campaign: Kennedy, Nixon, and the Election of 1960* (Lanham, MD: Rowman & Littlefield Publishers, Inc., 20070, p. 55; and Dallek, *An Unfinished Life*, pp. 253-54.

[47] Donaldson, *The First Modern Campaign*, p. 47.

primaries. In previous elections, candidates had focused their energy on securing their party's nomination at the national convention. Kennedy adopted a different approach.[48] He planned to campaign hard in the primaries to build momentum that the other candidates would not be able to overcome at the national convention.

In 1960, only sixteen states held primaries.[49] Furthermore, only in California, Florida, Maryland, New Hampshire, Ohio, Oregon, Wisconsin, and Indiana did the state primaries bind their respective delegates to the winning candidate.[50] In the forty-two remaining states, the delegates to the Democratic national convention remained free to pick which ever candidate they wanted. In previous campaigns, candidates focused on winning over state party leaders who would then bring their delegates in line.[51] The 1960 election was going to be different as Kennedy was making the primaries much more significant. The Massachusetts's senator ultimately secured the nomination by capitalizing on the other candidates' failure, with the exception of Humphrey, to run actively in the primaries.

Kennedy had a clear advantage over Humphrey going into the primary season. Humphrey had very limited resources, and the senator did not. To make the most of his resources, Humphrey focused on winning two state primaries—Wisconsin and West Virginia.[52] Since neighboring Minnesota was his home state, he believed he had a solid chance of winning in Wisconsin. Further, West Virginia Democrats tended to be Protestant and leaned more to the left, which was also more in tune with Humphrey's positions. He hoped to force Kennedy to withdraw from the campaign by winning these states and to emerge as the frontrunner. This strategy had little chance for success but provided him his best opportunity. Unfortunately for Humphrey, Kennedy proved too strong.

Kennedy started by campaigning hard in New Hampshire even though he really faced no opposition there and won with 85 percent in early March. He then ran unopposed in Indiana and Nebraska and brokered deals to gain the delegates in Ohio and California.[53] His first major challenge was to win a contested state, and he made a relatively bold move by challenging Humphrey in Wisconsin—the Minnesota senator's own backyard. Kennedy ran an

---

[48] Goodwin, *Remembering America*, pp. 79-80.
[49] Dalleck, *An Unfinished Life*, p. 239.
[50] See Donaldson, *The First Modern Campaign*, note 2, p. 170.
[51] Dallek, *An Unfinished Life*, p. 239.
[52] Donaldson, *The First Modern Campaign*, p. 47.
[53] Dallek, *An Unfinished Life*, p. 247.

excellent campaign and used his overwhelming advantage in organization and resources. For example, he toured the state in his family's personal jet, while Humphrey travelled from site to site in an old bus.[54] After winning a strong victory, Kennedy expected Humphrey to pull out, but the Minnesota senator, much to Kennedy's chagrin, decided to take his economically hamstrung campaign to do battle in West Virginia. Again, the Kennedy machine was simply too strong. By the time the votes were counted in West Virginia in early May, Humphrey knew his chance for the nomination was over, and he withdrew from the Democratic race.[55]

Although Kennedy clearly had the momentum, he definitely was not assured of the nomination. Former President Truman came out in support of Symington in May; Johnson officially declared his candidacy in early July and already controlled most of the southern states' delegates; and Stevenson remained the champion of most liberals and continued to hold out hope of securing his third nomination at the Democratic National Convention in Los Angeles in mid-July. While the Humphrey/Kennedy contests in the spring had produced some negative campaigning, the rhetoric in June and early July became particularly heated. Kennedy feared Symington's campaign only if a deadlock emerged at the convention and the party looked for a compromise candidate. Since Symington was well-liked and more importantly had fewer enemies, he could become the dark-horse candidate. Just days before the convention, Symington predicted such an outcome claiming a Kennedy/Johnson deadlock would lead to his nomination.[56]

Johnson and Stevenson were different opponents altogether. The Kennedys saw Johnson as the greatest threat to his nomination but also feared that Stevenson could emerge if the liberal wing of the Democratic Party gained prominence. While Stevenson had already received the nomination and lost the general elections in 1952 and 1956, many liberals saw him as the true champion of their cause.[57] They argued that any Democratic candidate would have lost against Eisenhower, and that Stevenson deserved another chance. One of them, Eleanor Roosevelt, urged Stevenson to run and for Kennedy to

---

[54] See W. J. Rorabaugh, *The Real Making of the President: Kennedy, Nixon, and the 1960 Election* (Lawrence, KS: University Press of Kansas, 2009), pp. 48-51; and Donaldson, *The First Modern Campaign*, p. 50.

[55] The best accounts of the Democratic primary campaign are Rorabaugh, *The Real Making of the President*, pp. 31-67; Dallek, *An Unfinished Life*, pp. 45-60; and Donaldson, *The First Modern Campaign*, pp. 46-60.

[56] Walter Trohan, "Johnson Arrives in Los Angeles to Marshall Forces," *Chicago Daily Tribune*, July 9, 1960, p. N1.

[57] Schlesinger, *Journals*, pp. 59-60.

join the ticket as the vice-president candidate. She explained that serving as vice president would give the Massachusetts senator "the opportunity to grow and learn."[58] Kennedy would have none of this. He worked diligently to gain Stevenson's endorsement, calling him in May to tell him that he wanted "to be nominated by the liberals. I don't want to go screwing around with all those [southerners]."[59] Stevenson, however, held out some hope that he might be drafted a third time by the Democrats and refused Kennedy's entreaties.[60]

Johnson was the clear choice of most Democrats who did not support Kennedy. Throughout the primary campaigns and heading up to the convention, key Democratic leaders, like Senator Robert Byrd of West Virginia and former President Truman, openly campaigned against Kennedy. Byrd had supported Humphrey in the West Virginia primary in his bid to derail Kennedy.[61] While Truman put his support behind Symington in May, he mainly did this in hopes of slowing the Kennedy machine until Johnson decided to enter the race.[62]

Truman came out most strongly on July 2 when he announced on television that he had resigned as a delegate to the Democratic National Convention because he feared that it was "taking on the aspects of a prearranged affair." He argued the party should nominate "someone with the greatest possible maturity and experience." Furthermore, he asked Kennedy "to be patient" and "that all personal ambitions be put aside and that we all join forces to seek out such a man who could unite us in purpose and action."[63] He identified Symington and Johnson as two leaders who met these qualifications. Kennedy responded angrily and demanded air time to refute Truman's claims. CBS (Columbia Broadcasting System) agreed to give him 30 minutes.[64] Kennedy vehemently denied that the results of the convention were "prearranged", and then raised the issue as to whether Truman and his generation should be the leaders anymore. He claimed, "It is time for a new generation of leadership to cope with new problems and new opportunities. For there is a new world to be won, a world of peace and goodwill, and a world of hope and abundance, and I want America to lead the way to that new

58 "Mrs. F.D.R.'s View," *The Washington Post and Times Herald*, June 11, 1960, p. A2.
59 Schlesinger, *Journals*, p. 60.
60 See Donaldson, *The First Modern Campaign*, pp. 73-74, and Dallek, *An Unfinished Life*, p. 259.
61 Dallek, *An Unfinished Life*, p. 255.
62 Donaldson, *The First Modern Campaign*, p. 72.
63 Donald Janson, "Truman Charges Kennedy Backers Run Convention," *New York Times*, July 3, 1960, p. 1.
64 Leo Egan, "Kennedy Demands Air Time To Reply," ibid., p. 1.

world." As to who was most qualified to be the leader Truman described, Kennedy concluded, "I am ready."[65]

A bigger potential threat was Johnson officially announcing his candidacy on July 5.[66] Johnson immediately went on the attack questioning Kennedy's health, limited experience, and ties to his father. Alluding to his experience in comparison to Kennedy's, Johnson claimed, "All the forces of evil in this world … will have no mercy for innocence, no gallantry toward inexperience, and no patience toward errors."[67] Both sides threw mud at the other. While Robert Kennedy raised questions about Johnson's alleged ties to the Teamsters and Jimmy Hoffa,[68] Johnson privately tried to get Eisenhower to speak out against Kennedy to help block his nomination, but the president refused. Johnson even went as far as to contend that Kennedy could serve as his vice president since "The Vice Presidency is a good place for a young man who needs experience. It's a good place to get that training."[69]

The Kennedys responded to Johnson's allegations about the senator's health and bravado by denying that Kennedy had Addison's disease and portraying the senator as being in excellent health.[70] Privately, however, they were fearful that the truth concerning Kennedy's health problems, including him having Addison's disease[71], would reach the voters. While the Kennedys were able to hide the senator's health problems, historian Robert Dallek argues that if the public had known about all of Kennedy's ailments, "it could have raised substantial doubts about his fitness for the presidency." Dallek also found that when Kennedy misplaced the bag containing all of his medications on a campaign trip, it caused a near panic until it was found.[72]

All the campaigning aside, Kennedy was virtually guaranteed the nomination once the convention began on July 11 as Johnson, Stevenson, and Symington could not muster the support to mount a serious challenge.[73] While

---

65 "Transcript of Senator Kennedy's News Conference Replying to Truman Attack," ibid., July 5, 1960, p. 20.

66 "Sen. Johnson in Race as 'Working' Leader: Texan's Formal Announcement Full of Gibes," *Chicago Daily Tribune*, July 6, 1960, p. 6.

67 Ibid.

68 Walter Trohan, "Johnson Arrives in Los Angeles to Marshall Forces," ibid., July 9, 1960, p. N1.

69 John D. Morriss, "Maturity Theme of Johnson Drive," *New York Times*, July 9, 1960, p. 8.

70 Dallek, *An Unfinished Life*, p. 262.

71 Addison's Disease is a disease where the adrenal glands do not release sufficient hormones to regulate the body's organs. The most common symptoms are fatigue, muscle weakness, weight loss, and irritability.

72 Dallek, *An Unfinished Life*, p. 262.

73 Herbert S. Parmet, *JFK: The Presidency of John F. Kennedy* (New York: The Dial Press, 1983), pp. 10-12.

Johnson kept up the attacks until the delegates began to vote, too many Democrats considered him too conservative, and more importantly, too "southern." Stevenson failed to seize whatever opportunity that might have existed to rally the liberal base when he did not openly seek the nomination. Symington simply was not a strong enough candidate. Kennedy won the nomination on the first ballot when Wyoming cast its 15 votes giving him two more than he needed for the nomination.[74]

Democrats quickly rallied around their nominee, as one editorial claimed Kennedy is "a healing rather than divisive figure."[75] Arthur Schlesinger, who had advised Kennedy but would have preferred Stevenson as the nominee, compared the young candidate to Franklin Roosevelt. Schlesinger wrote in his diary "The thought of power neither rattles nor discomposes him. He takes power in his stride. He had absolute assurance about his own capacity to do the job, and he was a sure instinct about how to get what he wants. In John Kennedy the will to victory and the will to command are both plain and visible." However, Schlesinger also had some reservations. "I believe him to be a liberal," Schlesinger noted, "but committed by a sense of history rather than consecrated by inner conviction. I also believe him to be a devious and, if necessary, ruthless man."[76]

One of the first major political decisions he had to make, deciding who would be his vice president, quickly gave this assessment some credence. The obvious choice was Lyndon Johnson, but there was bad blood between the Senate majority leader and some members of the Kennedy family. Further, many liberals viewed Johnson as way too conservative.[77] When word leaked out that Kennedy was leaning towards nominating Johnson, liberals "began raging with indignation."[78] In the end Kennedy made the practical decision that placing Johnson on the ticket would help him during the campaign and possibly remove a future opponent to his programs.[79] As Schlesinger concluded, Kennedy "believed that Johnson would add the most strength to the ticket. In addition, he knew it would greatly simplify his life … if he had

---

[74] See Rorabaugh, *The Real Making of the President*, pp. 72-80; Dallek, *An Unfinished Life*, pp. 265-66; and Donaldson, *The First Modern Campaign*, pp. 74-77.

[75] "Kennedy the Candidate," *The Washington Post and Times Herald,* July 14, 1960, p. A22.

[76] Schlesinger, *Journals*, pp. 69-70.

[77] O'Donnell and Power, *"Johnny, We Hardly Knew Ye"*, p. 213.

[78] *Time*, July 25, 1960; quoted in Donaldson, *The First Modern Campaign*, p. 80.

[79] O'Donnell and Power, *"Johnny, We Hardly Knew Ye"*, p. 217-18. See also Parmet, *JFK*, p. 26-29.

Johnson under his eye as vice president rather than running a competing administration as majority leader."[80]

While some may have doubted him, Kennedy moved with confidence, placing his sights on the national election and doing his best to get Americans to focus on the future. He announced in his acceptance speech, "Today our concern must be with that future. For the world is changing. The old era is ending. The old ways will not be." He asked Americans to not evaluate a candidate on his religious faith as had happened in past elections, particularly the 1928 presidential election, by emphasizing "It is not relevant." Kennedy further noted that the United States stood at the edge of a "New Frontier—the frontier of the 1960's—a frontier of unknown opportunities and perils—a frontier of unfulfilled hopes and threats" and called for "a new generation of leadership—new men to cope with new problems and new opportunities." Finally, he challenged all that were listening by asserting that "the New Frontier of which I speak is not a set of promises--it is a set of challenges. It sums up not what I intend to offer the American people, but what I intend to ask of them. It appeals to their pride, not to their pocketbook--it holds out the promise of more sacrifice instead of more security. ... I am asking you to be pioneers on that New Frontier."[81]

As Kennedy began the general campaign, he faced the presumptive Republican nominee, Richard Nixon, who was running basically unopposed for the Republican nomination. There was some question whether New York Governor Nelson Rockefeller would mount a challenge, but that never materialized. The Republicans met in Chicago at the end of July and quickly nominated Nixon. While nominated without much of a fight, the vice president was the nominee for a party that was showing some deep divisions, especially from moderate Republicans who supported Rockefeller. Nixon's efforts to reach out to Rockefeller's supporters angered many on the right, and his efforts to appease the right alienated some of the more moderate delegates. In the end this division did not amount to much in the 1960 campaign but marked

---

[80] Schlesinger, *Journals*, p. 68. Sorensen told Kennedy that Johnson "helps with the farmers, Southerners and Texas; easier to work with in this position than as Majority Leader." Kennedy retorted that if Johnson remained as majority leader he "would screw me all the time." Sorensen, *Counselor*, p. 243.

[81] Address of Senator John F. Kennedy Accepting the Democratic Party Nomination for the Presidency of the United States, July 15, 1960, found at the John F. Kennedy Presidential Library and Museum, http://www.jfklibrary.org/Historical+Resources/Archives/Reference+Desk/Speeches/JFK/JFK+Pre-Pres/Address+of+Senator+John+F.+Kennedy+Accepting+the+Democratic+Party+Nomination+for+the+Presidency+of+t.htm, accessed on January 17, 2008.

the initial stages of a major schism in the Republican Party that emerged in 1964. To balance his candidacy, Nixon selected Henry Cabot Lodge, the ambassador to the United Nations and the former senator from Massachusetts who Kennedy had beaten in the 1952 senatorial campaign, as his running mate.[82]

As Kennedy left the Democratic Convention, he did so confident in his abilities, but also knowing that Nixon was a worthy opponent who would pose a stiff challenge through the election in November. Although at one point early in their careers they had almost become friends, they had moved their separate ways in the 1950s.[83] They came to respect each other's political abilities, but they did not like one another.[84] As Kennedy laid out his views of the New Frontier, he made every effort to contrast his record with the Republican candidate. He claimed Nixon "has often seemed to show charity toward none and malice for all" and "after eight years of drugged and fitful sleep, this nation needs strong, creative Democratic leadership in the White House." Despite being only four years younger than Nixon, Kennedy opined that the Republican nominee's "approach is as old as McKinley. His party is the party of the past."[85]

Kennedy began his campaign as the Democratic nominee with an incredibly strong organization that in ways marked a break from the past. In prior elections, staffs remained relatively small and the candidate himself served in essence as the campaign manager. The 1960 election was going to be different at least for the Democratic nominee. Kennedy left the management side of the campaign to his brother, Robert, and to other loyal supporters. This tight structure, when coupled with his campaign's use of television, air travel, mass polling, and careful communication, gave Kennedy a clear advantage over Nixon. In contrast to Kennedy, the Republican nominee micromanaged his entire campaign. He spread himself very thin by keeping his promise to visit all of the fifty states. While a nice gesture, it prevented him from focusing as much time as necessary in key battleground states. The contrasting campaign strategies gave Kennedy a clear advantage.[86]

One of Kennedy's priorities after a brief vacation with Jackie and his daughter, Caroline, immediately following the Democratic Convention was to

---

82 Stephen E. Ambrose, *Nixon: The Education of a Politician, 1913-1962* (New York: Simon and Schuster, 1987), pp. 552-54.
83 See Christopher J. Matthews, *Kennedy & Nixon: The Rivalry that Shaped Postwar America* (New York: Simon & Schuster, 1996).
84 Schlesinger, *Journals*, p. 77.
85 Ibid.
86 Donaldson, *The First Modern Campaign*, pp. 94-7.

make sure the old stalwarts of the Democratic Party—Roosevelt, Stevenson, and Truman—rallied around the ticket. This was not a foregone conclusion as each of them had doubts about their party's nominee, and both Roosevelt and Truman had been openly critical of the Massachusetts senator. Fortunately for Kennedy, these three were party loyalists, and more importantly, they shared a common hatred of Nixon. While Truman saw Kennedy as "immature",[87] he loathed Nixon and even called him "Tricky Dicky" in private correspondence.[88] Truman later told Abe Ribicoff "I never liked Kennedy. I hate his father. Kennedy wasn't so great as a Senator.... However, ... Dick Nixon called me a Communist and I'll do anything to beat him."[89] Roosevelt and Stevenson also shared similar views and agreed to campaign for Kennedy.

Through August and into September, both Nixon and Kennedy moved to shore up their party's base and to reach out to the undecided. Unfortunately for the vice president he lost valuable time on the campaign trail when he hurt his knee and had to spend two weeks in the hospital. The key question in September was whether the two would engage in any debates. While they are the norm in modern elections, they were quite rare before 1960. In fact, televised debates had never occurred. Eisenhower warned Nixon not to debate Kennedy, as he believed the vice president really had nothing to gain, while the Democratic challenger would gain greater name recognition and be seen as the vice president's equal on the debate stage.[90] Commentators at the time recognized the same situation. *New York Times* columnist James Reston claimed that "Kennedy stands to gain the most from these confrontations [debates]. He has been laboring under the popular impression that he is too young and immature for the presidency.... But once he gets on the same screen with Nixon, this age difference of four years seems less important."[91] Nixon, however, could not resist the challenge. In the end, the two candidates met in four debates with the first proving the most monumental.

While Nixon recognized the value of the debates, he underestimated Kennedy and did not prepare as well as he should have. Kennedy, on the other hand, focused much of his attention in late September on debate preparation. Further, while Kennedy had numerous health concerns, he and his staff kept

---

87 Harry S. Truman to Dean Acheson, August 26, 1960 (never sent), in Robert H. Ferrell, ed., *Off the Record: The Private Papers of Harry S. Truman* (New York: Penguin Books, 1980), p. 390.

88 Harry S. Truman to Dean Acheson, August 22, 1959 (never sent), in ibid., p. 382.

89 Quoted in Dallek, *An Unfinished Life*, p. 278.

90 Ambrose, *Nixon*, pp. 558-59. See also Dwight D. Eisenhower, *Waging Peace, 1956-1961* (Garden City, NY: Doubleday & Company, Inc., 1965), p. 598.

91 James Reston, "Kennedy on First by Fielder's Choice," *New York Times*, Sept. 28, 1960, p. 38.

them hidden for the most part. On the outside, Kennedy seemed to epitomize strength and good health. He had a nice sun tan and showed no outward signs of any health problems. Nixon was a different story. He was still recovering from his knee injury, and any time he bumped it, as he did exiting the car at the TV studio, he felt excruciating pain.[92] Additionally, he had suffered a bad case of the flu and had pushed himself on the campaign to the point of near exhaustion. He looked haggard and much older then he really was. The television executives offered both candidates make-up, and to his later regret, Nixon declined.[93]

An estimated nearly 60 million Americans watched as Kennedy and Nixon gave their opening statements and then answered questions from four reporters.[94] Kennedy emphasized the importance of seeking a new direction and better future, while Nixon defended the Eisenhower administration's policies and the direction the country was headed. Kennedy argued, "I think we can do better. I don't want the talents of any American to go to waste." He concluded, "I think it is time America started moving again." Nixon followed by expressing his general agreement with Kennedy, "I subscribe completely to the spirit that Senator Kennedy has expressed tonight, the spirit that the United States should move ahead." However, Nixon then pointed to the acco-mplishments on the Eisenhower administration and noted that he planned "to build on" that record.[95] Overall, both men came across as qualified for the presidency. However, this was really a victory for Kennedy since there were still some who questioned his qualifications. Furthermore, those watching the debate on television, as opposed to those listening on the radio, came away with a much more favorable impression of Kennedy.[96] Unfortunately, this was mainly due to each candidate's appearance. While Kennedy looked young and fresh, Nixon "looked tired."[97] A Boston Republican who watched the debate even claimed Nixon's "grimness was shocking."[98]

While the remaining debates were significant, the first one had raised Kennedy's stature and introduced him to the entire nation. Going into the first debate a Gallup Poll had the race a statistical tie with Nixon leading 47 to

---

92 Clay Gowran, "Candidates Tell Aims," *Chicago Daily Tribune*, Sept. 27, 1960, p. 1.

93 Donaldson, *The First Modern Campaign*, pp. 110-15. See also Goodwin, *Remembering America*, p. 115.

94 "Debate's TV Audience Estimated at 60 Million," *New York Times*, Sept, 27, 1960, p. 29.

95 Transcript of Nixon-Kennedy Discussion, *Chicago Daily Tribune*, Sept. 27, 1960, p. 6.

96 Donaldson, *The First Modern Campaign*, p. 118.

97 Reston, "Kennedy on First by Fielder's Choice," *New York Times*, Sept. 28, 1960, p. 38.

98 "Both Candidates Retain Backers," ibid., p. 26.

46%. By the end of October, Kennedy led 51 to 45%.[99] While the debates were clearly not the only factor for the shift, they did play a role. Prior to the debates, Kennedy was still relatively unknown to the average American. After them, he was a known commodity who had shown a good command of the issues and an ability to lead the nation.[100] One reporter noted that while Kennedy was popular before the first debate, the enthusiasm at his campaign events afterwards, especially among women, was similar to "those evoked by Dick Clark or Frank Sinatra on personal-appearance tours."[101]

While the candidates' appearances, Kennedy's faith, and Kennedy's connection to his father all played a role in the election, there were several substantive issues that Kennedy emphasized to set himself apart from Nixon. As he had done prior to declaring his candidacy, he hammered the Eisenhower administration for not being strong enough against communism and for spending too little on defense programs. He criticized the administration's handling of the economy, often claiming that the administration's emphasis on a balanced budget undermined economic growth. Finally, he lambasted the administration's handling of civil rights issues. On each of these issues, Kennedy's views were not too different from Nixon's, but he did his best to paint his opponent in the worst possible light.

Kennedy was interested in defense and foreign policy issues more than others, and unfortunately for Nixon, Eisenhower's policies were an easy target. Eisenhower had deliberately designed his defense policies to be affordable for an indefinite period, or the "long haul" as he sometimes called it.[102] He believed the United States ultimately would win the Cold War but not through military force. Rather, he thought the United States would need to maintain a large enough military force to deter Soviet aggression until the Soviet Union eventually collapsed from what he saw as the inherent weaknesses in communism. To achieve this, he wanted to balance the budget and maintain a large enough military to do the job. He managed to do this by placing a much greater emphasis on nuclear weapons and their delivery systems—long-range bombers, intercontinental ballistic missiles, and intermediate-range ballistic missiles—while limiting conventional forces. He believed the United States had sufficient conventional forces to meet any

---

99 Donaldson, *The First Modern Campaign*, p. 123.

100 Ibid., pp. 123-25.

101 "Kennedy Dazzles Women on Tours," *New York Times*, Oct. 2, 1960, p. 54. See Parmet, *JFK*, p. 45.

102 For the best description of Eisenhower's national security policies, see Immerman and Bowie, *Waging Peace*.

challenge similar to the Korean War and that they did not need to be larger because any war with the Soviet Union would quickly involve nuclear weapons.[103] Kennedy disagreed as he believed the United States needed larger conventional and nuclear forces.

Kennedy, along with many other Eisenhower critics, argued that Eisenhower put too much emphasis on balancing the budget at the expense of national security. Critics did not make much headway in Eisenhower's first term, but his second term was different. Prior to October 1957, Eisenhower could rely on his vast prestige to assuage most Americans. However, after the Soviet Union launched *Sputnik* in October 1957 many Americans came to believe that the United States had fallen behind the Soviet Union in military capabilities, in particular missile delivery systems. Kennedy was one of them. He argued in November that the Soviets "appear to possess a marked lead in important phases of missile development and technology; their ballistic missiles are able--or soon will be-to strike any designated target anywhere in the world."[104] For the next three years, he frequently criticized the Eisenhower administration for allowing the United States to fall behind the Soviet Union and persistently claimed that a missile gap existed with the United States falling further and further behind the Soviet Union. He claimed that if the gap was not closed, the Soviet Union might decide to launch an attack.[105]

During the 1960 primary and general election campaign, Kennedy continually questioned the Eisenhower administration's positions on conventional forces and the missile gap. In a note to a constituent soon after declaring his candidacy, he wrote, "I am convinced that there are a number of serious deficiencies in our defense budget and program for the coming year."[106] He claimed in October that "we cannot afford to get into a position where Soviet aggression on a limited scale with conventional weapons forces

---

[103] David L. Snead, *The Gaither Committee, Eisenhower, and the Cold War* (Columbus: Ohio State University Press, 1999), pp. 154-55.

[104] Remarks of Senator John F. Kennedy, "The New Dimensions of American Foreign Policy," November 1, 1957, found at http://www.jfklibrary.org/Historical+Resources/Archives/Reference+Desk/Speeches/JFK/JFK+Pre-Pres/002PREPRES12SPEECHES_57NOV01.htm, accessed on January 30, 2008.

[105] For a summary of Kennedy's allegations about the missile gap between 1957 and 1960, see Appendix B to the Memorandum for the Record, June 17, 1963, JFKL, Kennedy Papers, National Security Files, Subjects, Box 298, Folder – Missile Gap 6/63-7/63.

[106] John F. Kennedy to John De Lowe, Jan. 18, 1960, JFKL, Kennedy Papers, Pre-Presidential Papers, Senate Files, Legislation, Legislation Files, 1953-1960, 1960, Defense: General – Education: General, Box 733, Folder – Economy, 1/60, 2/60.

us to choose between retreat and starting nuclear warfare."[107] Earlier in the campaign, he called for expanding conventional forces "to prevent brush-fire wars that our capacity for nuclear retaliation is unable to deter"[108] and supported an increase in defense spending of $2.5-3 billion, paid for by higher taxes if necessary.[109]

He argued on October 18 that "American strength in relation to that of the Sino-Soviet bloc has been slipping" as "the direct result of short-sighted budgetary policies and bad judgment in Washington." He called for "crash programs" to increase production of Polaris and Minuteman missiles that would "eventually close the missile gap". [110] In an earlier speech, he accused the Eisenhower administration with "gambling with our national survival." He added that "those of us who call for a higher defense budget are taking a chance on spending money unnecessarily. But those who oppose these expenditures are taking a chance on our very survival as a nation. ... The only real question is—which chance, which gamble, do we take—our money or our survival?" He called for expanding missile production across the board "to cover the current gap as best we can."[111] His arguments resonated with those who no longer thought that Eisenhower really understood the nature of the communist threat.

Kennedy tied his critique of Eisenhower's defense policies to what he contended was the growing threat of communism around the world. In 1960, there were numerous struggles and standoffs occurring across the globe. Most Americans still considered the Soviet Union the greatest threat to world peace and viewed most conflicts through the prism of the Cold War. Besides the general arms race, Kennedy focused much of his attention on Cuba and Berlin. He also mentioned problems in Laos, Vietnam, the Middle East, and elsewhere. His main critique was that Eisenhower's policies had allowed communism to spread into many new locations and that he would put an end to it. He told reporters in late July 1960, "I believe in T.R.'s [Teddy Roosevelt]

---

107 Quoted in John Raymond, "Kennedy Favors Pentagon Shift and Plane Alert," *New York Times*, Oct. 24, 1960, p. 1.

108 "Remarks of Senator John F. Kennedy, American State Legion Convention, Sioux Falls, South Dakota," June 19, 1960, JFKL, Kennedy Papers, Pre-Presidential Papers, '60 Campaign Press and Publicity, Speeches, Statements, and Sections 1958-1960, Agriculture-Defense-Disarmament: Increasing Perils of Radioactivity, Box 1028, Folder – Civil Rights, Job Discrimination, NAACP Policy.

109 Joseph A. Loftus, "Kennedy Favors Defense Outlay," *New York Times*, July 11, 1960, p. 18.

110 Quotes in Joseph Hearst, "Kennedy Asks U.S. Weapons Not Oratory," *Chicago Daily Tribune*, Oct. 19, 1960, p. 1; and "Excerpts from Kennedy Talk to Legion," *New York Times*, Oct. 19, 1960, p. 39. See also Preble, *John F. Kennedy and the Missile Gap*, p. 115.

111 "Kennedy Pursues Rise in Arms Funds," *New York Times*, Mar. 1, 1960, p. 4.

advice about carrying a big stick and speaking softly, and not the reverse, as this Administration has done."[112]

Questions concerning the status of Berlin played a critical role in U.S.-Soviet relations from the time the allies decided to divide Germany and Berlin into four occupation zones at the end of World War II, controlled by France, Great Britain, the Soviet Union, and the United States, respectively. Very quickly in the years after the war, the British, French, and American consolidated their zones into what became West Germany and the Soviet zone became East Germany. A similar division occurred in Berlin. Since Berlin was located within East Germany, the Soviets fruitlessly requested its former allies to turn over West Berlin to East German control. This standoff led to several crises, including in the famous Berlin Blockade and resulting allied airlift in 1948-1949, and lesser crises like in 1958. Kennedy believed that while Eisenhower had not given West Berlin to the Soviets as they demanded, the president had not been as clear as he should. He wrote a constituent in September 1960, "the preservation of the free world position in Berlin was a matter on which we must be willing, if necessary, to use whatever weapons we have at our command in order to meet or forestall any Communist attempt at military seizure or attack. … (W)ere the Russians to take reckless actions, I would want to meet that aggression by appropriate means, which might not at all involve nuclear weapons."[113]

Cuba was an even more pressing issue than Berlin. In January 1959, Fidel Castro seized power in Cuba by overthrowing Fulgencio Batista. Over the next several years, Castro consolidated his power and moved distinctly towards communism. While he was initially received with some enthusiasm by Americans, Eisenhower and most other American politicians had come to see Castro as a devoted communist by 1960. In fact, unbeknownst to most Americans, Eisenhower had ordered the Central Intelligence Agency (CIA) in 1960 to develop plans to remove Castro from power. Kennedy thought Eisenhower should have been doing more. While Kennedy wrote early in his presidential bid that the "Administration is moving with realism yet

---

[112] Carroll Kilpatrick, "Kennedy Meets Sen. Johnson on Strategy," *The Washington Post and Times Herald*, July 30, 1960, p. A1.

[113] John F. Kennedy to Henry P. Schroerluke, Sept. 16, 1960, JFKL, Kennedy Papers, Pre-Presidential Papers, Senate Files, Legislation, Legislation Files, 1953-1960, 1960, Foreign Policy: Bowles, Chester-Middle East, Box 737, Folder – Foreign Policy-Germany. See also George Schild, "The Berlin Crisis," in Mark J. White, ed., *Kennedy: The New Frontier Revisited* (New York: New York University Press, 1998), pp. 92-93.

prudence," he emphasized the need for a firm policy.[114] In the heat of the campaign he increased his rhetoric by claiming "that our own shores are for the first time since 1812 imperiled by chinks in our defense armor."[115] In October, he raised his criticisms to even higher levels. On October 6, he described Castro's rise as "a disaster that threatens the security of the whole Western Hemisphere."[116] A little over a week later he asked, "if you can't stand up to Castro, how can you be expected to stand up to Khrushchev?"[117] On October 21, he foreshadowed the Bay of Pigs invasion, when he claimed, "we must attempt to strengthen the non-Batista democratic anti-Castro forces in exile, and in Cuba itself, who offer eventual hope of overthrowing Castro. Thus far these fighters for freedom have had virtually no support from our government."[118]

Nixon castigated Kennedy for these statements but had a hard time refuting the Democratic nominee. While there was little the Eisenhower administration could have done to stop Castro's rise to power, the image of a communist country ninety miles south of Miami was alarming. Further, Nixon knew that the United States was already working with Cuban exiles to do exactly what Kennedy proposed but could not say anything because the information was top secret.[119] There are still debates among scholars as to whether Kennedy knew about the CIA operation to train Cuban exiles. After Kennedy won the Democratic nomination, President Eisenhower arranged for CIA Director Allen Dulles to brief Kennedy and later Johnson.[120] It is unclear how much information Dulles provided in the over two hour brief in July,

---

[114] John F. Kennedy to Robert C. Sprague, Jr., Feb. 9, 1960, JFKL, Kennedy Papers, Pre-Presidential Papers, Senate Files, Legislation, Legislation Files, 1953-1960, 1960, Foreign Policy: Bowles, Chester-Middle East, Box 737, Folder – Foreign Policy-Cuba, 2/60.

[115] W.H. Lawrence, "Kennedy Declares Castro Is Enemy; Sees U.S. Arms Lag," *New York Times*, Aug. 27, 1960, p. 1.

[116] Leo Egans, "Kennedy Assails Nixon Over Cuba," ibid., Oct. 7, 1960, p. 1.

[117] Edward T. Folliard, "Kennedy Asks Nixon Explain Cuba 'Disaster'," *The Washington Post and Times Herald*, Oct. 16, 1960, p. A16.

[118] "Text of Statement by Kennedy on Dealing With Castro Regime," *New York Times*, Oct. 21, 1960, p. 18.

[119] "Kennedy, Nixon Tangle on Policies For Dealing with Danger of Castro," *The Washington Post and Times Herald*, Oct. 22, 1960, p. A1. Nixon was also furious because he believed that Kennedy knew about the Eisenhower administration's efforts from briefings with CIA Director Allen Dulles. While Kennedy did receive briefings at Eisenhower's invitation from the CIA and Joint Chiefs of Staff during the campaign, he denied that information about the training of Cuban exiles was given to him. See Schlesinger, *Journals*, p. 131. For Eisenhower's invitation, see, Telegram from Dwight D. Eisenhower to John F. Kennedy, JFKL, Kennedy Papers, President's Office Files, Special Correspondence, Box 29A, Folder – Eisenhower, Dwight D., 3/30/60-12/6/60.

[120] Telegram from Dwight D. Eisenhower to John F. Kennedy, ibid.

although his notes from the meeting indicate he was prepared to tell Kennedy that the "CIA was training Cuban exiles as guerilla leaders and recruiting from refugees for more such training."[121] They did discuss the general world situation, and Kennedy was particularly interested in the situations in Cuba and the Congo.[122] While Nixon believed Kennedy knew, the Massachusetts senator later dismissed this claim.[123]

Besides foreign policy and defense issues, Kennedy focused a great deal of attention on the economy and civil rights. While Eisenhower's economic record was admirable overall, especially in successfully balancing the budget three of his eight years in office. His two terms did witness brief recessions in 1953-1954 and 1957-1958, but overall scholars generally note the positives like steady economic growth, low inflation, and balanced, or nearly balanced, budgets.[124] Kennedy believed Eisenhower placed too much emphasis on balancing the budget and did not use the government's full resources to stimulate the economy when needed. Kennedy claimed Eisenhower's obsession with achieving a balanced budget and low inflation had "had an adverse affect on the nation's economic growth."[125] He also argued that the president failed to recognize the needs of the working class by fighting for an increase in the minimum wage. He supported increasing the minimum wage from $1.00 to $1.25 claiming that, "There are those who say we cannot afford this increase—that it is inflationary—or that it is unnecessary. But I am convinced that we cannot afford to pay less."[126] He stressed it would give "the lowest paid workers ... a fairer opportunity to share our high standard of living. To pass them by—to water down the help they need—or merely

[121] Memorandum for the President, Mar. 14, 1962, JFKL, Kennedy Papers, National Security Files, McGeorge Bundy Correspondence, Box 405, Folder – Memos to the President, 2/62-3/62.

[122] Richard L. Lyons, "Kennedy Gets First Briefing by CIA Director," *The Washington Post and Times Herald*, July 24, 1960, p. A7. Eisenhower arranged additional briefings from the Joint Chiefs of Staff. See Eisenhower to Kennedy, Aug. 19, 1960, JFKL, Kennedy Papers, President's Office Files, Special Correspondence, Box 29A, Folder – Eisenhower, Dwight D. 3/30/60-12/5/60.

[123] Schlesinger, *Journals*, p. 131.

[124] See John W. Sloan, *Eisenhower and the Management of Prosperity* (Lawrence: University Press of Kansas, 1991), pp. 153-57.

[125] "Ike's Economic Policies Hit by Kennedy: Senator Meets with Reuther, Di Salle," *Chicago Daily Tribune*, August 4, 1960, p. E2.

[126] Remarks of Senator John F. Kennedy, Feb. 18, 1960, JFKL, Kennedy Papers, Pre-Presidential Papers, Senate Files, Holburn, Subject, 1957-1959, Press, Radio, TV-Urban Renewal, Box 365, Folder Unemployment Compensation.

assume that prosperity at the top will someday reach them—shocks the conscience of those who care."[127]

Besides the economy, the civil rights movement also played an important role in the campaign. Kennedy had not been a strong advocate for civil rights while a senator as he tried to take an approach that would not alienate either the liberal wing of the Democratic Party or more conservative Southern Democrats.[128] James Farmer recalled that "Kennedy was ignorant on civil rights in particular and blacks in general."[129] However, the Democratic Party platform asserted that "The time has come to assure equal access for all Americans to all areas of community life, including voting booths, schoolrooms, jobs, housing, and public facilities," and pledged to use the full force of the federal government to achieve equality.[130] Kennedy delivered one of his boldest statements in support of civil rights the week prior to the Democrat Convention when he exclaimed,

> "The next President of the United States cannot stand above the battle engaging in vague little sermons on brotherhood. The immense moral authority of the White House must be used to offer leadership and inspiration to those of every race and section who recognize their responsibilities. And the immense legal authority of the White House must be used to direct implementation of all Constitutional rights, protection of the right to vote, fulfillment of the requirement of school desegregation, and an end to discrimination in the government's own midst—in public contracts, in employment and in all Federal housing programs."

He concluded that "The place to begin is the White House itself, where the Chief Executive, with his prestige and influence, should exert firm and positive leadership."[131] His efforts to assign a moral tone to the civil rights

---

[127] Speech by John F. Kennedy, Aug. 10, 1960, ibid., '60 Campaign Press and Publicity, Speeches, Statements, and Sections 1958-1960, Foreign Affairs—Labor: Minimum Wage Bill, Box 1030, Folder – Labor, Fair Labor Standards.

[128] Sorensen, *Counselor*, p. 270. See also Mark Stern, *Calculating Visions: Kennedy, Johnson & Civil Rights* (New Brunswick, N.J.: Rutgers University Press, 1992), pp. 15-18.

[129] Quoted in Deborah Hart Strober and Gerald S. Strober, *The Kennedy Presidency: An Oral History of the Era*, Revised Edition (Washington, D.C.: Brassey's, Inc., 2003), p. 278.

[130] 1960 Democratic Party Platform, in Schlesinger (ed.), *History of American Presidential Elections*, vol. IV, p. 3509.

[131] Remarks of Senator John F. Kennedy, NAACP Rally, July 10, 1960, JFKL, Kennedy Papers, Pre-Presidential Papers, '60 Campaign Press and Publicity, Speeches, Statements, and Sections 1958-1960, Agriculture-Defense-Disarmament: Increasing Perils of Radioactivity, Box 1028, Folder – Civil Rights, Job Discrimination, NAACP Policy.

movement resonated with many Black Americans.[132] Further, his effort to reach out to Corretta King late in the campaign, after her husband, Martin Luther King, Jr. was arrested in Georgia, made a very positive impression in the black community.[133]

All of these issues played important roles in the election. Kennedy ended up winning one of the closest presidential elections in American history with a margin of victory of just over 100,000 votes out of the over 68,500,000 million cast. Kennedy won 34,220,984 votes or 49.7% of the vote, while Nixon won 34,108,157 votes, or almost 49.6% of the vote. In the electoral vote, Kennedy won 303 to 219.[134] Gallup polls from the time provide some insight into the breakdown of the vote. Men favored Kennedy slightly more than Nixon (52 to 48%), while women favored Nixon slightly more (51 to 49%). The candidates split the white vote with 51% voting for Nixon, but Kennedy overwhelming won the non-white vote winning 68% of the ballots cast. 54% of the voters under age 50 voted Kennedy, while Nixon won 54% of the votes cast by Americans older than 50. Finally, Nixon won 62% of the Protestant vote, while Kennedy won 78% of the Catholic vote.[135]

There were many reasons for Kennedy's close victory including the lagging economy and concerns about the country's security.[136] Furthermore, Kennedy's youth and enthusiasm offered a sense of a new direction in sharp contrast to the leadership provided by the 70-year old Eisenhower. More significantly, Kennedy won the minority vote. Had the same percentage of black Americans voted in 1960 like they had voted in 1956, Kennedy would have lost the election because he would not have won Delaware, Illinois, Michigan, New Jersey, and South Carolina.[137] He also offset his losses in areas dominated by Protestants by overwhelmingly winning the Catholic vote in urban areas which helped secure his victories in key areas in the Northeast and Midwest.[138] Finally, Chicago Mayor Richard Daľy probably fraudulently inflated the vote tallies in his city for Kennedy securing the Democratic candidate's victory in Illinois.[139]

---

[132] Garth E. Pauley, *The Modern Presidency and Civil Rights: Rhetoric on Race from Roosevelt to Nixon* (College Station: Texas A&M University Press, 2001), pp. 113-117.
[133] "Kennedy Calls Mrs. King," *New York Times*, Oct. 27, 1960, p. 22.
[134] Donaldson, *The First Modern Campaign*, pp. 152-53.
[135] Election Polls – Vote by Groups, 1960-1964, Gallup, Inc., http://www.gallup.com/poll/9454/Election-Polls-Vote-Groups-19601964.aspx, accessed on March 24, 2008.
[136] Dallek, *An Unfinished Life*, p. 295.
[137] Donaldson, *The First Modern Campaign*, p. 156.
[138] Carty, *A Catholic in the White House*, pp. 156-57.
[139] Rorabaugh, *The Real Making of the President*, pp. 188-91.

Kennedy's close victory left him as president-elect but with no true mandate for change. A small shift in the vote in just a few states would have given Nixon the victory. However, regardless of the margin, Kennedy had achieved his goal of winning the presidency and the country stood on the verge of a new era. Kennedy had shown that he was a tough campaigner and shrewd politician. The question before him and the country now was would he be able to handle the responsibilities that came with being the president?

Chapter 3

CAMPAIGN RHETORIC MEETS REALITY – FROM CUBA TO SOUTHEAST ASIA TO BERLIN

As his predecessors before him, Kennedy quickly became aware that being the president was very different from being a candidate for the presidency or even a senator. Candidates have a lot more freedom of action and do not necessarily have to be responsible for all of their words and promises. Further, unless seeking the limelight, senators can remain fairly obscure. Once elected president, however, this changes. Kennedy's first year as president tested him in ways he could have never imagined. Not surprisingly considering his interests while a member of the House of Representatives and Senate, Kennedy wanted to focus much of his attention on national security issues. By the end of 1961, he probably wished he could have reduced that focus as he had overseen the reshaping of the military, supported a disastrous invasion of Cuba, seen the limits of American power in Southeast Asia, and witnessed the construction of the Berlin Wall. Little in Kennedy's previous experiences offered him much guidance to meet the challenges he faced that year.

After winning the presidency, Kennedy quickly switched gears from presidential candidate to being the president-elect. One of his first needs was to reach out to the out-going administration—a difficult task considering the virulent nature of the recent campaign, and Kennedy's and Eisenhower's less than kind views of the other. Kennedy considered Eisenhower a "non-president" who relied on the government's structure to govern. Eisenhower sometimes called the president-elect "Little Boy Blue".[1] Despite their hard feelings, they sought as smooth a transition as possible and held meetings on December 6 and January 19.[2] They met for about three hours on December 6, and Kennedy's "pleasing personality, his concentrated interest and his receptiveness" impressed Eisenhower.[3] Their meeting was briefer on January 19, and they focused most of their discussion on the situation in Southeast Asia and to a lesser extent on Cuba.[4]

While meeting with Eisenhower was essential for his transition into the presidency, it was a relatively minor point when compared to selecting his cabinet and other key advisers.[5] By mid-December, he had selected most of them, including his brother Robert Kennedy as the Attorney General, J. Edward Day as the Postmaster General, Orville Freeman as the Secretary of Agriculture, Robert McNamara as the Secretary of Defense, Abraham Ribicoff as the Secretary of Health, Education, and Welfare, Stewart Udall as the Secretary of the Interior, Arthur Goldberg as the Secretary of Labor, Dean Rusk as the Secretary of State, Douglas Dillon as the Secretary of Treasury, and Luther Hodges as the Secretary of Commerce. He selected David Bell as the Director of the Bureau of Budget, Walter Heller to serve as the Chairman of the Council of Economic Advisers, Ted Sorensen to be Special Counsel to the President, and McGeorge Bundy to be his National Security Adviser.[6] Kennedy's brother became his most trusted adviser. As the *New York Times* noted, "When Robert Kennedy phones anyone about a political matter, he doesn't have to explain that he is speaking for the president. The implication is automatic."[7] Kennedy met most frequently with his national security team of

---

[1] Dallek, *An Unfinished Life*, p. 302. In 1959, Kennedy told Arthur Schlesinger that Eisenhower was "terribly cold and terribly vain." Schlesinger, *Journals*, p. 53.

[2] Eisenhower, *Waging Peace*, pp. 603, 617, and 712-17.

[3] Ibid., p. 603.

[4] Dallek, *An Unfinished Life*, p. 305. See also Robert S. McNamara, James C. Blight, and Robert K. Brigham, *Argument Without End: In Search of Answers to the Vietnam Tragedy* (New York: PublicAffairs, 1999), pp. 41-42.

[5] For a description of the process Kennedy followed in selecting advisers, see O'Donnell and Power, *"Johnny, We Hardly Knew Ye"*, pp. 258-75.

[6] Profiles of Kennedy's cabinet members and advisers can be found at the John F. Kennedy Library, Biographies and Profiles, http://www.jfklibrary.org/Historical+Resources/Biographies+and+Profiles/, accessed on Mar. 18, 2009.

[7] Sidney Hyman, "Inside the Kennedy 'Kitchen Cabinet'," *New York Times*, March 5, 1961, p. SM 27. See also Russell Baker, "Twelve Men Close to Kennedy: Close Because of Important Jobs," ibid., Jan. 22, 1961, p. SM6.

McNamara, Rusk, and Rostow as this is where his true interests lay. The president worked with the rest of his cabinet and advisers as the need arose.[8]

As his campaign had shown, Kennedy recognized the value of making a strong impression with the public; therefore, he spent a great deal of time during the transition period preparing his inaugural address. While Kennedy wanted the country to be fully aware of the problems it faced, he wanted to inspire Americans to look to the future with hope and a desire to change the world for the better. The result is one of the most remembered and quoted speeches in American History. "Let the word go forth from this time and place, to friend and foe alike," Kennedy announced,

> "that the torch has been passed to a new generation of Americans—born in this century, tempered by war, disciplined by a hard and bitter peace, proud of our ancient heritage—and unwilling to witness or permit the slow undoing of those human rights to which this nation has always been committed, and to which we are committed today at home and around the world.
>
> Let every nation know, whether it wishes us well or ill, that we shall pay any price, bear any burden, meet any hardship, support any friend, oppose any foe to assure the survival and the success of liberty."

He concluded, "And so, my fellow Americans: ask not what your country can do for you—ask what you can do for your country."[9]

Kennedy could not have known how difficult a transition it would be to manage the myriad number of national security and foreign policy issues the country faced. He was very cognizant of his campaign promises and his accusations that Eisenhower had not waged the Cold War very effectively. In his first weeks in office he continued to paint a dire picture of the future as he told Congress in his first annual message that even with some significant problems at home, they paled "when placed beside those which confront us around the world." "Each day," the new president added, "the crises multiply. Each day their solution grows more difficult. Each day we draw nearer the hour of maximum danger, as weapons spread and hostile forces grow stronger."[10] Kennedy had accused Eisenhower of not doing enough to fight the spread of communism and weakening the American military by cutting

[8] "Here's Top Team at White House: Young Men on Kennedy's Staff May Outrank Cabinet in Influence," *Los Angeles Times*, Mar. 13, 1961, p. 2.

[9] Inaugural Address, January 20, 1961, *Public Papers of the Presidents, John F. Kennedy*, http://www.presidency.ucsb.edu/ws/?pid=8032, accessed on March 18, 2009.

[10] Annual Message to the Congress on the State of the Union, Jan. 30, 1961, *Public Papers of the Presidents*, http://www.presidency.ucsb.edu/ws/?pid=8045, accessed on Oct. 26, 2007.

defense spending in order to balance the budget. Kennedy did not see these claims as simple campaign rhetoric, believing that the United States had indeed fallen behind the Soviet Union in military capabilities. However, he was also a politician at heart. He knew that he would have to adopt more assertive policies to avoid being seen as reneging on his campaign promises.

The Kennedy presidency began in an atmosphere of emerging crises in Africa, Southeast Asia, and Cuba. Underlying each of these issues was the ongoing Cold War which encouraged Kennedy to examine issues through a staunchly anti-communism prism. Kennedy's most basic critique of the Eisenhower administration was the latter's over reliance on nuclear weapons and delivery systems. Eisenhower consistently argued that the United States was maintaining adequate conventional forces to deal with limited wars like it had faced in Korea. However, he believed any war with the Soviet Union would quickly turn into a nuclear conflict and that large conventional forces beyond the initial stages of a war would be useless. Further, he did not see a nuclear war as winnable for any country involved; therefore, he believed the United States had to develop and expand its nuclear forces to levels that would deter the Soviet Union from ever attacking. By the time he left office, the United States was well on the way to establishing its nuclear triad of land-based bombers, land-based intercontinental ballistic missiles, and submarine-launched ballistic missiles.[11]

Kennedy actually supported Eisenhower's efforts to build the nuclear triad but believed it needed to be done more quickly and with larger force levels. He announced in late January that the Soviet Union still sought "world domination" and noted that "On the Presidential Coat of Arms, the American eagle holds in his right talon the olive branch, while in his left he holds a bundle of arrows. We intend to give equal attention to both."[12] He did not share his predecessor's belief that U.S. conventional force levels were adequate and called for their expansion and modernization. Additionally, he wanted to increase the country's civil defense capabilities. Influenced by his own assessment of America's national security needs and critics of the Eisenhower administration, Kennedy envisioned a military force that could

[11] Snead, *Gaither Committee*, p. 161.

[12] Annual Message to the Congress on the State of the Union, January 30, 1961, *Public Papers of the Presidents*, http://www.presidency.ucsb.edu/ws/?pid=8045, accessed on October 26, 2007.

meet any conceivable threat and a civil defense program that would protect the majority of the country's population if a war was to occur.[13]

Reviews of the country's national security programs began early in his presidency. National Security Adviser Bundy advised the president on January 30 that "the most urgent need is for a review of basic military policy." He added "a review of this sort should include at all stages the relevant political questions, and it should go along the whole spectrum from thermonuclear weapons systems to guerrilla action and political infiltration."[14] Bundy stressed that this review was "of literally life-and-death importance."[15] Bundy's memorandum resonated with Kennedy as the president was already requesting a Defense Department review. At a meeting with the Joint Chiefs of Staff (JCS), the president at least contemplated the possibility of the United States launching a preemptive or preventive war. He asked the chiefs, "if we decided to make the first strike, could we eliminate the Soviet strike-back?" They responded "no" and stressed that "under any circumstances the Soviet Union could strike back hard."[16]

Secretary of Defense McNamara completed his review of U.S. military programs in late February and briefed the president. McNamara stressed the vital importance of deterrence. He noted that "deterrence depends critically upon our ability to strike back after a direct Soviet attack designed to destroy our retaliatory forces. ... We must have survivable retaliatory power."[17] McNamara then went on to recommend specific program changes. Of utmost importance, he counseled the adoption of "a broadly flexible posture that can serve us well in a wide range of contingencies."[18] He outlined that the United States needed to reduce the vulnerabilities of its command and control of its nuclear weapons, its strategic bomber force, and its land-based missile systems. He pointed to the Eisenhower administration's overemphasis on preparing for a general nuclear war and recommended raising "the threshold of

---

13 Robert S. McNamara Oral History Interview, April 4, 1964, JFKL, pp. 1-2, http://www.jfklibrary.org/NR/rdonlyres/FCC01356-1AFA-46E0-818E-605360FF7D2B/43973/McNamaraRobertSJFK1_oralhistory.pdf, accessed on July 8, 2009.

14 Memorandum for the President, JFKL, Kennedy Papers, National Security Files, Meetings & Memoranda, Box 313, Folder – NSC Meetings, 1961 No. 475, 2/1/61, p. 1.

15 Ibid., p. 2.

16 Memorandum of Conference with the President, February 6, 1961, JFKL, Kennedy Papers, National Security Files, Chester V. Clifton, Box 345, Folder – Conferences with the President, JCS 1/61-2/61, pp. 1-2.

17 Review of FY 1961 and FY 1962 Military Programs and Budgets, February 21, 1961, ibid., President's Office Files, Departments & Agencies, Box 77, Folder – Defense FY61 and FY62, Military Programs and Budgets, 2/21/61, p. 2.

18 Ibid., p. 5.

our local non-nuclear defense capability" and reducing "our dependence on nuclear war, a type of warfare which will increasingly be in our interest to avoid."[19] He concluded by reiterating that the recommendations were directed at the "removal of dangerous inflexibilities and vulnerabilities in our posture" and creating military capabilities that would allow "a responsible, controlled power of selective response that can appropriately meet a wide range of possible threats."[20]

Kennedy quickly went to work developing a military force structure, nicknamed Flexible Response, which would provide the flexibility to meet any crisis from small brush-fire wars to World War III. In his first year in office, he expanded defense spending over $6 billion dollars—a 15% increase over Eisenhower's proposed $40 billion budget—and by 1963 had increased spending to almost $50 billion annually. He expanded America's ballistic missile capacity, and by his death, the United States had deployed 631 ICBMs and 10 nuclear powered submarines carrying a total of 160 Polaris nuclear-tipped missiles. In addition to these operational missiles, the United States planned to deploy 800 more ICBMs and 31 more submarines. He also increased the size of the strategic bomber force to 600 B-52s.[21] Together, these three weapons-systems created a virtually indestructible deterrent force.

Kennedy did not want to rely solely on a nuclear deterrent; so, he also supported the expansion of America's conventional forces. He believed Eisenhower's policies had reduced the country's ability to wage non-nuclear, limited wars and in turn, restricted its flexibility. Generals Maxwell Taylor and James Gavin profoundly influenced Kennedy's thinking during the presidential election campaign and while he was president. General Taylor served as Eisenhower's Army chief of staff from 1955 until 1959, but resigned because of his frustrations with Eisenhower's New Look policies. While serving as the chief of staff, Taylor was a constant advocate for expanding conventional force capabilities. After his resignation, he became an outspoken critic of Eisenhower's policies. In 1960, he published *The Uncertain Trumpet* and blasted what he perceived as Eisenhower's over reliance on nuclear forces at the expense of conventional force capabilities.[22] General Gavin retired from the army in 1958 also out of frustration at Eisenhower's policies. He wrote

[19] Ibid., p. 11.

[20] Ibid., p. 12.

[21] Snead, *Gaither Committee*, p. 177. See also Robert S. McNamara Oral History Interview, April 4, 1964, JFKL, pp. 3-4, http://www.jfklibrary.org/NR/rdonlyres/FCC01356-1AFA-46E0-818E-605360FF7D2B/43973/McNamaraRobertSJFK1_oralhistory.pdf, accessed on July 8, 2009.

[22] Maxwell D. Taylor, *The Uncertain Trumpet* (New York: Harper, 1960).

War and Peace in the Space Age, a devastating critique of current U.S. military polices.[23] Together, Taylor and Gavin argued that President Eisenhower had reduced defense spending to dangerous levels and limited the country's ability to wage smaller wars.

Based on their recommendations and the advice of others in his administration like Defense Secretary McNamara, Kennedy agreed that the country needed to increase its conventional forces, develop counterinsurgency units, expand its airlift capabilities, and boost weapons purchases. He announced to Congress on January 30 that he had ordered McNamara to immediately "increase our airlift capacity," "step up our Polaris submarine program," and "accelerate our entire missile program."[24] Kennedy also ordered an increase in the number of U.S. military personnel, and by the end of July 1961, he had enlarged the military from 2,493,000 to 2,743,000 with over half the increase going to the army.[25]

One other area that particularly caught Kennedy's attention was guerrilla warfare. In a meeting with the JCS in early February, the president asked about the unconventional tactics being used by guerrilla forces in Southeast Asia and elsewhere, and inquired as to what each military branch was doing to address them. He expressed a particular interest in Vietnam.[26] His interest in guerrilla warfare continued as he reminded Marine Corps Commandant General David Shoup that he wanted to discuss "the improvements or changes in the Marine Corps for guerrilla or counter guerrilla warfare."[27] Over the remainder of his administration, Kennedy encouraged the expansion of special operations forces, like the Green Berets, for counterinsurgency operations and the expansion of the army's limited war capabilities.[28]

The final characteristic of flexible responsible was for the United States to have the ability to survive a nuclear war. McNamara, in his review of U.S. military programs, noted that "While civil defense is not a Defense

---

23 James M. Gavin, *War and Peace in the Space Age* (New York: Harper, 1958).

24 Annual Message to the Congress on the State of the Union, January 30, 1961, *Public Papers of the Presidents*, http://www.presidency.ucsb.edu/ws/?pid=8045, accessed on October 26, 2007.

25 Snead, *Gaither Committee*, p. 178.

26 Memorandum of Conference with the President, February 6, 1961, JFKL, Kennedy Papers, National Security Files, Chester V. Clifton, Box 345, Folder – Conferences with the President, JCS 1/61-2/61, p. 2.

27 Memorandum for Commander Shepard, February 18, 1961, ibid., President's Office Files, Departments & Agencies, Box 68, Folder – JFK Memos to Departments and Agencies, Labor-Navy, p. 1.

28 Snead, *Gaither Committee*, p. 178. See also Special Message to the Congress on Urgent National Security Needs, May 25, 1961, *Public Papers of the Presidents*, http://www.presidency.ucsb.edu/ws/?pid=8045, accessed on October 26, 2007.

Department responsibility, the success of many of our programs depends on some expansion in civil defense."[29] Civil defense, or a country's ability to defend its citizens against an enemy attack, has been a significant issue in American military and political debates since colonial times. However, the surprise Japanese attack on Pearl Harbor in 1941 and the developments of nuclear weapons and improved delivery systems after World War II made civil defense a much more vital issue. Concerns about America's lack of civil defense capabilities accelerated in late 1957 when the combination of the Soviet launch of *Sputnik* and the completion of the Gaither Report seemed to indicate that the United States was vulnerable to a nuclear attack. *Sputnik* indicated that the Soviet Union was way ahead of the United States in missile development and the leak of the top-secret Gaither Report in December 1957 seemed to offer some corroboration.[30] While the United States was really far ahead of the Soviet Union in missile design, many Americans, including Kennedy, came to believe otherwise. The *Washington Post* noted "the United States took a licking in the race to launch the first satellite."[31] To address America's vulnerability, the Gaither Committee argued that if the United States built a nationwide system of fallout shelters it would be able to protect most of the civilian population in the event of a Soviet nuclear attack.

Kennedy alluded to the Gaither Report during the presidential campaign and spoke out in favor of a civil defense program.[33] However, he did not propose a detailed plan. His approach began to change in the spring of 1961. While he questioned whether "any particular fall-out shelter program would have enduring value" considering "rapidly changing weapons technology and military policy," the thought of the losses resulting from a nuclear war concerned him greatly.[34] One study completed late in the Eisenhower presidency concluded that a Soviet nuclear strike in 1970 could kill as many as 170 out of 206 million Americans.[35] In May, Kennedy ordered the government

[29] Review of FY 1961 and FY 1962 Military Programs and Budgets, February 21, 1961, ibid., President's Office Files, Departments & Agencies, Box 77, Folder – Defense FY61 and FY62, Military Programs and Budgets, 2/21/61, p. 9.

[30] Snead, *Gaither Committee*, p. 80.

[31] Chalmers M. Roberts, "Satellite Psychology: U.S. Misjudgment Indicated," *The Washington Post and Times Herald*, October 12, 1957, p. A13.

[33] Snead, *Gaither Committee*, 175. Kennedy even mentioned in a press conference on February 1, 1961, that he was reading the Gaither Report. See The President's News Conference, February 1, 1961, *Public Papers of the Presidents*, http://www.presidency.ucsb.edu/ws/?pid=8045, accessed on October 26, 2007.

[34] Memorandum: Civil Defense Meeting, May 9, 1961, JFKL, Kennedy Papers, National Security Files, Subjects, Box 295, Folder – Civil Defense 4/1/61-5/17/61, p. 2.

[35] Memorandum for Mr. Bundy, February 21, 1961, ibid., Folder – Civil Defense, 1/61-3/61, p. 1.

to identify fallout shelters in existing structures and requested that the federal, state, and local governments spend more on civil defense. In describing his civil defense proposals, he claimed "no insurance is cost-free; and every American citizen and his community must decide for themselves whether this form of survival insurance justifies the expenditure of effort, time and money. For myself, I am convinced that it does."[36]

During the height of the Berlin crisis in the summer of 1961, the Kennedy administration gave even more attention to civil defense. Bundy asked the director of the Office of Civil Defense Mobilization to "submit recommendations concerning additional measures which might be taken to reduce the vulnerability of the U.S. civilian population to nuclear attack."[37] In early July, Kennedy told Bundy to have the "Civil Defense" people develop an emergency plan that detailed what the government "could do in the next six months that would improve the population's chances of surviving if a war should break out."[38] Kennedy ultimately announced that the United States needed fallout shelters because "We owe that kind of insurance to our families, and to our country."[39] He then ordered McNamara to assume more responsibilities on civil defense matters because "adequate protection of the civilian population requires a substantial strengthening of the Nation's civil defense capability."[40] In this area, Congress gave a lukewarm reception to Kennedy's requests and failed to appropriate much money for shelters. While Kennedy mentioned civil defense programs on a few occasions over the remainder of his presidency, he never gave it the emphasis he did during his first summer in office.[41]

---

[36] Special Message to the Congress on Urgent National Security Needs, May 25, 1961, *Public Papers of the Presidents*, http://www.presidency.ucsb.edu/ws/?pid=8045, accessed on October 26, 2007.

[37] Memorandum for the Director, OCDM, June 30, 1961, JFKL, Kennedy Papers, National Security Files, Subjects, Box 295, Folder – Civil Defense, 6/1/61-7/11/61, p. 1.

[38] Memorandum for Mr. Bundy, July 5, 1961, JFKL, Kennedy Papers, President's Office Files, Staff Memos, Box 62, Folder – Bundy, McGeorge, 5/61-7/61, p. 1.

[39] Snead, *Gaither Committee*, p. 179.

[40] Executive Order 10952, July 20, 1961, *Public Papers of the Presidents*, http://www.presidency.ucsb.edu/ws/?pid=8045, accessed on October 26, 2007. See also Peter Braestrup, "Shelter Program: It Gets New Status From Kennedy," *New York Times*, August 6, 1961, p. E5.

[41] The decline in commitment to civil defense after the summer Berlin crisis was at least partly due to Kennedy's earlier concern about how enduring any program would be in light of developments in nuclear weapons and delivery capabilities. McGeorge Bundy captured this concern aptly when he told the president, "I must say I am horrified by the thought of digging deeper as the megatonnage gets bigger." Memorandum for the President, December 1, 1961, JFKL, Kennedy Papers, National Security Files, Subjects, Box 295, Folder – Civil Defense 12/61, p. 1.

As Kennedy took significant steps to strengthen national security programs, he did face one potential public relations crisis early in his presidency related to his national security review. In the late 1950s and during the presidential campaign, Kennedy was one of the Eisenhower administration's most vocal critics for allowing the so-called "Missile Gap". While Eisenhower had consistently denied that the United States was behind the Soviet Union in missile development and deployments, he did not offer much proof other than his own expertise. Kennedy and other Eisenhower critics took advantage of this to launch their attacks.[42] Unfortunately for Kennedy, Eisenhower was right. Now, as president, Kennedy had to deal with the reality that his campaign rhetoric concerning the "Missile Gap" was inaccurate.

In an off-the-record meeting with reporters on February 6, Secretary of Defense McNamara admitted that studies by the new administration revealed there was no missile gap. He evidently believed that off-the-record meant that the information would not be reported, not just accredited to an anonymous source. He could not have been more wrong. The headline the next morning in the *New York Times*, "Kennedy Defense Study Finds No Evidence of a 'Missile Gap'," proved his naiveté.[43] Kennedy was furious, and the White House went on the offensive denying the report.[44] Kennedy told reporters at a press conference on February 8 that "it would be premature to reach a judgment as to whether there is a gap or not a gap."[45] The editors of the *Chicago Daily Tribune* were not impressed with his denial. They claimed that the president "was visibly embarrassed" and his "response to questions ... showed a certain agility in broken field running."[46] Surprisingly the issue did not gain much traction, and the public quickly focused its attention on other issues.[47]

While the question of whether the missile gap existed did not resonate with the public for the remainder of his presidency, Kennedy remained concerned that it might. Soon after the Cuban missile crisis in October 1962,

---

42 For a summary of the missile gap claims, see "Chronology of Two-Year Dispute on 'Missile Gap'," *New York Times*, February 9, 1961, p. 4.

43 Jack Raymond, "Kennedy Defense Study Finds No Evidence of a 'Missile Gap': U.S. Studies Find No Missile Gap'," *New York Times*, February 7, 1961, p. 1.

44 See Preble, *John F. Kennedy and the Missile Gap*, pp. 155-60; and Michael R. Beschloss, *The Crisis Years: Kennedy and Khrushchev, 1960-63* (New York: HarperCollins Publishers, 1991), pp. 65-66.

45 The President's News Conference, February 8, 1961, *Public Papers of the Presidents*, http://www.presidency.ucsb.edu/ws/?pid=8200, accessed on March 30, 2009.

46 "Cat Out of Bag," *Chicago Daily Tribune*, February 9, 1961, p. 14.

47 Dallek, *An Unfinished Life*, p. 338.

he began asking for a report on the missile gap. In particular, he wanted to know the missile gap's "genesis."[48] In late March 1963, he showed some frustration with the lack of information and again asked for a report on the missile gap and "an appraisal of the military and space deficiencies which existed in January 1961."[49] Just over a month later, Kennedy was still not pleased by the reports he received, claiming they were "too superficial." He also revealed his motive for wanting the reports—he was concerned that his earlier claims of a missile gap could be used against him in the 1964 presidential campaign. "I want," Kennedy told National Security Adviser Bundy, "to be able to demonstrate that there was a military and intelligence lag in the previous administration that started the missile gap."[50] The president persisted in asking about the missile gap into the summer.[51] Finally, the president was satisfied when he received studies that concluded that "Senator Kennedy's statements on defense and the missile gap in the late 1950s were sensible and responsible."[52] Unfortunately for Kennedy, drawing attention away from the alleged missile gap would be one of the easier problems he faced in the early months of his administration.

One of the reasons Kennedy accelerated defense spending during his first year, beyond his desire for a stronger military, was because the United States faced a series of crises around the world. Cuba was particularly troublesome. American involvement there dates to the 19th century and became more significant during the 1898 Spanish-American War and its aftermath. After the United States defeated Spain, Cuba technically gained its independence. However, based on the 1901 Platt Amendment to the Cuban constitution the United States retained the right to intervene when it saw fit. In essence, the United States formed a virtual protectorate over Cuba. Over the next half century, American investments there increased dramatically, and by the 1950s American companies controlled 90% of Cuba's utilities, 50% of its mining

---

48 Preble, *John F. Kennedy and the Missile Gap*, p. 166.

49 Memorandum for Mr. Bundy, Mar. 30, 1963, JFKL, Kennedy Papers, National Security Files, Subjects, Box 298, Folder – Missile Gap, 2/63-5/63, p. 1.

50 Memorandum for Mr. Bundy, May 15, 1963, JFKL, Kennedy Papers, President's Office Files, Staff Memos, Box 62, Folder – Lincoln, Evelyn – Notebook of Memoranda to Staff, Bundy, p. 1.

51 Memorandum for Mr. Bundy, Jun. 3, 1963, JFKL, Kennedy Papers, National Security Files, Subjects, Box 298, Folder – Missile Gap, 6/63-7/63, p.1.

52 Paul Nitze to McGeorge Bundy, June 17, 1963, ibid., p. 2. See also Memorandum for the Record, June 17, 1963, ibid.; and Memorandum for Mr. Bundy, July 10, 1963, ibid., p. 3. For a fuller description of Kennedy's efforts to justify his remarks, see Preble, *John F. Kennedy and the Missile Gap*, pp. 166-74.

wealth, and 40% of its sugar.[53] From the American standpoint, who was in power in Cuba did not necessarily matter as long as that leader protected America's interests. During the 1950s that leader was Fulgencio Batista. He had ruled Cuba off and on since the 1930s and had seized power one last time in 1952. While Eisenhower did not particularly care for the dictator to the south, he accepted Batista because of his support for U.S. corporations and his anti-communist policies.[54]

As was unfortunately too common in the 20th century, the United States chose to side with a Latin American leader who was more interested in centralizing his power than in truly helping his own people. Many Cubans feared Batista and wanted him gone. They found a willing leader in Fidel Castro, a 32-year old leftist revolutionary, who seized power in January 1959 after several years of waging a guerilla war. Most Americans did not know initially what to make of the new Cuban leader. During his guerilla campaign, several U.S. reporters followed his operations and gave Americans the opportunity to see the revolutionary leader. Castro's image as the warrior against a despotic regime won him a great deal of support in the United States, but his political and social views were relatively unknown.[55] He continued to wow Americans when he toured parts of the United States in the spring of 1959. Nearly 1,500 people met Castro at the airport when he arrived in Washington, D.C. chanting "Viva Castro!"[56] At Princeton 2,000 students hailed the Cuban leader and other large crowds met him at Columbia and Harvard.[57]

While many Americans greeted Castro favorably, the Eisenhower administration did not. Castro's efforts to expropriate businesses and to seize land in Cuba, his association with known communists like his brother, Raul, and Ché Guevara, and his increasingly socialistic or communist rhetoric

---

[53] Stephen G. Rabe, *Eisenhower and Latin America: The Foreign Policy of Anticommunism* (Chapel Hill: The University of North Carolina Press, 1988), p. 120. See also Walter LaFeber, *The American Age: United States Foreign Policy at Home and Abroad since 1750* (New York: W.W. Norton & Company, 1989), p. 539; and Michael Grow, *U.S. Presidents and Latin American Interventions: Pursuing Regime Change in the Cold War* (Lawrence: University Press of Kansas, 2008), p. 29.

[54] Stephen E. Ambrose, *Eisenhower*, Volume 2: *The President* (New York: Simon and Schuster, 1984), pp. 504-5.

[55] Rabe, *Eisenhower and Latin America*, pp. 117-25.

[56] "Crowd Hail Castro As He Reached U.S. for an 11 Day Visit," *New York Times,* April 16, 1959, p. 1.

[57] Jules Du Bois, "Castro Tells Students His Plans for Cuba," *Chicago Daily Tribune*, April 21, 1959, p. A1.

grabbed the Eisenhower administration's attention.[58] When Castro visited the United States in 1959, Eisenhower refused to welcome him, although he did allow Vice President Nixon to meet with the new Cuban leader for over three hours.[59] The president recognized that Castro posed a possible challenge to the American leadership position in Latin America. Further, typical of the cold warriors of the 1940s and 1950s, he viewed any possible communist as little more than a stooge of the Soviet Union. However, there were not many possible alternative leaders for Cuba. Eisenhower did not want Batista to return to power, but he did want some middle ground between Batista and Castro.[60] Unfortunately, no such leader existed or, if one did, he was not known in the United States.

As 1960 progressed, Eisenhower and his advisers decided that Castro was indeed a threat to U.S. interests in Latin America and needed to go.[61] Eisenhower turned to the CIA as he had done previously for operations in Guatemala and Iran to facilitate a regime change. The CIA hatched several plans to remove Castro ranging from assassination to invading Cuba. Furthermore, in September 1960, the CIA's Director of Plans, Richard Bissell, began looking for assets that could carry out "a sensitive mission requiring gangster-type action." The CIA eventually made contact with Johnny Roselli who was part of an organized crime syndicate in Las Vegas and who also had connections to the mafia. Because Castro had seized many of their prostitution and gambling rings in Havana, many leading mafia figures, including

---

58 Eisenhower, *Waging Peace*, pp. 520-25.

59 See "Bay of Pigs, Chronology, 40 Years After," on National Security Archive, http://www.gwu.edu/~nsarchiv/bayofpigs/chron.html, accessed on July 19, 2007.

60 Fursenko and Naftali, *"One Hell of a Gamble,"* p. 7; and Eisenhower, *Waging Peace*, p. 614.

61 Howard Jones, *The Bay of Pigs* (New York: Oxford University Press, 2008), pp. 11-13. See chronology of the evolution of the Eisenhower administration's view of Castro and plans for removing him at "Bay of Pigs, Chronology, 40 Years After," on National Security Archive, http://www.gwu.edu/~nsarchiv/bayofpigs/chron.html, accessed on July 19, 2007. The CIA's official history of the Eisenhower's administration's efforts to deal with Castro is also available. See Official History of the Bay of Pigs Operation—Evolution of CIA's Anti-Castro Operations, 1959-January 1961, December 1979, Digital National Security Archives, in four parts (http://gateway.proquest.com/openurl?url_ver=Z39.88-2004&res_dat=xri:dnsa&rft_dat=xri:dnsa:article:CCU01456, http://gateway.proquest.com/openurl?url_ver=Z39.88-2004&res_dat=xri:dnsa&rft_dat=xri:dnsa:article:CCU01457, http://gateway.proquest.com/openurl?url_ver=Z39.88-2004&res_dat=xri:dnsa&rft_dat=xri:dnsa:article:CCU01458, and http://gateway.proquest.com/openurl?url_ver=Z39.88-2004&res_dat=xri:dnsa&rft_dat=xri:dnsa:article:CCU01459), accessed on June 12, 2009. See also Don Bohning, *The Castro Obsession: U.S. Covert Operations Against Cuba, 1959-1965* (Dulles, VA: Potomac Books, Inc., 2005), pp. 20-23; and Lawrence Freedman, *Kennedy's Wars: Berlin, Cuba, Laos, and Vietnam* (New York: Oxford University Press, 2000), pp. 123-27.

Salvatore Giancani and Santos Trafficant, shared the CIA goal of eliminating the new Cuban leader. Over the course of the next year, they made at least six attempts to assassinate Castro using poisoned pills provided by the CIA.[62]

As the assassination plans were being developed, the CIA also devised an operation to train and support anti-Castro forces in the overthrow of the Cuban government. By the fall of 1960, the CIA was actively training Cuban exiles at a base in Guatemala and developing plans for their use. CIA Director Allen Dulles briefed Kennedy on the operations to overthrow Castro after the election. While Richard Nixon claimed in *Six Crises* that Kennedy knew about the operation before the election,[63] Kennedy later told his friend and adviser, Arthur Schlesinger, Jr. in March 1962 that "Of course that is not true. I never heard of the Cuban operation until Dulles and Bissell told me about it at Palm Beach after the election."[64] Regardless of when Kennedy found out, he definitely knew about the operation soon after his election. In early December and then on January 19, Eisenhower and Kennedy met to discuss the anti-Castro operations. At both meetings, Eisenhower encouraged Kennedy to support the CIA's efforts to overthrow Castro, telling the president-elect at the January meeting that "the United States cannot allow the Castro Government to continue to exist in Cuba."[65] Kennedy inherited an evolving plan of intervention, and it ultimately fell to him to evaluate it and decide whether to proceed or not.

Kennedy told Congress on January 30 that "Our objection with Cuba is not over the people's drive for a better life. Our objection is to their domination by foreign and domestic tyrannies. Cuban social and economic reform should be encouraged. Questions of economic and trade policy can always be negotiated. But Communist domination in this Hemisphere can never be negotiated."[66] As Kennedy made this speech, the CIA was deep into planning

---

[62] See the "Family Jewels," an internal CIA report documenting some of its covert operations. Memorandum for the Executive Secretary, CIA Management Committee, May 16, 1973 found at http://www.gwu.edu/~nsarchiv/NSAEBB/NSAEBB222/family_jewels_pt1_ocr.pdf, accessed on July 19, 2007. See also Bohning, *The Castro Obsession*, pp. 178-80.

[63] Richard M. Nixon, *Six Crises* (Garden City, New York: Doubleday and Company, Inc., 1962), pp. 353-55. Richard Goodwin gives some credence to this claim in his memoir. See Goodwin, *Remembering America*, p. 125.

[64] Schlesinger, *Journals*, p. 131.

[65] Memorandum from McNamara to Kennedy, January 24, Washington National Records Center, RG 330, OSD Files: FRC 65 A 3464, 381 Cuba, 18 Jan. 61, quoted in Editorial Note Referencing January 19 Meeting between Eisenhower and Kennedy, *FRUS 1961-63*, Vol. X, http://www.state.gov/www/about_state/history/frusX/16_30.html, accessed on April 1, 2009. See also Schlesinger, *Journals*, p. 131.

[66] Annual Message to the Congress on the State of the Union, January 30, 1961, *Public Papers of the Presidents*, http://www.presidency.ucsb.edu/ws/?pid=8045, accessed on October 26, 2007.

what became the Bay of Pigs invasion. Little did the new president know that this operation would bring the first major crisis of his administration.

The CIA briefed the president on its plan on January 28, and Kennedy ordered them to proceed with additional planning.[67] During the same meeting, Kennedy asked the Joint JCS to offer an evaluation of the CIA's plan. General Lyman Lemnitzer, the JCS chairman, told the president "that in view of the strong forces Castro now had that the Cubans would have very little chance of success." Dulles expressed a different opinion and had a "very optimistic view of the force's ability to land and hold a beach head."[68] This early disagreement revealed some of the problems that were going to exist throughout the planning and execution of the invasion.[69]

Over the next two and a half months, Kennedy participated in numerous meetings that addressed the planning and feasibility of the operation. While at times he expressed misgivings and called for changes in the plans, he continued to allow the momentum for the operation to build. One of his biggest concerns was that the operation would be seen as an American invasion resembling a World War II amphibious assault, and he pressed "for alternatives."[70] In early March, "he was willing to take the chance of going ahead," but he wanted changes to the plan "where US assistance would be less obvious."[71] Less than two weeks prior to the invasion, he reiterated "a desire to use the force but he wanted to do everything possible to make it appear to be a Cuban operation partly from within Cuba but supported from without Cuba, the objective being to make it more plausible for U.S. denial of association with the operation although recognizing that we would be accused."[72] To achieve this deniability, Kennedy asked the CIA to change the

---

67 Memorandum of Discussion, January 28, 1961, *FRUS, 1961-1963*, Volume X: Cuba, 1961-1962, http://www.state.gov/www/about_state/history/frusX/16_30.html, accessed on April 1, 2009.

68 Review of Record of Proceedings Related to Cuban Situation, May 5; Naval Historical Center, Area Files, Bumpy Road Materials, quoted in Editorial Note, ibid., http://www.state.gov/www/about_state/history/frusX/16_30.html, accessed on April 1, 2009.

69 For a chronology of the Bay of Pigs planning, see Chronology of Events Leading to the Bay of Pigs Invasion, April 23, 1961, Digital National Security Archives, http://gateway.proquest.com/openurl?url_ver=Z39.88-2004&res_dat=xri:dnsa&rft_dat=xri:dnsa:article:CCU00154, accessed on June 12, 2009.

70 Memorandum of Meeting with President Kennedy, February 8, 1961, *FRUS, 1961-1963*, Volume X: Cuba, 1961-1962, http://www.state.gov/www/about_state/history/frusX/31_45.html, accessed on April 1, 2009.

71 Editorial Note Addressing Meeting at White House on March 11, 1961, ibid., http://www.state.gov/www/about_state/history/frusX/46_60.html, accessed on April 1, 2009.

72 Editorial Notes on Meeting with President, April 6, 1961, ibid., http://www.state.gov/www/about_state/history/frusX/76_90.html, accessed on April 1, 2009.

landing area from Trinidad to a more remote location.[73] The CIA chose a new landing area at the Bay of Pigs.[74]

Generally speaking, Kennedy's advisers offered mixed views of the chances of the operation's success. Bundy, an early skeptic to the plan, told Kennedy in early February that the Defense Department and CIA were quite enthusiastic about the potential success of the plan. However, he reported that the State Department was taking a much "cooler view" as it was fearful of the potentially "very grave" political consequences in Latin America.[75] Bundy warmed up to the operation in March and told the president that while he had been a "skeptic," he thought the CIA was "on the edge of a good answer."[76] The JCS at the same time was not as optimistic. Chief of Naval Operations Arleigh Burke told the president that the CIA's revised plan of operation only had about a 50 percent chance of success. Burke "emphasized that the plan was dependent on a general uprising in Cuba, and that the entire operation would fail without such an uprising."[77] Arthur Schlesinger questioned whether the risk was the worth the possible benefits. He advised the president that he would support an operation that eliminated the Castro regime with "a swift, surgical stroke." However, he argued that the operation as then planned "involved many hazards; and on balance—and despite the intelligence and responsibility with which the case for the action has been presented—I am against it."[78] As the failure of the landing became evident, he recorded in his

---

[73] Clandestine Services History: Record of Paramilitary Action against the Castro Government, 17 March 1960-May 1961, May 5, 1961, Digital National Security Archives, http://gateway.proquest.com/openurl?url_ver=Z39.88-2004&res_dat=xri:dnsa&rft_dat=xri:dnsa:article:CCU00171, accessed on June 12, 2009. See also Grow, *U.S. Presidents and Latin American Interventions*, p. 55.

[74] See Bohning, *The Castro Obsession*, p. 31; Fursenko and Naftali, *"One Hell of a Gamble,"* pp. 84-85, and Jones, *The Bay of Pigs*, p. 55.

[75] Memorandum of Meeting with President Kennedy, February 8, 1961, *FRUS, 1961-1963*, Volume X: Cuba, 1961-1962, http://www.state.gov/www/about_state/history/frusX/31_45.html, accessed on April 1, 2009.

[76] Memorandum for the President, March 15, 1961, JFKL, Kennedy Papers, National Security Files, McGeorge Bundy Correspondence, Box 405, Folder – Memos to the President, 3/1/61-4/4/61, p. 2.

[77] Review of Record of Proceedings Related to Cuban Situation, May 5; Naval Historical Center, Area Files, Bumpy Road Materials, quoted in Editorial Note, *FRUS, 1961-1963*, Volume X: Cuba, 1961-1962, http://www.state.gov/www/about_state/history/frusX/61_75.html, accessed on April 1, 2009.

[78] Memorandum for the President, April 5, 1961, Digital National Security Archive, http://nsarchive.chadwyck.com.ezproxy.liberty.edu:2048/nsa/documents/CU/00095/all.pdf, accessed on April 1, 2009. Schlesinger summarized a conversation he had with the president on March 28 that showed these misgivings. He asked the president, "What do you think about this damned invasion?" The president answered "I think about it as little as possible." Schlesinger noted, "We agreed that the critical point—and the weak part of the case for

journal, "… one cannot resist the belief that this was an ill-conceived and mistaken expedition."[79]

In the face of these mixed assessments, Kennedy reluctantly decided to proceed with the operations. However, he continued to insist on trying to hide U.S. involvement. While the original plan called for using sixteen B-26s to attack Cuban air bases, the president decided that such a large force would point to U.S. involvement. To placate the president, CIA Deputy Director Bissell cut the strike force in half. [80] Late on April 14 eight B-26s left their base in Nicaragua and dropped their ordinances early the next morning on several Cuban airfields, destroying between 50 and 60 percent of the Cuban Air Force. Fearing any greater U.S. involvement, Kennedy decided to cancel a planned follow-up bombing mission the next day despite protests from the CIA.[81] A Marine colonel, detailed to the CIA at the time of operation, concluded that this decision "doomed the operation to failure." He added, "Restrictions which prevented the full application of available airpower in accordance with sound tactical principles must be regarded as primarily responsible for [the] failure of the amphibious operation." [82] Even though the CIA knew that the invasion force was going to be at the mercy of the Cuban army without the second bombing mission, it decided to proceed with the landing on April 17, evidently hoping that the president would change his mind and not allow the operation to fail.

The invasion force of over 1,500 men, including 170 airborne forces, attempted to make landfall early on April 17 and met difficulties from the start.[83] The ship carrying one battalion of the attacking force became stuck on a reef 60 yards offshore and several miles from the landing area. The second battalion landed successfully but found itself facing nearly 20,000 Cuban forces. While several members of the CIA and the military recommended that the United States at least provide air support, Kennedy held to his conviction

action—lay in the theory of an immediate local response to a landing." Schlesinger, *Journals*, p. 94.

[79] Schlesinger, *Journals*, p. 97. See Parmet, *JFK*, pp. 161-62.

[80] Jones, *The Bay of Pigs*, pp. 76-78.

[81] Detailed Statement of All the Circumstances Surrounding the Cancellation of the D-Day Airstrike, May 3, 1961, Digital National Security Archive, http://gateway.proquest.com/openurl?url_ver=Z39.88-2004&res_dat=xri:dnsa&rft_dat=xri:dnsa:article:CCU00163, accessed on June 12, 2009.

[82] Clandestine Services History: Record of Paramilitary Action Against the Castro Government, 17 March 1960-May 1961, May 5, 1961, Digital National Security Archives, http://gateway.proquest.com/openurl?url_ver=Z39.88-2004&res_dat=xri:dnsa&rft_dat=xri:dnsa:article:CCU00171, accessed on June 12, 2009.

[83] Jones, *The Bay of Pigs*, p. 96.

that the United States should not take such an obvious role in the operation. Whether the air support would have made any difference in the ultimate outcome of the operation is unknown; however, without it, it was "doomed." While most of the attackers fought bravely and caused significant casualties among Castro's forces, after several days of heavy fighting, 1,189 men from the invasion force surrendered. 140 others died in the fighting, with the rest either never making it ashore or escaping to ships at sea.[84]

The entire Bay of Pigs operation was a disaster, and "The President was really quite shattered."[85] Schlesinger probably captured it best when he wrote in his journal, "It is evident that the Cuban affair has done us immense damage ... . We not only look like imperialists, we look like ineffectual imperialists, which is worst; and we look like stupid, ineffectual imperialists, which is worst of all."[86] While Kennedy publically shouldered the blame for the operation, he was outraged at the CIA and JCS. He believed they had misled him or, at least, not adequately informed him of the dangers involved in the operation.[87] There is an element of truth in Kennedy's charges. The CIA was overconfident about its abilities to manipulate the internal affairs of other countries and underestimated Castro's popular support. In doing so, it presented a flawed plan to the president that had little chance of success. Additionally, the Joint Chiefs did not forcefully express the reservations that many of them had concerning the operation.[88] If they would have, it is possible that Kennedy would have chosen a different course of action.

Others could be blamed as well for not speaking up forcefully against the plan like Secretary of State Rusk and Secretary of Defense McNamara, or

---

[84] Freedman, *Kennedy's Wars*, p. 145. Four Americans, who piloted two B-26s, also died in the fighting. Two of them were apparently executed after safely bailing out of their planes. See Jones, *The Bay of Pigs*, p. 119.

[85] Notes on Cabinet Meeting, April 20, 1961, *FRUS, 1961-1963*, Volume X: Cuba, 1961-1962, http://www.state.gov/www/about_state/history/frusX/151_165.html, accessed on April 1, 2009.

[86] Schlesinger, *Journals*, p. 104. Goodwin later captured Kennedy's emotions at the time: "Kennedy was furious—furious at the advisers whose persuasions were mingled with misjudgments so grotesque as to constitute misrepresentations; furious at Castro, who had humiliated his fledgling administration; furious, most of all, at himself for having approved and commanded this comic-opera fiasco whose failure, in the new clarity of retrospect, was quickly seen to be inevitable." Goodwin, *Remembering America*, p. 180.

[87] Jones, *The Bay of Pigs*, p. 131. Kennedy exclaimed to Arthur Schlesinger, "It is a hell of way to learn things, but I have learned one thing from this business—that is, that we will have to deal with the CIA." Schlesinger, *Journals*, p. 98. See also Dallek, *An Unfinished Life*, pp. 367-68.

[88] Jones, *The Bay of Pigs*, pp. 139-42.

initiating the operation like former President Eisenhower.[89] Schlesinger believed that the secretary of state deserved most of the blame since he did not question the operation with any "vigor." Schlesinger wrote, "I would regard his failure as almost the most reprehensible of all."[90] While all of this is true, the ultimate responsibility for the operation lay with the president. While reluctant at times, Kennedy continually approved the planning during his first three months in office and made critical decisions that altered its implementation. He requested a change in the landing site that made a successful mission even more unlikely, and then he cancelled the second day of bombing raids, allowing Castro's Air Force to control the skies over the beachhead. While the likelihood of the mission's success was never great, these two changes ensured its failure.

Numerous factors help explain Kennedy's actions and decisions. As a new president, he faced difficult questions with limited experience and was unclear which of his advisers he should trust. He also wanted to fulfill his campaign promises to stand up to communism more than his predecessor. While removing Castro provided him the opportunity to burnish his credentials as a strong leader, the failure to follow through with an operation initiated by President Eisenhower could have led to claims that he was weak. Robert Armory, from the CIA, believed that "the total political risk" of not doing something Eisenhower planned was critical.[91] Ted Sorensen later asserted that Kennedy initially approved the operation because of "his unwillingness to be labeled 'soft'." Beyond these considerations, at least two other factors played a role. First, "he was unable to devise any politically acceptable means of dismantling and dispersing the brigade assembled by the CIA."[92] The 1,500 Cuban exiles in training would have been a political liability if dispersed and an international embarrassment if their full story became public. Second, Kennedy personally hated Castro and simply could not see how the will of the United States could be thwarted. Flushed with confidence that the United States could do nothing but succeed, Kennedy authorized a mission that had little chance of success.

---

89 For McNamara's assessment, see Robert S. McNamara Oral History Interview, April 4, 1964, JFKL, p. 12-14, http://www.jfklibrary.org/NR/rdonlyres/FCC01356-1AFA-46E0-818E-605360FF7D2B/4
3973/McNamaraRobertSJFK1_oralhistory.pdf, accessed on July 8, 2009.

90 Schlesinger, *Journals*, p. 104.

91 Second Oral History Interview with Robert Armory, February 17, 1966, JFKL, p. 32. See also Dallek, *An Unfinished Life*, p. 358; and Beschloss, *The Crisis Years*, p. 132.

92 Sorensen, *Counselor*, p. 315. See also O'Donnell and Power, *"Johnny, We Hardly Knew Ye"*, p. 306.

The fiasco had a lasting impact. In Cuba, Castro used the invasion to consolidate his position and to openly embrace socialism. The Soviet Union took the opportunity to strengthen its military ties to Cuba, and Khrushchev set his sights on proving his superiority to the American president.[93] Kennedy came out of the crisis with a lasting mistrust of the CIA and the military. He ultimately replaced both Dulles and Bissell at the CIA. Further, Kennedy and his brother became obsessed with removing Castro from power.[94] At a National Security Council meeting just days after the failed invasion, Robert Kennedy "took the lead … slamming into anyone who suggested that we go slowly and try to move calmly and not repeat previous mistakes." The focus of the intensely "emotional" meeting was to identify ways "to harass Castro."[95] The Kennedys' desire to eliminate the Cuban leader led to the initiation of Operation Mongoose in November 1961 with the expressed purpose of removing Castro from power.[96] Lasting over a year, this $50 million operation failed to remove Castro and raised the Cuban leader's concerns about the U.S. threat, ultimately encouraging him to seek missiles from the Soviet Union.[97]

While Cuba, Berlin, and Vietnam receive the lion-share of attention in analyses of Kennedy's presidency, one of the first crises he had to deal with involved Laos. Kennedy inherited a problem in 1961 that had already been festering for many years. In the aftermath of World War II, former colonial territories around the world sought their independence, sometimes peacefully but often not. The French hoped to regain their empire in Indochina, which today comprises Cambodia, Laos, and Vietnam, and attempted to reassert control after Japan's defeat. Vietnamese nationalists, led by Ho Chi Minh, had different plans and on September 2, 1945, they declared Vietnam independent, marking the beginning of a colonial struggle with France. While the United States ideally did not want France or the other colonial powers to reestablish their empires, the onset of the Cold War and growing concerns about the

---

[93] Fursenko and Naftali, *"One Hell of a Gamble,"* pp. 99-100. See also Beschloss, *The Crisis Years*, p. 177.

[94] Bohning, *The Castro Obsession*, pp. 68-70.

[95] Notes on the 478th Meeting of the National Security Council, April 22, 1961, *Foreign Relations of the United States* [hereafter *FRUS*], Volume X: Cuba, 1961-1962 (Washington, D.C.: U.S. Government Printing Office, 1997), http://www.state.gov/www/about_state/history/frusX/166_175.html, accessed on June 19, 2009.

[96] Memorandum for the Record, November 4, 1961, ibid., http://www.state.gov/www/about_state/history/frusX/271_285.html, accessed on June 19, 2009. See also, Inter-Agency Staff Study, undated, ibid.

[97] Ibid., p. 79. CIA Deputy Director Robert Amory remembered that "Bobby was convinced that we could upset Castro by a long campaign of meddling, infiltration and so on." See Oral History Interview with Robert Armory, February 9, 1966, JFKL, p. 7.

spread of communism led it to change its views. After initially hoping France would relinquish its empire, the United States began offering aid to the French so that they would continue to resist the communist menace posed by Ho Chi Minh.[98]

President Truman began to believe that if Vietnam fell to communism, then the other states and territories would also fall. This belief, growing out of the strategy of containment that the United States had adopted in the late 1940s, led Truman and most other American political leaders to believe that the United States had to resist the spread of communism wherever it was occurring. The CIA argued in 1948 that "The growth of nationalism in colonial areas ... has major implications for US security.... Should the recently liberated and currently emergent states become oriented toward the USSR, US military and economic security would be seriously threatened."[99] The fall of mainland China to communism in 1949, the Soviet test of an atomic bomb during the same year, and North Korea's attack on South Korea in 1950 all seemed to confirm the growing threat of communism. By the time Truman left office in January 1953, the United States was paying most of the costs of France's continuing involvement in Indochina.[100]

President Eisenhower shared the beliefs of many in the Truman administration that the spread of communism had to be stopped. In April 1954 Eisenhower explained his "falling domino principle:"

> "You have a row of dominoes set up, you knock over the first one, and what will happen to the last one is the certainty that it will go over very quickly.... Then with respect to more people passing under this domination, Asia, after all, has already lost some 450 million of its peoples to the Communist dictatorship, and we simply can't afford greater losses.... When we come to the possible sequence of events, the loss of Indochina, of Burma, of Thailand, of the Peninsula, and Indonesia following, now you begin to talk about areas that not only multiply the disadvantages that you would suffer

---

[98] See Ronald H. Spector, *Advice and Support: The Early Years of the U.S. Army in Vietnam, 1941-1960* (New York: The Free Press, 1985), pp. 77-78, 83-84, and 95-104; and Melvyn P. Leffler, *A Preponderance of Power: National Security, the Truman Administration, and the Cold War* (Stanford, CA: Stanford University Press, 1992), pp. 165-66 and 382-83.

[99] ORE 25-48: The Breakup of the Colonial Empires and Its Implications for US Security, September 3, 1948 in *Estimative Products on Vietnam, 1948-1975* (Pittsburgh, PA: National Intelligence Council and the Government Printing Office, 2005), p. 4.

[100] George C. Herring, *America's Longest War: The United States and Vietnam, 1950-1975*, 3rd ed. (New York: McGraw-Hill, Inc., 1996), pp. 27-29; Leffler, *A Preponderance of Power*, pp. 436-37 and 475; LaFeber, *The American Age*, pp. 494 and 521-22.

through loss of materials ..., but now you are talking really about millions and millions and millions of people."[101]

The situation in Indochina in the spring of 1954 had turned perilous for the French. In 1953, French soldiers had occupied Dien Bien Phu, a small city in northwest Vietnam, to create a forward operating base. However, the Viet Minh controlled the hills surrounding the base and in March 1954 began a two month siege. French efforts to send reinforcements and ultimately to evacuate failed, and on May 7 almost 8,000 French soldiers had to surrender.[102] The Battle of Dien Bien Phu effectively marked the end of the French effort to control Indochina.

Immediately following the fall of Dien Bien Phu, a conference opened in Geneva where representatives from France, the Viet Minh, Great Britain, the Soviet Union, and several other countries discussed the future of Indochina. In July 1954 they signed the Geneva Accords which recognized the independence of Laos and Cambodia and the temporary division of Vietnam into northern and southern parts. Communists under the leadership of Ho Chi Minh controlled the north and non-communists, ultimately led by Ngo Dinh Diem, controlled the south.[103] The accords called for a national election in 1956 to unify the country. When the time for the elections came, Diem refused to allow them to occur in the south and began a course to maintain South Vietnam as an independent country. President Eisenhower, fearing the loss of South Vietnam, decided he had little choice but to support Diem.[104] The CIA concluded in July 1956 that "Despite the moderately favorable outlook projected for South Vietnam, the situation contains many elements of instability, and progress will continue to depend on firm US support."[105] Between 1956 and 1961, the United States provided over $1 billion in aid to

---

[101] The President's News Conference, April 7, 1954, *Public Papers of the Presidents, Dwight D. Eisenhower*, found at John T. Woolley and Gerhard Peters, *The American Presidency Project*, http://www.presidency.ucsb.edu/ws/?pid=10202, accessed on March 18, 2009.

[102] Spencer C. Tucker, ed., *The Encyclopedia of the Vietnam War: A Political, Social, and Military History* (New York, Oxford University Press, 1998), p. 102.

[103] Seth Jacobs, *Cold War Mandarin: Ngo Dinh Diem and the Origins of America's War in Vietnam, 1950-1963* (Lanham, MD: Rowman & Littlefield Publishers, Inc., 2006), pp. 3 and 100.

[104] Address at Annual Dinner of the American Society of Newspaper Editors, April 21, 1956, *Public Papers of the Presidents, Dwight D. Eisenhower*, http://www.presidency.ucsb.edu/ws/?pid=10786, accessed on March 18, 2009. See also Herring, *America's Longest War*, pp. 48-60.

[105] NIE 63-56: Probable Developments in North and South Vietnam Through Mid-1957, July 17, 1956 in *Estimative Products on Vietnam*, p. 101.

South Vietnam and sent almost 700 military advisers as part of its Military Assistance and Advisery Group to help train the South Vietnamese military.[106]

Besides the tenuous situation in Vietnam, there was also a crisis in Laos. The Geneva Accords had granted Laos full independence and there were immediate questions as to who would be its legitimate leaders. For example, Souvanna Phouma served as the prime minister from 1956 to 1958, again in 1960, and then from 1962 to 1975.[107] Phouma hoped to establish a coalition government that could remain neutral in the Cold War. However, he faced opposition from the military and from the communist Pathet Lao organization, which was supported by North Vietnam. Eisenhower tried to create a non-communist Laos that could resist the Pathet Lao's efforts without much success. Eisenhower noted in his memoirs that he "regretted deeply" that his administration had "left a legacy of strife and confusion in Laos."[108] The CIA shared the pessimism and concluded in late 1960 that "The non-Communist political factions have never achieved unity or cohesion and have tended to view one another with as much suspicion as they do the Communist left. As a result, no strong, effective non-Communist leadership has emerged since Laos achieved independence."[109] The CIA told Kennedy soon after he came into office that, "By far the most serious problems are the deteriorating situation in Laos and the mounting Communist threat and precarious governmental situation in South Vietnam."[110] It stressed "the loss of Laos would severely damage the US position and its influence in Thailand and South Vietnam."[111]

Kennedy inherited a situation in Laos where the government was unpopular and relatively weak, and the only viable alternative was from the Pathet Lao. One of the president's advisers described the Laotian army as "clearly inferior to a battalion of conscientious objectors from World War I."[112] According to Robert Dallek, "No foreign policy issue commanded as much attention during the first two months as this tiny, impoverished,

---

[106] Herring, *America's Longest War*, p. 62. For a critical evaluation of Eisenhower's policies towards Southeast Asia and Vietnam, in particular, see David Kaiser, *American Tragedy: Kennedy, Johnson, and the Origins of the Vietnam War* (Cambridge, MA: The Belknap Press of Harvard University Press, 2000), pp. 10-35.

[107] Background Notes: Laos, U.S. Department of State, http://www.state.gov/r/pa/ei/bgn/2770.htm, accessed on June 25, 2009.

[108] Eisenhower, *Mandate for Change*, p. 612

[109] SNIE 68-60: The Situation and Short-Term Outlook in Laos, December 6, 1960 on CD in *Estimative Products on Vietnam*, p. 4.

[110] NIE 50-61: Outlook in Mainland Southeast Asia, March 28, 1961 on CD in *Estimative Products on Vietnam*, p. 5.

[111] Ibid., p. 6.

[112] Quoted in Dallek, *An Unfinished Life*, p. 351.

landlocked country's civil war."[113] In late January, the president indicated his willingness to accept Laos as "an independent country not dominated by either side but concerned with the life of the people within the country."[114] Two months later, Kennedy noted "The security of all Southeast Asia will be endangered if Laos loses its neutral independence."[115] At a meeting involving the president and Congressional and military leaders in late April, they discussed the Laotian situation. Admiral Arleigh Burke cautioned against war, but stressed "we must hold Laos or face the loss of Southeast Asia."[116] The consensus at the meeting, however, was that "the worst possible mistake we could make would be to intervene."[117]

The Laotian question continued to stew the rest of the Kennedy administration. However, Kennedy recognized that it would be virtually impossible to win a war in Laos; therefore, he decided to pursue a policy of neutrality.[118] As he told some of his advisers, he would have liked nothing better than "to get out of Laos."[119] Since Khrushchev also wanted to avoid a crisis in Laos and also supported neutrality, this was one area where the two Cold War leaders actually agreed.[120] By June 1962, the various factions, with a push from the United States and the Soviet Union, reached a compromise which left Souvanna Phouma again the leader of a coalition government that was supposed to remain neutral in the Cold War. Kennedy pursued this solution to avoid committing combat troops, but by focusing so much attention on it, he made it a larger issue than it needed to be.[121] Unfortunately, the Pathet

---

[113] Ibid., pp. 350-51.

[114] The President's News Conference, January 25, 1961, *Public Papers of the Presidents, Dwight D. Eisenhower*, http://www.presidency.ucsb.edu/ws/?pid=8533, accessed on June 25, 2009.

[115] The President's News Conference, March 23, 1961, ibid., http://www.presidency.ucsb.edu/ws/?pid=8547, accessed on June 25, 2009.

[116] Memorandum on the President's Meeting with Congressional Leaders on April 27, 1961, May 4, 1961, JFKL, Kennedy Papers, National Security Files, Chester V. Clifton, Box 345, Folder – Conferences with the President, Congressional Leaders, 1961-1962, p. 4.

[117] Ibid., p. 3.

[118] Kaiser, *American Tragedy*, pp. 37-38.

[119] Minutes of Discussion on Southeast Asia, August 29, 1961, JFKL, Kennedy Papers, National Security Files, Meetings and Memoranda, Box 317, Folder – Meetings with the President General, 9/61-1/62, p. 2.

[120] Fursenko and Naftali, *Khrushchev's Cold War*, pp. 334 and 345-46.

[121] Freedman, *Kennedy's Wars*, pp. 293-304 and 350. George Ball later claimed "we were treating it [Laos] as a matter of far greater importance than the facts justified. But, nevertheless, the amount of time and effort that was devoted to this was very considerable. As far as the President was concerned, I think this situation had a kind of fascination for him." George W. Ball Oral History Interview, February, 16, 1968, JFKL, p. 1, http://www.jfklibrary.org/NR/rdonlyres/7EC43350-74D1-420B-96A2-44E5A728FCFA/43845/BallGeorgeW3_oralhistory.pdf, accessed on July 8, 2009.

Lao still offered opposition and the conflict in Vietnam continued to spill into Laos.

Until the summer of 1963, other Cold War events generally overshadowed Southeast Asia in the minds of Kennedy and his advisers. However, on occasion, events there took prominence. While Kennedy was willing to see Laos established as a neutral state, he could not accept the loss of South Vietnam. Having criticized the Eisenhower administration for not doing enough to contain communism, he could not accept defeat there.[122] His problem was the Diem government faced some of the same difficulties as the one in Laos. "In South Vietnam," the CIA advised the president, "the situation of the Diem government seems likely to become increasingly difficult, not only because of rising Communist guerrilla strength and declining internal security but also because of widening dissatisfaction with Diem's government."[123]

Kennedy struggled to determine what to do. He sent Lyndon Johnson to Vietnam on a fact-finding mission in the spring of 1961, and Walt Rostow and Maxwell Taylor on another one that fall. They both argued that Diem and South Vietnam had to be saved. Johnson reported to the president that "The battle against Communism must be joined in Southeast Asia with strength and determination to achieve success there—or the United States, inevitably, must surrender the Pacific and take up our defenses on our own shores."[124] He stressed, however, that "it is not desirable" to place American troops in Southeast Asia as the biggest dangers were from "hunger, ignorance, poverty and disease."[125] Taylor told the president the United States needed "an integrated strategy for the entire area because the position in Southeast Asia is precarious."[126]

In the fall of 1961, Kennedy received a report from Senator Mike Mansfield and another from his ambassador to India, John Kenneth Galbraith, that both addressed the difficulties of developing effective policies in Southeast Asia, and more specifically in Vietnam. Mansfield told Kennedy that the decision to send U.S. troops to Vietnam "should be approached with

---

122 Carroll Kilpatrick, "Kennedy Meets Sen. Johnson on Strategy," *The Washington Post and Times Herald*, July 30, 1960, p. A1.

123 NIE 50-61: Outlook in Mainland Southeast Asia, p. 5.

124 Memorandum to the President, May 23, 1961, JFKL, Kennedy Papers, President's Office Files, Special Correspondence, Box #30, Folder – Johnson, Lyndon B., 1/61-5/61, p. 4.

125 Ibid., p. 5. See also Jacobs, *Cold War Mandarin*, pp. 123-24.

126 Memorandum for the President, July 27, 1961, JFKL, Kennedy Papers, National Security Files, McGeorge Bundy Correspondence, Box 405, Folder – Memos to the President, 7/61, p. 1.

the greatest caution" as it "could become a quicksand for us."[127] Galbraith told Kennedy that South Vietnam "is certainly a can of worms" and raised serious questions about Diem's ability to rule.[128] He argued that Diem was more concerned about a coup against his government than fighting the Viet Cong.[129]

The caution of Galbraith, Mansfield, and others was met by calls for greater U.S. involvement. Taylor delivered an ominous report in early November claiming "Communist strategy aims to gain control of Southeast Asia" and in Vietnam, "This strategy is well on the way to success." He recommended increasing U.S. military, economic, and political support.[130] The Secretary of State, the Secretary of Defense, and the JCS sent a memorandum a few days later arguing that "The fall of South Viet-Nam to Communism would lead to the fairly rapid extension of Communist control, or complete accommodation to Communism, in the rest of mainland Southeast Asia and in Indonesia." They advised that the United States would need to introduce up to 205,000 troops to stabilize the situation.[131] Kennedy struggled with what to do. He was "instinctively against" the introduction of American combat forces[132] but also wanted to prove to the world and his domestic opponents that the United States was committed to fighting communism.[133] After his meeting with Senator Mansfield, he told one of his aides, "I got angry with Mike for disagreeing with our policy so completely, and I got angry with myself because I found myself agreeing with him."[134] Regardless of his apparent misgivings, he decided to act, but with much more moderation than Taylor and the others recommended.[135] In mid-November, he ordered the Defense Department to prepare contingency plans for introducing U.S. combat forces

---

[127] Letter to John F. Kennedy, November 2, 1961, JFKL, Kennedy Papers, President's Office Files, Special Collections, Box 31, Folder – Mansfield, Mike, 2/13/61-2/11/62, p. 1. See also Jacobs, *Cold War Mandarin*, pp. 137-39.

[128] Letter to Mr. President, November 28, 1961, JFKL, Kennedy Papers, President's Office Files, Special Collections, Box 29A, Folder – Galbraith, John Kenneth, 11/61-12/61, p. 1.

[129] Ibid., pp. 1-3.

[130] Letter From the President's Military Representative (Taylor) to the President, November 3, 1961, *FRUS, 1961-1963*, Volume 1: Vietnam, 1961, http://www.state.gov/www/about_state/history/vol_i_1961/u.html, accessed on June 26, 2009.

[131] Draft Memorandum From the Secretary of State to the President, November 7, 1961, *FRUS, 1961-1963*, Volume 1: Vietnam, 1961 (Washington, D.C.: U.S. Government Printing Office, 1988), http://www.state.gov/www/about_state/history/vol_i_1961/v.html, accessed on June 26, 2009; and Memorandum From the Secretary of Defense (McNamara) to the President, November 8, 1961, ibid.

[132] Memorandum for the Record, November 6, 1961, ibid.

[133] Dallek, *An Unfinished Life*, pp. 453-54.

[134] O'Donnell and Power, *"Johnny, We Hardly Knew Ye"*, p. 15.

[135] See Herring, *America's Longest War*, p. 91; Kaiser, *American Tragedy*, pp. 113-21; Dallek, *An Unfinished Life*, pp. 454-55; and Freedman, *Kennedy's Wars*, pp. 332-33.

to South Vietnam under certain circumstances and ordered significant increases in American military and economic aid.[136] Over the next year, the number of U.S. advisers in Vietnam jumped from 3,205 to over 9,000 and the amount of military aid more than doubled.[137] While the president had stopped short of directly sending American forces into combat, he raised American involvement in South Vietnam to an unprecedented level and left room for future combat operations.[138]

The crises in Cuba, Laos, and Vietnam reflected the magnitude of the Cold War. Relations between the United States and the Soviet Union were precarious and the advent of more advanced nuclear weapons and delivery systems threatened the world's very survival. As Kennedy dealt with each of these crises, his focus remained on the Soviet Union. He believed in standing firm against communism, but he also hoped to reduce tensions between the two nations. Early in his administration, the president wrote Soviet leader Nikita Khrushchev requesting that they "meet personally for an informal exchange of views."[139] While Khrushchev did not respond immediately, Kennedy did not give up on holding a summit with the Soviet leader. In early April, the United States suggested that the two leaders meet in early June in Vienna for a two-day "get acquainted" meeting.[140] Khrushchev accepted in mid-May, and the two leaders planned to meet on June 3 and 4.[141]

---

136 Draft National Security Action Memorandum, November 13, 1961, *FRUS, 1961-1963*, Volume 1: Vietnam, 1961, http://www.state.gov/www/about_state/history/vol_i_1961/x.html, accessed on June 26, 2009

137 Herring, *America's Longest War*, p. 95.

138 David Halberstam, *The Making of a Quagmire: America and Vietnam during the Kennedy Era*, revised edition (Lanham, MD: Rowman & Littlefield Publishers, Inc., 2008), pp. 39-42. George Ball told Kennedy that he thought it was a mistake to increase American military involvement in South Vietnam as it could lead to much larger increases in the future. Kennedy told Ball, "George, you're just crazier than hell! This decision doesn't mean that." Ball later recalled, "I think we were then caught in a developing situation where it was manifestly difficult to turn back." George W. Ball Oral History Interview, February, 16, 1968, JFKL, pp. 8-9, http://www.jfklibrary.org/NR/rdonlyres/7EC43350-74D1-420B-96A2-44E5A728FCFA/43845/BallGeorgeW3_oralhistory.pdf, accessed on July 8, 2009.

139 Letter From President Kennedy to Chairman Khrushchev, February 22, 1961, *FRUS, 1961-1963*, Volume VI: Kennedy-Khrushchev Exchanges (Washington, D.C.: U.S. Government Printing Office, 1996), http://www.state.gov/www/about_state/history/volume_vi/volume i.html, accessed on June 19, 2009.

140 Telegram From the Department of State to the Embassy in the Soviet Union, April 5, 1961, *FRUS, 1961-1963*, Volume V: Soviet Union (Washington, D.C.: U.S. Government Printing Office, 1998), http://www.state.gov/www/about_state/history/vol_v/50_59.html, accessed on June 19, 2009.

141 Telegram From the Department of State to All Diplomatic Posts, May 18, 1961, ibid., http://www.state.gov/www/about_state/history/vol_v/70_79.html, accessed on June 19, 2009.

Kennedy flew to Paris on his way to the Vienna Summit in order to meet with French President Charles De Gaulle. Kennedy and his wife arrived in Paris on May 31 and stayed until June 3. While Jackie was the star of the visit as she dazzled De Gaulle with her elegance, the president took the opportunity to talk to the French leader about Khrushchev. De Gaulle advised Kennedy that Khrushchev often used bluffs to get his way and noted that if the Soviet leader was really serious about going to war over Berlin he would have done so already. He explained that it was important for Kennedy to make the Soviet premier understand that the United States was committed to defending Western Europe and Berlin. Beyond these points, De Gaulle made it clear that France would act independently on some issues, including the need to develop its own means to retaliate against the Soviet Union if necessary.[142]

Kennedy flew from Paris to Vienna on June 3 for his two-day summit with Khrushchev. After the Bay of Pigs debacle, the president wanted to make a strong impression on the Soviet leader who was his elder by over 20 years. Khrushchev saw an opportunity to push around the young president.[143] The summit began during the mid-morning on June 3 and the differences between the two leaders quickly became apparent. Other than agreeing that Laos should be neutral, the two leaders found little common ground.[144] Kennedy had high hopes that they could reach an agreement on limiting nuclear testing and was shocked when Khrushchev announced the Soviet Union would have to have veto power over any enforcement measures and would allow only three on-site inspections to evaluate suspicious seismic activity. Kennedy had expected Khrushchev to accept ten on-site inspections a year. With little room for agreement, the chances of reaching any substantial arms control agreements or limits on nuclear testing were virtually negligible.[145]

In reality, while Kennedy had ambitions to talk about a range of issues from Laos to arms control to Berlin, Khrushchev wanted to focus on Berlin and specifically on getting NATO forces out of West Berlin. When the

---

[142] Memorandum of Conversation with the President and the Congressional Leadership, June7, 1961, JFKL, Kennedy Papers, National Security Files, Meetings & Memoranda, Box 317, Folder – Meeting with the President – General, p. 1. See also Josephine Brain, "Dealing with DeGaulle," in White, ed., *Kennedy*, p. 166. Beschloss, *The Crisis Years*, pp. 183-186; Giglio, *The Presidency of John F. Kennedy*, pp. 73-74; and Dallek, *An Unfinished Life*, pp. 396-97 and 402-3.

[143] Quoted in Fursenko and Naftali, *Khrushchev's Cold War*, p. 355.

[144] Memorandum of Conversation, June 3, 1961, *FRUS, 1961-1963*, Volume VII: Arms Control and Disarmament (Washington, D.C.: U.S. Government Printing Office, 1995), http://www.state.gov/r/pa/ho/frus/kennedyjf/vii/50950.htm, accessed on June 26, 2009.

[145] Memorandum of Conversation, June 4, 1961, *FRUS, 1961-1963*, Volume V: Soviet Union, http://www.state.gov/www/about_state/history/vol_v/80_85.html, accessed on June 26, 2009.

meeting turned to the Berlin question on the second day, the tone of discussions went from bad to worse.[146] Khrushchev presented Kennedy with an ultimatum. The Soviet Union was going to sign a separate peace treaty with East Germany within six months and with that treaty all special air, road, and rail corridors between West Germany and Berlin would be ended. Kennedy reacted with dismay and announced that while the United States could accept the peace treaty, it could not accept the loss of access to West Berlin.[147] Khrushchev announced, "The USSR will sign a peace treaty and the sovereignty of the GDR [East Germany] will be observed. Any violation of that sovereignty will be regarded by the USSR as an act of open aggression against a peace-loving country."[148] Kennedy "concluded the conversation by observing that it would be a cold winter."[149] On that dire note, the summit soon came to an end.[150] Kennedy knew he had been bested at the summit and later exclaimed to journalist James Reston, a family friend, that Khrushchev had "just beat the hell out of him."[151]

The 1961 Berlin Crisis was really a continuation of a dispute with the Soviet Union that had existed since the end of World War II. The former allies—the United States, Soviet Union, Great Britain, and France—had not specified when Germany would be unified. Ultimately, reunion depended on the agreement of all four. After the Cold War began, there was little room for agreement and two Germanys soon emerged. West Germany resulted from the union of the American, British, and French zones, while East Germany originated from the Soviet zone. The same split occurred in Berlin. Disputes over Berlin, located in the middle of East Germany, remained a centerpiece of the Cold War with the most contentious times being during the Soviet blockade of the land routes in and out of West Berlin and the allied airlift to supply the city in 1948 and 1949. However, prior to 1961, nothing the Soviet Union did shook the West's resolve to hold onto the city.

Khrushchev's threats at the Vienna summit were the Soviet Union's latest attempts to force a resolution to the crisis. West Berlin was a major problem for the Soviet Union and East Germany as it was a beacon for those who

---

146 Schild, "The Berlin Crisis," pp. 100-1.
147 Ibid.
148 Ibid.
149 Memorandum of Conversation, June 4, 1961, JFKL, Kennedy Papers, President's Office Files, Countries, Box 126, Folder – USSR-Vienna Meeting, Memos of Conversations, 6/61 (I), p. 3.
150 For fuller descriptions of the Vienna Summit, see Beschloss, *The Crisis Years*, pp. 192-226; and Fursenko and Naftali, *Khrushchev's Cold War*, pp. 360-66.
151 Quoted in Beschloss, *The Crisis Years*, p. 225.

wanted to escape communism. Khrushchev told Kennedy adviser, John McCloy, that "Lancing [the] West Berlin boil" would offer the opportunity for greatly improved relations between the two countries.[152] Khrushchev and the East Germans realized the West's freedoms and economic prosperity attracted many people in communist-controlled areas. From East Germany's perspective, literally a "Brain Drain" was occurring as many of its most educated people were fleeing to the west.[153] During the first six months of 1961, 100,000 people left East Germany through Berlin.[154] In July, almost 1,000 East Germans fled each day across the border and the numbers only increased in August.[155] If those numbers had continued, East Germany's economy would have had little chance of improving.

After the Vienna summit, Kennedy was determined to not let Khrushchev get the better of him again.[156] He decided that Berlin would be where he made his stand, even if he desired to avoid a war. He told the American people in a radio address on June 6 that the Soviet Union and the United States "have wholly different views of right and wrong, of what is an internal affair and what is aggression, and, above all, we have wholly different concepts of where the world is and where it is going." He announced the United States would protect the rights of West Berlin "at any risk."[157] A few weeks later at a news conference, he stressed, "There is peace in Germany and in Berlin. If it is disturbed, it will be a direct Soviet responsibility."[158] On July 25, he told the American public "We cannot and will not permit the Communists to drive us out of Berlin, either gradually or by force." He added, "The world is not

---

152 Telegram From the Embassy in the Soviet Union to the Department of State, July 28, 1961, *FRUS, 1961-1963*, Volume VIX: Berlin Crisis, 1961-1962 (Washington, D.C.: U.S. Government Printing Office, 1993), http://www.state.gov/r/pa/ho/frus/kennedyjf/xiv/15860.htm, accessed on June 30, 2009.

153 Schild, "The Berlin Crisis," p. 111.

154 Fursenko and Naftali, *Khrushchev's Cold War*, p. 373.

155 Warren I. Cohen, *The Cambridge History of American Foreign Relations*, Volume IV: *America in the Age of Soviet Power, 1945-1991* (New York: Cambridge, University Press, 1993), p. 133. See also "Refugees Shun Threats: More Pour to West: Record for July May Be Near 40,000," *Chicago Daily Tribune*, August 2, 1961, p. 10; and Harry Gilroy, "Berlin Crisis Tied to Refugee Flow: East Needs Workers but They Prefer West's Jobs," *New York Times*, August 6, 1961, p. 2.

156 Others were also expressing doubts about the president's performance. Former President Truman wrote Dean Acheson in early July, "The performance of our Chief Executive worries me." Harry S. Truman to Dean Acheson, July 7, 1961 in Ferrell, ed., *Off the Record*, p. 395.

157 Radio and Television Report to the American People on Returning From Europe, June 6, 1961, *Public Papers of the Presidents, John F. Kennedy*, http://www.presidency.ucsb.edu/ws/?pid=8180, accessed on June 26, 2009.

158 The President's News Conference, June 28, 1961, ibid., http://www.presidency.ucsb.edu/ws/?pid=8209, accessed on June 26, 2009.

deceived by the Communist attempt to label Berlin as a hot-bed of war. There is peace in Berlin today. The source of world trouble and tension is Moscow, not Berlin. And if war begins, it will have begun in Moscow and not Berlin."[159] With this message, the president announced military and civil defense preparations in case the Soviet Union or East Germany shut off access to West Berlin.[160]

The crisis came to a head in early August, and war was a definite possibility. *Pravda*, the main Soviet newspaper, claimed "The bellicose imperial circles are fanning the arms race and threatening the peoples with war."[161] The headlines blared in Chicago, "Nikita Warns of War Peril Over Berlin."[162] Neither side wanted war, however, as both Kennedy and Khrushchev were looking for ways to bring closure to the crisis.[163] This was no easy task as the recalcitrance of West German leader Konrad Adenaur and East German leader Walter Ulbrecht made the process more difficult. However, both Kennedy and Khrushchev worked to restrain them.[164] While neither leader knew it, a resolution to the war scare was near.

The reality for both the United States and the Soviet Union was that neither thought a war over Berlin was worth it. In late July, Khrushchev decided to construct a wall, or "an iron ring", to separate West Berlin from the rest of East Berlin and East Germany.[165] East German leader Ulbrecht responded enthusiastically to the idea, and they decided to initially place a barbed wire barrier around West Berlin on August 13 and to follow that with a more permanent barrier. The world awoke that morning to a 96-mile long barbed wire barrier that "sliced through 192 streets, thirty-two railway lines, eight S-Bahn (city train lines), four subway lines, and three autobahns."[166] Over the next several weeks, the East Germans added concrete barriers. Importantly, however, while the barbed wire blocked East Germans from crossing to the west without permission, it did not cut off the West's access.

---

[159] Radio and Television Report to the American People on the Berlin Crisis, July 25, 1961, ibid., http://www.presidency.ucsb.edu/ws/?pid=8259, accessed on June 26, 2009.

[160] Memorandum of Minutes of the National Security Council Meeting, July 19, 1961, *FRUS, 1961-1963*, Volume VIX: Berlin Crisis, 1961-1962, http://www.state.gov/r/pa/ho/frus/kennedyjf/xiv/15860.htm, accessed on June 30, 2009.

[161] Seymour Topping, "Soviet Stresses Military Aspects of New Program: Emphasis Seen as Warning to West and Steeling of People for Berlin Test Soviet Stresses Military Goals Of Program as Warning to West," *New York Times* August 1, 1961, p. 1.

[162] "Nikita Warns of War Peril Over Berlin," *Chicago Daily Tribune*, August 5, 1961, p. S1.

[163] Record of Meeting, August 3, 1961, *FRUS, 1961-1963*, Volume VIX: Berlin Crisis, 1961-1962, http://www.state.gov/r/pa/ho/frus/kennedyjf/xiv/15861.htm, accessed on June 30, 2009.

[164] Beschloss, *The Crisis Years*, pp. 266-70.

[165] Fursenko and Naftali, *Khrushchev's Cold War*, p. 377.

The barrier did not block the three highways and railways across East Germany that connected West Germany to West Berlin.[167] Through the remainder of the summer and fall tensions remained high, including one stand-off between American and Soviet tanks at a crossing point. However, the wall actually began to remove Berlin as a pivotal issue because it stabilized the post-World War II settlement.[168] As Kennedy told one of his aides, "It's not a very nice solution, but a wall is a hell of a lot better than a war."[169]

The gradual settling of these crises in the fall of 1961 marked the end of the series of very difficult foreign and national security policy issues that the Kennedy administration faced during its first year in office. None of the crises had been completely resolved, and the problems with Cuba and Vietnam would especially rear their heads in the coming years. Kennedy made numerous mistakes, but most are understandable considering he was a new president. He struggled at times to determine which advisers he could trust and how to juggle different policy options. He sometimes took events and issues too personally, as his hatred of Castro and his desire to prove himself led to some questionable decisions. However, he generally remained composed during crises and resisted pressures to make quick decisions that could have made the situation worse. His decision to support the neutralization of Laos, while not necessarily popular, represented a wise course. However, his efforts to leave his options open often left it unclear what direction his policies would ultimately follow. For example, while he limited American involvement in Vietnam compared to what many of his advisers recommended, he still increased the number of American military advisers and aid sent to that country, and left open the possibility for future expansion. He had not had a completely successful year, but his handling of different crises showed definite promise.

---

[166] Ibid., p. 383.
[167] Ibid., pp. 378-83.
[168] Freedman, *Kennedy's Wars*, p. 75.
[169] O'Donnell and Power, *"Johnny, We Hardly Knew Ye"*, p. 343.

Chapter 4

THE NEW FRONTIER AND THE COLD WAR

When John F. Kennedy accepted the Democratic Party's nomination to run for president in July 1960, he asked Americans to join him as the country faced the "opportunities and perils" of a "New Frontier".[1] The perils fell in many areas as the last chapter indicated, and there were additional ones at home as the country faced a stagnant economy, difficulties in race relations,[2] and the coming of age of the first baby boomers. However, as challenging as some of these issues were, Kennedy also saw opportunities. In his inaugural address, he called for Americans to "explore the stars, conquer the deserts, eradicate disease, tap the ocean depths and encourage the arts and commerce."[3] As his administration got underway, he set out to cross that new frontier and pursue policies that would lead to "a much better life for people" and strengthen American prestige around the world.[4]

Starting with the launch of Sputnik in October 1957, the United States faced new questions concerning its relative strength compared to the Soviet Union. As detailed in previous chapters, the launch led to claims that the United States was behind the Soviet Union in missile development and may

---

[1] Address of Senator John F. Kennedy Accepting the Democratic Party Nomination for the Presidency of the United States, July 15, 1960, found at the John F. Kennedy Presidential Library and Museum, http://www.jfklibrary.org/Historical+Resources/Archives/Reference+Desk/Speeches/JFK/JFK+Pre-Pres/Address+of+Senator+John+F.+Kennedy+Accepting+the+Democratic+Party+Nomination+for+the+Presidency+of+t.htm, accessed on July 9, 2009.

[2] Kennedy's Civil Rights policies are discussed in Chapter 5.

[3] Inaugural Address, January 20, 1961, *Public Papers of the Presidents, John F. Kennedy*, http://www.presidency.ucsb.edu/ws/?pid=8032, accessed on July 9, 2009.

[4] Transcript of Remarks During an Interview for British Television, April 19, 1961, ibid., http://www.presidency.ucsb.edu/ws/?pid=8071, accessed on July 9, 2009.

have been vulnerable to a communist attack. It also raised questions about what country would lead the world in the development of the science and technology to explore outer space. As one government study noted in 1959,

> "The most significant and enduring result ... of the launching of the first earth satellite by the USSR was a revolutionary revision of estimates of Soviet power and standing. Prior to the launching of Sputnik I there was a very general belief that the Soviet Union was a long way from offering a serious challenge to the US lead in science, technology, and productive power. Sputnik and subsequent Soviet space achievements appeared as a dramatic demonstration that the USSR was able to challenge the US successfully in an endeavor where US pre-eminence had been widely taken for granted."[5]

While President Eisenhower recognized the public relations hit it had taken in the field of space exploration, he urged a "cautious and modest" approach to advancing the American space program.[6]

The Eisenhower administration sought the "development and exploitation of U.S. outer space capabilities as needed to achieve U.S. scientific, military, and political purposes, and to establish the U.S. as a recognized leader in this field."[7] In March 1958 Eisenhower had a bill, officially known as the National Aeronautics and Space Act of 1958, drafted for Congress to create the National Aeronautics and Space Administration (NASA) to "plan, direct, and conduct aeronautical and space activities."[8] The president signed the bill into

[5]Impact of US and Soviet Space Programs on World Opinion: A Summary Assessment, July 7, 1959, found at http://www.hq.nasa.gov/office/pao/History/sputnik/july59.html, accessed on July 9, 2009.

[6] Introduction to Outer Space, March 26, 1958, found at http://www.hq.nasa.gov/office/pao/History/sputnik/16.html, accessed on July 9, 2009. For an assessment of Eisenhower's space policy, see David Callahan and Fred I. Greenstein, "The Reluctant Racer: Eisenhower and U.S. Space Policy," in Roger D. Launius and Howard E. McCurdy, eds, *Spaceflight and the Myth of Presidential Leadership* (Urbana: University of Illinois Press, 1997), pp. 41-45; and John M. Logsdon, *The Decision to Go to the Moon: Project Apollo and the National Interest* (Cambridge, MA: The MIT Press, 1970), p. 12.

[7] National Security Council, NSC 5814/1, "Preliminary U.S. Policy on Outer Space," August 18, 1958, in John M. Logsdon, ed., *Exploring the Unknown: Selected Documents in the History of the U.S. Civil Space Program*, Volume 1: *Organizing for Exploration* (NASA, 1995), p. 360, found at http://history.nasa.gov/SP-4407/vol1/chapter2-4.pdf, accessed on July 9, 2009.

[8] "National Aeronautics and Space Act of 1958," July 29, 1958, in ibid., p. 337, found at http://history.nasa.gov/SP-4407/vol1/chapter2-4.pdf, accessed on July 9, 2009.

law in July and for the remainder of his administration NASA directed the country's space programs.[9] In its final statement on space policy, the Eisenhower administration called for the United States to "carry out energetically a program for the exploration and use of outer space … based upon sound scientific and technological progress" with the purpose of enhancing the country's "scientific knowledge, military strength, [and] economic capabilities" while obtaining "the advantages which come from successful achievements in space."[10] Eisenhower specifically noted that he was "not about to hock his jewels" to reach the moon.[11]

Considering his criticisms of other Eisenhower policies, it is not surprising that Kennedy concluded that the Eisenhower administration was not doing enough combat the Soviet advantages in the space race. He announced in late 1957 that the United States was "behind, possibly as much as several years, in the race for control of outer space."[12] During the campaign, the question of the space race was part of the larger debate concerning whether the Soviet Union had passed the United States militarily. As with his claims of a missile gap, Kennedy accused the Eisenhower administration of allowing the Soviet Union to take the lead in the space race.[13] Indeed, the Soviet Union had beaten the United States in many areas. It had put the first satellite in space, sent the first animals to space and brought them back safely, and launched the first probe that reached the moon.[14] With each success, Soviet prestige increased around the world. As Lyndon Johnson later claimed, the Eisenhower space program "represented an effort for a second place runner."[15] After winning the election, Kennedy began to look for ways to overcome the deficiencies he saw in the Eisenhower space program and to regain American prestige around the world.

Prior to his inauguration, President-elect Kennedy received several recommendations concerning space programs, one from Richard Neustadt,

---

[9] For a description of the political negotiations behind the creation of NASA, see Walter A. McDougall, *...the Heavens and the Earth: A Political History of the Space Age* (New York: Basic Books, Inc., Publishers, 1985), pp. 172-76.

[10] National Aeronautics and Space Council, "U.S. Policy on Outer Space," January 26, 1960, in Logsdon, ed., *Exploring the Unknown*, Volume 1, p. 367, found at http://history.nasa.gov/SP-4407/vol1/chapter2-4.pdf, accessed on July 9, 2009.

[11] Quoted in Logsdon, *The Decision to Go to the Moon*, p. 35.

[12] "Sen. Kennedy Fears Soviet Atom Planes," *Chicago Daily Tribune*, December 4, 1957, p.3.

[13] "Split Over Space Issue: Kennedy Says U.S. Has Lost Lead—Nixon Differs," *New York Times*, October 26, 1960, p. 28. See also Giglio, *The Presidency of John F. Kennedy*, p. 150.

[14] See Chronology of Space, http://www.russianspaceweb.com/chronology_XX.html, accessed on July 10, 2009.

[15] Lyndon B. Johnson, Vice President, to the President, May 13,1963, in Logsdon, ed., *Exploring the Unknown*, Volume 1, p. 430, found at http://history.nasa.gov/SP-4407/vol1/chapter3-2.pdf, accessed on July 10, 2009.

who was serving as one of his consultants, and the other from a task force headed by Jerome Wiesner. Neustadt sent the president-elect a report in December 1960 where he described the relationship between the civil and military components of the space program and briefly explained the current program. He noted that "Since Sputnik we have been in a race to be "first" in physical achievements of a dramatic sort—the sort which has high visibility and thus makes an impression on mass opinion, especially abroad." He then described to Kennedy a booster technology in development that would be needed "to put a man on the moon and get him back before or soon after the Russians do."[16] The Wiesner task force identified the main activities involving space, including ballistic missiles, the use of satellites for scientific observations, and sending men into orbit. While noting that national security was the primary reason for having a space program, it also stressed the importance of national prestige. It claimed that "space exploration and exploits have captured the imagination of the peoples of the world. During the next few years the prestige of the United States will in part be determined by the leadership we demonstrate in space activities. It is within this context that we must consider man in space." It recommended improving the management and coordination of the space effort and the development of a rocket booster sufficient to lift large payloads. Finally, it emphasized that the United States needed to "push forward in space science as effectively and as forcefully as we can."[17]

Other issues occupied Kennedy's time in the early months of his administration; therefore, he initially moved slowly on space related items.[18] After he appointed James Webb as the NASA administrator in February, the president told Congress he would not be asking for any significant changes to the Eisenhower budget for space until his administration completed a "hard-boiled reappraisal" of the space program.[19] In March, Kennedy began to reformulate his goals for space and had meetings with Vice President Johnson,

---

[16] Richard E. Neustadt, "Problems of Space Programs," December 20, 1960, in John M. Logsdon, ed., *Exploring the Unknown*, Volume 1, p. 414, found at http://history.nasa.gov/SP-4407/vol1/chapter3-1.pdf, accessed on July 10, 2009.

[17] Wiesner Committee,"Report to the President-Elect of the Ad Hoc Committee on Space," January 10, 1961, found at http://www.hq.nasa.gov/office/pao/History/report61.html, accessed on July 10, 2009.

[18] McDougall, *...the Heavens and the Earth*, p. 310; and Logsdon, *The Decision to Go to the Moon*, p. 75.

[19] John W. Finney, "Kennedy Plans Few Changes in Eisenhower's Space Budget," *New York Times*, February 28, 1961, p. 4. For a description of Webb's appointment, see W. Henry Lambright, *Powering Apollo: James Webb of NASA* (Baltimore: Johns Hopkins University Press, 1995), pp. 82-84.

who he had asked to head the National Aeronautics and Space Council, Webb, and others to establish NASA's direction. Hugh Dryden, NASA's deputy administrator, later explained that "The President was obviously interested in what could be done to get out of this difficult position of being second place to the Russians in space, and he urged that every effort ought to be made to accelerate the program that we had."[20] NASA administrators also recommended giving priority to making a lunar-landing, claiming they could achieve it within the decade for between $20 and 40 billion.[21]

The president began giving more attention to the space program after Yuri Gagarin, a Soviet cosmonaut, became the first man to fly in space in early April and the Bay of Pigs debacle a few days later.[22] Although another Soviet achievement in space was not a surprise at all, it was still a major propaganda victory.[23] Democratic Senator Stuart Symington captured this concern when he noted that Gagarin's flight was "just another illustration of the fact that the nation or any group of nations who control space will control the world."[24] Kennedy conceded in a press conference, "the news will be worse before it is better, and it will be some time before we catch up."[25] The humiliation of the Bay of Pigs also played a role. Kennedy wanted a victory in the Cold War, and he decided to increase U.S. efforts to "catch up" as soon as possible.[26]

On April 20, he asked his vice president to make "an overall survey of where we stand in space" and deliver his report "at the earliest possible moment." He particularly asked Johnson to determine if there was "any other space program which promises dramatic results if we could win," how much the program would cost, and whether the country was "making maximum

---

20 Hugh L. Dryden Oral History Interview, April 4, 1964, JFKL, p. 14, http://www.jfklibrary.org/NR/rdonlyres/619862E4-5727-41B2-B38F-3B2B1BE2742E/44001/DrydenHughL_oralhistory.pdf, accessed on July 10, 2009. Walter MacDougall argues "The brief Kennedy years were those in which American space policy fell captive to the image makers." McDougall, *...the Heavens and the Earth*, p. 305.

21 Ibid., p. 18.

22 Sorensen, *Counselor*, pp. 334-6. See also Derek W. Elliott, "Space: The Final Frontier of the New Frontier," in White, *Kennedy*, p. 197; Michael Beschloss, "Kennedy and the Decision to Go to the Moon," in Launius and McCurdy, *Spaceflight and the Myth of Presidential Leadership*, p. 56; and Logsdon, *The Decision to Go to the Moon*, pp. 101-105 and 111-12.

23 "Man in Space," *New York Times*, April 16, 1961, p. E1.

24 Philip Dodd, "Behind in Space Race: Kennedy Denies Weakness in Struggle on Ideology," *Chicago Daily Tribune*, April 13, 1961, p. 3.

25 The President's News Conference, April 12, 1961, *Public Papers of the Presidents, John F. Kennedy*, http://www.presidency.ucsb.edu/ws/?pid=8055, accessed on July 10, 2009.

26 See McDougall, *...the Heavens and the Earth*, pp. 318-19; and Dallek, *An Unfinished Life*, pp. 392-94.

effort."[27] At a news conference the next day, he told a reporter "if we can get to the moon before the Russians, we should."[28] Johnson delivered a preliminary report on April 28 and highlighted the importance of space accomplishments. The vice president noted that "dramatic accomplishments in space are being increasingly identified as a major indicator of world leadership," and "if we do not make the strong effort now, the time will soon be reached when the margin of control over space and over men's minds through space accomplishments will have swung so far on the Russian side that we will not be able to catch up, let alone assume leadership."[29] He then went through and answered the questions the president had sent in his previous memorandum. He explained that it would be difficult, but not impossible, to beat the Soviet Union to the moon if the country was willing to increase the NASA budget by roughly $1 billion annually.[30]

One of Johnson's advisers and one of the world's leading experts on rockets and space, Dr. Wernher von Braun, addressed Kennedy's questions in a separate letter. He stressed that "we have an excellent chance of beating the Soviets to the *first landing of a crew on the moon*."[31] He concluded "in the space race we are competing with a determined opponent whose peacetime economy is on a wartime footing. Most of our procedures are designed for orderly, peacetime conditions. I do not believe that we can win this race unless we take at least some measures which thus far have been considered acceptable only in times of a national emergency."[32]

Johnson continued to work feverously with his advisers to formulate a new U.S. space program and on May 8 Webb and McNamara delivered a report that laid the foundation for the race to the moon. They recommended that the "National Space Plan include the objective of manned lunar exploration before the end of this decade."[33] They recognized that "to achieve the goal of landing a man on the moon and returning him to earth in the latter

27 Memorandum for the Vice President, April 20, 1961, JFKL, Kennedy Papers, President's Office Files, Special Correspondence, Box #30, Folder – Johnson, Lyndon B., 1/61-5/61, p. 1.

28 The President's News Conference, April 21, 1961, *Public Papers of the Presidents, John F. Kennedy*, http://www.presidency.ucsb.edu/ws/?pid=8077, accessed on July 10, 2009.

29 Memorandum for the President, April 28, 1961, JFKL, Kennedy Papers, President's Office Files, Special Correspondence, Box #30, Folder – Johnson, Lyndon B., 1/61-5/61, p. 2.

30 Ibid., p. 4.

31 Wernher von Braun to the Vice President of the United States, April 29, 1961, in Logsdon, ed., *Exploring the Unknown*, p. 430, found at http://history.nasa.gov/SP-4407/vol1/chapter3-2.pdf, accessed on July 10, 2009. Emphasis in original.

32 Ibid., p. 433.

33 James E. Webb, NASA Administrator, and Robert S. McNamara, Secretary of Defense, to the Vice President, May 8,1961, ibid., p. 446.

part of the current decade requires immediate initiation of an accelerated program of spacecraft development" as the program, nicknamed Apollo, would require tremendous technological improvements and numerous test flights.[34] Finally, they estimated that total spending for space programs, including NASA and the Defense Department's space budget, would have to increase dramatically. In 1962 they proposed $2.8 billion in spending with an increase to over $6 billion by 1965.[35]

Kennedy formally announced to Congress on May 25 that it was "time for this nation to take a clearly leading role in space achievement," and "we go into space because whatever mankind must undertake, free men must fully share." He then set the dramatic goal: "I believe that this nation should commit itself to achieving the goal, before this decade is out, of landing a man on the moon and returning him safely to the earth." He challenged "Congress and the country to accept a firm commitment to a new course of action-a course which will last for many years and carry very heavy costs: 531 million dollars in fiscal '62--an estimated seven to nine billion dollars additional over the next five years." He called for the entire nation to "move forward, with the full speed of freedom, in the exciting adventure of space."[36] Congress approved the funding with little dissention, and the space race had begun.[37]

Over the next two years, despite some concerns about the costs, the president persisted in pursuing the goal of placing a man on the moon by the end of the decade. In November 1961, he told a gathering of young Democrats that "while many may think that it is foolish to go to the moon, I do not believe that a powerful country like the United States, which wishes to demonstrate to a watching world that it is first in the field of technology and science, … [would] want to permit the Soviet Union to dominate space, with all that it might mean to our peace and security in the coming years."[38] To confirm his commitment, he issued Executive Order 10976 which declared "an extraordinary emergency exists" which required that laborers and mechanics employed by NASA be able to work more than eight hours a day as long as

---

34 Ibid., p. 441.

35 Ibid., p. 452. For the development of the Webb-McNamara Plan, see Lambright, *Powering Apollo*, pp. 97-98.

36 Special Message to the Congress on Urgent National Needs, May 25, 1961, *Public Papers of the Presidents, John F. Kennedy*, http://www.presidency.ucsb.edu/ws/?pid=8151, accessed on July 10, 2009.

37 Logsdon, *The Decision to Go to the Moon*, p. 129.

38 Address in Los Angeles at a Dinner of the Democratic Party of California, November 18, 1961, *Public Papers of the Presidents, John F. Kennedy*, http://www.presidency.ucsb.edu/ws/?pid=8452, accessed on July 10, 2009.

they were paid overtime for their work. This broke with long-standing regulations that government workers could work no more than eight hours in a day unless there was a national emergency.[39] In September 1962, he made probably his most famous call for going to the moon. "We choose to go to the moon and do the other things," Kennedy told an audience at Rice University, "not because they are easy, but because they are hard, because that goal will serve to organize and measure the best of our energies and skills, because that challenge is one that we are willing to accept, one we are unwilling to postpone, and one which we intend to win."[40]

Kennedy's unswerving commitment to landing a man on the moon by the end of the decade even brought him into conflict with NASA administrator Webb. While Webb was fully committed to the Apollo mission, he wanted to make sure other NASA programs continued to receive funding.[41] Webb told the president in late November 1962 that "we believe it would not be in the nation's long-range interest to cancel or drastically curtail on-going space science and technology development programs in order to increase the funding of the manned lunar landing program."[42] While Webb was able to keep the funding, Kennedy made it clear that Apollo was the priority.[43] The president continued to emphasize the importance of the space race to the nation's prestige for the remainder of his administration, arguing "an energetic continuation of our strong space effort is essential."[44] Increases in funding for NASA reflected this commitment. In FY 1962, $500 million of NASA's $1.7 billion budget went to manned flight. In FY 1963, the NASA budget increased to $3.7 billion with roughly two-thirds dedicated to putting a man on the moon. In the next year, NASA's budget increased to $5.1 billion.[45] By the

---

[39] Executive Order 10976 – Suspension of Eight-hour Law as to Laborers and Mechanics Employed by the National Aeronautics and Space Administration, November 15, 1961, found at http://www.lib.umich.edu/govdocs/jfkeo/eo/10976.htm, accessed on July 10, 2009.

[40] Address at Rice University in Houston on the Nation's Space Effort, September 12, 1962, *Public Papers of the Presidents, John F. Kennedy*, http://www.presidency.ucsb.edu/ws/?pid=8862, accessed on July 10, 2009.

[41] Glen E. Swanson, ed., *"Before This Decade is Out ...": Personal Reflections on the Apollo Program* (Washington, D.C.: National Aeronautics and Space Administration, NASA History Office, Office of Policy and Plans, 1999), p. xi; and Lambright, *Powering Apollo*, pp. 7-8.

[42] James E. Webb to the President, November 30, 1962, in Logsdon, ed., *Exploring the Unknown*, Volume 1, p. 430, found at http://history.nasa.gov/SP-4407/vol1/chapter3-2.pdf, accessed on July 10, 2009.

[43] JFK Library Releases White House Tape on Space Race, August 22, 2001, found at http://www.jfklibrary.org/JFK+Library+and+Museum/News+and+Press/JFK+Library+Releases+White+House+Tape+on+Space+Race.htm, accessed on July 10, 2009.

[44] Quoted in Dallek, *An Unfinished Life*, p. 654.

[45] James L. Kaufmann, *Selling Outer Space: Kennedy, the Media, and Funding for Project Apollo, 1961-1963* (Tuscaloosa: The University of Alabama Press, 1994), p. 2.

time the crew of Apollo 11 landed on the moon, the United States had spent $25.4 billion and used 400,000 workers to get them there.[46] In the end, while the president did not live to see Neil Armstrong land on the moon on July 20, 1969, he deserves more credit than anyone for setting the country on that course.

In addition to placing the country on the path to the moon, the president also wanted to encourage new policies towards the underdeveloped countries in the world. With much fanfare, he introduced two programs in 1961— the Alliance for Progress and the Peace Corps—to address problems in Latin America and elsewhere. The president was not personally acquainted with poverty and oppression, but he did recognize that these problems were at the heart of the struggle in the Cold War to win the support of underdeveloped regions.[47] During the election campaign, Kennedy noted "unless we begin to identify ourselves not only with the anti-communist fight but also with the fight against poverty and hunger, these people are going to begin to turn to the Communists."[48] Further, many of his advisors, including Adolf Berle, Richard Goodwin, Walt Rostow, and Arthur Schlesinger, believed that the United States needed to be doing more to combat suffering inside and outside the United States.[49] Further, Kennedy and advisers accepted a key Cold War belief that "foreign aid could create stability abroad."[50] Out of these desires emerged the new programs to create different and more positive U.S. policies.

Kennedy formally called for a new policy towards Latin America on October 18, 1960 in an address in Tampa, Florida. After accusing the Eisenhower administration of being "indifferent" to the plight of Latin American peoples, he pledged to "fight for, the most revolutionary of all doctrines, the right of people to be free."[51] He claimed that "The people of Latin America want better homes, better schools, and better living standards. They want land reform, and tax reform, and an end to the corruption which drains off a nation's resources. In short, they want a new deal for South

---

46 Swanson, *"Before This Decade is Out ..."*, p. 2.

47 Stephen G. Rabe, *The Most Dangerous Area in the World: John F. Kennedy Confronts Communist Revolution in Latin America* (Chapel Hill: The University of North Carolina Press, 1999), pp. 19-22. See also Jeffrey F. Taffet, *Foreign Aid as Foreign Policy: The Alliance for Progress in Latin America*, (New York: Routledge, 2007), pp. 12-13.

48 "Here Is What They Said in 2d Show," *Chicago Daily Tribune*, October 8, 1960, p. W8.

49 Edwin McCammon Martin, *Kennedy and Latin America* (New York: University Press of America, 1994), pp. 21-22 and 26.

50 Taffet, *Foreign Aid as Foreign Policy*, p. 2.

51 Speech of Senator John F. Kennedy, Tampa, FL, Hillsborough County Courthouse, October 18, 1960, *Public Papers of the Presidents, John F. Kennedy*, http://www.presidency.ucsb.edu/ws/?pid=74098, accessed on July 14, 2009.

America." "Our new policy," Kennedy asserted, "can best be summed up in the Spanish words 'alianza para progreso,' an alliance in progress—an alliance of nations with a common interest in freedom and economic advance in a great common effort to develop the resources of the entire hemisphere, strengthen the forces of democracy, and widen the vocational and educational opportunities of every person in all the Americas."[52] After winning the election, Kennedy created a task force to offer him recommendations to initiate this new program.[53]

The task force delivered its report to the incoming president on January 4, 1961 and called for the new administration to give greater attention to Latin America, to focus on the importance of freedom and freely elected governments, and to advance the social well-being of everyone. It stressed "men are not free when enslaved by disease, ignorance, poverty, and inhuman conditions, or where their creative energies are thwarted by hopelessness."[54] Kennedy adopted this theme in his inaugural address when he reached out "to our sister republics south of our border" and pledged "to convert our good words into good deeds—in a new alliance for progress—to assist free men and free governments in casting off the chains of poverty."[55] In the months that followed, the president tasked Richard Goodwin with developing a policy based on these recommendations and an additional study.[56] He told Goodwin that Latin America "could blow up on us" and added, "we can't embrace every tinhorn dictator who tells us he's anticommunist while he is sitting on the necks of his own people."[57]

---

[52] Speech by Senator John F. Kennedy, Hillsborough County Courthouse, Tampa, FL - (Advance Release Text), October 18, 1960, ibid., http://www.presidency.ucsb.edu/ws/?pid=74097, accessed on July 14, 2009. See also Robert C. Albright, "Kennedy Taunts His Opponent: Charges Neglect of Cuban Situation; Pledges Rebuilding," *Washington Post, Times Herald*, October 19, accessed July 14, 2009.

[53] See Goodwin, *Remembering America*, p. 134; and Taffet, *Foreign Aid as Foreign Policy*, p. 22.

[54] Report From the Task Force on Immediate Latin American Problems to President-elect Kennedy, January 4, 1961, *FRUS, 1961-1963*, Volume XII: American Republics, 1961-1963 (Washington, D.C.: U.S. Government Printing Office, 1996), http://www.state.gov/r/pa/ho/frus/kennedyjf/xii/, accessed on July 14, 2009.

[55] Inaugural Address, January 20, 1961, *Public Papers of the Presidents, John F. Kennedy*, http://www.presidency.ucsb.edu/ws/?pid=74098, accessed on July 14, 2009.

[56] See Draft Memorandum From the Consultant to the Task Force on Latin America (Gordon) to the President's Assistant Special Counsel (Goodwin), March 6, 1961 and Memorandum From the President's Special Assistant (Schlesinger) to the President's Assistant Special Counsel (Goodwin), March 8, 1961, *FRUS, 1961-1963*, Volume XII: American Republics, 1961-1963, accessed on July 14, 2009. See also Goodwin, *Remembering America*, pp. 150-51.

[57] Goodwin, *Remembering America*, p. 147.

Kennedy announced his administration's new policy at the White House on March 13 before a group of ambassadors from the Latin American countries.[58] He told them "our continents are bound together by a common history, the endless exploration of new frontiers. Our nations are the product of a common struggle, the revolt from colonial rule. And our people share a common heritage, the quest for the dignity and the freedom of man." He announced "our unfulfilled task is to demonstrate to the entire world that man's unsatisfied aspiration for economic progress and social justice can best be achieved by free men working within a framework of democratic institutions." He then proposed a ten-year plan and "called on all people of the hemisphere to join in a new Alliance for Progress--Alianza para Progreso--a vast cooperative effort, unparalleled in magnitude and nobility of purpose, to satisfy the basic needs of the American people for homes, work and land, health and schools." He stressed that while each nation had to take the lead in making progress, the United States would provide resources and assistance in the effort. He concluded "unless the great mass of Americans share in increasing prosperity—then our alliance, our revolution, our dream, and our freedom will fail."[59]

He asked Congress the next day to authorize the $500 million dollars promised the previous fall by the Act of Bogota to initiate the Alliance for Progress.[60] He told Congress that "poverty, illiteracy, hopelessness and a sense of injustice—the conditions which breed political and social unrest—are almost universal in the Latin American countryside;" therefore, "if this momentum is lost, through failure of the United States to act promptly and fully, we may not have another chance."[61] The administration planned to use this initial funding to increase literacy, to improve land use, to combat the spread of disease, and to increase educational opportunities.[62] Congress

---

[58] Rabe, *The Most Dangerous Area in the World*, p. 9.

[59] Address at a White House Reception for Members of Congress and for the Diplomatic Corps of the Latin American Republics, March 13, 1961 *Public Papers of the Presidents, John F. Kennedy*, http://www.presidency.ucsb.edu/ws/?pid=8531, accessed on July 14, 2009.

[60] Martin, *Kennedy and Latin America*, pp. 54-55.

[61] Special Message to the Congress Requesting Appropriations for the Inter-American Fund for Social Progress and for Reconstruction in Chile, March 14, 1961, *Public Papers of the Presidents, John F. Kennedy*, http://www.presidency.ucsb.edu/ws/?pid=8535, accessed on July 14, 2009.

[62] Memorandum by the Acting Executive Secretary of the National Security Council, March 20, 1961, *FRUS, 1961-1963*, Volume XII: American Republics, 1961-1963, http://www.state.gov/r/pa/ho/frus/kennedyjf/xii/, accessed on July 14, 2009.

approved the funding in May and the president initiated planning for implementing the Alliance for Progress.[63]

Over the coming months, Kennedy and his advisers discussed the best ways to fully implement the program. He sent Adlai Stevenson on a tour of South America in June with the express purpose of consulting with various national leaders,[64] and in the ten capitals Stevenson "encountered a unanimous and intense interest in the Alliance for Progress."[65] The president had also organized a task force on Latin America chaired by Adolf Berle in February that met almost every two weeks through June to make recommendations to the president. Berle noted in his final report that the opportunities for success were great but warned that the administration needed to avoid supporting "transitory power-holders or forces whose objectives are basically hostile to the peoples they dominate" as "the forces sweeping Latin America today demand progress, and a better life for the masses of their people, through evolution if possible, or through revolution if that price must be paid. A preponderance of these forces want the resulting forms to provide liberty, rejecting tyranny whether from the right or from the left."[66]

Representatives from the United States headed by Secretary of Treasury Douglas Dillon and every Latin American nation, including Ché Guevara from Cuba, began meeting at Punta del Este, Uruguay on August 5 to discuss the Alliance for Progress. While Kennedy could not attend due to the on-going Berlin Crisis, he sent a message that was read at the opening of the conference. He again reiterated how important improving the situation in Latin America was and pledged that the United States would offer at least $1 billion in aid over the coming year.[67] The conference met the better part of two weeks to hammer out the main provisions of the program and Dillon telegraphed the president at the end telling him that the "Final result is … everything we could

[63] Letter From the Chairman of the Task Force on Latin America to President Kennedy, July 7, 1961, ibid.

[64] Memorandum of Conversation, May 24, 1961, ibid. See also Statement by the President Concerning Adlai Stevenson's Special Mission to South America, May 29, 1961, *Public Papers of the Presidents, John F. Kennedy*, http://www.presidency.ucsb.edu/ws/?pid=8157, accessed on July 14, 2009.

[65] Report From the Representative to the United Nations (Stevenson) to President Kennedy, June 27, 1961, *FRUS, 1961-1963*, Volume XII: American Republics, 1961-1963, http://www.state.gov/r/pa/ho/frus/kennedyjf/xii/, accessed on July 14, 2009.

[66] Letter From the Chairman of the Task Force on Latin America to President Kennedy, July 7, 1961, ibid.

[67] Message to the Inter-American Economic and Social Conference at Punta del Este, Uruguay, August 5, 1961, *Public Papers of the Presidents, John F. Kennedy*, http://www.presidency.ucsb.edu/ws/?pid=8271, accessed on July 14, 2009.

have hoped for and the Alliance for Progress has now been fully and successfully launched."[68]

The conference concluded with the representatives from every nation, except Cuba, signing the Charter of Punta del Este. They agreed the purpose of the Alliance for Progress was "to enlist the full energies of the people and governments of the American republics in a great cooperative effort to accelerate the economic and social development of the participating countries of Latin America, so that they may achieve maximum levels of well-being, with equal opportunities for all, in democratic societies adapted to their own needs and desires." They set as a goal that the economy of every country should grow by at least 2.5% annually, pledged to raise the standard of living of all peoples, promised to encourage industrialization and land reform, called for the elimination of illiteracy by requiring all children to attend school for at least six years, and encouraged increasing life expectancy by at least five years as soon as possible by concentrating on eradicating diseases. The signatories agreed to raise at least $20 billion, the majority coming from the United States, over the next decade to be used along with internal sources to meets these goals and promises.[69]

The charter was a major success, but its creation was to prove relatively easy when compared to the actual implementation of the Alliance for Progress.[70] The effectiveness of the program required the cooperation of the U.S. government, private investors, and each state in Latin America. Several advisers in the months after the Punta del Este Conference pointed to the difficulties ahead. Goodwin told the president in late September that the United States needed "good people to run the program" but noted that "nothing is more discouraging than to compare the caliber of people who were drafted into the Marshall Plan effort with those who now run our Latin American Aid program."[71] U.S. Ambassador to Mexico Thomas Mann

68 Telegram From the Embassy in Uruguay to the Department of State, August 16, 1961 11 pm, *FRUS, 1961-1963*, Volume XII: American Republics, 1961-1963, http://www.state.gov/r/pa/ho/frus/kennedyjf/xii/35148.htm, accessed on July 14, 2009.

69 The Charter of Punta del Este, Establishing an Alliance for Progress Within the Framework of Operation Pan America, August 17, 1961, found at The Avalon Project: Documents in Law, History and Diplomacy at the Yale Law School, http://avalon.law.yale.edu/20th_century/intam16.asp, accessed on July 14, 2009. See also Peter H. Smith, *Talons of the Eagle: Dynamics of U.S. Latin American Relations* (New York: Oxford University Press, 1996), p. 150; and Taffet, *Foreign Aid as Foreign Policy*, p. 33.

70 Taffet, *Foreign Aid as Foreign Policy*, p. 29.

71 Memorandum From the President's Assistant Special Counsel (Goodwin) to President Kennedy, September 28, 1961, *FRUS, 1961-1963*, Volume XII: American Republics, 1961-1963, http://www.state.gov/r/pa/ho/frus/kennedyjf/xii/35148.htm, accessed on July 14, 2009.

explained the "governments of most Latin American countries have not yet grasped what this program calls for in the way of economic and social change, nor do the economically privileged groups understand the sacrifices which will be required of them." He added, "The obstacles to change vary from country to country but they are all deep-seated and each will be extremely difficult to remove." He also pointed out that if the United States pressed for the reforms called for in the Charter of Punta del Este, it would lead to widespread opposition from the established governments and ruling families. He concluded by noting that "Most Latin Americans whom I have met do not think we have the guts to do it."[72]

Over the remainder of the Kennedy administration, the president remained committed to the Alliance for Progress.[73] Under Kennedy, Latin America received approximately 18% of total U.S. foreign aid, as compared to 3% under Truman and 9% under Eisenhower. In financial terms, the United States provided an average of $1.4 billion per year in aid to Latin American countries from June 1962 to June 1967. Adding in other sources of aid from private investors and other countries brought the total to $3.3 billion per year.[74] In the decade of the Alliance's existence, the United States spent over $22 billion.[75] Just before his death, Kennedy continued to exhort Americans to support the program. He told them the Alliance for Progress "is a battle for the progress and freedom of all of our nations. And it must be fought on every front of national interest and national need.[76]

Despite all of the aid, the Alliance on the whole did not succeed.[77] In September 1963 Richard Goodwin sent a damming memo to Kennedy where he explained, "the most serious single problem [with the Alliance for Progress] is personnel. The Alianza has the same trouble as the Washington Nats--they don't have the ballplayers. There are, of course, some very good people, but

[72] Memorandum From the President's Assistant Special Counsel (Goodwin) to President Kennedy, September 28, 1961, ibid.

[73] Taffet, *Foreign Aid as Foreign Policy*, pp. 38-39 and 45.

[74] Smith, *Talons of the Eagle*, p. 151.

[75] Ibid., p. 219. See also see L. Ronald Scheman, "The Alliance for Progress: Concept and Creativity," in L. Ronald Scheman, ed., *The Alliance for Progress: A Retrospective* (New York: Praeger, 1988), pp. 10-11.

[76] Address in Miami Before the Inter-American Press Association, November 18, 1963, *Public Papers of the Presidents, John F. Kennedy*, http://www.presidency.ucsb.edu/ws/?pid=9529, accessed on July 29, 2009.

[77] Taffet, *Foreign Aid as Foreign Policy*, pp. 45-58. See also See also Howard J. Wiarda, "Did the Alliance 'Lose its Way,' or Were Its Assumptions All Wrong from the Beginning and Are Those Assumptions Still with Us?," in Scheman, ed., *The Alliance for Progress*, pp. 100-115.

there is also a tremendous amount of mediocrity in high places."[78] As Stephen Rabe argues "the Kennedy administration found the challenge of nation building in Latin America far more daunting than it had envisioned. The Alliance for Progress proved a notable policy failure of the 1960s, superseded only by the U.S. debacle in Vietnam."[79]

The program did provide some help.[80] Latin American countries increased their tax collection by 30% and there was a decline in diseases.[81] Further, there was real progress in the Gross National Project (GNP) of most Latin American countries, improved adult literacy, reduced infant mortality rates, and increased life expectancy.[82] These successes, however, have to be balanced with far greater failures. While the GNP of most countries did improve, growth for most countries did not reach the 2.5% goal set in the Punta del Este Charter. In fact only seven countries reached 2.5% per capita annual growth in the 1960s, while another twelve fell short and two saw declines. When the population growth in Latin America during the 1960s is taken into the equation, there was only a per capita increase of 1.5% during the decade. Furthermore, progress in income distribution was virtually non-existent.[83]

More telling than the economic figures is the fact that despite some improvements, Latin America became less democratic in the years following the start of the Alliance for Progress. Kennedy's Assistant Secretary of State for Inter-American Affairs Edwin Martin later explained some of the difficulties: "while the AFP had imaginative goals, wise policy recommendations and challenging targets as measures of performance, its implementation, unfortunately, required choices and actions over a ten-year period of a difficulty which was far beyond the capacities of the human beings

78 Memorandum From the Secretary General of the International Peace Corps Secretariat (Goodwin) to President Kennedy, September 10, 1963, *FRUS, 1961-1963*, Volume XII: American Republics, 1961-1963, http://www.state.gov/r/pa/ho/frus/kennedyjf/xii/35149.htm, accessed on July 29, 2009. In making reference to the Washington Nats, Goodwin was pointing to the Washington Senators, a major league baseball team that finished the 1963 season with a record of 56 wins and 106 losses. See 1963 Washington Senators Batting, Pitching, & Fielding Statistics, Baseball-Reference.com, http://www.baseball-reference.com/teams/WSA/1963.shtml, accessed on July 29, 2009.

79 Rabe, *The Most Dangerous Area in the World*, p. 148. See also Michael E. Latham, *Modernization as Ideology: American Social Science and "Nation Building" in the Kennedy Era* (Chapel Hill: University of North Carolina Press, 2000), p. 99; and Taffet, *Foreign Aid as Foreign Policy*, p. 5.

80 For a more positive interpretation of the Alliance for Progress, see Scheman, "The Alliance for Progress," pp. 5-7, 12-50, and 56-62.

81 Federico G. Gil, *Latin American-United States Relations* (New York: Harcourt Brace Jovanovich, Inc., 1971), pp. 246-68.

82 Martin, *Kennedy and Latin America*, pp. 459-60.

83 Smith, *Talons of the Eagle*, p. 152.

who lived in the Western Hemisphere at the time."[84] Unfortunately, many of the Latin American ruling elites fit this description. In fact, the number of dictators in Latin America increased from six in 1960 to ten in 1963 and fourteen by 1980.[85] While Kennedy at times would oppose these dictators, he was not consistent as his administration "frequently demonstrated that it preferred anti-Communist authoritarians over left-leaning leaders who respected constitutional processes."[86] When it came to choosing between a government supporting democratic reform and one committed to anti-communist principles, Kennedy always placed greater weight on waging the Cold War.[87]

In the midst of the 1960 presidential campaign, Kennedy arrived at the University of Michigan from New York at 2 in the morning after his third debate with Richard Nixon. His plan was to get some sleep and resume campaigning the next morning. However, to his surprise, 10,000 students were waiting for him to say a few words.[88] He delivered a short, impromptu speech where he asked them, "How many of you who are going to be doctors, are willing to spend your days in Ghana? Technicians or engineers, how many of you are willing to work in the Foreign Service and spend your lives traveling around the world?"[89] With these remarks he laid the groundwork for one of his most innovative programs, the Peace Corps. A few weeks later in San Francisco, he formally called for volunteers to be part of a "peace corps" to combat the "missionaries for world communism" that the Soviet Union and China were sending to the underdeveloped regions of the world. He told the audience, "I am convinced that our men and women, dedicated to freedom, are able to be missionaries, not only for freedom and peace, but [to] join in a worldwide struggle against poverty and disease and ignorance."[90] While believing his new proposal would indeed benefit the United States, Kennedy

---

[84] Martin, *Kennedy and Latin America*, pp. 458-59.

[85] Ibid., p. 460. See also Lincoln Gordon, "The Alliance at Birth: Hopes and Fears," in Scheman, ed., *The Alliance for Progress*, p. 78; and Memorandum for the President, June 22, 1962, JFKL, Kennedy Papers, President's Office Files, Staff Memos, Box #62A, Folder – Dungan, Ralph A., 2/62/6/62.

[86] Rabe, *The Most Dangerous Area in the World*, p. 56.

[87] Ibid., pp. 197-98.

[88] Elizabeth Cobbs Hoffman, *All You Need Is Love: The Peace Corps and the Spirit of the 1960s* (Cambridge, MA: Harvard University Press, 1998), p. 11.

[89] Remarks of Senator John F. Kennedy, October 14, 1960, http://www.peacecorps.gov/index.cfm?shell=learn.whatispc.history.speech, accessed on July 15, 2009. See Sargent Schriver, *Point of the Lance* (New York: Harper & Row, Publishers, 1964), p. 10.

[90] Speech of Senator John F. Kennedy, Cow Palace, San Francisco, CA, November 2, 1960, *Public Papers of the Presidents, John F. Kennedy*, http://www.presidency.ucsb.edu/ws/?pid=25928, accessed on July 15, 2009. See also Sorensen, *Counselor*, pp. 329-30.

made the proposal in the last week of the campaign at least in part to squeeze out a few more votes in a very close election. Whether his proposal changed any voters' minds is unclear, but polls showed it was very popular, and he received more mail related to the Peace Corps in the coming months than any other topic.[91]

As with the Alliance for Progress and the space program, Kennedy set up a task force, headed by his brother-in-law Sargent Shriver, to study the establishment of the program and offer recommendations.[92] The task force met frequently throughout February 1961, and Shriver delivered its report to the president late in the month.[93] He called for the "immediate establishment" of the Peace Corps through an executive order.[94] He explained that waiting for Congressional approval could delay the program for months and cause it to lose momentum. By using an executive order, the president could get the program started and then turn to Congress for formal approval.[95] Finally, he recommended that the Peace Corps be established as an autonomous entity within the State Department because it needed "great flexibility to experiment with different methods of operation" in order to operate as a bold program.[96]

On March 1, 1961, President Kennedy issued an executive order establishing the Peace Corps as an agency in the State Department and requested that Congress make the Peace Corps a permanent organization.[97] A few days later he appointed Shriver as its first director.[98] According to Ted Sorensen, "Shriver was the perfect choice to run the new program—idealistic, tireless, and deeply committed to public service."[99] While Shriver immediately began organizing the Peace Corps, Kennedy began shaping the legislation to

---

91 Giglio, *The Presidency of John F. Kennedy*, p. 155.

92 Scott Stossel, *Sarge: The Life and Times of Sargent Shriver* (Washington, D.C.: Smithsonian Books, 2004), pp. 193-95. See also Hoffman, *All You Need Is Love*, p. 44; and Gerard T. Rice, *The Bold Experiment JFK's Peace Corps* (Notre Dame, IN: University of Notre Dame Press, 1985), pp. 35-43.

93 Summary of Report to the President on the Peace Corps, February 28, 1961, JFKL, Kennedy Papers, White House Staff Files, Carmine S. Bellino File, Box #1, Folder – Peace Corps General, 1961, p. 1.

94 Ibid., p. 1.

95 Stossel, *Sarge*, p. 205.

96 Summary of Report to the President on the Peace Corps, February 28, 1961, p. 3. For its relationship within the State Department, see ibid., p. 8.

97 See Executive Order 10924 – Establishment and Administration of the Peace Corps in the Department of State, March 1, 1961, *Public Papers of the Presidents, John F. Kennedy*, http://www.presidency.ucsb.edu/ws/?pid=58862, accessed on July 15, 2009; and Special Message to the Congress on the Peace Corps, March 1, 1960, ibid., http://www.presidency.ucsb.edu/ws/?pid=8515, accessed on July 30, 2009.

98 Schriver, *Point of the Lance*, p. 12.

99 Sorensen, *Counselor*, p. 331.

change it from a temporary agency created by an executive order to a permanent one established by Congress.[100] On May 30 he sent identical letters to the President of the Senate, Lyndon Johnson, and the Speaker of the House, Sam Rayburn, calling for Congressional approval of the Peace Corps. He recommended Congress authorize $40 million for the program in FY 1962 so that the Peace Corps could have between 500 and 1,000 volunteers abroad by the end of 1961 and 2,700 either in service or in training by the summer of 1962. He noted that the volunteers should receive a modest living allowance, health care, and a small monthly payment that would be given to them at the completion of their service. Finally, he stressed that while the Peace Corps should be within the State Department and work closely with other aid agencies, it should have a "separate identity and unique role".[101]

This last request was not what the president originally intended. He initially tried to place the Peace Corps under the direction of another aid agency within the State Department. However, both Shriver and the vice president questioned whether the Peace Corps would be effective if it was buried in the State Department's bureaucracy and strongly lobbied to create it as an autonomous agency there.[102] Johnson met with Kennedy to fight for the independence of the Peace Corps and ultimately "badgered" him until he relented.[103] Because of Johnson's strong support, Shriver goes as far as to call him "a founding father of the Peace Corps."[104]

While Shriver and Johnson's efforts to create the Peace Corps as an independent agency were successful, they angered a lot of people, including the president. Kennedy told Shriver's wife, his sister Eunice, that he was not going to push for Congressional authorization beyond what he had already done. He told her, "they wanted it that way [as an independent agency] ... so let them go ahead and put [it] through."[105] Shriver and his aides took up the challenge and actively lobbied senators and congressmen throughout the summer.[106] He even asked Secretary of State Rusk to talk to key senators to

---

[100] For Shriver's efforts at organizing the Peace Corps, see Stossel, *Sarge*, pp. 210-17.

[101] Letter to the President of the Senate and to the Speaker of the House Proposing the Establishment of a Permanent Peace Corps, May 30, 1961, *Public Papers of the Presidents, John F. Kennedy*, http://www.presidency.ucsb.edu/ws/?pid=8160, accessed on July 30, 2009.

[102] See Stossel, *Sarge*, pp. 218-25; and Rice, *The Bold Experiment*, pp. 60-67.

[103] Quoted in ibid., p. 225.

[104] Schriver, *Point of the Lance*, p. 15. For the Peace Corps relationship to the State Department, see Martin, *Kennedy and Latin America*, p. 38.

[105] Quoted in Stossel, *Sarge*, p. 234.

[106] Ibid., pp. 240-45; and Rice, *The Bold Experiment*, pp. 74-90.

smooth passage of the program.[107] At the conclusion of the signing ceremony on September 22, Kennedy expressed his "esteem for the most effective lobbyist on the Washington scene, Mr. Sargent Shriver."[108]

The legislation stated the Peace Corps' purposes were "to promote world peace and friendship," to assist countries "in meeting their needs for trained manpower," and "to help promote a better understanding of other peoples on the part of the American people." It authorized the full amount, $40 million, requested by the president for the FY 1962, and left the Peace Corps virtually autonomous within the State Department. It provided volunteers with living allowances and a termination payment of up to $75 per month upon completion of their service. Additionally, the government covered their health care costs. The legislation finally spelled out the role of the director of the Peace Corps and his staff.[109]

Even while fighting for the passage of the Peace Corps bill in Congress, Shriver actively recruited the first volunteers. He generally did not face too many difficulties getting volunteers as within the first three months of Kennedy announcing the program over 7,000 people had filled out applications.[110] However, he had to make sure that volunteers met very high standards. This was in part to make the program more palatable to Congress, but it also reflected Shriver's desire to include only the best candidates possible. Each applicant had to provide six references and undergo a battery of tests, including a six-hour exam, before being selected for training. Only one in five applicants made it through this process. The Peace Corps made further cuts during the training phase that culled the number of volunteers further. To ensure that the Peace Corps maintained these rigorous standards and still received enough volunteers, Shriver met frequently with business leaders and college presidents, and initiated a very successful advertising blitz to reach the American public.[111]

---

107 Letter From the Director of the Peace Corps (Shriver) to Secretary of State Rusk, June 26, 1961, *FRUS, 1961-1963*, Volume XXV: Foreign Relations, Organization of Foreign Policy; Information Policy; United Nations; Scientific Matters, (Washington, D.C.: U.S. Government Printing Office, 2001), http://www.state.gov/r/pa/ho/frus/kennedyjf/xxv/6007.htm, accessed on July 30, 2009.

108 Remarks Upon Signing the Peace Corps Bill, September 22, 1961, *Public Papers of the Presidents, John F. Kennedy*, http://www.presidency.ucsb.edu/ws/?pid=8345, accessed on July 30, 2009.

109 Public Law 87-293, 87th Congress, H.R. 7500, 75 Stat. 612, September 22, 1961, JFKL, Kennedy Papers, White House Staff Files, Carmine S. Bellino File, Box #1, Folder – Peace Corps General, 1961, pp. 1-4.

110 Press Release, Office of the White House Press Secretary, May 16, 1961, ibid., p. 1.

111 Stossel, *Sarge*, pp. 238-9; and Rice, *The Bold Experiment*, pp. 145-7 and 160-63.

The Peace Corps was already beginning to train its first volunteers when it announced in early June its first six projects in Tanganyika, Columbia, the Philippines, Ghana, Chile, and St. Lucia.[112] Each volunteer, after completing the rigorous evaluations to be accepted into the Peace Corps, generally went through three phases of training. In the first phase, the volunteers usually trained approximately ten hours a day, six days a week for eight to ten weeks at an American university or college. This phase was normally followed by four weeks of training in Puerto Rico, Hawaii, or New Mexico. Finally, the volunteers spent 2-4 weeks training in the host country.[113] Despite some weaknesses, most volunteers found the training at least adequate preparation for their field experience.[114]

The volunteers came from all walks of like. During the Kennedy years, there were approximately three men for every two women volunteers. Most were unmarried and between 22 and 28 years old. In fact, less than one percent of them were over 60. Eighty-six percent had a college degree, and two-thirds were Democrats.[115] Finally, most of the volunteers were white as no more than 5% of them were black at any time in the 1960s.[116] They volunteered for a variety of reasons, but most simply wanted to help. An analysis of questionnaires filled out by volunteers in 1962 found that the most selected answer to the question, "What do you hope to accomplish by joining the Peace Corps?" was "to help people and humanity in general."[117] In the end, according to Shriver, the Peace Corps volunteers went to countries around the world "to work with people, not to employ them, use them or advise them."[118]

Applications poured into the Peace Corps office throughout the Kennedy Administration. By the end of June 1963, over 66,000 Americans had submitted applications, and there were over 6,600 volunteers in the field.[119] By far the largest number of volunteers served as teachers with around 2,400 in the field. Other volunteers worked with agricultural extension agencies, in

---

[112] Stossel, *Sarge*, p. 232. See also The President's Remarks to the Advisory Council Peace Corps, May 22, 1961, JFKL, Kennedy Papers, White House Staff Files, Carmine S. Bellino File, Box 1, Folder – Peace Corps General, 1961, p. 1. Tanganyika is located in present day Tanzania.

[113] Velma Adams, *The Peace Corps in Action* (Chicago, IL: Follett Publishing Company, 1968), pp. 15-17; and Roy Hoopes, *The Complete Peace Corps Guide* (New York: The Dial Press, 1966), pp. 174-180.

[114] Rice, *The Bold Experiment*, p. 158.

[115] Ibid., p. 167.

[116] Hoffman, *All You Need Is Love*, p. 126.

[117] Rice, *The Bold Experiment*, p. 168.

[118] Schriver, *Point of the Lance*, p. 50.

community action groups, as health providers, and on engineering projects.[120] Between the start of the program in summer of 1961 and the end of 1964, over 13,000 volunteers served in 46 countries with the largest contingent of over 1,000 in the Philippines and the smallest group of 22 in Cyprus.[121]

The Peace Corps was one of the most successful of President Kennedy's New Frontier programs. As could be expected with any program that grew as fast as the Peace Corps did, there were a few problems, including one volunteer accidently dropping a postcard that inadvertently disparaged the people of Nigeria, a few cases of illegal drug use, and some sexual indiscretions.[122] However, most reports from the field were glowing. Alluding to the importance of the Peace Corps in waging the Cold War, the JCS noted in January 1962 that "the Peace Corps program in Ghana has been highly successful."[123] After a trip to Africa and a visit with some volunteers, Kennedy advisor Harris Wofford told him, "I know we have struck gold."[124] The situation in Malawi is an example of this. When forty volunteer teachers arrived there in January 1963, it doubled the number of secondary school teachers in the entire country.[125] Finally, when Arthur Schlesinger visited Venezuela in 1963, one of the locals told him: "The Peace Corps has been wonderful. It has worked miracles in changing the Venezuelan image of North Americans. Before the Peace Corps, the poor Venezuelan supposed all Americans to be rich, selfish, callous, [and] reactionary. Now they are seeing

---

119 Hoffman, *All You Need Is Love*, p. 262. This number includes those that were still in training in their assigned countries.

120 Adams, *The Peace Corps in Action*, p. 21.

121 Schriver, *Point of the Lance*, pp. 231-33. The following countries had Peace Corps volunteers: Afghanistan, Bolivia, Brazil, British Honduras, Cameroon, Ceylon, Chile, Columbia, Costa Rica, Cyprus, Dominican Republic, Ecuador, El Salvador, Ethiopia, Gabon, Ghana, Guatemala, Guinea, Honduras, Indonesia, India, Iran, Ivory Coast, Jamaica, Liberia, Malawi, Malaysia, Morocco, Nepal, Niger, Nigeria, Pakistan, Panama, Peru, Philippines, Senegal, Sierra Leone, Somali, St. Lucia, Tanganyika, Thailand, Togo, Tunisia, Turkey, Uruguay, and Venezuela.

122 Rice, *The Bold Experiment*, pp. 230-34 and 241-44.

123 Memorandum on the Substance of Discussions at the Department of State - Joint Chiefs of Staff Meeting, January 6, 1962, *FRUS, 1961-1963*, Volume XXI: Africa (Washington, D.C.: U.S. Government Printing Office, 2001), http://www.state.gov/r/pa/ho/frus/kennedyjf/50755.htm, accessed on July 30, 2009.

124 Memorandum for the President, January 20, 1962, JFKL, Kennedy Papers, President's Office Files, Staff Memos, Box #67, Folder – Wofford, Harris, 1962, p. 1.

125 Memorandum From the Department of State Executive Secretary (Brubeck) to the President's Special Assistant for National Security Affairs (Bundy), January 23, 1963, *FRUS, 1961-1963*, Volume XXI: Africa, http://www.state.gov/r/pa/ho/frus/kennedyjf/50763.htm, accessed on July 30, 2009. At the time, Malawi was a British Protectorate called Nyasaland.

an entirely different kind of American, and it is transforming their whole theory of the United States."[126]

President Kennedy initiated numerous programs in his first year that produced mixed results. His efforts to start the Alliance for Progress built on programs initiated in the previous administration to alleviate the poverty and desperation in much of Latin America. While the motives were good, the Alliance for Progress fell far short of its original goals. A limited commitment by the president and resistance to change by many Latin American leaders doomed it from the beginning. The president's efforts for space exploration and in creating the Peace Corps were much more successful. While expensive, the United States succeeded in placing a man on the moon in 1969 and more importantly from Kennedy's perspective, beat the Soviet Union in doing so. The success of the Peace Corps is probably one of President Kennedy's most significant legacies. While Lyndon Johnson and Sargent Shriver deserve significant credit for establishing and leading the Peace Corps in its early years, Kennedy's support made their actions meaningful. The Peace Corps volunteers raised the U.S. image in many countries around the world and came to be one of the truly new frontiers of the Kennedy administration.

[126] Schlesinger, *Journals*, p. 191.

Chapter 5

THE NEW FRONTIER AT HOME

The Peace Corps joined with the Alliance for Progress and the Apollo program to show how the Kennedy administration tried to reach for the "New Frontier" in different areas. However, while they influenced domestic issues and policies, they were very much tied to the country's efforts in waging the Cold War. The Kennedy administration also pursued the New Frontier at home, but with noticeably less vigor. The president entered office wanting to stimulate the economy which had been in a recession since the middle of 1960 and planned to address some of the issues faced by the working class, elderly, and the poor. With varying levels of commitment, he pushed programs which would bring the country out of the recession and lead to social progress. He had success in several areas but struggled to get some of his proposals accepted by Congress.

The recession of 1960 and 1961 was one of the most significant domestic issues facing the country at the time of Kennedy's inauguration and resulted from several economic difficulties in the late 1950s.[1] Overall, the Eisenhower years were not bad from an economic standpoint.[2] The economy had witnessed considerable growth, and most Americans were generally confident in the country's economic future. However, recessions in 1958 and 1960 had led an increase in the unemployment rate, larger budget deficits, and a decline in the balance of the payments between the United States and other countries. Throughout his presidency, Eisenhower had emphasized a program of limited inflation, steady economic growth, and balanced budgets. While he achieved three balanced budgets while president, something no president has achieved since, the country had entered a recession in 1960. In his campaign, Kennedy

[1] "State of Economy Tops Kennedy Agenda," *New York Times*, February 5, 1961, p. E1.
[2] Sloan, *Eisenhower and the Management of Prosperity*, p. 154.

claimed “not even the rose-colored glasses monotonously peddled by the present administration with Madison Avenue slogans can hide the problems.” He then went on to point to the country’s anemic economic growth and Eisenhower’s general lack of leadership on economic issues.[3]

While he had been critical of the Eisenhower administration’s handling of the economy, Kennedy came into office like most of his predecessors with a limited understanding of economic principles.[4] He had shown only minimal interest in economic policies throughout his career, but his main focus had almost always been on national security policies and issues related directly to Massachusetts. To his credit, Kennedy recognized many of his limitations in these areas and assembled a team of able economic advisers including Douglas Dillon as Secretary of the Treasury and Walter Heller as the chairman of the Council of Economic Advisers.[5] He also asked Dr. Paul Samuelson, a professor of economics at M.I.T., to head a task force that would examine the country’s economic situation and provide him recommendations. Kennedy’s economic team included members with diverging economic viewpoints on such issues as public spending, tax cuts, and deficits. Kennedy had to deal with numerous economic issues while president with the most important being the loss of gold because of a negative balance of payments with other countries, high unemployment, and deficits.[6]

Soon after his inauguration, Kennedy received Samuelson’s task force report. The M.I.T. professor began by noting the difficulties arising from the recession but stressed “with proper actions by the government, the contraction in business can be brought to a halt within 1961 itself and converted into an upturn.”[7] He argued that high employment and real growth should be the primary goals with worries about deficit spending and inflation being of secondary importance. He also explained that the balance of payment deficit the United States was experiencing in its relationships with other countries limited what his administration could do, but did not preclude it from acting. Samuelson stressed that the keys to developing sound economic policies were to be flexible and to search for the balance between action and inaction. He

---

[3] Special Labor Day Message from Democratic Presidential Candidate John F. Kennedy, September 5, 1960, *Public Papers of the Presidents, John F. Kennedy*, http://www.presidency.ucsb.edu/ws/?pid=60413, accessed on January 6, 2010.

[4] Seymour E. Harris, *Economics of the Kennedy Years and a Look Ahead* (New York: Harper & Row, Publishers, 1964), pp. 17-20.

[5] Ibid., pp. 21-23.

[6] Ibid., pp. 27-29.

[7] *New Frontiers of the Kennedy Administration: The Texts of the Task Force Reports Prepared for the President*, (Washington, D.C.: Public Affairs Press, 1961), p. 24.

understood that this balance would be hard to discern but emphasized "it must be resolutely sought."[8] He then made recommendations for what Kennedy should do. He argued that planned government expenditures should be accelerated and that new spending of around $3-5 billion in areas like education and urban renewal would be good. He also strongly recommended addressing the balance of payments deficit and considering temporary tax cuts. He finally cautioned that the administration could not continue to allow the wage-price spiral to continue.[9]

Kennedy accepted much of the report's advice but moved rather cautiously despite rhetoric indicating a more forceful approach. The president told Congress in his first annual message that "the American economy is in trouble" and argued that the United States "must show the world what a free economy can do—to reduce unemployment, to put unused capacity to work, to spur new productivity, and to foster higher economic growth within a range of sound fiscal policies and relative price stability."[10] Over the next week he sent Congress his plans for economic recovery and growth. He argued "The nation cannot—and will not—be satisfied with economic decline and slack." He called for the lowering of long-term interest rates, a thirteen week extension of unemployment insurance, raising the Social Security payments for those eligible by roughly 1/3, and accelerating procurement and construction for already existing plans. He finally argued for wage and price stability. He stressed "We cannot afford unsound wage and price movements which push up costs, weaken our international competitive position, restrict job opportunities, and jeopardize the health of our domestic economy."[11]

Kennedy delivered a separate message to Congress concerning the balance of payments deficit. At its most basic level, this problem "resulted when more dollars flowed out—via business investment, tourist spending, import purchases, and foreign and military aid—than came in."[12] Over the last three years of the Eisenhower administration, the deficit totaled over $10 billion and resulted in a decline in America's gold reserve and the fear that the value of the dollar would fall. Because the dollar was so important to both the

---

[8] Ibid., p. 30.
[9] Ibid., pp. 31-39.
[10] Annual Message to the Congress on the State of the Union, January 30, 1961, *Public Papers of the Presidents, John F. Kennedy*, http://www.presidency.ucsb.edu/ws/?pid=8045, accessed on January 5, 2010.
[11] Special Message to the Congress: Program for Economic Recovery and Growth, February 2, 1961, ibid., http://www.presidency.ucsb.edu/ws/?pid=8111, accessed on January 5, 2010.
[12] Jim F. Heath, *John F. Kennedy and the Business Community* (The University of Chicago Press, 1969), p. 39.

American and world economies, Kennedy explained the country had to "take its balance of payments into account when formulating its economic policies and conducting its economic affairs." He called for eliminating the deficit by developing constructive measures that would "strengthen our dollar position and insure that our gold reserves are employed effectively to facilitate the commerce of the free nations and to protect the stability of their currencies." He mainly argued for promoting exports and achieving cost and price stability.[13]

While he spoke boldly, Kennedy proceeded cautiously on most economic issues during his first year and half in office. He asked Congress to provide more assistance to the jobless and children from needy families.[14] He lobbied hard for a thirteen-week extension of unemployment benefits that would provide additional assistance to the roughly 700,000 whose benefits had recently run out or were about to do so. After a hard struggle in the Senate where Republicans and conservative Democrats, led by Virginia Senator Harry Byrd, tried to require the states and not the federal government to pay for the extra benefits, Kennedy won the extension in late March.[15] In May, he also signed legislation extending additional federal aid to needy families with children for fourteen months.

President Kennedy also advanced social programs that he believed would rectify some of the inequalities in American society while also providing some stimulus to the economy. As he had done with most issues, he established several task forces after his election and met with key congressional leaders before Christmas 1960 to evaluate key domestic programs.[16] After his meeting with Vice President-elect Lyndon Johnson, House Majority Leader Sam Rayburn, and Senator Mike Mansfield, who was expected to take over Johnson's role as Senate majority leader, he told reporters that he had five legislative priorities: increasing the minimum wage, making housing more affordable, providing hospital insurance for the elderly, increasing federal

---

[13] Special Message to the Congress on Gold and the Balance of Payments Deficit, February 6, 1961, *Public Papers of the Presidents, John F. Kennedy*, http://www.presidency.ucsb.edu/ws/?pid=8178, accessed on January 5, 2010.

[14] Letter to the President of the Senate and to the Speaker of the House Transmitting Bills Extending Unemployment Benefits and Providing Aid to Needy Children, February 6, 1961, ibid., http://www.presidency.ucsb.edu/ws/?pid=8167, accessed on January 5, 2010.

[15] Russell Baker, "Senate Approves Jobless Aid, 84:4, Backing Kennedy: Votes Extension of Benefits After Rejection of Byrd's Financing Amendment," *New York Times*, March 17, 1961, p. 1.

[16] For copies of each task force report, see *New Frontiers of the Kennedy Administration*.

assistance for public education, and expanding aid to depressed areas.[17] Most of the ideas were not new as they had been proposed by Democrats on other occasions. However, Kennedy adopted an approach on domestic policy that he was going to follow throughout most of his presidency—to "tread carefully … despite its New Frontier rhetoric."[18]

Kennedy moved has quickly as he believed he could on domestic issues, but he operated within distinct limits. With few exceptions, Kennedy had always been more interested in foreign policy issues, and this did not change while he was president. He simply saw them as more important. In his first State of the Union address to Congress, he noted that all of the country's many domestic problems "pale when placed beside those which confront us around the world."[19] Second, the president had an eye on what polices would garner congressional approval. While he had Rayburn and Mansfield's support on most issues, he knew he might face trouble in Congress. On the surface, he was in a great position. Democrats had a 65 to 35 majority in the Senate and a 262 to 174 advantage in the House of Representatives. However, these numbers were not has overwhelming as they seemed as there was a division between conservatives and liberals that crossed party lines.[20] Southern Democrats were opposed to most of the new president's domestic agenda and frequently sided with Republicans. The difficulties could best be seen with the House Rules Committee. Senator Howard Smith, a Democrat from Virginia, chaired the twelve-member committee and had to approve most legislation that reached the House floor. While the Democrats had eight seats on the committee, two of them typically voted with the four Republicans, causing many bills to languish and die before reaching a full House vote. Rayburn and the new administration wanted to expand the membership of the committee in order to break this deadlock. It took all the persuasion of Rayburn and officials

---

17 "Transcript of Joint News Conference of Kennedy, Johnson, Rayburn and Mansfield," *New York Times*,
December 21, 1960, p. 20. See also Giglio, *Presidency of John F. Kennedy*, p. 97; and Irwin Unger, *The Best of Intentions: The Triumph and Failure of the Great Society Under Kennedy, Johnson and Nixon* (New York: Doubleday, 1996), p. 23.

18 Georg Schild, "John F. Kennedy and the American Social Welfare Debate in the Early 1960s," in Manfred Berg, and Andreas Etges, eds., *John F. Kennedy and the 'Thousand Days': New Perspectives on the Foreign and Domestic Policies of the Kennedy Administration* (Heidelberg: Universitätsverlag, 2007), p. 261. See also ibid., pp. 273-5.

19 Annual Message to the Congress on the State of the Union, January 30, 1961, *Public Papers of the Presidents, John F. Kennedy*, found http://www.presidency.ucsb.edu/ws/?pid=8045, accessed on August 5, 2009.

20 Alan Shank, *Presidential Policy Leadership: Kennedy and Social Welfare* (Lanham, MD: University Press of America, 1980), p. 260.

from the Kennedy administration to eke out a 217 to 212 victory.[21] While successful, the close vote was a clear sign of how difficult it might be to get substantial domestic legislation passed.

Kennedy began to move forward with his domestic social agenda in January when he asked Congress to pass legislation to help distressed areas. The president had been genuinely moved by the poverty he encountered while campaigning in West Virginia in 1960. From his privileged background, he had not known such problems existed in the United States, and after seeing them, pledged to use the powers at his disposal to address them.[22] In his request to congressional leaders, he noted that there were almost 100 areas in the country with "substantial and persistent unemployment." He asked Congress to consider legislation that would "strengthen and improve the economic climate of the communities affected."[23]

The problems that Kennedy saw in West Virginia symbolized many of the problems faced by Americans living in Appalachia. The 1950s had been a particularly challenging time for this region as the country moved away from coal as its primary energy source. Coal provided 51 percent of the country's energy supplies in 1951 but only 23 percent in 1960. This decline led to widespread unemployment and poverty in coal-producing areas. In fact, as of 1959, more than 50 percent of Appalachian families lived below the poverty line.[24] The Kennedy administration proposed legislation that would provide financial assistance to chronically depressed areas like this. Since most of the planned spending was designated for the southern states, Congress passed legislation in late April without much of a fight. Congress provided $394 million in grants and loans to help "create new jobs by attracting new industries to urban areas having chronic unemployment and to underdeveloped rural areas."[25] Almost 130 industrial urban areas and over 650 rural areas were eligible for funding. Unfortunately, the large number of areas proved the

---

[21] Dallek, *An Unfinished Life*, p. 329; Giglio, *Presidency of John F. Kennedy*, pp. 98-99; and Unger, *The Best of Intentions*, pp. 23-25.

[22] Dallek, *An Unfinished Life*, p. 255.

[23] Letter to the President of the Senate and to the Speaker of the House Urging Enactment of a Distressed Area Redevelopment Bill, January 25, 1961, *Public Papers of the Presidents, John F. Kennedy*, http://www.presidency.ucsb.edu/ws/?pid=8522, accessed on August 5, 2009.

[24] Petra Dolata-Kreutzkamp, "Kennedy and Central Appalachia: Fighting Unemployment and Poverty," in Berg and Etges, *John F. Kennedy and the 'Thousand Days'*, p. 244.

[25] Russell Freeburg, "Kennedy Signs 394 Million Depressed Aid: Names Labor Expert to Administer It," *Chicago Daily Tribune*, May 2, 1961, p. 6. For a history of the legislation, see "Congress Enacts Area Redevelopment Bill," CQ Press Electronic Library, CQ Almanac Online Edition, cqal61-1373049. Originally published in *CQ Almanac 1961* (Washington,

program's ultimate undoing.[26] As one historian has noted, because so many different areas requested assistance, recipients of funding only "received a diet portion."[27]

While seeking aid for depressed areas was one of his first initiatives, Kennedy saw improving the housing market as a way to stimulate urban renewal, increase consumer spending, and provide the American dream of home ownership.[28] The president asked Congress for new housing legislation in March arguing "a nation that is partly ill-housed is not as strong as a nation with adequate homes for every family."[29] Congress completed debate on the bill in June and sent the president the Housing Act of 1961 where Kennedy called it "the most important and far-reaching Federal legislation in the field of housing since the enactment of the Housing Act of 1949."[30] The legislation increased the availability of low interest loans to moderate income families and the elderly, lowered the required down payment for the loans to 3 percent, authorized the construction of 100,000 additional public housing units, and expanded federal urban renewal grants by $2 billion.[31]

Kennedy also called for increasing the minimum wage in his February speech to Congress. The minimum wage in 1961 was $1.00 per hour and had not been increased since 1955. As a senator, Kennedy had advocated increasing the wage but failed in the face of Republican and conservative Democrat opposition.[32] In early February, Kennedy asked Congress to increase the minimum wage to $1.25 and increase the number of people eligible to be covered by the wage by 4.3 million. He argued "our nation can

---

D.C.: Congressional Quarterly, 1961). http://library.cqpress.com/cqalmanac/cqal61-1373049, accessed August 5, 2009.

26 Dolata-Kreutzkamp, "Kennedy and Central Appalachia," pp. 250-52.

27 Carl M. Brauer, "Kennedy, Johnson, and the War on Poverty," *Journal of American History*, 69:1 (June 1982), p. 110. See also Giglio, *Presidency of John F. Kennedy*, p. 104.

28 Remarks at the Swearing In of Robert C. Weaver as Housing and Home Finance Administrator, February 11, 1961, *Public Papers of the Presidents, John F. Kennedy*, http://www.presidency.ucsb.edu/ws/?pid=8267, accessed on August 5, 2009. See also Shank, *Presidential Policy Leadership*, pp. 51-54.

29 Special Message to the Congress on Housing and Community Development, March 9, 1961, *Public Papers of the Presidents, John F. Kennedy*, http://www.presidency.ucsb.edu/ws/?pid=8529, accessed on August 5, 2009.

30 Remarks Upon Signing the Housing Act, June 30, 1961, ibid., http://www.presidency.ucsb.edu/ws/?pid=8216, accessed on August 5, 2009.

31 "Administration Wins Victory on Housing Bill," CQ Press Electronic Library, CQ Almanac Online Edition, cqal61-1372857. Originally published in *CQ Almanac 1961* (Washington, D.C.: Congressional Quarterly, 1961). http://library.cqpress.com/cqalmanac/cqal61-1372857, accessed August 5, 2009.

32 See Tom Nelson, "GOP Blasts Democrats' Wage Bill: Goldwater Says It Would End 500,000 Jobs," *The Washington Post, Times Herald*, August 12, 1960, p. A1.

ill afford to tolerate the growth of an under-privileged and underpaid class. Substandard wages lead necessarily to substandard living conditions, hardship and distress."[33] Republican senators claimed the bill would prevent businesses from hiring new workers and possibly lead to job losses because they could not afford the new expense.[34] In the end, however, the Democrats were able to push through legislation that achieved most of what the president wanted. They increased the minimum wage to $1.15 per hour in September and to $1.25 the following year. They expanded the number of workers, mainly in retail, eligible for the minimum wage by 3.6 million.[35] Despite covering fewer workers than Kennedy wanted, the legislation was a clear victory for the new administration.

While Kennedy had some success in getting part of his domestic agenda passed, he ran into difficulties with two of his legislative priorities: providing hospital insurance for the elderly and increasing federal assistance for public education. Both programs required much greater federal government spending and involvement in society. The president put forward his plan for expanding Social Security to include hospital insurance for the elderly in February. He argued that many of the 16 million Americans older than 65 "simply do not obtain and cannot afford the care they need." He called for covering most of the bills for hospital stays up to ninety days, skilled nursing care for up to 180 days, and medical diagnosis tests. He proposed a quarter percent increase in the Social Security payroll tax on employers and employees to cover the additional costs. He stressed that he was not proposing "socialized medicine" and explained that each participant in the program would still "choose his own doctor and hospital."[36]

His proposal met almost immediate opposition as one report noted the president had "prodded a dormant hornet's nest." Most Republicans and many conservative Democrats opposed the bill because of the extension of federal

---

[33] Letter to the President of the Senate and to the Speaker of the House Transmitting a Minimum Wage Bill, February 7, 1961, *Public Papers of the Presidents, John F. Kennedy*, http://www.presidency.ucsb.edu/ws/?pid=8189, accessed on August 5, 2009.

[34] William Moore, "Minimum Wage Bill Foes Lash Its Provisions," *Chicago Daily Tribune*, April 15, 1961, p. 4.

[35] "Kennedy Wins Minimum Wage Victory," CQ Press Electronic Library, CQ Almanac Online Edition, cqal61-1372039, originally published in *CQ Almanac 1961* (Washington, D.C.: Congressional Quarterly, 1961), http://library.cqpress.com/cqalmanac/cqal61-1372039, accessed August 5, 2009. See also Robert J. Williams and David A. Kershaw, "Kennedy and Congress: The Struggle for the New Frontier," *Political Studies* 27:3 (September 1979), pp. 393-94.

power and the financial burden it would place on businesses. They were supported by the American Medical Association (AMA), National Association of Manufacturers, the Chamber of Commerce of the United States, and American Farm Bureau Federation.[37] The AMA distributed flyers to its doctors entitled, "Socialized Medicine and You," to post in their offices and claimed that Kennedy's plan was a "deadly challenge."[38] Senator Robert Kerr, a leading Democrat from Oklahoma, urged the defeat of the Kennedy bill because he charged it would be too expensive.[39] By the fall the bill had stalled, and Kennedy decided to wait until 1962 to push the legislation again.

The president renewed his call for health insurance for the aged in February 1962 and asked Congress to pass the same plan he put forward the previous year. He again stressed that "this program ... would not interfere in any way with the freedom of choice of doctor, hospital or nurse."[40] Over the coming months he continued to advocate for the bill. On May 20, his administration orchestrated thirty-three meetings around the country to generate support for the legislation. Kennedy spoke at a rally before close to 20,000 people in Madison Square Garden, and told the crowd that "this bill serves the public interest."[41] Unfortunately, he met the same resistance as in 1961. The AMA called the bill "a cruel hoax and a delusion" and mounted a strong campaign against the legislation.[42] The bill died in the Senate in July on a 52-48 vote with Democratic Senator Kerr leading the opposition.[43] While Kennedy did not publicly give up on achieving legislation the next year, he

36 Special Message to the Congress on Health and Hospital Care, February 9, 1961, *Public Papers of the Presidents, John F. Kennedy*, http://www.presidency.ucsb.edu/ws/?pid=8222, accessed on August 5, 2009.

37 John D. Morris, "Fight Looms Over Medical Plan: Kennedy Message Stirs Partisans in the Strongly Opposed Camps," *New York Times,* February 12, 1961, p. E10.

38 Donald Janson, "A.M.A. Maps Fight on Aged-Care Bill: Calls Kennedy Plan 'Deadly Challenge' -- National Ad Campaign Is Planned," *New York Times,* February 15, 1961, p. 18.

39 Morris Kaplan, "Kerr Advocates Own Health Bill: Senator Calls on Insurance Heads to Fight Kennedy's," *New York Times*, May 11, 1961, p. 26.

40 Special Message to the Congress on National Health Needs, February 27, 1962, *Public Papers of the Presidents, John F. Kennedy*, http://www.presidency.ucsb.edu/ws/?pid=9077, accessed on August 6, 2009.

41 "Text of President Kennedy's Address to Senior Citizens' Rally at Garden," *New York Times*, May 21, 1962, p. 20.

42 Peter Kihss, "A.M.A. Rebuttal To Kennedy Sees Aged Care 'Hoax': Surgeon Spokesman on TV Says Federal Plan Would Not Cover Millions Limited Benefits Cited Senior Citizens'," *New York Times*, May 22, 1962, p. 1. See also Shank, *Presidential Policy Leadership*, pp. 143-44.

43 Robert C. Albright, "Bipartisan Vote Tables Proposal For the Session: Senate Kills Administration's Aged Care Bill," *The Washington Post, Times Herald*, July 18, 1962, p. A1.

told his new Health, Education, and Welfare Secretary Anthony Celebrezze that "events will not permit legislative action in 1963."[44]

Kennedy's efforts to increase federal spending for education met a similar fate.[45] In February 1961, he told Congress, "Too many state and local governments lack the resources to assure an adequate education for every child. Too many classrooms are overcrowded. Too many teachers are underpaid. Too many talented individuals cannot afford the benefits of higher education. Too many academic institutions cannot afford the cost of, or find room for, the growing numbers of students seeking admission in the 60's." He called for the federal government to provide states and localities almost $2.4 billion over a three year period for public elementary and secondary schools. He also requested making greater funding available to colleges and universities for them to provide more scholarship aid to students and so that they could expand their facilities.[46]

His program ran into opposition from the beginning from a variety of opponents including House Majority Leader Rayburn.[47] The bill deliberately excluded Catholic parochial schools from receiving assistance because Kennedy knew that if he offered federal assistance to Catholic schools, he would be accused of doing the bidding of the Pope. However, by excluding these schools, he set-off a ground swell of opposition.[48] Almost immediately after the president announced his plan, Bishop Lawrence Shehan noted his "keen disappointment" that it "denies even the least bit of help" to the millions of children who attended Catholic schools.[49] Francis Cardinal Spellman argued that it was "unthinkable that any American child be denied the Federal funds allotted to other children which are necessary for his mental development

---

44 Quoted in Giglio, *Presidency of John F. Kennedy*, p. 103. See also Shank, *Presidential Policy Leadership*, p. 146.

45 Shank, *Presidential Policy Leadership*, pp. 110-12.

46 Special Message to the Congress on Education, February 20, 1961, *Public Papers of the Presidents, John F. Kennedy*, http://www.presidency.ucsb.edu/ws/?pid=8433, accessed on August 6, 2009.

47 Laurence Burd, "Kennedy Offers 5.6 Billion School Aid: Fate in Congress Uncertain," *Chicago Daily Tribune*, February 21, 1961, p. 2. See also Cabell Phillips, "School Aid Facing Fight on 3 Fronts: Integrationist, Catholic and Conservative Blocs Push Drives for Own Goals," *New York Times*, March 5, 1961, p. 58.

48 Williams and Kershaw, "Kennedy and Congress," pp. 395-96.

49 "A Catholic Bishop Hits School Plan: Educator Urges Congress to Broaden Bill—Protestants Back Kennedy Measure," *New York Times*, February 22, 1961, p. 16. See also Fred M. Hechinger, "Education: Church and State Catholic Hierarchy Hardens Stand On Aid to Parochial Schools," *New York Times*, March 12, 1961, p. E9.

because his parents chose for him a God-centered education."[50] As of 1965, there were 14,000 Catholic elementary and secondary schools in the United States, and the Catholic Church paid $3 billion annually to run them. The Catholic Church made two basic arguments. First, for every child it educated, there was one less student in the public schools to pay for. Second, the parents who sent their children to Catholic schools were paying taxes that supported the public schools. They questioned why they should not get at least some benefit from their taxes.[51]

Other opponents spoke against the plan for different reasons. Virginia Senator Harry Byrd and many other Southern politicians feared that the plan would lead to the forced integration of schools. "No one," Byrd argued, "can guarantee that there will not be Federal efforts to control our schools."[52] When the Kennedy administration tried to compromise, the National Education Association (NEA) came out against parts of the plan as well. Provisions in the compromise that could allow private schools to receive some funding raised its alarm.[53] While it was definitely concerned about whether providing funds to private religious schools would violate Constitutional provisions concerning the separation of church and state, the NEA also knew that "sharing the tax pie with Catholic schools would leave their members with a smaller slice."[54]

In the end there was too much opposition to the bill, and it died in the House Rules Committee in July when one Democrat representative rejected Kennedy's personal appeals and cast the deciding vote against sending the legislation to the floor.[55] Another effort to revive the legislation in the House fell on a vote of 242-170.[56] Similar legislation in 1962 and 1963 met some of the same results. Only near the end of his administration did the president have even modest success when Congress passed the Higher Education Facilities

---

50 "Spellman Pushes Effort to Widen School Measure: Calls Kennedy's Bill Unfair—Cites Ways of Including Non-Public Institutions," *New York Times*, March 14, 1961, p. 1.

51 Unger, *The Best of Intentions*, p. 44.

52 "Byrd Opposes Education Plan," *The Washington Post, Times Herald*, February 24, 1961, p. A1.

53 Cabell Phillips, "Ribicoff Demands School Bill Now: Tells N.E.A. Compromise Is Only Hope This Year," *New York Times*, July 22, 1961, p. 20.

54 Unger, *The Best of Intentions*, p. 45.

55 Drew Pearson, "The Washington Merry-Go-Round: Cardinal Blamed for School Defeat Strange Apathy," *The Washington Post, Times Herald,* July 22, 1961, p. B21. For a more thorough examination of the administration's efforts, see Huge Davis Graham, *The Uncertain Triumph: Federal Education Policy in the Kennedy and Johnson Years* (Chapel Hill: University of North Carolina Press, 1984), pp. 18-22.

56 Giglio, *Presidency of John F. Kennedy*, p. 104. See also John D. Morris, "First Kennedy Congress Responded Coolly to the Call of the New Frontier: Appeals to Blaze Trails Rebuffed," *New York Times*, September 28, 1961, p. 32.

Act of 1963.[57] This legislation provided $230 million in grants over a three year period for colleges to use for construction. Lyndon Johnson signed it into law in December 1963 after Kennedy's assassination.[58] While definitely an achievement, this legislation fell well short of Kennedy's education program announced in 1961.

While he did not obtain all the social legislation he wanted, Kennedy's programs, in conjunction with increases in defense spending in 1961, did help stimulate the economy and quicken the pace of the recovery after the recession.[59] However, several economic problems remained. The efforts to extend unemployment benefits helped the jobless, but they did not address the fundamental issue that the unemployment rate in 1961 was 6.7 percent, up from the 5.5 percent level in 1960.[60] While the level dropped back to 5.5 percent in 1962, it was still higher than Kennedy wanted. Furthermore, the budget deficits in 1961 and 1962 grew from $3.4 to $7.1 billion.[61] Finally, the balance of payments deficit had been lowered but was still a problem. Adding to these problems, Kennedy faced two new hurdles in the first half of 1962: the decision by steel executives to raise prices in April and a stock market crash in May.

The balance of payment deficit had improved during 1961, but it still worried Kennedy greatly.[62] He told Congress in his 1962 Annual Budget Message that "basic improvement in our balance of payments will depend primarily upon our ability to continue a high degree of overall price stability and to improve the competitive position of U.S. goods in world markets."[63] A week later he proposed legislation that would lower the balance of payments deficit by encouraging more American exports. He asked Congress to give him the authority to negotiate reductions in tariffs of up to 50 percent, specifically with the European Economic Community. He claimed "a new American trade initiative is needed to meet the challenges and opportunities of a rapidly

[57] Graham, *The Uncertain Triumph*, pp. 26-52.

[58] Giglio, *Presidency of John F. Kennedy*, pp. 106-7; and Unger, *The Best of Intentions*, pp. 448-49. See also "Congress Enacts Broad Education Program," CQ Press Electronic Library, CQ Almanac Online Edition, cqal63-1316861, originally published in *CQ Almanac 1963* (Washington, D.C.: Congressional Quarterly, 1964), http://library.cqpress.com/cqalmanac/cqal63-1316861, accessed August 7, 2009.

[59] Heath, *John F. Kennedy and the Business Community*, pp. 22-30.

[60] *The Statistical History of the United States: From Colonial Times to the Present* (New York: Basic Books, 1976), p. 135.

[61] Ibid., p. 1105.

[62] Dallek, *An Unfinished Life*, pp. 481-82.

changing world economy." Kennedy argued that the Trade Expansion Act, if passed, would lead to increased exports, economic growth, and, most importantly, obtaining "the equilibrium in our balance of payments which is essential to our economic stability and flexibility."[64]

The trade act moved slowly through Congress as there were concerns that the legislation would give the president too much authority over negotiating trade agreements and hurt some American industries that could be negatively affected by lower tariffs. Kennedy continued to push for ratification of the legislation noting that former Presidents Truman and Eisenhower and former Vice President Nixon supported passage.[65] The Senate passed the bill in late September by an overwhelming margin, giving Kennedy a clear victory. The trade bill did not end the balance of payments deficits, but it did improve the government's ability to negotiate more favorable tariff policies. The legislation ultimately led to an average tariff reduction of 35 percent on 6,300 trade items by 1967.[66] Kennedy told Congress in July 1963 that the country had made progress but that "more remains to be done today to eliminate the continuing payments deficit." He continued to support increasing exports and foreign tourism to the United States, while adjusting American military spending abroad.[67] However, he never resolved the balance of payments problem.

One reason Kennedy pursued the Trade Expansion Act so hard was his desire to build a working relationship with business leaders. When he initially called for the legislation, his relationships with the business community were generally favorable, but they soured in April 1962 due to a dispute between the Kennedy administration and the steel industry. Since the rise of big business in the late 19th century, the steel industry had assumed a particularly important place in the American economy, and Kennedy even claimed "Steel is a bellwether" of the American economy.[68] A 116-day steel strike in 1959 had

---

[63] Annual Budget Message to the Congress, Fiscal Year 1963, January 18, 1962, *Public Papers of the Presidents, John F. Kennedy*, http://www.presidency.ucsb.edu/ws/?pid=8588, accessed on January 6, 2010.

[64] Special Message to the Congress on Foreign Trade Policy, January 25, 1962, ibid., http://www.presidency.ucsb.edu/ws/?pid=8688, accessed on January 6, 2010. See Heath, *John F. Kennedy and the Business Community*, pp. 89-91.

[65] Address Before the Conference on Trade Policy, May 17, 1962, *Public Papers of the Presidents, John F. Kennedy*, http://www.presidency.ucsb.edu/ws/?pid=8664, accessed on January 6, 2010.

[66] Heath, *John F. Kennedy and the Business Community*, p. 93.

[67] Special Message to the Congress on Balance of Payments, July 18, 1963, *Public Papers of the Presidents, John F. Kennedy*, http://www.presidency.ucsb.edu/ws/?pid=9349, accessed on January 6, 2010.

[68] Letter to Leaders of the Steel Industry on the Need for Price Stability, September 7, 1961, ibid., http://www.presidency.ucsb.edu/ws/?pid=8316, accessed on January 2, 2010. See also

paralyzed the economy, and no one wanted such an important industry disrupted that way again.[69] Prior to Kennedy coming into office, the steel industry and the United Steelworkers of America had reached a labor agreement that scheduled wage increases over a three year period with the last one coming on October 1, 1961. During the period of the contract, wages for workers increased, while the steel industry maintained its prices at 1958 levels. As the time came to renegotiate the labor contract, the Kennedy administration became concerned that the steel executives would seek to raise prices.

Having grown up in a house led by an entrepreneur, Kennedy believed in private enterprise and generally pro-business policies. However, he also had come to see the importance of labor unions in securing the rights of workers. As president, he sought to balance the steel companies' need to make reasonable profits with the workers' desire for competitive wages and benefits. Early in his administration he mentioned that changes in manufacturing, especially the increase in automation, had allowed companies to continue to earn profits while they increased wages. However, he also knew that the efficiency brought by automation reduced the demand for workers. He noted that one of the problems was "the steel companies were able to maintain rather substantial profits at a time … with a good many more than 100,000 steel workers out of work."[70] Kennedy desired an arrangement that protected profits, guaranteed fair wages, and increased employment opportunities.

The fall of 1961 was a critical time for the steel industry as workers were scheduled to receive a wage increase on October 1, and there were reports that the steel executives were considering increasing the price of steel.[71] Kennedy decided to place public pressure on the steel companies to keep their prices at current levels. He feared that if the companies raised their prices it could lead to "an inflationary spiral" and "serve as a brake on our recovery" from the recession. He asserted that "the inflation which marked our economy before 1958 was … tied very closely to the increases in steel prices." He explained that his economic advisers had assured him that the steel companies could

Kim McQuaid, *Big Business and Presidential Power: From FDR to Reagan* (New York: William Morrow and Company, Inc., 1982), p. 205.

[69] See Edward B. Shils, "Arthur Goldberg: Proof of the American Dream," *Monthly Labor Review* (January 1997), pp. 63-65, http://www.bls.gov/mlr/1997/01/art5full.pdf; accessed on January 2, 2010; and Henry P. Guzda, "James P. Mitchell: Social Conscience of the Cabinet," *Monthly Labor Review* (August 1991), p. 3, http://www.bls.gov/OPUB/MLR/1991/08/art3full.pdf, accessed on January 2, 2010.

[70] The President's News Conference, February 8, 1961, *Public Papers of the Presidents, John F. Kennedy*, http://www.presidency.ucsb.edu/ws/?pid=8200, accessed on January 2, 2010.

[71] Shils, "Arthur Goldberg: Proof of the American Dream," p. 66.

absorb the wage increase and still make a solid profit. He finally expressed his hope that the steel industry leaders would act with the "public interest" in mind.[72]

The president followed these statements with a letter to the twelve leading steel manufacturers that he made public. He reiterated the inflationary impact of the increases in steel prices and wages prior to 1958 and stressed that the United States had lost market share because of them. He then noted that even with the upcoming wage increase for steel workers, the steel companies could still "look forward to good profits without an increase in prices." While assuring them that they would continue to make good profits, he hoped they would recognize the positive good arising from holding prices steady. He explained that by committing to maintain prices in October the steel industry would increase its "moral position" in the negotiation of a new collective bargaining agreement in the spring. He concluded by emphasizing the importance of price stability in the steel industry to maintaining "the economic vitality necessary to face confidently the trials and crises of our perilous world" and was sure the steel executives shared his "conviction that the clear call of national interest must be heeded."[73]

While the president of the United Steelworkers Union responded favorably to the president's efforts, steel company executives generally did not. Roger Blough, the chairman of U.S. Steel, spoke for most of the executives when he claimed that by limiting profits of steel companies the president was unfairly restricting free enterprise. He wrote a letter to the president that was also released to the public. He was critical of some of the president's statistics, arguing that they overstated the profits steel companies had made in previous years. He then pointed out that even if the president's figures were correct, they were not sufficient to cover the costs of the depreciation of machinery, repay loans, pay dividends, and buy new

---

[72] The President's News Conference, August 30, 1961, *Public Papers of the Presidents, John F. Kennedy*, http://www.presidency.ucsb.edu/ws/?pid=8294, accessed on January 2, 2010.

[73] Letter to Leaders of the Steel Industry on the Need for Price Stability. In a separate letter to David MacDonald, the president of the United Steelworkers of America, Kennedy reiterated some of the same points. He explained "the Steelworkers Union can make a significant contribution to the public interest by following, in the forthcoming negotiations, policies that will ensure that their collective bargaining proposals are fashioned so that, in meeting the needs of workers in the industry, the interests of stockholders are safeguarded and the public interest in price stability is protected." Letter to the President, United Steelworkers of America, on the Importance of Price Stability, September 14, 1961, *Public Papers of the Presidents, John F. Kennedy*, http://www.presidency.ucsb.edu/ws/?pid=8329, accessed on January 2, 2010.

equipment. He stressed "if the profit is not good enough to do these things, they cannot and will not be done; that would not be in the national interest."[74]

The tense relationship between the steel executives and the Kennedy administration remained unsettled for the remainder of 1961 and the first part of 1962. As required in the collective bargaining agreement, the steel industry enacted a wage increase on October 1, raising wages between 10 and 13 cents an hour.[75] It did so without raising steel prices. However, there were no promises that they would not do so in the future.

The collective bargaining agreement was in place until June 30, 1962, and the Kennedy administration wanted a new one completed by that date. Early in the year, Kennedy and his advisers began placing pressure on both labor and management to negotiate with the public interest in mind. Kennedy met with Blough and David MacDonald, the president of the United Steel Workers of America, for three hours in late January strongly encouraging them to negotiate in good faith and to get a new agreement completed.[76] When negotiations reached an impasse in late February, Kennedy again put pressure on the negotiators from both sides to get back to the table quickly.[77] At the end of March, the two sides came to an agreement that left wages the same, but provided for increases in fringe benefits equivalent to an approximate 2.5 percent raise.[78] Kennedy commended both sides for their efforts and was particularly impressed "by their desire to meet their responsibilities to the country here and abroad."[79]

The euphoria in the White House was short-lived. Less than two weeks after the new labor agreement was signed, Blough met Kennedy at the White House and informed the president that U.S. Steel was raising the price of steel $6 per ton, a 3.5 percent increase.[80] Seven other steel companies followed U.S. Steel's lead.[81] Believing he had been lied to, Kennedy was furious. In a private, profanity laced tirade, Kennedy blasted the steel executives and

---

[74] "Text of Blough's Letter to the President," *New York Times*, September 14, 1961, p. 18.

[75] Emanuel Perlmutter, "Steel Wage Rise Effective Today: Companies Give No Word on an Increase in Prices," *New York Time*, October 1, 1961, p. 64.

[76] Richard E. Mooney, "U.S. is Optimistic on Drama in Steel: Officials Hopeful on Drive to Forestall Strike but Bar Inflationary Pact," *New York Times*, February 11, 1962, p. 133.

[77] Norman Walker, "U.S. Is Seeking Early Renewal Of Steel Talks," *The Washington Post, Times Herald*, March 4, 1962, p. A2.

[78] Bernard D. Nossiter. "Steel Pay Agreement Is Reached: Pact Skips Any Raise For Year New Benefits Won," *The Washington Post, Times Herald*, March 29, 1962, p. A1.

[79] The President's News Conference, March 29, 1962, *Public Papers of the Presidents, John F. Kennedy*, http://www.presidency.ucsb.edu/ws/?pid=8573, accessed on January 2, 2010.

[80] McQuaid, *Big Business and Presidential Power*, pp. 207-8. See also "Text of U.S. Steel's Statement on Prices," *New York Time*, April 11, 1962, p. 28.

businessmen in general.[82] At a press conference the next day, he was still visibly angry and called the increase "a wholly unjustifiable and irresponsible defiance of the public interest" and claimed the steel executives "pursuit of private power and profit exceeds their sense of public responsibility" and showed "utter contempt for the interests of 185 million Americans."[83] Over the next three days, the Kennedy administration brought tremendous pressure on the steel companies to rescind their price increases. The Department of Justice and Federal Bureau of Investigation began investigations to determine if any laws related to collusion had been broken, the Defense Department announced that it would begin shifting its businesses to steel companies that had not raised their prices, and Congressional Democrats threatened to launch formal committee hearings.[84] Facing this pressure and knowing that several steel companies did not raise their prices, U.S. Steel and the other seven companies decided to rescind their increase three days later.[85] Prices for steel held steady for another year before the steel companies raised prices about 3 percent in the face of only mild protests.[86]

Although clearly a victory, Kennedy moved quickly to minimize the divide between his administration and business leaders. After the steel crisis, the president tried to "make it clear that this administration harbors no ill will against any individual, any industry, corporation, or segment of the American economy." He added "our goals of economic growth and price stability are dependent upon the success of … corporations, business, and labor and there can be no room on either side … for any feelings of hostility or vindictiveness." He then explained that "while our chief concern last week was to prevent an inflationary spiral, we were not then and are not now unmindful of the steel industry's needs for profits, modernization, and investment

[81] Heath, *John F. Kennedy and the Business Community*, p. 68.

[82] Dallek, *An Unfinished Life*, p. 484.

[83] The President's News Conference, April 11, 1962, *Public Papers of the Presidents, John F. Kennedy*, http://www.presidency.ucsb.edu/ws/?pid=8598, accessed on January 2, 2010. One reporter noted "As he spoke in a voice edged with bitterness, Mr. Kennedy fingered the dias [sic] before him with trembling hands. At no time during the half hour press conference did he smile or joke with reporters as he often does. Robert Thompson, "Steel Uproar!: Kennedy Calls Council of War After Denouncing Price Hike," *Los Angeles Times*, April 12, 1962, p. 2.

[84] Heath, *John F. Kennedy and the Business Community*, p. 69. See also Shils, "Arthur Goldberg: Proof of the American Dream," p. 67; and E. Ray Canterbery, *Economics on a New Frontier* (Belmont, CA: Wadworth Publishing Company, Inc., 1968), pp. 250-53.

[85] "Steel Companies Give In, Rescind Price Increases under Pressure from Kennedy," *New York Times*, April 14, 1962, p. 10. See Denise M. Bostdorff and Daniel J. O'Rourke, "The Presidency and the Promotion of Domestic Crisis: John Kennedy's Management of the 1962 Steel Crisis," *Presidential Studies Quarterly* 27:2 (Spring 1997), pp. 343-62.

[86] Giglio, *The Presidency of John F. Kennedy*, p. 133.

capital."[87] He also made efforts to show that unions also had responsibilities by telling the United Auto Workers union that "unjustified wage demands … are equally as contrary to the national interest as unjustified profit demands which require price increases."[88]

Concerns about the president's handling of the economy in the wake of steel crisis and fears that stock prices were overvalued led prices to decline in May and finally to the largest single-day drop in the stock market since 1929. On May 28, the stock market lost $21 billion in value as the Dow Jones Industrial Average fell almost 35 points to just under 577. Altogether, the Dow had lost 23 percent of its value since the previous December.[89] Some even called it "The Kennedy Crash."[90] The president and his advisers went back and forth over exactly what to do. There were real fears that the sluggish recovery from the 1960-61 recession might end and the economy might fall back into a new recession.[91]

As Kennedy and advisers debated how to address the country's continuing economic problems, they realized one of the major impediments to getting their programs moving was that the conservative Congress was reluctant to support many of his administration's policies. As one scholar has noted, "the President's power struggle with Congress was almost equal to that of his struggle with the Communist leaders abroad."[92] After the defeat of his plan for health care for the elderly in July 1962, he went on the offensive. He announced to Americans "we have to decide, the United States, in 1962, in November, in the Congressional elections, whether we want to stand still or whether we want to support this kind of legislation for the benefit of the people."[93] A week later he reiterated the importance of the fall elections.

[87] The President's News Conference, April 18, 1962, *Public Papers of the Presidents, John F. Kennedy*, http://www.presidency.ucsb.edu/ws/?pid=8613, accessed on January 2, 2010. See Kennedy's comments on the importance of bargaining in good faith, Television and Radio Interview: "After Two Years - a Conversation With the President," December 17, 1962, ibid., http://www.presidency.ucsb.edu/ws/?pid=9060, accessed on January 2, 2010.

[88] Address in Atlantic City at the Convention of the United Auto Workers, May 8, 1962, ibid., http://www.presidency.ucsb.edu/ws/?pid=8637, accessed on January 2, 2010.

[89] Peter T. Earle, "Stock Market Decline Is Sharpest Since '29," *The Washington Post, Times Herald*, May 29, 1962, p. A1. See also Canterbery, *Economics of a New Fronteir*, p. 254; McQuaid, *Big Business and Presidential Power*, pp. 210-11; and Heath, *John F. Kennedy and the Business Community*, pp. 73-74.

[90] "The Kennedy Crash," *Chicago Daily Tribune*, May 29, 1962, p. 14.

[91] Dallek, *An Unfinished Life*, pp. 506-7.

[92] Carroll Kilpatrick, "The Kennedy Style and Congress," *The Virginia Quarterly Review* 39:1 (Winter 1963), p. 1.

[93] Statement by the President on the Defeat of the Medical Care Bill, July 17, 1962, *Public Papers of the Presidents, John F. Kennedy*, http://www.presidency.ucsb.edu/ws/?pid=8772, accessed on January 4, 2010.

"November 1962," Kennedy explained, "presents the American people with a very clear choice between the Republican Party … and the Democratic Party…. Fortunately, the American people will have a choice. And they will choose … either to put anchor down or to sail." He added, "I'm going to help elect Democrats who support this program. The areas I will be campaigning in are seats where there will be a very clear choice between Republicans who oppose these actions and Democrats who support them."[94]

Going into the fall elections, the Democrats had strong majorities in both the House and the Senate.[95] The fall was a difficult time for the president and the country. There was widespread tension over the civil rights movement, especially in the south, and the Cuban missile crisis brought attention to the real dangers of a nuclear war.[96] Kennedy campaigned when he could and constantly advocated the election of candidates who supported "progress." He announced at a campaign event in Michigan "the decision is yours. Every off year in this century, with the exception of once, the party in power has lost votes. And I can tell you after the razor-thin majorities by which we have won or lost, that we need every vote we can get; otherwise this country will stand still."[97] He told a crowd in Kentucky "I don't think there is anything better to do than to … go around the country and ask for Democrats."[98]

Kennedy's efforts and the general mood of the country helped produce results that were "the best Congressional election showing since 1934 for the party occupying the White House" during a midterm election.[99] Democrats emerged from the elections with a 68 to 32 majority in the Senate and a 259 to 176 majority in the House. As significant, conservatives within the Democratic Party lost some influence, allowing the party to pursue a more progressive agenda.[100] Kennedy believed the Democrats "did better than we had hoped in

---

94 The President's News Conference, July 23, 1962, ibid., http://www.presidency.ucsb.edu/ws/?pid=8784, accessed on January 2, 2010.

95 Kilpatrick, "The Kennedy Style and Congress," p. 3.

96 These issues are discussed in detail in later chapters.

97 Remarks at a Democratic Rally in Detroit, October 6, 1962, *Public Papers of the Presidents, John F. Kennedy*, http://www.presidency.ucsb.edu/ws/?pid=8932, accessed on January 4, 2010.

98 Remarks at the State Fairgrounds in Louisville, October 13, 1962, ibid., http://www.presidency.ucsb.edu/ws/?pid=8956, accessed on January 4, 2010.

99 Paul Duke, "Election & Congress: Vote Likely to Benefit Kennedy Proposals as Liberals Score Gains," *Wall Street Journal*, November 8, 1962, p. 1

100 Cabell Phillips, "Survey of New Congress Finds Kennedy Stronger," *New York Times*, December 27, 1962, p. 1.

the election," but was not sure whether there was enough change to produce better results in the next Congress.[101]

While he tried to persuade the American people to elect a more cooperative Congress, Kennedy continued to evaluate the best ways to tackle the country's economic problems. In a break with the views he held the first year and a half of his administration, he decided the best approach was to reform the tax system and reduce taxes significantly. Previously, Kennedy had resisted tax cuts because of their potential to drive up the deficit, but by the summer of 1962 he had come to accept that deficits could be helpful in times of high unemployment and tax cuts would not only stimulate economic growth but would "extend the recovery and weaken recessionary forces."[102] Kennedy came to this position under the prodding of Walter Heller and others in his administration who had been advising the president of these views for a year and a half.[103] Kennedy argued in early June that "our tax structure as presently weighted exerts too heavy a drain on a prospering economy." He then laid out the need for major tax reforms "to make certain that recovery is stronger and longer than before and is not cut short by a new recession."[104]

In August Kennedy announced that while he did not support immediate tax cuts in 1962 he would put forward a plan in 1963 that would reform the tax system and provide tax relief to most Americans. He argued "the facts of the matter are that our present tax system is a drag on economic recovery and economic growth, biting heavily into the purchasing power of every taxpayer and every consumer." He added "Our tax rates ... are so high as to weaken the very essence of the progress of a free society, the incentive for additional return for additional effort." He announced that his administration would propose legislation that would cut both corporate and personal taxes starting in 1963. He acknowledged that cutting taxes would reduce government revenue in the short term, but stressed the economic growth stimulated by the cuts

---

[101] The President's News Conference, November 20, 1962, *Public Papers of the Presidents, John F. Kennedy*, http://www.presidency.ucsb.edu/ws/?pid=9020, accessed on January 2, 2010.

[102] Harris, *Economics of the Kennedy Years and A Look Ahead*, p. 14.

[103] Ibid., pp. 22-23; Canterbery, *Economics on a New Frontier*, pp. 14-15; McQuaid, *Big Business and Presidential Power*, pp. 214-15; Heath, *John F. Kennedy and the Business Community*, p. 115; and Paul M. Simpson, "John F. Kennedy and the 1964 Revenue Act: The Politics of Formulation/Legitimation," in Harper and Krieg, eds., *John F. Kennedy*, pp. 195-97.

[104] The President's News Conference, June 7, 1962, *Public Papers of the Presidents, John F. Kennedy*, http://www.presidency.ucsb.edu/ws/?pid=8698, accessed on January 6, 2010.

would lead to larger federal revenues in the future.[105] He reiterated his support for tax cuts when he told a group of economists "this Nation can afford to reduce taxes, we can afford a temporary deficit, but we cannot afford to do nothing."[106]

The tax system in 1963 was based on legislation passed in 1954 and included personal income tax rates ranging from 20 percent to 91 percent. Married couples who earned less than $4,000 and singles making less than $2,000 were subject to the lowest tax brackets, while married couples making over $400,000 and singles making over $200,000 paid the highest amount. Altogether, there were 24 separate income tax brackets.[107] Corporations had to pay a 30 percent tax on the first $25,000 in profit they made and 52 percent on the rest.[108] In his annual budget message to Congress in January 1963, Kennedy proposed cutting taxes across the board "to help speed the economy toward full employment and a higher rate of growth with price stability."[109] A week later he presented his formal plan calling for a reduction in personal income taxes to a range of between 14 and 65 percent and corporate taxes to 22 percent on the first $25,000 and 47 percent on amounts above that by January 1965. Altogether, his administration calculated these cuts would reduce tax liabilities $13.6 billion—$11 billon for individuals and $2.6 billion for corporations. He concluded that while the tax cuts would benefit all Americans, the greatest gains would be made by lower income families with five out of every 6 taxpayers seeing at least a 20 percent drop in their tax liabilities.[110]

The immediate reactions to his budget and tax proposals were mixed. Democratic House Speaker James McCormack called the budget containing

---

105 Radio and Television Report to the American People on the State of the National Economy, August 13, 1962, ibid., http://www.presidency.ucsb.edu/ws/?pid=8812, accessed on January 7, 2010.

106 Address and Question and Answer Period at the Economic Club of New York, December 14, 1962, ibid., http://www.presidency.ucsb.edu/ws/?pid=9057, accessed on January 8, 2010.

107 Joseph A. Pechman, "Individual Income Tax Provisions of the Revenue Act of 1964," *The Journal of Finance*, 20:2, Papers and Proceedings of the Twenty-Third Annual Meeting of the American Finance Association, Chicago, IL, December 28-20, 1964 (May 1965), p. 257.

108 Louis Alan Talley, "Federal Taxation: An Abbreviated History," January 19, 2001, CRS Report for Congress, http://www.taxhistory.org/thp/readings.nsf/cf7c9c870b600b9585256df80075b9dd/2d52a4cfd2844fab85256e22007840e6?OpenDocument, accessed on July 31, 2009.

109 Annual Budget Message to the Congress, Fiscal Year 1964, January 17, 1963, *Public Papers of the Presidents, John F. Kennedy*, http://www.presidency.ucsb.edu/ws/?pid=9241, accessed on January 7, 2010.

110 Special Message to the Congress on Tax Reduction and Reform, January 24, 1963, ibid., http://www.presidency.ucsb.edu/ws/?pid=9387, accessed on January 8, 2010.

the tax cuts "a sound and progressive one … geared to the nation's actual and potential fiscal policy." Democratic Representative Clarence Cameron thought the budget was "entirely too big" when taking into consideration the tax cuts. Senate Minority Leader Everett Dirksen claimed the whole budget was based on faulty principles and ultimately concluded that the Kennedy administration must have determined "that the best way to correct mistakes is to create bigger ones."[111] Virginia Senator Harry Byrd called for Kennedy to fire his budget director. "If we do not get crack-pot economists out of these positions," he argued, "the American system will be lost."[112] The issues that bothered most officials were not the tax cuts but the deficits that would result from them. Former President Eisenhower wrote a letter to House Republican leader Charles Halleck explaining "if the Government is to accept deliberately a massive deficit, and then simultaneously embark on lavish new spending and a huge tax cut, the nation is headed for trouble."[113]

Kennedy pushed back against the opposition.[114] In response to the former president's claims, Kennedy argued that if Congress cut the budget as Eisenhower suggested it would put the country "in an economic decline instead of a rise."[115] He continued to campaign for the cuts telling a group in favor of his plan in May "it is my hope that a tax program will be enacted along lines I believe to be in the overall national interest—a balanced program that will benefit both consumers and producers, both workers and investors, with a consequently cumulative benefit for incomes and jobs, profits and incentives, consumption and productivity."[116] His efforts continued during the summer when he wrote the chairman of the House Ways and Means Committee, that "it is most important now that the bill be enacted this year as rapidly as possible." He furthered cautioned that any further delay "would substantially reduce the effectiveness of the legislation in stimulating the economy, reducing unemployment and increasing incentives."[117]

The efforts of Kennedy and others who supported the legislation ultimately led to the passage of a major tax reform bill. While the president did

[111] "Leaders in Both Parties Blast Request," *Chicago Daily Tribune*, January 18, 1963, p. 1.

[112] Russell Freeburg, "Byrd Urges Dismissal of Budget Boss," ibid., January 31, 1963, p. N1.

[113] "Text of Eisenhower's Budget Letter," *New York Times*, March 30, 1963, p. 4

[114] Simpson, "John F. Kennedy and the 1964 Revenue Act," pp. 197 and 202.

[115] The President's News Conference, April 3, 1963, *Public Papers of the Presidents, John F. Kennedy*, http://www.presidency.ucsb.edu/ws/?pid=9139, accessed on January 8, 2010.

[116] Remarks to Representatives of the Citizens Committee for Tax Reduction and Revision in 1963, May 9, 1963, ibid., http://www.presidency.ucsb.edu/ws/?pid=9201, accessed on January 8, 2010.

[117] Letter to the Chairman, House Ways and Means Committee, on Tax Reduction, August 21, 1963, ibid., http://www.presidency.ucsb.edu/ws/?pid=9375, accessed on January 8, 2010.

not live to see his legislation enacted into law, it was passed in early 1964 as the Revenue Act of 1964. Kennedy did not get everything he requested, but he came close. The lowest tax bracket for married couples making less than $1,000 and singles making less than $500 was reduced to 14 percent as Kennedy proposed. Congress set the highest tax bracket for married couples making over $200,000 and singles making over $100,000 at 70 percent whereas Kennedy wanted the highest rate to be 65 percent for those married couples making over $400,000 and singles making over $200,000.[118] The legislation further reduced corporate taxes from 30 percent on the first $25,000 and 52 percent on the rest to 22 percent and 48 percent respectively.[119] Again, these numbers were very close to what Kennedy had proposed.

Kennedy deserves a great deal of credit for successfully pushing through this legislation. Unlike on some issues, he truly led the efforts to get tax reform. While Lyndon Johnson's efforts to obtain final passage should not be overlooked, Kennedy laid the groundwork for the legislation.[120] The tax cuts achieved what Kennedy wanted—a growing economy. It grew at a 6 percent rate in 1964 and unemployment dropped to 4 percent by 1966. Tax revenues also increased.[121] Further, while the deficit did rise in 1964 to almost $6 billion, it declined the following year to $1.4 billion.[122] It is virtually impossible to determine the tax cuts long-term ramifications, but at least in the short-term they had achieved what the president wanted.

The New Frontier at home produced notable successes. After the end of the recession in 1961, the American economy entered a period of sustained growth that lasted through most of the decade. While Kennedy was unable to get major tax legislation passed in 1963 as he hoped, he laid the foundation for the Revenue Act of 1964 which reduced taxes for all Americans and stimulated economic growth. He was also able to push through legislation to increase the minimum wage and assistance for the needy, especially in depressed areas in the country. However, he had little success obtaining a government supported health care for the elderly or in providing more funding for education. When compared to what he set out to do, Kennedy

118 Pechman, "Individual Income Tax Provisions of the Revenue act of 1964," p. 257.
119 Talley, "Federal Taxation: An Abbreviated History".
120 Simpson, "John F. Kennedy and the 1964 Revenue Act," pp. 201-2; and Dallek, *An Unfinished Life*, p. 708.
121 Heath, *John F. Kennedy and the Business Community*, p. 122; and Giglio, *The Presidency of John F. Kennedy*, pp. 139-40.
122 Budget of the United States Government: Historical Tables Fiscal Year 2010, Table 1.1 — Summary of Receipts, Outlays, and Surpluses or Deficits (-): 1789–2014, http://www.gpoaccess.gov/usbudget/fy10/hist.html, accessed on January 8, 2010.

accomplished a great deal. While he could have been a stronger advocate in some areas, he was able to get much of his legislative program adopted.

Chapter 6

THE CIVIL RIGHTS MOVEMENT AND KENNEDY

Kennedy's "New Frontier" seemingly heralded a new age for Black Americans, but the reality was quite different. Black Americans voted in great numbers for Kennedy in 1960 hoping that they finally would have a president who could understand their plight, and their votes helped him win several northern states. However, for most of the Kennedy administration, they could not have been more wrong. Kennedy had reached out to black voters in 1960 because he believed it was politically expedient to do so. His commitment did not go much deeper than that until the realities of their plight jarred his consciousness in 1963.[1] In was only in May of that year that he finally realized that the civil rights question truly needed presidential leadership. Over the last six months of his life, he became much more committed to advancing civil rights and began to offer some of the leadership that many Black Americans had been expecting in January 1961.

As Kennedy entered the White House in January 1961, many Black Americans waited anxiously to see his first actions related to civil rights. They remembered his campaign rhetoric when he had argued in regards to civil rights that "The place to begin is the White House itself, where the Chief Executive, with his prestige and influence, should exert firm and positive leadership."[2] They also remembered his critique of former President

---

[1] Shank, *Presidential Policy Leadership*, p. 157.

[2] Remarks of Senator John F. Kennedy, NAACP Rally, July 10, 1960, JFKL, Kennedy Papers, Pre-Presidential Papers, '60 Campaign Press and Publicity, Speeches, Statements, and Sections 1958-1960, Agriculture-Defense-Disarmament: Increasing Perils of Radioactivity, Box 1028, Folder – Civil Rights, Job Discrimination, NAACP Policy.

Eisenhower's civil rights record where he argued the Republican president could have made a significant contribution to civil rights with "one stroke of the pen."[3] His rhetoric and the results of the election raised expectations for many black Americans. Roy Wilkins captured this sense when he claimed, "I know everybody is claiming to have elected Mr. Kennedy, but the Negroes had a particular role here, because they helped the South to elect him."[4] Republican Congressman Seymour Halpern from Queens, New York wrote Kennedy and explained, "The sincerity of the Democratic platform and its candidates is now ready for the test. The American people will be watching with concern and anticipation."[5]

Some of Kennedy's advisors on civil rights shared this view. Harris Wofford served as the president-elect's principal adviser on civil rights and became the White House's Coordinator for Civil Rights Policy in the new administration. In a memorandum to Kennedy, Wofford noted that "It took a strong civil rights platform and campaign, and Lyndon Johnson and substantial southern support to win in 1960."[6] He suggested that the new president not propose new civil rights legislation but to use "a large measure of executive action."[7] He hoped that through "vigorous and inventive efforts" Kennedy could "produce a new Negro and a new South."[8] He finally stressed that the president needed to keep "in touch with the top Negro leaders," and especially Martin Luther King and Roy Wilkins.[9]

Kennedy did reach out to civil rights leaders in the weeks prior to his inauguration. In late December 1960, he selected Dr. Robert Weaver to be the Housing and Home Finance Administrator. Weaver became the first black American to serve in a presidential cabinet.[10] He also met with Wilkins for a little over thirty minutes in early January. Wilkins came away satisfied with new president's understanding of "the place and importance of civil rights" and with his commitment to support the civil rights plank of the Democratic

---

[3] Laurence Burd, "Charges Ike Drags Feet on Civil Rights," *Chicago Daily Tribune*, Aug. 9, 1960, p. 9.

[4] "Kennedy Tactics Disturb Wilkins," *New York Times*, Dec. 29, 1960, p. 13.

[5] "Kennedy is Prodded on Civil Rights Bill," ibid., Jan. 6, 1961, p. 19.

[6] Memorandum to President-Elect Kennedy on Civil Rights – 1961, Dec. 30, 1960, JFKL, Kennedy Papers, Pre-Presidential Papers, Transition Files, Task Force Reports, Task Reports 1960, Domestic Affairs: Agriculture-Housing, Box 1071, Folder – Civil Rights—Harris Wofford Memorandum, p. 1.

[7] Harris Wofford, Jr. to President-Elect Kennedy, Dec. 30, 1960, ibid.

[8] Memorandum to President-Elect Kennedy on Civil Rights – 1961, ibid.

[9] Harris Wofford, Jr. to President-Elect Kennedy, Dec. 30, 1960, ibid.

[10] Alvin Shuster, "Robert Weaver Is Picked As Federal Housing Chief," *New York Times*, Dec. 31, 1960, p. 1.

Party platform.[11] These initial steps seemed to indicate that Kennedy would keep civil rights near the top of his agenda, but they proved to be among the few steps he would take in his first year in office.

During the opening months of his administration, Kennedy set the slow pace for civil rights he would follow through most of his presidency. Concerned that he might alienate southern Democrats and not holding firm convictions that he should take a leading role in furthering civil rights, Kennedy took only moderate steps to help black Americans.[12] What Kennedy did not realize was the movement was growing faster than he realized, and his administration was about to witness the full onslaught of a national crisis that had been building for over a decade. Early in his presidency, he received a report from the Southern Regional Council, a biracial group based in Atlanta, encouraging him to forcefully lead the federal government in standing in favor of civil rights. The group emphasized, "the presidency is the center of American energy. What the President says and does will mark the direction and the speed with which the country moves to perfect its racial relations."[13] It added, "a President of robust conviction will lose no occasion, however trivial, to show by purely personal action his admiration of principles of equality."[14] Unfortunately, Kennedy's lack of a "robust conviction" led to a very limited commitment to civil rights.

Kennedy decided the best approach was to avoid confrontations in Congress over civil rights that might stall some of his other priorities. In fact, "there was no Kennedy administration civil rights program in 1961."[15] He felt some pressure from Republicans who pointed out that Kennedy had not included civil rights legislation in the agenda he presented to Congress. One Republican leader lamented "nothing has been done, nothing has been advanced."[16] Martin Luther King encouraged Kennedy to act, especially using the unique powers that the president possessed. "I was amazed," King wrote to one of the president's aides, "to find the powerful things that the President can do in the civil rights area through executive orders."[17] King's advice reflected

---

[11] "Negro Leader Sees Kennedy on Rights," *New York Times*, Jan. 7, 1962, p. 40.

[12] Stern, *Calculating Visions*, pp. 40 and 63.

[13] Joseph H. Baird, "Kennedy Prodded on Negro Rights," *Christian Science Monitor*, Jan. 30, 1961, p. 5.

[14] Claude Sitton, "Southerners Ask Kennedy to Lead Civil-Rights Drive," *New York Times*, Jan. 30, 1961, p. 1.

[15] Sorensen, *Counselor*, p. 272.

[16] Russell Baker, "G.O.P. Will Offer Civil Rights Bill: Kennedy Chided. *New York Times*, Feb. 24, 1961, p. 1.

[17] Martin Luther King, Jr. to Frank D. Reeves, Feb. 28, 1961, John F. Kennedy Presidential Library,

Kennedy's thinking as to how he could advance civil rights without alienating others in the process. He believed offering economic aid to the poor would help more black Americans than symbolic civil rights legislation and that executive orders could advance civil rights in specific ways.[18]

On March 7, he issued Executive Order 10925 to establish the President's Committee on Equal Employment Opportunity with the main purpose "to scrutinize and study employment practices of the Government of the United States, and to consider and recommend additional affirmative steps which should be taken by executive departments and agencies to realize more fully the national policy of nondiscrimination within the executive branch of the government."[19] While this action met with some praise, many black leaders did question Kennedy's reluctance to present civil rights legislation to Congress. Wilkins, for one, welcomed the executive order, but criticized the president for not fighting harder for actual legislation. He claimed "an administration gets as much by whacking them [legislators] as wooing them." From Wilkins' perspective, "wooing" was not working; therefore, the president needed to go ahead and put "a civil rights bill in the hopper." A few months later Wilkins chastised Kennedy for not confronting southern senators and congressmen more directly with civil rights legislation. When Kennedy did not publicly back civil rights legislation, Wilkins noted that the Soviet Union was not the only threat to the United States. He claimed "both the jackals [from the South] and the bears [from the Soviet Union] are reaching for our vitals" and the United States needed to protect its interests at home and abroad.[20] Little did Wilkins know that he would have to wait another two years for any type of real presidential leadership on civil rights.

While Kennedy may have wanted a go slow approach, events outside his control actually drove the civil rights movement. In the years prior to his administration, Martin Luther King had emerged as the key civil rights leader and encouraged a civil disobedience or non-violence to protest discrimination. The movement had gained momentum in the 1950s with the *Brown* v. *Board*

http://www.jfklibrary.org/Asset+Tree/Asset+Viewers/Image+Asset+Viewer.htm?guid={58337A97-5722-4613-BAC9-E5422945B297}&type=mpd&num=1, accessed on May 12, 2008.

18 Anthony Lewis, "Economic Aid for Negroes Gets White House Priority," *New York Times*, Mar. 6, 1961, p. 1.

19 Executive Order 10925 – Establishing the President's Committee on Equal Employment Opportunity, March 7, 1961, JFKL, Kennedy Papers, Presidential Papers, White House Staff Files, Lee C. White File, Civil Rights File, Box 20, Folder – Equal Employment Opportunity, March 7-Dec. 12, 1961.

20 "Presidents View on Rights Scored: N.A.A.C.P. Cites Failure to Back New Legislation," *New York Times*, May 11, 1961, p. 24.

of Education decision, the success of the Montgomery Bus Boycott, the desegregation of schools in Little Rock, and the passage of the 1957 Civil Rights Act. These were all important steps, but the most significant progress did not occur until the 1960s. On February 1, 1960, four black students from North Carolina A & T State University began at sit-in at the lunch counter at a Woolworth's in downtown Greensboro that lasted until it was desegregated in late July.[21] Further, in December 1960 the Supreme Court ruled in *Boynton* v. *Virginia* that discrimination in interstate transportation, including in the transportation terminals, was unconstitutional.[22] While these issues were not directly related, they did come together to encourage a new challenge to discrimination in the spring and summer of 1961.

From the president's perspective, one of the first true civil rights crises that he had to face could not have occurred at a more inopportune time. In April 1961, the United States had supported an invasion by Cuban exiles at the Bay of Pigs. It was an unmitigated disaster and damaged Kennedy's and America's prestige internationally. The spring had also seen rising tensions between the United States and the Soviet Union. Accordingly, Kennedy was not interested in tackling major domestic issues at that time. Unfortunately for him, James Farmer and the Congress of Racial Equality (CORE) had a different idea. They planned to test whether the South would accept the desegregation of interstate commerce as ordered by the Supreme Court. On April 26, Farmer wrote Kennedy explaining the organization's plans. Kennedy evidently never read the letter, as he and his advisers were later caught by surprise when some southerners attacked the riders in Alabama.[23] Farmer explained that CORE planned to have approximately fifteen of its members travel as passengers on interstate buses in the south. The riders planned to board a Greyhound bus and a Trailways bus in Washington, D.C. and travel to New Orleans from May 4 to 17. Farmer told the president that the main purpose of the Freedom Ride "is to make bus desegregation a reality instead of merely an approved legal doctrine. By demonstrating that a group can ride

---

21 Greensboro Sit-ins: The Launch of a Civil Rights Movement, http://www.sitins.com/index.shtml, accessed on May 7, 2008.

22 U.S. Supreme Court, *Boynton* v. *Virginia*, 364 U.S. 454 (1960), http://supreme.justia.com/us/364/454/case.html, accessed on May 7, 2008.

23 Dallek, *An Unfinished Life*, p. 384. Dallek did not believe the White House had been informed of the upcoming Freedom Rides, but James Farmer did send the president a letter and notified Bobby Kennedy and the FBI. See Nick Bryant, *The Bystander: John F. Kennedy and The Struggle for Black Equality* (New York: Basic Books, 2006), pp. 262-63.

buses in a desegregated manner even in the Deep South, CORE hopes to encourage other people to do likewise."[24]

On May 4, thirteen black and white members of CORE boarded buses in D.C. for their trip through the South. They met relatively little resistance until they arrived in Rock Hill, S.C. where several teenagers accosted some of the riders. None of the riders needed medical attention, and they reported that the local police intervened quickly to protect them.[25] Unfortunately, they did not receive the same sort of protection just a few days later.

On May 14, the buses left Atlanta on their way to Birmingham and made a stop in Anniston, Alabama. The Greyhound bus arrived about an hour before the Trailways one. As the Greyhound bus pulled into the terminal, a group of protestors threw rocks at its windows and slashed its tires. The bus driver drove a few more miles away from the terminal before the tires went flat. At that point a group of southerners surrounded the bus, and one of them threw a Molotov cocktail through the back window.[26] The bus riders scrambled off the burning bus where they were met by a white mob that beat them with their fists, clubs, and iron bars. Despite numerous injuries to the protestors and the destruction of the bus, the police made no arrests.[27] When the Trailways bus arrived an hour later, protestors dragged several passengers off the bus and beat them before the bus was allowed to leave for Birmingham.[28] The passengers who had to go to the hospital were later taken to Birmingham without incident.

The riders met even more violence in Birmingham. Despite the Supreme Court decision ruling segregation in bus terminals as unlawful, most terminals in the South remained segregated. When the black passengers entered the waiting area labeled for whites only, a group of white men attacked them. One eyewitness explained, "When the bus arrived, the toughs grabbed the passengers into alleys and corridors, and pounding them with pipes, with key rings and with fists." In one particular case, around a dozen attackers beat and kicked one passenger until his face was "a bloody pulp."[29] Little did the

---

[24] James Farmer to the President, Apr. 26, 1961, John F. Kennedy Presidential Library, http://www.jfklibrary.org/Asset+Tree/Asset+Viewers/Image+Asset+Viewer.htm?guid={83B6CAA1-F101-4DB9-82F2-F1DD5E323AD0}&type=mpd, accessed on May 12, 2008.

[25] "Biracial Unit Tells of Beating in South," *New York Times*, May 11, 1961, p. 25.

[26] A Molotov cocktail is an improvised incendiary device. Usually, an attacker will fill a bottle with gasoline an insert a cloth into the top of the bottle to use as a wick. The assailant would light the cloth and then throw the bottle.

[27] "Mob Burns Bus in Race Row: 9 Riders Get Treatment For Injuries," *Chicago Daily Tribune*, May 15, 1961, p. 1.

[28] Bryant, *The Bystander*, p. 263.

[29] "Bi-Racial Buses Attacked, Riders Beaten in Alabama," *New York Times*, May 15, 1961, p. 1.

passengers know that Birmingham Police Chief Eugene "Bull" Conner had made arrangements with the local Ku Klux Klan (KKK) to allow them at least 10 minutes to confront the bus riders before the police arrived, even though the police station was only two blocks away.[30]

While a Gallup poll showed only 24 percent of Americans approving the efforts of the freedom riders, the violence still horrified most.[31] A *Washington Post* editorial described the "Darkest Alabama" and claimed, "The plain fact is that Americans cannot be assured in Alabama of the equal protection of the laws guaranteed by the Fourteenth Amendment." The writer then added that black Americans "are quite justified … into looking to the United States Department of Justice for the protection of their rights as American citizens."[32] The Reverend Billy Graham lamented "I think it is deplorable when certain people in any society have been treated as second class citizens." He called for the prosecution of the attackers "to the full extent of the law."[33]

Farmer telegrammed the president and pleaded with him for the federal government to intervene and for the president to launch an investigation in Alabama since "white mobs over ruled the law of the land and desecrated the face of our nation before the world." He challenged the president to exert the "moral force" of his office and to speak forcefully against the violence.[34] After the crisis, Kennedy's Coordinator of Federal Civil Rights Policy, Harris Wofford, sent a memorandum to the president seeking more leadership. He explained the growing frustration in the black community with the administration's unwillingness "to say anything about the right of Americans to travel without discrimination." He encouraged Kennedy to speak out about the moral dimension of the crisis and explained, "How much good this kind of moral leadership can do is unknown—and cannot be known until it is tried. This seems to me to be the time to give it a try."[35]

Despite the urgings of those in and out of the government, Kennedy did not want to get involved. In fact, he was furious at the freedom riders for instigating a crisis. He asked Wofford, "Can't you get your … friends off

---

30 Bryant, *The Bystander*, pp. 263-64.
31 Dallek, *An Unfinished Life*, p. 384.
32 "Darkest Alabama," *The Washington Post and Times Herald*, May 16, 1961, p. A12.
33 John Wicklein, "Graham Deplores Alabama Bus Riot: Says Southerners Should Be Prosecuted in Beatings," *New York Times,* May 18, 1961, p. 27.
34 James Farmer to the President, May 15, 1961, John F. Kennedy Presidential Library, http://www.jfklibrary.org/Asset+Tree/Asset+Viewers/Image+Asset+Viewer.htm?guid={83B6CAA1-F101-4DB9-82F2-F1DD5E323AD0}&type=mpd&num=7, accessed on May 13, 2008.
35 Memorandum for the President (from Harris Wofford), May 29, 1961, JFKL, Kennedy Papers, President's Office Files, Staff Memos, Box 67, Folder – Wofford, Harris, 1961.

those buses?"[36] Because Kennedy believed the Constitution limited what he could do involving issues under a state's jurisdiction, he thought local police officials should deal with the crisis. Further, he wanted to focus his attention on upcoming trips to Canada and Europe where he would hold a summit with Soviet leader Nikita Khrushchev.[37] He relied heavily on his brother to resolve the crisis without his involvement. When the riders decided to abandon the rest of their trip and fly to New Orleans, Robert Kennedy was quite relieved, and he sent one of his assistants, John Seigenthaler, to Birmingham to escort the riders on their flight out of Alabama.[38]

The attorney general's relief was short-lived as another group of riders from the Student Nonviolent Coordinating Committee (SNCC) decided to renew the freedom ride from Birmingham. They planned go from Birmingham to Montgomery, Alabama then to Jackson, Mississippi, and finally to New Orleans. In the early morning on May 20, the new group climbed on the bus. Unbeknownst to the freedom riders, one of the biggest obstacles that morning was finding a bus driver. The scheduled one initially refused to risk his life, but later relented after Robert Kennedy pressured Greyhound executives to put a driver on the bus.[39] When the bus arrived in Montgomery, upward of a thousand angry whites attacked the riders.

Amidst screams of "get those niggers," chaos reigned around the bus terminal for at least ten minutes until the police arrived and continued sporadically afterwards. One group of white protestors threw a flammable liquid on one of the riders and lit it. The fire went out quickly, but the victim was badly burned. A group of women attacked two white women who had ridden in with the freedom riders with their purses and fists. When a white man tried to intervene to protect them, a group of men "attacked him, clubbed him to the ground, kicked him, and left him lying motionless and bloody on the ground." When the attorney general's aide, John Seigenthaler, tried to help some of the victims he was hit over the back of the head with a led pipe and knocked unconscious.[40]

The violence in Montgomery finally convinced the attorney general and, to a lesser extent the president, that they had to act. President Kennedy issued a short statement condemning the violence and urging restraint on both sides.

---

[36] Dallek, *An Unfinished Life*, p. 284.

[37] Mary L. Dudziak, *Cold War Civil Rights: Race and Image of American Democracy* (Princeton University Press, 2000), pp. 158-61.

[38] Bryant, *The Bystander*, p. 266.

[39] Ibid., p. 268.

[40] "Freedom Riders Attacked By Whites in Montgomery: President's Aide Hurt by Rioters," *New York Times*, May 21, 1961, p. 1.

While he called upon Alabama's local and state law enforcement officials "to exercise their lawful authority to prevent any further outbreaks of violence," he also asked that "any persons, whether a citizen of Alabama or a visitor there, would refrain from any action which would in any way tend to provoke further outbreaks."[41] Robert Kennedy had been much more shaken by the violence, especially against his aide, and ordered 400 federal marshals to go to Montgomery.[42] The attorney general wanted to avoid sending federal troops if at all possible.

The crisis in Montgomery threatened to explode into a full-scale confrontation as Martin Luther King came to the city to speak to a group of black leaders at the First Baptist Church. While officials from the Kennedy administration tried to dissuade him from going, they had little choice but to protect him. At the church on the evening of May 22, 100 marshals formed a cordon and faced close to 3,000 protestors. The protestors threw rocks, Molotov cocktails, and clubs at the marshals. Even after more marshals arrived, the protestors managed to break into the church before being driven back. At that moment the attorney general asked his brother for permission to send in federal troops. However, the president demurred, unsure whether he had the constitutional authority to do so. While the president deliberated, Alabama governor John Patterson declared martial law and sent in the Alabama National Guard to relieve the marshals. After spending a very uneasy night in the church, King and the rest of the people at the meeting quietly left the next morning.[43]

Only the final act of the May Freedom Rides remained. The Kennedys hoped that the rides were over as King and his supporters left the church. The attorney general claimed that "a cooling-off period" was needed "until the present state of confusion and danger" had passed.[44] Uriah Fields, the president of a group favoring integration in Montgomery, telegrammed Robert Kennedy and asked, "Isn't ninety-nine years long enough to cool off, Mr. Attorney General?"[45] James Farmer exclaimed, "Negroes have been cooling off for a hundred years" and would be "in a deep freeze if they cooled any further."[46] Rather than abide by the attorney general's request, twenty-seven

---

41 "Statement by the President Concerning Interference With the "Freedom Riders" in Alabama," May 20, 1961, *Public Papers of the Presidents, John F. Kennedy*, http://www.presidency.ucsb.edu/ws/?pid=8142, accessed on May 13, 2008.

42 Bryant, *The Bystander*, pp. 271-2.

43 Ibid., pp. 271-74.

44 "Attorney General's Pleas," *New York Times*, May 25, 1961, p. 25.

45 "Negroes to Continue." ibid., p. 25.

46 Quoted in Dallek, *An Unfinished Life*, p. 387.

freedom riders boarded two buses in Birmingham and rode to Jackson. In an effort to avoid further confrontations that no one wanted, Robert Kennedy opened negotiations with Alabama Governor Patterson and Mississippi Governor Ross Barnett to arrange safe passage for the riders. The governors agreed on the condition that the Jackson police could arrest the riders once they arrived. After the buses arrived in Jackson under heavy escort, the local police arrested the riders for "refusing to disperse" and put them in jail.[47]

The arrest of the freedom riders in Jackson brought some closure to this civil rights crisis. Some freedom rides continued through the rest of year, but the violence seen in Alabama was normally avoided. The Kennedy administration acted behind the scenes to desegregate interstate transportation and had the Interstate Commerce Commission issue a statement in September prohibiting segregation on buses engaged in interstate transportations and in terminals serving them. However, as he had been during most of the crisis over the Freedom rides in May, President Kennedy remained silent and relied on his brother to deal with civil rights concerns. Their relative silence and willingness to do only the perceived minimum in fighting discrimination angered civil rights leaders and heartened southern segregationists.[48]

While it took crises to often get the Kennedy administration's attention on civil rights, the president did make important decisions at other times that impacted black Americans. In February, he asked Congress to create new federal court judgeships to relieve the congestion in federal cases and over the next several months Congress deliberated.[49] During the heart of the confrontation over the freedom rides, Congress approved and Kennedy signed a judicial bill creating seventy-three new judgeships. He pledged at the signing ceremony to "choose men and women of unquestioned ability. I want for our courts individuals with respected professional skill, incorruptible character, firm judicial temperament, the rare inner quality to know when to temper justice with mercy, and the intellectual capacity to protect and illuminate the Constitution and our historic values in the context of a society experiencing profound and rapid change."[50] Since there were already twenty-two judicial vacancies, Kennedy now had the authority to appoint ninety-five judges.

[47] Bryant, *The Bystander*, pp. 276-78.
[48] Ibid., pp. 280-82.
[49] Letter to the President of the Senate and to the Speaker of the House Proposing Creation of Additional Federal Judgeships, Feb. 10, 1961, *Public Papers of the Presidents, John F. Kennedy*, http://www.presidency.ucsb.edu/ws/?pid=8233, accessed on May 14, 2008.
[50] Statement by the President Upon Signing Bill Providing for an Increase in the Federal Judiciary.

Unfortunately for the cause of civil rights, Kennedy did not always uphold the principles he had espoused. While he did appoint Thurgood Marshall to the Second Circuit Court of Appeals—only the second black American to serve at that high a level—his overall record for appointing judges sympathetic to civil rights was mixed at best. To get the 1961 judicial bill creating the new judgeships passed by Congress, Kennedy negotiated with Democratic Senator James Eastland from Mississippi who chaired the powerful Senate Judicial Committee. Without Eastland's support, it would have been difficult for any judicial appointment to survive in the Senate. In return for supporting the creation of the new judgeships, Eastland requested that he be consulted on appointments and the first judge to be appointed to be from Mississippi.[51] President Kennedy agreed and with his first appointment, he nominated William Harold Cox, Eastland's former college roommate and a leading segregationist, to a judgeship in Mississippi. Within a week of his appointment, Cox called several black litigants in his court "niggers", and his court became widely known for its racially charged atmosphere.[52] Over the next year, Kennedy put forward other segregationist judges including E. Gordon West, Robert Elliott, and Clarence Allgood.[53] Even Arthur Schlesinger, one of Kennedy's staunchest supporters, contends that "damage was done" to civil rights by these appointments.[54]

Inconsistent standards in appointing judges were not the only problem the Kennedy administration had. At a press conference on January 15, 1962, a reporter asked the president why he had not issued an executive order prohibiting racial segregation in federally assisted housing as he had pledged to do in the 1960 campaign. He claimed that he would issue the order when it was in the "public interest" and then argued that his "administration in the last 12 months made more progress in the field of civil rights on a whole variety of fronts than were made in the last 8 years." He concluded "we are proceeding ahead in a way which will maintain a consensus, and which will advance this cause."[55] The slow pace of change and Kennedy's reluctance to follow through

---

May 19, 1961, ibid., http://www.presidency.ucsb.edu/ws/?pid=8139, accessed on May 14, 2008.

51 David A. Nichols, *A Matter of Justice: Eisenhower and the Beginning of the Civil Rights Revolution* (New York: Simon & Schuster, 2007), pp. 266-67.

52 Giglio, *The Presidency of John F. Kennedy*, p. 43.

53 Bryant, *The Bystander*, pp. 286-87.

54 Arthur M. Schlesinger, Jr., *Robert Kennedy and His Times* (New York: Ballantine Books, 1978), p. 334.

55 The President's News Conference, Jan. 15, 1962, *Public Papers of the Presidents, John F. Kennedy*, http://www.presidency.ucsb.edu/ws/?pid=9093, accessed on May 20, 2008.

on his campaign pledge infuriated many. In late 1961, the White House began receiving parcels containing bottles of inks and pens reminding the president of his failure to fulfill his pledge.[56] Republican legislative leaders "chided" the administration's civil rights record.[57] Representative John Lindsay, the Republican representative from Manhattan and future mayor of New York City, wrote a letter to Kennedy complaining about his "abandonment of solemn pledges."[58] House Republican leader Charles Halleck later in the month accused the president of "employing sham tactics in an effort to cover Democratic shortcomings on the civil rights issue."[59] Later in the spring, Martin Luther King criticized Kennedy for his "failure to stand up vigorously" for the concerns of black Americans.[60]

Views of President Kennedy's civil rights record were not all negative and there was at least one positive achievement in the summer of 1962. The Southern Regional Council, a biracial group based in Atlanta, gave the president good marks in many areas and claimed 1961 was "a year of establishing a national mood and direction" and had "built momentum for civil rights in the structure and the policies of government."[61] The Kennedy administration also deserves credit for supporting a constitutional amendment banning the poll tax that Congress passed in August 1962.[62] However, there were more negatives than positives.

A racial standoff in Albany, Georgia dominated the civil rights movement in the summer of 1962. Martin Luther King and Ralph Abernathy stood trial on July 10 for leading a protest march the previous December. The presiding judge sentenced each man to spend 45 days in jail or pay a $178 fine. To emphasize the injustice of the sentence, King and Abernathy chose jail. The negative publicity generated by the imprisonment of the civil rights leaders horrified the president and Attorney General Robert Kennedy. They quietly arranged to have the fines paid and both leaders released from jail. However,

---

[56] Manfred Berg, "'Ink for Jack': John F. Kennedy and the Promise of Racial Liberalism," in Berg, and Etges, *John F. Kennedy and the 'Thousand Days'*, p. 221.

[57] Julius Duscha, "GOP Chides Kennedy on Civil Rights: Leaders Assert Schools Need Aid in Desegregation," *The Washington Post and Times Herald*, Jan. 15, 1962, p. A1.

[58] Anthony Lewis, "Kennedy Says Civil Rights Pace is Geared to National Opinion," *New York Times*, Jan. 16, 1962, p. 1.

[59] "Literacy Bill Sparks Early Senate Battle on Civil Rights Issue," *The Washington Post and Times Herald*, Jan. 31, 1962, p. A1.

[60] William M. Beecher, "Civil Rights Drive: Kennedy Plans a Series of Actions to Soothe Critics, Sway Voters," *Wall Street Journal*, May 10, 1962, p. 1.

[61] Claude Sitton, "Civil Rights Report Applauds Kennedy," *New York Times*, Mar. 26, 1962, p. 1.

the crisis did not end as the Albany City Commission still refused to meet with the protestors.[63] For the rest of the summer, the crisis simmered and President Kennedy received almost constant pleas to intervene. Roy Wilkins urged the president "to speak out in condemnation of the persecution in Albany."[64] Whitney Young called the Albany City Commission's actions "tragic" and "grossly repugnant to Americans everywhere."[65] While Kennedy did eventually speak out against the discrimination in Albany, civil rights activists were growing weary of the lack of executive action. As Robert Dallek explains "conditions in the South cried out not for prose but for action, and action now."[66]

The Kennedy administration faced an even more volatile crisis over civil rights in the fall of 1962 that *The Washington Post* called the "Greatest Test since Civil War."[67] Twenty-nine year old, James Meredith, a nine-year veteran in the Air Force, sued in January 1961 so that he could enroll at the University of Mississippi. The Supreme Court ultimately agreed with him in September 1962.[68] Mississippi Governor Ross Barnett and the Mississippi state legislature attempted to block his enrollment with the support of many southerners. Bumper stickers began showing up on cars in Mississippi castigating the Kennedys. One claimed, "THE CASTRO BROTHERS 'Have Moved Into the White House'," while another took a swipe at Robert Kennedy by asserting, "WE'RE BACKING ROSS: BEAT 'LIL' BROTHER."[69] Barnett delivered a state-wide radio and television address pledging to go to jail rather than enforce the Supreme Court ruling. "I now call," he announced, "on every public official and every private citizen of our great state to join with me in refusing, in every legal and constitutional manner available, to submit to

---

62 For a copy of the amendment, see http://www.archives.gov/exhibits/charters/constitution_amendments_11-27.html, access on May 20, 2008. In January 1964, the thirty-eighth state ratified the amendment and it became part of the constitution.

63 Bryant, *The Bystander*, pp. 315-24.

64 Roy Wilkins to the President, July 30, 1962, John F. Kennedy Presidential Library, http://www.jfklibrary.org/Asset+Tree/Asset+Viewers/Image+Asset+Viewer.htm?guid={3833512A-D34A-456F-B15B-076C65CB934F}&type=mpd&num=11, accessed on May 20, 2008.

65 Whitney M. Young to the President, Aug. 1, 1962, John F. Kennedy Presidential Library, http://www.jfklibrary.org/Asset+Tree/Asset+Viewers/Image+Asset+Viewer.htm?guid={35557BBF-90FA-400D-AF04-15CF90B67E88}&type=mpd&num=6, accessed on May 20, 2008.

66 Dallek, *An Unfinished Life*, p. 514.

67 James E. Clayton, "Greatest Test Since Civil War Takes Shape in Mississippi: News Analysis," *The Washington Post and Times Herald,* September 23, 1962, p. A7.

68 An excellent chronology of the issues and events surrounding Meredith's efforts to enter the University of Mississippi can be found at http://jfklibrary.org/meredith/chronfr.html, accessed on May 22, 2008.

69 Bumper Stickers from the Conflict, John F. Kennedy Presidential Library, http://jfklibrary.org/meredith/pubfr.html, accessed on May 22, 2008.

illegal usurpation of power by the Kennedy administration."[70] A few days later the Mississippi legislature passed a resolution supporting the governor.[71]

Both John and Robert Kennedy wanted to head off the crisis before it became another Little Rock. The attorney general tried to work with Barnett behind the scenes prior to the start of the fall semester on September 25. They spoke at least twenty times over a two week period in the latter part of September but came to no arrangement concerning how to admit Meredith without Barnett losing face.[72] Barnett told the attorney general on September 25 that he would not let Meredith into the University of Mississippi and "would rather spend the rest of my life in a penitentiary than do that."[73] The Kennedys looked at cutting off federal aid to the state since it received about twice as much federal money as its citizens paid in taxes, but Barnett still insisted that he would not "agree to let that boy get to Ole Miss."[74] The crisis escalated beginning on September 25 when Barnett personally barred Meredith from registering at the state office building in Jackson with protestors in the background yelling "Go Home Nigger."[75] The next day Meredith decided to register on-campus in Oxford and was escorted by a representative from the Justice Department and the chief U.S. marshal. Several blocks from the school, the state and local police along with the sheriff's office had established a road block under the supervision of Mississippi Lieutenant Governor Paul Johnson.[76] The lieutenant governor refused to allow them to pass and after some shoving between some U.S. marshals and Mississippi patrolmen, Meredith and his escort withdrew. Meredith tried to enroll again on September 27, but this time he was stopped by a mob of around 2,000 people even though Barnett had secretly made a deal to allow him to register for classes that day.[77] The presence of the mob thwarted that plan.[78]

As the crisis grew, President Kennedy decided he had to personally get involved. He still wanted to avoid sending federal troops or the National

---

[70] "Gov. Barnett Defies Order to Integrate." *Chicago Daily Tribune*, September 14, 1962, p. A3.

[71] "Legislature Backs Up Barnett: Robert Kennedy Calls Board Has Final Say," *The Washington Post and Times Herald,* September 19, 1962, p. A9.

[72] Dallek, *An Unfinished Life*, pp. 514-5.

[73] Schlesinger, *Robert Kennedy and His Times*, p. 342.

[74] Ibid., p. 515. For a description of the federal money that Mississippi received, see Memorandum for the President, Sept. 28, 1962, JFKL, Papers of Individuals and Organizations, Papers of Dave E. Bell, Box 16, Folder – Mississippi – 1962.

[75] Bryant, *The Bystander*, p. 334.

[76] Jonathan Rosenberg and Zachary Karabell, *Kennedy, Johnson, and the Quest for Justice: The Civil Rights Tapes* (New York: W.W. Norton & Company, 2003), pp. 34-35.

[77] "Miss. U. Bars Negro Again: Police Repulse U. S. Escort at Campus Gate," *Chicago Daily Tribune*, September 27, 1962, p. 1.

Guard if at possible. However, he was facing growing pressure to act. James Farmer wrote Kennedy on September 28 that it was "imperative that the insurrection of Governor Barnett and his cohorts be put down quickly, firmly, and decisively." He added, "We urge you personally to escort Meredith to his classes and thus demonstrate to the world that the American way of life means a life of justice, equality, and democracy for all."[79] Kennedy knew that if he did what Farmer asked, it would bring the full weight of southern racism against him. Alabama Governor John Patterson came out fully in support of Governor Barnett and Mississippi. He told the president that if sent federal troops to Mississippi, "your action would establish the Federal Government as a dictatorship of the foulest sort." He added, "If troops are sent to Mississippi, I ask you if you are prepared to invade Alabama? We stand united in this fight and we will resist all unlawful encroachments by the Federal Government."[80]

President Kennedy called Governor Barnett in an effort to negotiate an end to the standoff. Both men pleaded their cases with the other. Kennedy explained, "I didn't put him in the university, but on the other hand, under the Constitution … I have to carry out the orders, carry that order out."[81] Barnett responded, "You know what I am up against, Mr. President. I took an oath, you know, to abide by the laws of this state."[82] They continued their conversation briefly and the president assured the governor, "we don't want to have a lot of people getting hurt or killed down there."[83] They agreed to talk more later in the day after Barnett's assistant and the attorney general tried to work out a settlement to the crisis. They agreed to several different deals late on September 29 and early the next day only to see them fall through. Finally on September 30, they agreed to sneak Meredith onto campus later that day and Barnett would then issue a statement that he had resisted but had been tricked and now Meredith was already on campus.[84]

---

[78] Rosenberg and Karabell, *Kennedy, Johnson, and the Quest for Justice*, pp. 34-35.

[79] Roy Wilkins to the President, July 30, 1962, John F. Kennedy Presidential Library, http://www.jfklibrary.org/Asset+Tree/Asset+Viewers/Image+Asset+Viewer.htm?guid={3833 512A-D34A-456F-B15B-076C65CB934F}&type=mpd&num=11, accessed on May 20, 2008.

[79] James Farmer to the President, Sept. 28, 1962, John F. Kennedy Presidential Library, http://www.jfklibrary.org/Education+and+Public+Programs/For+Students/Materials+Resources+and+Activities+for+Students/Leaders+in+the+Struggle+for+Civil+Rights/James+Farmer.htm, accessed on May 20, 2008.

[80] "Kennedy Warned by Gov. Patterson: Alabaman Says Troops' Use in Mississippi Would Be 'Foulest Dictatorship'," *New York Times*, September 28, 1962, p. 1.

[81] Rosenberg and Karabell, *Kennedy, Johnson, and the Quest for Justice*, p. 36.

[82] Ibid., p. 38.

[83] Ibid., p. 39.

[84] Ibid., pp. 44-47.

Considering the collapse of other agreements, Kennedy had also begun preparations for intervening with military forces if necessary. He issued an executive order just after midnight on September 30 authorizing "the Secretary of Defense to call into the active military service of the United States … any or all of the units of the Army National Guard and of the Air National Guard of the State of Mississippi to serve in the active military service of the United States for an indefinite period."[85] He also sent troops from the 101st Airborne Division to a base near Memphis, Tennessee in case they were needed in Oxford.[86] He issued a second statement calling for all persons engaged in the obstruction of justice in Mississippi "to cease and desist".[87] Finally, he announced plans to speak to the nation that evening about the crisis.

The agreement with the governor unraveled soon after Meredith arrived on campus as a mob converged on Oxford to protest his presence. Rather than resolving the crisis, the behind-the-scenes deal had led to a very dangerous situation. Meredith was on campus but with only limited protection against a growing mob. About 500 federal marshals faced a mob of several thousand men and women who were yelling, carrying clubs and guns, and throwing rocks and Molotov cocktails.[88] The marshals guarded the Lyceum where Meredith was supposed to register the next day and Meredith who was in a nearby dormitory. The original plan called for the president to speak to the nation at 8:00 pm, but he delayed his speech to make sure that Meredith was safe and that Barnett was keeping his end of the agreement. He explained "We can't take a chance with Meredith's life or let [Barnett] make the Federal government look foolish."[89]

While the president waited, Barnett gave an impassioned speech where he castigated the Kennedys for sneaking Meredith on campus. He accused them of "trampling on the sovereignty of this great state and depriving it of every of vestige of honor and respect as a member of the union of states." He added "you are destroying the Constitution of this great nation." He then pledged to continue to fight the case in the courts to the bitter end. While blasting the

---

[85] Executive Order 11053, Sept. 30, 1962, *Public Papers of the Presidents, John F. Kennedy*, http://www.presidency.ucsb.edu/ws/index.php?pid=58992&st=&st1, accessed on May 21, 2008.

[86] "Call for Troops for Miss. U.: Federalize State's National Guard," *Chicago Daily Tribune*, September 30, 1962, p. 1.

[87] Proclamation 3497 Obstructions of Justice in the State of Mississippi, Sept. 30, 1962, *Public Papers of the Presidents, John F. Kennedy*, http://www.presidency.ucsb.edu/ws/?pid=24042, accessed on May 21, 2008.

[88] "2 Die, 75 Hurt in Miss. Riot: Marshalls Hurl Gas at Mob of Attackers," *Chicago Daily Tribune*, October 1, 1962, p. 1.

[89] Quoted in Bryant, *The Bystander*, p. 345.

Kennedys, he did call for his officials and the people of Mississippi "to preserve peace and avoid violence in any form."[90]

After Barnett's speech, Kennedy had his speech writers re-write his address and also waited to see how events on the ground were unfolding before he spoke to the nation. Tensions on the University of Mississippi were very high. The roughly 500 federal marshals on campus initially were supported by just over 200 Mississippi highway patrolmen. However, just before his speech Barnett ordered the patrolmen to withdraw. The marshals then faced an onslaught of verbal and physical abuse that only grew worse as the evening went on. The presence of the former commander of the 101st Airborne Division General Edwin Walker, who saw the Kennedys as waging a pro-communist crusade, only made matters worse. When he arrived in Oxford, he encouraged Americans to "rally to the cause of freedom in righteous indignation." He called the government's actions "a disgrace to the nation."[91] As the protestors confronted the federal marshals, he encouraged them to "keep it up!"[92]

As Kennedy finally began his address, he was unaware how bad the situation was on the ground. He was getting fairly constant reports of the growing tensions but the worst had not occurred by the time he went on the air. Kennedy's speech writers had built the speech around the concept of obeying the law. The president announced that "Americans are free … to disagree with the law but not to disobey it." He expressed deep regret that the federal government had to intervene, but noted that "all other avenues and alternatives, including persuasion and conciliation, had been tried and exhausted." He then attempted to shift the blame for the problems in race relations. "Neither Mississippi nor any other southern State deserves," Kennedy explained, "to be charged with all the accumulated wrongs of the last 100 years of race relations. To the extent that there has been failure, the responsibility for that failure must be shared by us all, by every State, by every citizen."[93] Never in the speech did Kennedy applaud Meredith's efforts or

---

90 "2 Die, 75 Hurt in Miss. Riot," p. 1.

91 "Walker Demands a 'Vocal Protest': Texan, in Mississippi, Hits Plan to Use U.S. Troops," *New York Times*, September 30, 1962, p. 69.

92 Claude Sitton, "Negro at Mississippi U. as Barnett Yields," ibid., October 1, 1962, p. 1. For Kennedy's reaction, see Rosenberg and Karabell, *Kennedy, Johnson, and the Quest for Justice*, p. 64.

93 Radio and Television Report to the Nation on the Situation at the University of Mississippi, Sept. 30, 1962, *Public Papers of the Presidents, John F. Kennedy*, http://www.presidency.ucsb.edu/ws/index.php?pid=8915&st=&st1, accessed on May 21, 2008.

even recognize his right to attend the University of Mississippi as a moral issue.

After the speech, Kennedy received reports that the situation in Oxford was deteriorating. In a series of conversations, the president and his advisors discussed how to handle the situation. By 11:00 pm they decided to order federal troops being held in reserve in Memphis to fly to Oxford to relieve the marshals. After some frustrating delays in getting the troops to Oxford, the first soldiers arrived to help the marshals around 12:30 am. Kennedy had another conversation with Barnett just after midnight where they again discussed how to end the crisis. As Robert Kennedy recalled, "We could just visualize another great disaster, like the Bay of Pigs, and a lot of marshals being killed or James Meredith being strung up."[94] Fortunately, things turned out better than this. The governor wanted the president to remove Meredith from the campus, and for the next several hours Kennedy considered how to do this. However, he insisted on having security on the ground before Meredith's status was even discussed. Kennedy stayed up until 5:30 am to make sure tensions were dying down before going to bed for a few hours.[95] As morning dawned in Oxford, 160 marshals had been injured, including 27 with gunshot wounds. Two bystanders had also been killed.[96]

On the morning of October 1, Meredith, with an escort of federal marshals, registered for courses and attended his first class. By the end of the day there were around 10,000 soldiers and federalized national guardsmen in Oxford and more nearby. On October 3, close to 10,000 soldiers remained and another 10,000 were within an hour's drive.[97] Federal troops remained in Oxford through the next summer although their numbers began to decline significantly by the middle of October.[98] Meredith stayed in school until he graduated in 1963.[99]

President Kennedy's handling of the crisis in Mississippi drew generally positive responses outside of the South, but even there, the response was mixed. He deserves credit for ultimately intervening in the crisis, sending in

---

[94] Quoted in Schlesinger, *Robert Kennedy and His Times*, p. 349.

[95] For transcripts of the conversations going on involving Kennedy and his advisors, see Rosenberg and Karabell, *Kennedy, Johnson, and the Quest for Justice*, pp. 50-81. See also Bryant, *The Bystander*, p. 348-50; Schlesinger, *Robert Kennedy and His Times*, p. 348; and Dallek, *An Unfinished Life*, pp. 516-17.

[96] Dallek, *An Unfinished Life*, pp. 516-517

[97] Memorandum for the President, Oct. 3, 1962, JFKL, Kennedy Papers, President's Office Files, Subjects, Box 96, Folder – Civil Rights-General, 1962.

[98] Bryant, *The Bystander*, p. 351.

[99] Schlesinger, *Robert Kennedy and His Times*, p. 349.

federal troops when necessary, and getting Meredith registered for classes. However, he also made the situation potentially worse by trying to deal with Barnett behind the scenes and never truly appreciating the stance Meredith was taking. He couched the federal intervention in legal terms and did not take the opportunity to make a strong commitment to the morality of civil rights as he promised in his campaign. Further, after the crisis died down, "Kennedy showed no more enthusiasm for federal action on civil rights than he had earlier in his presidency."[100] Many black leaders noted the lack of true concern from the president. Martin Luther King later said that the president's dealings with Barnett "made Negroes feel like pawns in a white man's political game."[101]

In the months after the Mississippi crisis, the civil rights movement saw some limited advances but also a growing sense of frustration at the slow pace of change. President Kennedy sensed no reason to move any faster on civil rights as he was still overwhelmingly popular with 62 percent of Americans approving his job as president a little over a week after Meredith registered. While this was lower than his 77 percent approval at the beginning of the year, it was still a very high rating.[102] Further, the pace of integration divided Americans. In May 1962, 35 percent believed the pace was about right, 32 percent thought it was too fast, and 11 percent viewed it as not fast enough. The figures did not change much over the next year. Among black Americans, 48 percent believed the pace of integration was about right in May 1962, while only 31 percent thought it was too slow.[103] Without a true commitment from most Americans to advance civil rights at a quicker pace, Kennedy was not willing to try to lead the nation in a new direction on the issue. As Bayard Rustin, one of the founders of CORE, remarked "anything we got out of Kennedy came out of the objective situation and the political necessity, and not out of the spirit of John Kennedy. He was a reactor."[104]

Kennedy's decision to finally sign an executive order outlawing discrimination in federal housing reflected his approach to maintaining what he had earlier called a national consensus. On November 20, 1962, Kennedy issued the executive order guaranteeing equal opportunity in federal housing

---

100 Rosenberg and Karabell, *Kennedy, Johnson, and the Quest for Justice*, p. 84. See also Bryant, *The Bystander*, pp. 353-56; and Dallek, *An Unfinished Life*, p. 518.

101 Schlesinger, *Robert Kennedy and His Times*, p. 351.

102 Hazel Gaudet Erskine, "The Polls: Kennedy as President," *The Public Opinion Quarterly* 28:2 (Summer 1964), p. 334.

103 Ibid., p. 339.

104 Quoted in Dallek, *An Unfinished Life*, p. 381.

that he had promised two years prior in the presidential campaign.[105] Despite the efforts of some within his administration and the chiding of many civil rights leaders, he had equivocated to this point.[106] While acclaimed by Martin Luther King, who called it a "courageous action,"[107] the executive order really was not. When asked why he had waited so long, the president responded, "I said that I would issue it at the time when I thought it was in the public interest, and now is the time."[108] It is unclear why exactly he chose this time, but it was probably because it was after the 1962 midterm elections and at a time when most people were focused on the upcoming holiday and not on news coming out of Washington.

The housing order was a definite step forward, but it did not provide any real immediate assistance. Tensions still simmered and occasionally boiled over. In mid-December, someone threw a bomb at a black church in Birmingham that injured two children.[109] King telegraphed Kennedy, "a virtual reign of terror is still alive in Birmingham, Alabama. … If such acts of violence go unchecked and the Gestapo like methods of police officials not halted, we may see in this city a tragic and devastating racial holocaust." He then called for more direct leadership.[110] However, no new direction or comments came from the White House. In fact, the only mention of civil rights that came up in a major radio and television interview with the president on December 17 was the crisis over James Meredith's admission to the University of Mississippi.[111]

---

105 Executive Order – Equal Opportunity in Housing, JFKL, Kennedy Papers, Presidential Papers, White House Staff Files, Lee C. White File, Civil Rights File, Box 21, Folder – Housing-Executive Order Background, 9/10/62-11/20/62.

106 Harris Wofford, *Of Kennedys & Kings: Making Sense of the Sixties* (University of Pittsburgh Press, 1992), pp. 124-25.

107 Martin Luther King, Jr. to The President, Nov. 20, 1962, John F. Kennedy Presidential Library, http://www.jfklibrary.org/Asset+Tree/Asset+Viewers/Image+Asset+Viewer.htm?guid={58337A97-5722-4613-BAC9-E5422945B297}&type=mpd&num=5, accessed on May 22, 2008.

108 The President's News Conference, Nov. 20, 1962, *Public Papers of the Presidents, John F. Kennedy*, http://www.presidency.ucsb.edu/ws/index.php?pid=9020&st=&st1, accessed on May 22, 2008.

109 "Bomb Negro Church; 2 Are Injured," *Chicago Daily Tribune*, Dec. 15, 1962, accessed on May 22, 2008.

110 Martin Luther King, Jr. to The President, Dec. 15, 1962, http://www.jfklibrary.org/Asset+Tree/Asset+Viewers/Image+Asset+Viewer.htm?guid={58337A97-5722-4613-BAC9-E5422945B297}&type=mpd&num=6

111 Television and Radio Interview: "After Two Years - a Conversation With the President", Dec. 17, 1962, *Public Papers of the Presidents, John F. Kennedy*, http://www.presidency.ucsb.edu/ws/index.php?pid=9060&st=&st1, accessed on May 22, 2008.

1963 was a special year in the history of the civil rights movement as it marked the 100th anniversary of Abraham Lincoln's Emancipation Proclamation. After receiving a report from the Commission on Civil Rights explaining that while many advances had been made, citizenship had not been "fully realized for the American Negro,"[112] Kennedy announced, "it must be our purpose to continue steady progress until the promise of equal rights for all has been fulfilled."[113] Kennedy asserted himself a little more at the end of February when he delivered his first message to Congress specifically on civil rights. He told Congress that despite progress over the past 100 years, "the harmful, wasteful and wrongful results of racial discrimination and segregation still appear in virtually every aspect of national life, in virtually every part of the Nation." He then stressed the importance of guaranteeing the right to vote, desegregating public schools, extending the Commission on Civil Rights, prohibiting discrimination in employment, and ending discrimination in public accommodations.[114] This powerful and moving speech seemed to note a change in the administration's approach to civil rights, but again the rhetoric proved much stronger than any actions.

Appeals for action came from across the country in March for the president to do more for black Americans. The president had previously encouraged the appointment of more black Americans to policy level positions in his administration. By March 1963, one of his special assistants, Ralph Dungan, told the president that the administration had not made much progress. Part of the problem was the difficulty in finding qualified candidates, but a larger issue was "the lack of personal attention if not indifference of certain departments and agency heads to this problem." He concluded that "in view of the lack of interest and foot-dragging demonstrated thus far …, it is apparent that it will take strong and vigorous efforts to overcome the inertia in certain agencies."[115] Roy Wilkins wrote Kennedy a few weeks later decrying the discrimination faced by black Americans around Cape Canaveral, Florida. He noted "there is a particular irony when the soaring aspirations exemplified

---

112 Carroll Kilpatrick, "Rights Fight at Peak, Is Report to Kennedy," *The Washington Post and Times Herald,* February 13, 1963, p. A1.

113 Remarks Upon Receiving Civil Rights Commission Report "Freedom to the Free," Feb. 12, 1963, *Public Papers of the Presidents, John F. Kennedy*, http://www.presidency.ucsb.edu/ws/index.php?pid=9060&st=&st1, accessed on May 22, 2008.

114 Special Message to the Congress on Civil Rights, Feb. 28, 1963, ibid., http://www.presidency.ucsb.edu/ws/index.php?pid=9581&st=&st1, accessed on May 22, 2008.

115 Memorandum for the President, Mar. 4, 1963, JFKL, Kennedy Papers, President's Office Files, Subjects, Box 97, Folder – Civil Rights-General, 1/1/63-6/4/63.

in the United States government's programs for probing the far reaches of space are contrasted with the harsh reality faced by Negros who are contributing to those programs.... There is a sharp contrast between the world leadership we seek in space achievement and the handicaps resulting from job discrimination."[116] By the end of month, both King and A. Philip Randolph were asking the president to stop the violence in Greenwood, Mississippi where segregationists were assaulting civil rights protestors. King asked Kennedy "to personally intervene" and offered a veiled threat about the future. "In spite of our persistant [sic] council for the people to remain nonviolent," King explained, "I fear that if something is not done immediately to relieve this situation, a night will soon come darker than that night in Oxford."[117]

A flare up of violence soon overshadowed these issues and dominated the civil rights movement well into the summer. King and his advisers decided in the aftermath of the Mississippi crisis in late 1962 and early 1963 that the only way to get Kennedy to act was to give him no choice. One of King's assistants explained, "We've got to have a crisis to bargain with. ... To take a moderate approach hoping to get white help doesn't help. They nail you to the cross, and it saps the enthusiasm of the followers. You've got to have a crisis."[118] King and the Southern Christian Leadership Conference (SCLC) decided that Birmingham would be the perfect place to have a crisis. They knew that Birmingham's police commissioner, Eugene "Bull" Conner, was a noted racist and would resist any efforts to integrate the city.[119] Recently, Conner had promised, "We're not going to have white folks and nigras segregatin' together in this man's town."[120] King and the SCLC organized Project C, with the C standing for confrontation, in an effort to challenge the widespread racial discrimination in Birmingham and to spur the president to action. The protests began with sit-down protests at local restaurants on April 3 and grew into small marches over the next several days. Conner arrested the marchers and

---

[116] Roy Wilkins to John F. Kennedy, Mar. 18, 1963, John F. Kennedy Presidential Library, http://www.jfklibrary.org/Asset+Tree/Asset+Viewers/Image+Asset+Viewer.htm?guid={3833 512A-D34A-456F-B15B-076C65CB934F}&type=mpd&num=12, accessed on May 22, 2008.

[117] Martin Luther King, Jr. to John F. Kennedy, Mar. 28, 1963, JFKL, http://www.jfklibrary.org/Asset+Tree/Asset+Viewers/Image+Asset+Viewer.htm?guid={5833 7A97-5722-4613-BAC9-E5422945B297}&type=mpd&num=7, accessed on May 22, 2008. For A. Philip Randolph's request to the president, A. Philip Randolph to the President, Mar. 27, 1963, ibid., http://www.jfklibrary.org/Asset+Tree/Asset+Viewers/Image+Asset+Viewer.htm?guid={EFEE62B7-3B32-43F2-86CE-247673E440A9}&type=mpd&num=6, accessed on May 22, 2008.

[118] Quoted in Harvard Sitkoff, *The Struggle for Black Equality* Revised Ed. (New York: Hill and Wang, 1993), p. 120.

[119] Dallek, *An Unfinished Life*, p. 594.

even used the police dogs to disperse onlookers. By the middle April, King and many other activists had been arrested and were being held in the Birmingham jail.[121]

King took the opportunity while in jail to write his now famous, "Letter from Birmingham." He wrote his letter after reading an article about white clergymen who were criticizing his position. He told his readers that he was "in Birmingham because injustice is here" and stressed "Injustice anywhere is a threat to justice everywhere." To those who criticized his actions, he and his followers "had no alternative except to prepare for direct action, whereby we would present our very bodies as a means of laying our case before the conscience of the local and the national community." In a jab at the Kennedy's, he asserted, "I have been gravely disappointed with the white moderate ...who is more devoted to 'order' than to justice" and "who constantly advises the Negro to wait for a "more convenient season."[122] While not because of the letter, Kennedy did pressure officials in Birmingham to release King from jail hoping that would settle the crisis.[123]

King and his supporters continued their efforts the rest of April and on May 2 instituted a new and controversial tactic, a children's protest march. Several thousand children met at a local church before leaving in groups of 10 to 50 to march in different parts of the city. Conner did not know how react initially, but by the end of the day his forces had arrested several hundred of them.[124] The next day was one of the most important days of the entire movement. Children and adult protestors headed to the streets again, and Conner finally lost almost all restraint. He unleashed the police dogs which savagely attacked several protestors. He told one of his police officers, "I want them to see the dogs work. Look at those niggers run."[125] He also ordered the fire department to use water from fire hoses to disperse the marchers. The water "bowled over the marchers and sent several sprawling across the

---

120 Quoted in Sitkoff, *The Struggle for Black Equality*, p. 121.

121 Rosenberg and Karabell, *Kennedy, Johnson, and the Quest for Justice*, pp. 87-90.

122 Letter from Birmingham Jail, in David Howard-Pitney, *Martin Luther King, Jr., Malcolm X, and the Civil Rights Struggles of the 1950s and 1960s: A Brief History with Documents* (Boston: Bedford/St. Martin's, 2004), pp. 75-82.

123 Rosenberg and Karabell, *Kennedy, Johnson, and the Quest for Justice*, p. 90.

124 "750 Arrested in Alabama Race March," *Chicago Daily Tribune*, May 3, 1963, p. 1.

125 "Fire Hoses and Police Dogs Quell Birmingham Segregation Protest," *The Washington Post and Times Herald*, May 4, 1963, p. A1.

pavement." One policeman even used his motorcycle to catch up with some of the marchers and beat them with his nightstick.[126]

James Farmer sent the president a telegram warning him that "Alabama now rivals racist police state of South Africa."[127] For once, Kennedy did not need any encouragement. He saw the pictures in the newspapers and was horrified. After seeing a picture of a police dog biting a black man, Kennedy exclaimed – "I think it is terrible the picture in the paper. ... Birmingham is the worst city in the south. They have done nothing for the Negroes in that community, so it is an intolerable situation."[128] Unfortunately, things did not approve for several more days. While Kennedy sent Burke Marshall to try to mediate the crisis, the protestors continued to march and Conner continued to respond. On May 7, one of King's key allies, Rev. Fred Shuttlesworth, was blasted by the water from a fire hose against a brick building. Conner laughed after hearing of Shuttlesworth's injuries and said, "I wish they'd carried him away in a hearse."[129]

President Kennedy faced growing pressure to intervene. Farmer expressed his frustrations in a telegram to Kennedy:

> "Tactics of Birmingham Police appear to be aimed at intentionally provoking wide scale violence. There can be no truce with police brutality and police lawlessness such as we witness in Birmingham. Even if guns of Alabama succeed in quelling the nonviolent struggle in Birmingham, it will rise up again in place after place until such time as the president of the United States overcomes his fear of speaking out and decides to act forcefully to secure freedom of Negro Americans."[130]

Civil Rights commissioner Erwin Griswold argued that the president "hasn't even started to use the powers that are available to him."[131] Kennedy did not

---

[126] "Dogs and Fire Hoses Turned on Negroes: Marchers Sent Sprawling Fire Hoses and Dogs Halt Birmingham Negro March Protesting Segregation," *Chicago Daily Tribune*, May 4, 1963, p. N1.

[127] James Farmer to The President, May 3, 1963, JFKL, http://www.jfklibrary.org/Asset+Tree/Asset+Viewers/Image+Asset+Viewer.htm?guid={83B6CAA1-F101-4DB9-82F2-F1DD5E323AD0}&type=mpd&num=12

[128] "Tape Reveals JFK's Frustration on Civil Rights Progress," May 4, 1963, JFKL, http://www.jfklibrary.org/JFK+Library+and+Museum/News+and+Press/Tape+Reveals+JFKs+Frustration+on+Civil+Rights+Progress.htm

[129] Sitkoff, *The Struggle for Black Equality*, p. 131.

[130] James Farmer to the President, May 8, 1963, JFKL, http://www.jfklibrary.org/Asset+Tree/Asset+Viewers/Image+Asset+Viewer.htm?guid={83B6CAA1-F101-4DB9-82F2-F1DD5E323AD0}&type=mpd&num=13, accessed on May 23, 2008.

[131] Quoted in Dallek, *An Unfinished Life*, p. 595.

appreciate the criticism as he was considering a range of alternatives for dealing with the crisis but believed his options were limited in what he saw as a state and local issue.[132] He did send Marshall to negotiate behind the scenes with some Birmingham officials negotiated to bring the stand-off to a close. They emerged with an agreement on May 10. City officials agreed to the desegregation of lunch counters and restrooms, provide better job opportunities for black Americans, and form a biracial committee to study race relations.[133]

Unfortunately, Conner and some other Birmingham officials did not agree, and the sense of peace that initially resulted from the agreement fell to the wayside. On May 11, the KKK held a rally in support of Conner, and bombs exploded at Martin Luther King's brother's house and at the hotel where many civil rights activists stayed. Many young blacks began rioting and for four hours fighting raged on Birmingham's streets. The *New York Times* reported that "Showers of gravel, bottles, rocks, and bricks struck police cruisers" as many blacks released pent up anger from their earlier abuse.[134] The escalation of the violence shocked King and the Kennedys, and they all sought ways to bring it to an end.

Kennedy met with his brother, Marshall, and several others late in the afternoon on May 12 to determine how they should handle the resurgence of violence that had occurred the night before. They faced the dilemma that there were many groups and individuals involved with different agendas. Many Birmingham business leaders supported the earlier agreement with King, but there were others like Conner and the KKK that opposed it. Further, while King continued to preach the use of non-violent tactics, a growing number of black Americans were growing frustrated with the pace of change and wanted to openly resist. Finally, Kennedy still feared that he might be overstepping federal authority by intervening in a local and state crisis. After considerable deliberation, the president decided he had little choice but to intervene but to shape it in a way that would minimize the concerns of those who viewed this as a state's rights issue.[135]

Kennedy issued a statement decrying the violence from the night before. He highlighted how the bombings had instigated the rioting and condemned

---

132 Memorandum for the President, May 7, 1963, JFKL, Kennedy Papers, President's Office Files, Staff Memos, Box 66A, Folder – Sorensen, Theodore, 1962-1963.

133 Sitkoff, *The Struggle for Black Equality*, p. 131.

134 Hedrick Smith, "Bombs Touch Off Widespread Riot at Birmingham: Negroes Attack Police After Blasts Rip Home of King's Brother and a Motel," *New York Times*, May 12, 1963, p. 1.

135 Rosenberg and Karabell, *Kennedy, Johnson, and the Quest for Justice*, pp. 99-104.

the efforts "by a few extremists" who saw themselves as above the law. He then called upon Birmingham's citizens "to live up to the standards their responsible leaders set last week ... and to realize that violence only breeds more violence." To insure order, he sent Marshall back to Birmingham to facilitate negotiations, put military forces specially trained in riot control on alert and moved some near Birmingham, and took steps to nationalize the Alabama National Guard. He concluded by expressing hope that local officials and citizens could "maintain standards of responsible conduct" so that further federal action would be unnecessary.[136]

The president's efforts along with those of many others on the ground helped bring the immediate violence to a close. Alabama Governor George Wallace did posture some claiming that the president's actions violated the Constitution.[137] An upcoming visit to Alabama also raised some concerns as there were some fears that Wallace might institute a suit against Kennedy and issue a summons for his arrest.[138] In the end, nothing came from the threats. In fact, Kennedy visited Alabama on May 18 to celebrate the thirtieth anniversary of the Tennessee Valley Authority and flew with Wallace to Huntsville. During their flight, they discussed the Birmingham situation. Wallace insisted that local and state officials could maintain the peace, while Kennedy insisted that there would have to be positive changes for black Americans to truly see improvements. Wallace did blame King for most of the tensions and denigrated his character.[139]

The Birmingham crisis had a tremendous influence on Kennedy.[140] While still reluctant to forcefully intervene, the president began to speak more openly in support of civil rights. He told graduates at Vanderbilt University that the determination of any oppressed group "to secure these rights is in the highest traditions of American freedom." He added that "any educated citizen who seeks to subvert the law, to suppress freedom, or to subject other human beings to acts that are less than human, degrades his heritage, ignores his

[136] Statement by the President, May 12, 1963, JFKL, Kennedy Papers, Presidential Papers, White House Staff Files, Lee C. White File, Box 19, Folder – Alabama 5/2/63-10/9/63.

[137] Governor George Wallace to The President, May 13, 1963, ibid., President's Office Files, Subjects, Box 96, Folder – Civil Rights Alabama 5/12/63-5/14/63.

[138] Memorandum for the Honorable Lee C. White, May, 17, 1963, ibid., Presidential Papers, White House Staff Files, Lee C. White File, Box 19, Folder – Alabama 5/2/63-10/9/63.

[139] Memorandum of Conversation, May 18, 1963, JFKL, Kennedy Papers, President's Office Files, Subjects, Box 96, Folder – Civil Rights Alabama 5/12/63-5/14/63.

[140] Shank, *Presidential Policy Leadership*, p. 200.

learning, and betrays his obligation."[141] At a news conference a few days later, he noted that the administration was considering submitting new civil rights legislation to Congress so that those who were "denied equal rights, would have a remedy."[142] He still was not moving as quickly as many civil rights advocates wanted. As one black man in a political cartoon noted while standing outside the president's office, "Please Remind Him That We've Been Waiting a Long Time."[143]

On June 11, he delivered a radio and television address announcing that he would be submitting new civil rights legislation to Congress to address discrimination in public accommodations. Kennedy explained to the American public,

> "We are confronted primarily with a moral issue. It is as old as the scriptures and is as clear as the American Constitution.
>
> The heart of the question is whether all Americans are to be afforded equal rights and equal opportunities, whether we are going to treat our fellow Americans as we want to be treated. If an American, because his skin is dark, cannot eat lunch in a restaurant open to the public, if he cannot send his children to the best public school available, if he cannot vote for the public officials who will represent him, if, in short, he cannot enjoy the full and free life which all of us want, then who among us would be content to have the color of his skin changed and stand in his place? Who among us would then be content with the counsels of patience and delay?
>
> One hundred years of delay have passed since President Lincoln freed the slaves, yet their heirs, their grandsons, are not fully free. They are not yet freed from the bonds of injustice. They are not yet freed from social and economic oppression. And this Nation, for all its hopes and all its boasts, will not be fully free until all its citizens are free. …
>
> Now the time has come for this Nation to fulfill its promise. The events in Birmingham and elsewhere have so increased the cries for equality that no city or State or legislative body can prudently choose to ignore them. …

---

141 Remarks in Nashville at the 90th Anniversary Convocation of Vanderbilt University, May 18, 1963, *Public Papers of the Presidents, John F. Kennedy*, http://www.presidency.ucsb.edu/ws/?pid=9218, accessed on May 23, 2008.

142 The President's News Conference, May 22, 1963, ibid., http://www.presidency.ucsb.edu/ws/?pid=9233, accessed on May 23, 2008.

143 William H. Stringer, "State of the Nations: The President and Racial Issue," *Christian Science Monitor*, June 6, 1963, p. 1.

> I am, therefore, asking the Congress to enact legislation giving all Americans the right to be served in facilities which are open to the public--hotels, restaurants, theaters, retail stores, and similar establishments."[144]

Both Martin Luther King and Jackie Robinson lauded the president's speech and the upcoming civil rights legislation. Having previously been an outspoken critic of the president, Robinson announced that he would now support the president as "Kennedy's statement may well have stopped Americans from heading for cooperative suicide."[145] King congratulated Kennedy and claimed his speech "was one of the most eloquent, profound, and unequivocal pleas for justice and the freedom of all men ever made by any president."[146] One historian with a generally negative view of how the president handled civil rights called it "the most courageous of Kennedy's presidency."[147]

A little over a week later and after intense negotiations with both Republicans and members of his own party, and continued racial strife in different parts of the country, Kennedy called on Congress to pass new civil rights legislation because "persisting inequalities and tensions make it clear that Federal action must lead the way, providing both the Nation's standard and a nationwide solution." He continued "in too many communities, in too many parts of the country, wrongs are inflicted on Negro citizens for which no effective remedy at law is clearly and readily available." Kennedy warned Congress, "the result of continued Federal legislative inaction will be continued, if not increased, racial strife--causing the leadership on both sides to pass from the hands of reasonable and responsible men to the purveyors of hate and violence, endangering domestic tranquility, retarding our Nation's economic and social progress and weakening the respect with which the rest of the world regards us." He then requested that Congress guarantee equal accommodations to public facilities, take decisive action in support of desegregating schools, and support fair and full employment opportunities. He concluded by reminding the senators and congressmen that "racial injustices

---

[144] John F. Kennedy, "Radio and Television Report to the American People on Civil Rights," June, 11, 1963, http://www.jfklibrary.org/Historical+Resources/Archives/Reference+Desk/Speeches/JFK/003POF03CivilRights06111963.htm, accessed on December 9, 2008.

[145] "Jackie Robinson Says He Would Cast His Ballot for Kennedy," JFKL, Kennedy Papers, President's Office Files, Subjects, Box 97, Folder – Civil Rights General, 6/5/63-6/13/63.

[146] Martin Luther King, Jr. to The President, June 11, 1963, http://www.jfklibrary.org/Asset+Tree/Asset+Viewers/Image+Asset+Viewer.htm?guid={58337A97-5722-4613-BAC9-E5422945B297}&type=mpd&num=13, accessed on December 9, 2008.

[147] Bryant, *The Bystander*, p. 423.

are real" and without significant progress the violence of recent months would only get worse.[148]

With legislation now before Congress, Kennedy hoped the civil rights' debates would quiet down so that he could focus on other issues. They did not. He met with black civil rights leaders on June 22 to discuss the civil rights legislation and to try to dissuade them from holding a planned march in Washington, D.C. at the end of August. The president feared the march could turn violent and that it might also anger congressmen and senators who otherwise might support the legislation. The president relented after King and others remained adamant that the march would go on.[149] His legislation also ran into problems or as the *Wall Street Journal* put it, "Civil Rights Push, Rebellious Congress Bedevil Kennedy Plans."[150] Even after the March on D.C. took place on August 28 without a hitch and King delivered his eloquent "I Have A Dream" speech, the legislation remained stuck in Congress. A. Philip Randolph told the president "it's going to take nothing less than a crusade to win approval for these civil rights measures…. And if it is going to be a crusade, I think that nobody can lead this crusade but you."[151]

Kennedy had shown he was not a crusader for civil rights throughout his presidency and even his new commitment over the previous few months did not mark that type of leadership. After a bomb killed four black children and the murder of two others in Birmingham in mid-September, Kennedy condemned the murderers but ultimately decided that local officials in Birmingham could handle the situation without federal intervention.[152] He did not want federal action at this stage of the legislative process. To keep that process going, he did continue to work with Congress in the fall to get the civil rights legislation passed, but not with a great deal of force.[153] He even decided that a weaker bill was better than no bill at all. However, by mid-November he had to admit that Congress would not pass any civil rights legislation in

148 Special Message to the Congress on Civil Rights and Job Opportunities, June 19, 1963, *Public Papers of the Presidents, John F. Kennedy*, http://www.presidency.ucsb.edu/ws/?pid=9283, accessed on May 23, 2008.

149 Marjorie Hunter, "Negroes Inform Kennedy of Plan for New Protests: Demonstrations Needed to Assure Civil Rights Law, Leaders Say at Parley," *New York Times*, June 23, 1963, p. 1.

150 Jerry Landauer, "Civil Rights Push, Rebellious Congress Bedevil Kennedy Plans," *Wall Street Journal*, July, 9, 1963, p. 1.

151 Rosenberg and Karabell, *Kennedy, Johnson, and the Quest for Justice*, p. 140.

152 Tom Wicker, "Kennedy Says Birmingham Can Solve Own Problems: After Meeting 5 White Civic Leaders, He Asserts Officials Can Work at the Local Level With Team He Is Sending," *New York Times*, September 24, 1963, p. 1.

1963.[154] Kennedy's assassination just a few days later precludes knowing exactly how the civil rights legislation would have turned out. However, under Lyndon Johnson's leadership, Kennedy's civil rights bill became a reality the following summer and a major step was taken to end racial inequality in the country.[155]

President Kennedy left a mixed legacy on civil rights. He was not a strong leader on civil rights through most of his legislative career and that carried over into his presidency. Ultimately, however, events outside of his control forced his hand and led him to assert a leadership role that he had refused to take previously. While never to the satisfaction of most civil rights supporters, Kennedy's leadership in the summer and fall of 1963 helped lead to fundamental advances for black Americans through the eventual passage of the 1964 Civil Rights Act and the 1965 Voting Rights Act. His leadership late in his administration should not overshadow his lack of commitment to civil rights through most of his presidency.[156] Many reasons help explain his limited leadership on civil rights including the fact that more important issues, at least in his mind, often dominated his attention, particularly those related to the Cold War. Furthermore, he did not want to "rock the boat" as he announced in early 1962 that he would pursue policies that "will maintain a consensus."[157] Finally, he believed in a limited federal role in local and state issues. His brother captured this best in a memorandum to the president where he stated that "We know that you feel strongly that these matters [civil rights issues] should be resolved at the local and state level and the Federal Government should intervene only if all other efforts have failed."[158]

Overall, Kennedy's unwillingness to keep his campaign promises and take a leadership role on civil rights throughout his administration reflects poorly on his presidency. However, his efforts over the last six months of his life do seem to reflect a new and truer commitment to achieve positive change for

---

[153] Anthony Lewis, "President Joins Drive to Soften Civil Rights Bill: Meets House Leaders and Wins Delay in Vote, but Gets No Commitment," ibid., October 24, 1963, p. 1.

[154] For an excellent description of Kennedy's efforts, including transcripts of some of the president's conversations, see Rosenberg and Karabell, *Kennedy, Johnson, and the Quest for Justice*, pp. 174-93.

[155] For a description of the debates surrounding the passage of the 1964, see ibid., pp. 194-331.

[156] Berg, "'Ink for Jack'", p. 240.

[157] Anthony Lewis, "Kennedy Says Civil Rights Pace Is Geared to National Opinion," *New York Times*, Jan. 16, 1962, p. 1.

[158] Report of the Attorney General to the President on the Department of Justice's Activities in the Field of Civil Rights, Dec. 29, 1961, JFKL, Kennedy Papers, Presidential Papers, White House Staff Files, Meyer Feldman File, General File, Box 5, Folder – Civil Rights, 10/60-1/61.

black Americans. Without his efforts in 1963, the racial strife seen in Birmingham and elsewhere would have intensified more quickly and dangerously than it actually did, and black Americans' desires for equality would have been delayed even longer. For his leadership and efforts at this time, he deserves a lot of credit.

Chapter 7

CUBAN MISSILE CRISIS

One of the tensest moments of the Cuban Missile Crisis was only known to a few men until the early part of the 21st century. Surprisingly, these men did not include the well-known players like Kennedy, Khrushchev, or McNamara, but rather, a few officers on a Soviet submarine. During the crisis, U.S. destroyers tracked Soviet diesel-powered submarines in the Caribbean, and on at least two occasions, they forced them to the surface using so-called practice depth charges. Unbeknownst to the U.S. commanders each of these submarines carried one torpedo armed with a nuclear warhead. As a Soviet submarine, the B-59, struggled underwater to elude an American destroyer, its batteries began to run out, and its crew became very tense. Its commanding officer, Captain Valentin Savitsky, was nearly exhausted and furious at the Americans. As the American practice depth charges exploded nearby, he supposedly yelled, "We're going to blast them now! We will die, but we will sink them all." His second in command calmed him down, but the world had come to the brink of war that would have been initiated by two captains out of touch with their respective commanders.[1]

The key question is how did the United States and Soviet Union get into such a dire situation? The answer is complex and in many ways remains incomplete. Formerly classified documents from the United States and the Soviet Union are generally available, but only a few documents from the Cuban regime are. However, it is clear that Kennedy, Khrushchev, and Castro

---

[1] "The Submarines of October: U.S. and Soviet Naval Encounters During the Cuban Missile Crisis", National Security Archive Electronic Briefing Book No. 75, October 31, 2002, The National Security Archive, http://www.gwu.edu/~nsarchiv/NSAEBB/NSAEBB75/#3, accessed on May 26, 2008.

all played significant roles. Several different problems came together to precipitate the crisis. As detailed earlier, the United States had been opposed to Castro's emergence as the leader of Cuba since late 1959 and first under Eisenhower and then under Kennedy had devised plans to remove him. The Bay of Pigs debacle, in particular, had several long-term effects. Kennedy and his brother, Robert, became obsessed with Cuba and were willing to support almost any measure to remove Castro.[2] The Cuban leader became almost equally paranoid about the United States and turned even more to the Soviet Union for help in expanding his country's military's capabilities to resist a potential American invasion. While the Soviet Union had no specific stake in the Bay of Pigs, it did have its own share of problems that when joined with the U.S.-Cuban animosity set the stage for a crisis. Khrushchev knew that despite his earlier bluster to the contrary, the Soviet Union was far behind the United States in its strategic nuclear capabilities. Khrushchev admitted in a meeting with members of the Soviet Presidium in early 1961 that the United States was "not weaker than we are."[3] Furthermore, Khrushchev was facing a great deal of pressure from within the Kremlin and from China, which had emerged from the Soviet shadow, to be more assertive in the Cold War.[4] Placing missiles armed with nuclear warheads in Cuba would go a long way towards improving the Soviet Union's deterrent capabilities and quieting Khrushchev's critics.

Tensions between the United States and Cuba remained high after the Bay of Pigs fiasco. The continuation of the American economic embargo against Cuba placed strains on Castro's efforts to build a new socialist state. When combined with the American effort to overthrow him in 1961, Castro cast a wary eye to the north. Further, Kennedy approved a top-secret operation, code named Mongoose, soon after the failed invasion to destabilize and hopefully topple the communist regime. As Richard Goodwin told the president, "The beauty of such an operation over the next few months is that we cannot lose. If the best happens we will unseat Castro. If not, then at least we will emerge with a stronger underground, better propaganda and a far clearer idea of the dimensions of the problems which affect us."[5] By 1962, Operation Mongoose

---

[2] Don Bohning, *The Castro Obsession: U.S. Covert Operations Against Cuba, 1959-1965* (Washington, D.C.: Potomac Books, Inc., 2005), pp. 7-9.

[3] Quoted in Fursenko and Naftali, *Khrushchev's Cold War*, p. 412.

[4] Michael R. Beschloss, *The Crisis Years: Kennedy and Khrushchev, 1960-1963* (New York: Edward Burlingham Books, 1991), pp. 42-45.

[5] Memorandum for the President, November 1, 1961, The National Security Archive, http://nsarchive.chadwyck.com/nsa/documents/CU/00219/all.pdf. accessed on May 26, 2008. See also Memorandum From President Kennedy, November 30, 1961, in *FRUS, 1961-1963,*

operated with an annual budget of almost $50 million and involved over 400 Americans and 2,000 Cubans. While Castro did not necessarily know the full extent of Mongoose's activities, he was fully aware that the United States desired his removal from office. For example, after a series of explosions during a Castro address in October 1961, the Cuban government claimed that the bombs had been planted by "counter-revolutionary elements in the service of Yankee imperialism."[6] Later in the year, Castro accused Kennedy directly of sending "saboteurs and assassins."[7] In this atmosphere, Castro turned even more to the Soviet Union for military and economic assistance.[8]

While the Kennedy administration and Castro sparred constantly, Khrushchev's role in the crisis is the most critical. The Soviet leader had come to power in the mid-1950s after Joseph Stalin's death. He was a realist in many ways and recognized his own country's weaknesses, even if he tried to conceal them from others. As Melvyn Leffler argues, Khrushchev "was a man of paradox: practical yet ideological, impulsive yet prudent."[9] After the Soviet Union launched *Sputnik* in October 1957, Khrushchev announced to the world that the Soviet military was second to none. He further boasted that his country could produce large numbers of nuclear missiles. His claims fueled the "Missile Gap" argument made by Eisenhower's critics.[10] Khrushchev knew, however, that he was playing a dangerous game. While the Soviet Union was rightly proud of its satellite program, the reality was that it lagged behind the United States in actual missile and nuclear warhead development. Khrushchev attempted to hide the Soviet deficiencies with his bluster.[11] He claimed in October 1960 that the Soviet Union was producing missiles "like sausage out of a machine," and in an arms race, the Soviet Union would "win."[12] However,

Volume X: Cuba, 1961-1962 (Washington, D.C.: United States Government Printing Office, 1997), http://www.state.gov/www/about_state/history/*FRUS*X/391_405.html, accessed on May 26, 2008.

6 "1 Killed, 6 Hurt by Bomb Blasts During Castro Speech in Havana," *The Washington Post and Times Herald*, October 22, 1961, p. A22.

7 Jules Dubois, "U.S. Agents Captured: Castro Assails Kennedy in Speech," *Chicago Daily Tribune*, Dec. 23, 1961, p. 3.

8 Fursenko and Naftali, *"One Hell of a Gamble,"* pp. 134-7 and pp. 151-4. For a chronology of U.S. involvement in Cuba, see Bay of Pigs – Forty Years After: Chronology, The National Security Archive, http://www.gwu.edu/~nsarchiv/bayofpigs/chron.html, accessed on May 26, 2008.

9 Melvyn P. Leffler, *For the Soul of Mankind: The United States, The Soviet Union, and the Cold War* (New York: Hill and Wang, 2007), p. 173.

10 For an excellent study of the missile gap controversy, see Preble, *John F. Kennedy and the Missile Gap*.

11 See McDougall, *...the Heavens and the Earth*, pp. 237-49.

12 Murrey Marder, "K Defeated in U.N., 62 to 12: Arms Talk Move Killed In Assembly," *The Washington Post and Times Herald,* October 12, 1960, p. 1.

just a few months later he revealed to some of his colleagues in the Kremlin that the Soviet Union was behind in missile technology.[13]

The "Missile Gap" allegations arose from perceptions of the Soviet threat, the closed nature of Soviet society, inaccurate assessments of Soviet capabilities, and partisan politics. The leading proponents of the charge in the late 1950s feared Soviet military developments and saw a war with the Soviet Union as a distinct possibility. They were not the only ones fearing the Soviet Union, and based on the evidence available to them, it was to some degree understandable. Furthermore, the lack of access to the Soviet Union made it very difficult to develop accurate assessments of what its military was doing.[14] While the United States gathered value information from U-2 overflights and starting in late 1960 from satellites, it had no reliable source of information from within the Soviet Union. This did begin to change in 1960 when Soviet Lieutenant Colonel Oleg Penkovsky began sending information to Great Britain and the United States. After questioning Penkovsky's authenticity a great deal, the CIA received invaluable intelligence from the Soviet colonel until his arrest in October 1962.[15]

To complicate the matter further, intelligence estimates produced by the CIA, the Defense Department, and each military branch varied from each other and often reflected worst-case scenarios rather than the most likely alternatives. As one historian has noted, "Given the paucity of estimates [in the 1950s and early 1960s] based on concrete intelligence, [intelligence] analysts tended to credit the Soviet Union with capabilities based on the maximum that Soviet industry could produce."[16] The result was estimates that exaggerated Soviet military capabilities and misjudged its intentions. Finally, Senators Johnson, Kennedy, and Symington knew that they could possibly acquire political capital by championing this issue.[17]

Eisenhower did not share these concerns and was very disappointed in his critics. He knew from U-2 photography that the Soviet Union was not nearly as far along in rocket development as Khrushchev claimed. He also recognized that while the Soviet Union had made a great achievement in launching

---

[13] Fursenko and Naftali, *Khrushchev's Cold War*, pp. 43-48.

[14] Snead, *The Gaither Committee*, pp. 170-3.

[15] See collection of formerly classified documents detailing Penkovsky's entreaties to the British and Americans, the materials he gave to the allies, and his ultimate fate entitled, "Lt. Col. Oleg Penkovsky: Western Spy in Soviet GRU", that can be found at the Central Intelligence Agency, http://www.foia.cia.gov/penkovsky.asp, accessed on December 11, 2007. See also Oral History Interview with Robert Armory, February 9, 1966, JFKL, 7.

[16] Snead, *The Gaither Committee*, p. 118.

[17] Preble, *John F. Kennedy and the Missile Gap*, p. 59.

Sputnik, the United States was still well ahead in missile and guidance system design. One of the reasons the Soviet Union was able to launch its satellite was that it focused its attention on developing liquid-propelled rockets or first-generation technology. This propulsion system was difficult to use and often unstable. On the other hand, the United States was already moving to second-generation missile technology where solid fuels would be used for propulsion. With this information in mind, Eisenhower remained confident that the United States was not only ahead in the quantity of nuclear delivery systems but also in their quality. His problem was that he could not reveal the U-2 intelligence to public because it was a top-secret project.[18]

The claims of a missile gap and Eisenhower's unwillingness to make the U-2 intelligence public had the effect of making Khrushchev sound credible. Published estimates of Soviet and U.S. missile capabilities showed a growing gap; the fact that many Americans had heard the beeping radio signal from *Sputnik* as it passed over the United States seemed to indicate the Soviet's superiority in technology; and the claims of Eisenhower's critics seemed to offer compelling evidence. However, the façade began to crumble after the Soviet Union shot down the U-2 in May 1960 forcing the United States to acknowledge the existence of the top-secret program and when the United States began to receive the first satellite intelligence from its Corona satellite program in late 1960 and early 1961. By early in 1961, even the new Kennedy administration had to back away from its earlier claims of a missile gap. In fact, it was becoming ever more apparent in particular to Khrushchev that the opposite was occurring. The Soviet Union was actually on the wrong end of a real missile gap.[19]

With the growing evidence, including public reports, dismissing the missile gap, Khrushchev's bluff fell apart. Instead, he faced a situation where the United States was well ahead of the Soviet Union in every type of delivery system. The United States had a true nuclear triad: land-based intercontinental and intermediate range ballistic missiles (ICBMs and IRBMs), strategic bombers like the B-52, and submarine-launched ballistic missiles (SLBMs). The Soviet Union had a handful of ICBMs and was approaching production stage for a submarine-launched ballistic missile system, but they were far behind the United States. Most U.S. policy makers really had no idea how superior American nuclear forces were, although Khrushchev was under no illusions. In 1960, the United States had almost 7,000 strategic warheads and

[18] Dwight D. Eisenhower, *Waging Peace: The White House Years, 1956-1961* (Garden City, N.Y.: Doubleday & Company, Inc., 1965), pp. 225 and 483.
[19] Preble, *John F. Kennedy and the Missile Gap*, pp. 153-60.

another 13,000 tactical ones.[20] At the same time, the Soviet Union had around 400 strategic and 1,200 tactical warheads.[21]

To make matters worse for Khrushchev, America's strategy of containment included the establishment of military bases near the borders of Soviet and/or communist-controlled territories. While the United States viewed the bases as defensive measures to prevent Soviet expansion, Khrushchev saw them very differently. He had lived through two invasions of his country and the deaths of over 30 million of its citizens. He did not trust the United States and feared that someday the Americans might be the invaders. Particularly troublesome to him were the presence of American IRBMs in Turkey, Italy, and Great Britain. These missiles could reach the Soviet Union in a matter of minutes, and the Russians had no comparable force. Khrushchev later revealed to Averell Harriman how he perceived the Cuban situation. He explained, "Cuba. What can Cuba do with her seven millions? You have laid a dozen Cubas around us, Turkey, Greece, Iran, Norway, Germany, Italy, United Kingdom, Pakistan, and Japan."[22] For a state paranoid about its security, this was not an acceptable situation.[23]

The Soviet plan to install missiles in Cuba with nuclear warheads arose from this conglomeration of ideas and issues. Khrushchev initiated Operation Anadyr to narrow the gap between U.S. and Soviet forces and to address other issues he was facing. He knew the Soviet Union would construct its own nuclear triad in the fairly near future, but the placement of missiles in Cuba would enhance the Soviet ability to strike the United States. Further, the missiles would strengthen Soviet ties to Castro and offer the Cuban leader some assurance that the Soviet Union would defend his island in case of an U.S. invasion. Finally, the missiles would offer Khrushchev a bulwark against the criticism he was facing at home and from the Chinese for not standing firm against the United States. Khrushchev gambled that if his forces could install the missiles before they were detected, then the United States would have had

[20] Table of U.S. Nuclear Warheads, 1945-1975, National Research Defense Council, http://www.nrdc.org/nuclear/nudb/datab9.asp, accessed on May 26, 2008. See also David Allen Rosenberg, "The Origins of Overkill: Nuclear Weapons and American Strategy, 1945-1960, International Security 7:4 (Spring 1983), p. 66.

[21] Table of USSR/Russian Nuclear Warheads, 1949-1975, National Research Defense Council, http://www.nrdc.org/nuclear/nudb/datab10.asp, accessed on May 26, 2008.

[22] Memorandum for the President, April 30, 1963, JFKL, Kennedy Papers, President's Office Files, Special Correspondence, Box 30, Folder – Harriman, W. Averell 4/61-1/63, p. 16.

[23] See Fursenko and Naftali, *Khrushchev's Cold War*, pp. 424 and 431; and Philip Nash, *The Other Missiles of October: Eisenhower, Kennedy, and the Jupiters, 1957-1963* (Chapel Hill: University of North Carolina Press, 1997), p. 99.

little choice but to accept their existence.[24] The key was secrecy. Could the Soviet Union transport and install the missiles, nuclear warheads, and other support equipment 8,000 miles without the United States knowing?

The first ships carrying equipment to Cuba arrived in July, and from that point until the discovery of the missile sites in mid-October, 85 merchant ships delivered almost 190 ship loads of military personnel, equipment, weapons, and supplies. There is no evidence that the United States ever clearly understood what was going on until the development of the U-2 photographs on October 14. The Russians carried out the mission with the utmost secrecy. Military personnel had to remain below ship the entire journey. They hid most of the equipment and weapons below deck and skillfully camouflaged any of the materials that could only fit on deck. Further, after reaching Cuba, the Russians only unloaded and moved equipment at night. Cuban troops always cleared the streets or kept them closed to allow the transit of the military hardware.[25]

Reports did begin to trickle out of Cuba that something was happening. A Spanish-language radio station in Miami announced on August 7 that 4,000 Soviet soldiers had landed in Cuba.[26] The CIA received an intelligence report in early August detailing the extraordinary precautions taken in unloading a recently arrived Soviet ship. No Cubans, including the local custom officials, were allowed near the ship. They only unloaded the cargo after all the regular workers had been sent away. The Russians hoisted empty trucks into the ship's hold where they were loaded out of sight. The loaded trucks were then off-loaded as if "they were made of glass." The report speculated that "the trucks were loaded with rockets, nose cones for rockets, or most probably atomic bombs."[27] Although the Kennedy administration initially denied the landings, the State Department announced a few weeks later that around five shiploads of communist technicians had arrived with an additional ten other ships carrying unknown equipment.[28] At a news conference a few days later, Kennedy denounced a call by Republican Senator Homer Capehart to invade

---

[24] Fursenko and Naftali, *"One Hell of a Gamble,"* pp. 182-83.

[25] Norman Polmar and John D. Gresham, *DEFCON-2: Standing on the Brink of Nuclear War During the Cuban Missile Crisis* (Hoboken, NJ: John Wiley & Sons, Inc.), pp. 62-63.

[26] "Red Troop Landing Reported," *New York Times*, August 8, 1962, p. 11.

[27] Telegram – Information Report – Central Intelligence Agency, August 10, 1962, Central Intelligence Agency, http://www.foia.cia.gov/ under search Arrival of Soviet Vessel in Port of Mariel, Cuba, accessed on June 13, 2008.

[28] "14 Soviet Vessels Carry Aid to Cuba," *New York Times*, August 21, 1962, p. 12. See also Status of Soviet Merchant Shipping to Cuba, August 23, 1962, National Security Archive, http://www.nsa.gov/cuba/images/image00034.pdf, accessed on June 13, 2008.

Cuba to stop the influx of supplies. Kennedy claimed that there was no evidence that the Soviet Union had landed troops. Instead, he believed they were sending technicians to help the Cuban economy. He said that at this time, "it would be a mistake to invade Cuba, because I think it … could lead to very serious consequences for many people."[29] In early September, the administration also discounted reports concerning the construction of missile bases in Cuba even though a U.S. U-2 plane photographed surface-to-air missile sites under construction. When Kennedy got the information from the U-2 flight, he asked the acting director of the CIA to "to put it back in the box and nail it tight."[30] Eventually, the reports leaking out from Cuba led South Carolina Senator Strom Thurmond to call for an invasion claiming "Inaction can be justified at this point only by a no-win policy of paralysis."[31]

Behind the scenes, President Kennedy was acting with more concern. He asked the secretaries of state and defense, the attorney general, the acting director of the CIA, and General Maxwell Taylor to investigate different issues in light of the Soviet military activity in Cuba. He asked the Defense Department to determine what action could be taken to get the U.S. Jupiter IRBMs out of Turkey and to study "various military alternatives which might be adopted in executing a decision to eliminate any installations in Cuba capable of launching [a] nuclear attack on the U.S." He ordered the State Department to persuade America's NATO allies of the seriousness of the threat in Cuba; to investigate how much information to make available to the rest of the world; and to explore how the situation in Cuba might aggravate the Berlin Crisis. Finally, he encouraged General Taylor to move forward with Operation Mongoose "with all possible speed."[32]

His advisers began delivering their advice over the next week. National Security Advisor McGeorge Bundy warned the president that it did not look like Cuba had any Soviet missiles with nuclear capability; therefore, he advised that a wait and watch approach was the best policy. However, he did warn that "surface-to-surface missiles with nuclear warheads would constitute a very significant military threat to the continental U.S.," and if the Soviet

[29] The President's News Conference, August 29, 1962, *Public Papers of the Presidents, John F. Kennedy*, http://www.presidency.ucsb.edu/ws/?pid=8839, accessed on May 27, 2008.

[30] Editorial note, in *FRUS, 1961-1963,* Volume X: Cuba, 1961-1962, http://www.state.gov/www/about_state/history/*FRUS*X/271_285.html, accessed on May 29, 2008.

[31] "Senators Ask Armed Move on Castro," *Los Angeles Times*, September 3, 1962, p. 1.

[32] National Security Action Memorandum No. 181, August 23, 1962, JFKL, Kennedy Papers, President's Office Files, Box – 125a, Folder – USSR Security, 1962.

Union attempted to deploy them in Cuba, it "would be unacceptable."[33] On September 3 Deputy Special Assistant for National Security Affairs Walt Rostow advised Kennedy that "on the basis of existing intelligence the Soviet military deliveries to Cuba do not constitute a substantial threat to U.S. security." He recommended that the president make a "low key" but "confident" speech that would warn the Soviet Union and Cuba and alert America's allies of the seriousness of the situation.[34] The next day after a series of meetings,[35] Kennedy announced that the Soviet Union had constructed some anti-aircraft defense missiles sites and deployed radar equipment. He noted that there was "no evidence of any organized combat forces in Cuba from any Soviet bloc country; ... [or] of the presence of offensive ground-to-ground missiles; or of other significant offensive capability." He emphasized, however, that if those things were to take place, "the gravest issues would arise."[36]

Reports continued to filter out of Cuba of the growing Soviet presence and the construction of missile bases, and there was growing pressure on the Kennedy administration to do more. One Cuban exile group reported in early September that close to 20,000 communist troops, disguised as technicians, were in Cuba fortifying defensive positions and constructing missile bases in the northwest part of the country.[37] While the president knew that reports from Cuban exiles generally highlighted the worse-case scenario, this report proved quite accurate in identifying the locations where communist forces and missile sites were concentrated. Republican Senator Capehart called for a blockade of Cuba to prevent additional communist military supplies, troops, and weapons from reaching the island. He added that an invasion should not be ruled out if the situation did not improve.[38] Other senators, led by Everett Dirksen and Charles Halleck, called for Congress to pass a resolution authorizing the

[33] Memorandum From the President's Special Assistant for National Security Affairs (Bundy) to President Kennedy, August 31, 1962, *FRUS, 1961-1963,* Volume X: Cuba, 1961-1962, http://www.state.gov/www/about_state/history/*FRUS*X/271_285.html, accessed on May 29, 2008.

[34] Memorandum to the President, September 3, 1962, JFKL, Kennedy Papers, President's Office Files, Countries, Box 115, Folder – Cuba Security, 1962.

[35] See Ernest R. May and Philip D. Zelikow, eds., *The Kennedy Tapes: Inside the White House During the Cuban Missile Crisis* (New York: W.W. Norton & Company, 2002), pp. 3-19.

[36] "Kennedy's Cuba Statement," *New York Times*, September 5, 1962, p. 2.

[37] Jamie Plenn, "Exiles Release Details of Cuba Arms Buildup," ibid., September 6, 1962, p. A23.

[38] "Sen. Capehart Wants U.S. To Isolate Cuba," *Chicago Daily Tribune*, September 7, 1962, p. 3.

president to employ American military forces if necessary.[39] In response to the crisis and criticism, Kennedy did ask Congress for the authority to call up 150,000 reservists for active duty.[40]

President Kennedy's request and the recommendations for more action from Congress did not go unnoticed in Cuba and the Soviet Union. Castro denounced the warmongering of the United States and claimed an invasion would be a mistake as "we the leaders of this revolution are disposed to die alongside our people. We will not vacillate. We will remain firm."[41] The Soviet government released a statement that also warned the world of U.S. "provocations" that "might plunge the world into the disaster of a universal world war with the use of thermonuclear weapons." It added "the Soviet Government would like to draw attention to the fact that one cannot now attack Cuba and expect that the aggressor will be free from punishment for this attack. If this attack is made, this will be the beginning of the unleashing of war." It concluded that the Soviet Union had only peaceful intentions, and that it was the United States that was threatening the world with a nuclear "hurricane."[42]

President Kennedy's own party was growing uneasy with the situation as the November mid-term elections approached. There was some concern that voters would see the president's policy towards Cuba as weak and move to support Republicans in the election. Arthur Schlesinger told the president, "it need hardly be pointed out that the fall campaign vastly heightens the pressures and emotions surrounding the Cuban issue."[43] Key Senate Democrats, led by Senate Majority Leader Mike Mansfield, met on September 12 to discuss what Congress should do. They considered "the need for action ranging all the way from a Congressional resolution to a "quarantine" of Cuba … to all out war, at least with Cuba and perhaps with Russia as well." Mansfield warned the president that he "was disturbed by the intensity of the expressions on this issue" and that some Democrats running for re-election might decide to break with the president if they perceived his policy was a

---

39 "Texts of Two Republicans' Statements on Using Troops in Cuba," *New York Times*, September 8, 1962, p. 1.

40 Edward T. Folliard, "Kennedy Asks Power To Call Up Reserves: Would Order 150,000 Men To Active Duty," *The Washington Post and Times Herald*, September 8, 1962, p. A1.

41 Jules DuBois, "Attack by U.S. Would Fail, Castro Says," *Chicago Daily Tribune*, September 11, 1962, p. 2.

42 "Text of Soviet Statement Saying That Any U.S. Attack on Cuba Would Mean War," *New York Times*, September 12, 1962, p. 16.

43 Memorandum from the President's Special Assistant (Schlesinger) to President Kennedy, September 5, 1962, *FRUS, 1961-1963,* Volume X: Cuba, 1961-1962, http://www.state.gov/www/about_state/history/*FRUSX*/406_420.html, accessed on May 29, 2008.

political liability. In the end, he did not make specific recommendations but did encourage the president to be as "blunt and as frank as possible" when addressing the Cuba question.[44]

The first true indications that something was happening in Cuba was the discovery in late August of the construction of SA-2 anti-aircraft missiles sites. This was the type of missile that had shot down the U.S. U-2 plane in May 1960 over the Soviet Union, was used to guard important military targets, and posed a potentially lethal threat to any aerial surveillance. The presence of the SA-2 missile sites worried CIA Director John McCone. He was out of town on his honeymoon in late August and September but received regular updates on the intelligence situation from his deputy director, Marshall Carter. McCone did not believe the Soviet Union would invest so much money to deploy the SA-2 unless it was trying to protect a high value target. He told Carter on September 7 that "my hunch is we might face a prospect of Soviet short-range surface-to-surface missiles of portable type in Cuba which could command important targets of Southeast United States and possibly Latin American Caribbean areas." He recommended more reconnaissance flights to confirm his fear. Although told by Carter and others in the CIA that they did not think Khrushchev would take such a great risk in deploying nuclear missiles, McCone insisted that "we must carefully study the prospect of secret importation and placement of several Soviet MRBMs[45] which could not be detected by us if Cuban defenses deny overflight."[46] McCone's assessment was not accepted by his colleagues, as the CIA released an estimate in mid-September that warned the placement of intermediate-range ballistic missiles in Cuba would be a definite threat but believed this was "incompatible with Soviet policy as we presently estimate it."[47]

With conflicting information on the exact nature of the Soviet threat, President Kennedy was reluctant to order further overflights as he was fearful

---

44 Senator Mike Mansfield to the President, September 12, 1962, JFKL, Kennedy Papers, President's Office Files, Special Correspondence, Box 31, Folder – Mansfield, Mike, 3/1/62-8/4/63.

45 Kennedy and his advisors often used MRBMs and IRBMs interchangeably, even though they represented missiles with different ranges. The MRBM typically had a range of between 600 and 1,800 miles and the IRBM had a range between 1,800 and 3,400 miles. See "Ballistic and Cruise Missile Threat," National Air and Space Intelligence Center, March 2006, p. 3, http://www.nukestrat.com/us/afn/NASIC2006.pdf, accessed on June 13, 2008.

46 Editorial Note, *FRUS, 1961-1963,* Volume X: Cuba, 1961-1962, http://www.state.gov/www/about_state/history/*FRUS*X/406_420.html, accessed on May 29, 2008.

47 Special National Intelligence Estimate 85-3-62, September 19, 1962, *FRUS, 1961-1963,* Volume X: Cuba, 1961-1962, http://www.state.gov/www/about_state/history/*FRUS*X/421_443.html, accessed on May 29, 2008.

of the repercussions of having a U-2 shot down over Cuba.[48] Complicating the situation was the fact that it was the heart of hurricane season in the Caribbean and weather conditions limited or prohibited flights on 30 out of the 40 days between September 4 and October 14.[49] Because of these factors, there were only a few U-2 flights in late September, and none of them occurred over western Cuba where the Russians were constructing the missile bases.[50] Not wanting to be caught completely unprepared, Kennedy did ask Secretary of Defense Robert McNamara to make sure "contingency plans with relation to Cuba are kept up-to-date, taking into account the additions to their armaments resulting from the continuous influx of Soviet equipment and technicians."[51]

In late September more definite intelligence arrived that the Russians were probably building something more significant as McCone had concluded. The Joint Chiefs received an intelligence report on September 21 that indicated that the Soviet Union had unloaded 20 objects, measuring 65 to 70 feet long that resembled missiles. Over the next week, intelligence analysts compared this new information to other data and determined that the Soviet Union was probably in the process of deploying missiles in northwest Cuba and that if this was indeed happening, it "would give the Soviets a great military asset."[52]

As Kennedy deliberated over what to do, one of his greatest concerns was the losses the United States could expect if it launched air attacks against the SA-2 sites and other Soviet military installations in Cuba. McNamara reported to him on October 4 that the SA-2 would not be effective against the low-level attacks that the navy and air force had planned. Instead, anti-aircraft guns on the ground posed the greatest danger. Nevertheless, McNamara reported that while a good estimate of the losses in such an attack was unknowable, the military did not expect major difficulties. He concluded that both the navy and

48 Memorandum Prepared in the Central Intelligence Agency for the Executive Director, September 10, 1962, ibid., accessed on May 29, 2008. See also Memorandum, Feb. 27, 1963, Central Intelligence Agency, http://www.foia.cia.gov/ under search U-2 Overflights of Cuba, accessed on June 13, 2008.

49 Memorandum, Feb. 27, 1963, Central Intelligence Agency, http://www.foia.cia.gov/ under search Forecast Weather Over Cuba and Missions Status, accessed on June 13, 2008.

50 Fursenko and Naftali, *"One Hell of a Gamble"*, p. 214.

51 Memorandum From President Kennedy to Secretary of Defense McNamara, September 21, 1962, *FRUS, 1961-1963,* Volume X: Cuba, 1961-1962, http://www.state.gov/www/about_state/history/*FRUS*X/421_443.html, accessed on May 29, 2008.

52 Analysis of SAM Sites, October 1, 1962, *FRUS, 1961-1963,* Volume XI: Cuban Missile Crisis and Aftermath (Washington, D.C.: United States Government Printing Office, 1996), http://www.state.gov/www/about_state/history/*FRUS*XI/01_25.html, accessed on June 12, 2008.

air force had plans in place and crews that were already trained in these missions to take out the missile sites.[53]

Tensions increased over the ensuing weeks as the Kennedy administration attempted to determine what direction to go. Since early September it had limited U-2 and other intelligence flights over Cuba out of fear of one of them being shot down. Unfortunately, "the decisions to restrict U-2 flights had placed the United States Intelligence Community in a position where it could not report with assurance the development of offensive capabilities in Cuba."[54] Frustrations within the intelligence community spilled over in a meeting involving Robert Kennedy, CIA Director McCone, General Taylor, General Lansdale, and others. The central focus of the meeting was the lack of progress of Operation Mongoose and the restrictions on overflights of Cuba. The attorney general expressed the president's dissatisfaction with Mongoose's limited activities and several at the meeting expressed their dissatisfaction with the president's restrictions on the overflights. After a "sharp exchange," they agreed that the "hesitancy about overflights must be reconsidered." While the attorney general made no promise to resume the flights, he did agree that the intelligence community should develop alternatives including "the use of U-2s on complete sweeps (as contrasted with peripheral or limited missions), the use of firefly drones, the use of ... other reconnaissance planes on low level, intermediate level, and high level missions, and other possible reconnaissance operations."[55] After another meeting on October 9, President Kennedy finally relented and authorized U-2 flight over western Cuba but deferred making a decision about lower altitude overflights.[56] The U-2 flight would not take place for a few more days because of weather related issues, but the CIA was relieved to have the authorization.

At this stage in the crisis, President Kennedy was not sure what to do and was worried that it could become a major issue in the upcoming midterm elections. On October 10, CIA Director McCone reported that based on photographic evidence, the Soviet Union had probably sent IL-28s, a medium-range bomber with a range of 750 miles and capable of carrying nuclear bombs, to Cuba.[57] The CIA had photographs of large-crates on a Soviet ship in Havana that it presumed contained the planes. The president asked CIA

---

[53] Memorandum from Secretary of Defense McNamara to President Kennedy, October 4, 1962, ibid., accessed on June 12, 2008.

[54] Memorandum of Discussion with the President's Special Assistant for National Security Affairs (Bundy), October 5, 1962, ibid., access on June 12, 2008.

[55] Memorandum of Mongoose Meeting, October 4, 1962, ibid., accessed on June 12, 2008.

[56] Editorial Note, ibid., accessed on June 12, 2008.

[57] May and Zelikow, *The Kennedy Tapes*, p. 30.

director to withhold the information as, in McCone's words, "a new and more violent Cuban issue would be injected into the campaign." After McCone noted that the photos had already received widespread dissemination within the defense and intelligence communities, the president asked that "all future information be suppressed" except for those giving advice directly to the president. Although he did so reluctantly, McCone agreed to the restriction.[58]

The fear of information unwittingly reaching the public increased dramatically on October 14 as the first U-2 flight over the length of Cuba since early September occurred. Once the U-2 plane landed in Florida, the film from its two cameras was quickly removed and sent to Offutt Air Force Base in Nebraska and the Naval Photographic Interpretation Center (NPIC) in Washington. By the afternoon of the 15th analysts had reached their conclusions. The U-2 had discovered crews working on a SS-4 site in the vicinity of San Cristobal that was nearly operational. Art Lundahl, the director of the NPIC, called CIA Deputy Director of Intelligence Ray Cline and informed him that his team had definitely identified a Soviet missile site in Cuba. Cline immediately called National Security Adviser McGeorge Bundy who told him to be prepared to brief Kennedy and his national security team the next morning.[59] Altogether, the U-2 flight on October 14 and two additional flights the next day revealed several SS-4 and SS-5 missile sites and crates containing twenty-one IL-28 medium range bombers.[60] The SS-4 had a range of roughly 1,100 miles and the SS-5 could hit targets about twice as far. The power of these missiles was striking. The bomb dropped on Hiroshima equaled the equivalent of 14,000 tons of TNT, while the warhead carried by the SS-4 amounted to 1 million tons of TNT and the one on the SS-5 up to 5 million tons.[61] Bundy deliberately decided to wait a few hours before informing the president figuring correctly that there would be a number of sleepless nights ahead, and the president and his advisers should get at least one more good night's sleep before decisions had to be made.[62]

---

[58] Memorandum by Director of Central Intelligence McCone, October 11, 1962, *FRUS, 1961-1963,* Volume XI: Cuban Missile Crisis and Aftermath, http://www.state.gov/www/about_state/history/*FRUS*XI/01_25.html, accessed on June 12, 2008.

[59] Norman Polmar and John D. Gresham, *DEFCON-2*, pp. 89-92.

[60] Editorial Notes, *FRUS, 1961-1963,* Volume XI: Cuban Missile Crisis and Aftermath, http://www.state.gov/www/about_state/history/*FRUS*XI/01_25.html, accessed on June 12, 2008.

[61] See Fursenko and Naftali, *"One Hell of a Gamble"*, pp. 216 and 230; and May and Zelikow, *The Kennedy Tapes*, p. 76.

[62] See Memorandum for the President, March 4, 1963, in McGeorge Bundy, *Danger and Survival: Choices about the Bomb in the First Fifty Years* (New York: Random House, 1988), pp. 684-85.

The meetings began at 7:30 a.m. the next morning when Lundahl and his team briefed senior CIA officials and then went to the White House, where at 9:00 am they made a presentation to Robert Kennedy. Over the next several hours Bundy prepared for a meeting including the president and his chief advisors. The group, the Executive Committee of the National Security Council or ExComm for short, began its first meeting just before noon on October 16. ExComm consisted of Robert Kennedy, Bundy, McNamara, Rostow, Undersecretary of Defense Roswell Gilpatrick, Assistant Secretary of Defense Paul Nitze, Secretary of State Dean Rusk, Undersecretary of State George Ball, Deputy Undersecretary of State Alexis Johnson, Assistant Secretary of State for Latin American Affairs Edwin Martin, Secretary of the Treasury Douglas Dillon, Director of the CIA McCone, Special Counsel to the President Ted Sorensen, JCS Chairman Maxwell Taylor, and Ambassador Llewellyn Thompson. Other officials joined ExComm when required.[63] Over the next week, Kennedy and the members of ExComm felt pressures that they could have only previously imagined in their worst nightmares. As Ted Sorensen later noted, he gave his deputy "several grim assignments: Find out all you can about the bomb shelter under the White House and how to access it; obtain copies of previous U.S. declarations of war; determine who would be in charge of the government if the president, vice president, and senior cabinet members were all killed in an attack; and what plans, if any, exist for the evacuation of Washington."[64]

At its first meeting late that morning, Kennedy and his advisors discussed the situation and evaluated possible courses of action. He asked for Secretary of State Rusk's views first and then solicited comments from his other advisors. The president remained remarkably quiet throughout the meeting, listening while his advisors discussed the situation. Rusk rambled for a while but ultimately concluded that the United States had two options: "one, the quick strike; the other, to alert our allies and Mr. Khrushchev that there is [an] utterly serious crisis in the making." In the meantime, he suggested isolating Cuba and instituting a forceful blockade. Defense Secretary McNamara did not support or oppose military action but stressed that any attack should occur before the missiles were operational and had to include the destruction of the surrounding military facilities. He advocated a blockade after the missiles had been destroyed. Finally, he raised a disconcerting issue that hung over the entire crisis more than any of its participants knew. He questioned, "we don't

[63] Polmar and Gresham, *DEFCON-2*, pp. 102-3.
[64] Sorensen, *Counselor*, p. 288.

know what kinds of communications the Soviets have with those sites. We don't know what kinds of control they have over the warheads." President Kennedy leaned toward a limited airstrike throughout the meeting. He believed the United States had four options—an airstrike against only the missiles, wide-ranging air strikes against targets throughout Cuba, air strikes and a blockade, or an invasion. On more than one occasion, he said, "We're certainly going to do number one."[65]

At a meeting later the day, the president still focused on airstrikes and again, his military advisors emphasized if he selected this route that he needed to attack a broad-range of targets not just the missiles. General Taylor noted that there was no guarantee "of getting everything down there." He added, "there was unanimity among all the commanders involved in the Joint Chiefs … that … it would be a mistake to take this very narrow, selective target because it invited reprisal attacks and it may be detrimental." He was concerned that if the Soviet Union was willing to deploy nuclear-tipped missiles, it would probably deploy nuclear bombs for its airplanes. He recommended that the military "get complete intelligence" over "the next two or three days …. Then look at this target system. If it really threatens the United States, then take it right out with one hard crack."

McNamara then went through three possibilities—negotiation, instituting a blockade, or launching some sort of military attack. He recommended against negotiation without some action, because it would make any future military attacks more dangerous. He suggested the blockade as an intermediate step between negotiations and military strikes. Temporarily at least, the focus remained on launching an airstrike with the only real question being whether some sort of political statement should be made first. General Taylor and Secretary McNamara stressed that making an announcement before launching a military strike would significantly lessen its chances of success. McNamara bluntly told the gathering "before you make any announcements, you should decide whether you're going to strike. If you are going to strike, you shouldn't make an announcement." Taylor warned the president that "the Chiefs and the commanders feel so strongly about … the dangers inherent in the limited strike, that they would prefer taking no military action rather than" launch one.

---

[65] Transcript of a Meeting at the White House, October 16, 1962, *FRUS, 1961-1963,* Volume XI: Cuban Missile Crisis and Aftermath, http://www.state.gov/www/about_state/history/*FRUS*XI/01_25.html, accessed on June 12, 2008.

Before the end of the meeting, the discussion moved to McNamara's suggestion of a blockade, but without any consensus being formed.[66]

CIA Director McCone, who had been away to deal with a family tragedy, offered his advice on the situation the next day. He told the president that "the situation cannot be tolerated," but cautioned against military action without prior warning as to do otherwise would force the country "to live with a 'Pearl Harbor indictment' for the indefinite future." He recommended warning the Soviet leadership and Castro, giving them 24-hours to begin dismantling the missiles and bombers, notifying the American public and world of the threat, and if the communist leaders did not respond favorably, launching a "massive surprise strike at air fields, MRBM sites and SAM sites concurrently."[67]

ExComm now convened regularly to discuss just how the United States should respond to this October surprise. Their first decision was to fully consider every possible option from diplomatic maneuverings to military actions. By the end of the second day of deliberations on October 17, they had pretty much narrowed their focus to five options:

1) Limited air strikes preceded by a warning to Khrushchev;
2) Limited air strikes without warning;
3) Announcement and implementation of a naval blockade;
4) Large-scale air strikes; and/or
5) Invade Cuba[68]

Each option offered its share of risks. Air strikes, whether limited or large-scale, could not guarantee the destruction of all the missiles. As General Maxwell Taylor told the president in projecting the success rates of an attack, "I would stress the point … that we'll never be guaranteeing 100 percent."[69] Furthermore, the strikes would result in Soviet casualties which could trigger a military reaction. Chester Bohlen advised that a large air strike followed by an invasion "would probably be the most dangerous course of action we would

---

[66] Off the Record Meeting on Cuba, October 16, 1962, ibid., accessed on June 12, 2008. See also Robert S. McNamara Oral History Interview, April 4, 1964, JFKL, pp. 14-20, http://www.jfklibrary.org/NR/rdonlyres/FCC01356-1AFA-46E0-818E-605360FF7D2B/43973/McNamaraRobertSJFK1_oralhistory.pdf, accessed on July 8, 2009.

[67] Memorandum for Discussion, October 17, 1962, *FRUS, 1961-1963,* Volume XI: Cuban Missile Crisis and Aftermath, http://www.state.gov/www/about_state/history/*FRUS*XI/26_50.html, accessed on June 13, 2008.

[68] See Polmar and Gresham, *DEFCON-2*, p. 109; and May and Zelikow, *The Kennedy Tapes*, p. 75.

[69] May and Zelikow, *The Kennedy Tapes*, p. 83.

take" as it "would confront the Soviets with a series of very difficult choices."[70] Further, an invasion would have produced thousands of American casualties and could have easily sparked a larger confrontation. The blockade limited the risk of casualties but would allow the Soviet Union time to continue working on the missile sites. One of the biggest fears was that the missiles would become operational before anything was done. Kennedy noted his own misgivings about the blockade when he told some of his advisers, "The blockade wouldn't be sufficient. Because he could go on developing what he's got there. We don't know how much he's got there."[71]

Kennedy's advisors continued to discuss possible courses of actions and potential Soviet reactions. Most of them shifted positions at least once, as they looked at the real possibility that any action could precipitate a general nuclear war, or at a minimum, spread to conflicts elsewhere. Secretary of State Rusk captured it succinctly when he told the president that you "have to have in the back of your own mind … the possibility—if not the likelihood—of a Soviet reaction somewhere else running all the way from Berlin right around to Korea, and the possibility of a reaction against the United States itself."[72]

While the president and most ExComm initially leaned towards at least a precision air strike, opinions began to move towards a blockade as October 18 progressed. The risks of a large number of casualties and the fear that the crisis might escalate to a nuclear war, or "the final failure" as Kennedy called it, if the United States adopted military options weighed heavily on ExComm.[73] Another issue that grabbed a lot of attention was one that McCone had raised privately with the president earlier and was raised again by George Ball. The undersecretary of state hypothesized about the repercussions of not giving some warning to the world before launching a military strike. He warned the committee members, "a course of action where we strike without warning is like Pearl Harbor. It's the conduct that one might expect of the Soviet Union. It is not the conduct that one expects of the United States." McNamara quickly agreed, and while acknowledging that giving a warning would eliminate the chance of a surprise attack, he believed that it possibly gave Khrushchev "an out that would reduce the requirement that we enter with military force." Robert Kennedy later added, "I think George Ball has a hell of a point."[74]

---

[70] "Possible Soviet Reactions to the Following Alternatives," October 17, 1962, JFKL, Kennedy Papers, President's Office Files, Countries, Box 115, Folder – Cuba Security, 1962.
[71] May and Zelikow, *The Kennedy Tapes*, p. 89.
[72] Quoted in ibid., p. 78.
[73] Ibid., p. 93.
[74] Ibid., pp. 91-96.

Over the next two days, the president and his advisers went back and forth over what to do with a general recognition that with each day that passed the situation in Cuba grew more perilous. President Kennedy pointed out "that the missile threat became worse each day, adding that we might wish, looking back, that we had done earlier what we are now preparing to do."[75] The problem they faced was that no alternative seemed to lead to a good outcome. On October 21 he met with his brother, McNamara, McCone, and the Joint Chiefs to discuss air strikes against just the missile locations. The military chiefs told him it would take at least 350 sorties to be "successful", but General Taylor also told him, "The best we can offer you is to destroy 90% of the known missiles." Kennedy recognized that such an attack would escalate the crisis and probably would lead to some sort of Soviet retaliation. He also realized, however, that he could not let the missiles remain. At the end of the meeting he ordered his military advisers to be prepared to launch the air strikes the next morning or at any point after that upon receiving final orders.[76]

After all the discussions, President Kennedy and a majority of the ExComm members concluded that the best option was the blockade, or as it was called, quarantine, in combination with a strong statement from the president demanding the removal of the offensive weapons from Cuba under the threat of the United States taking military action if they were not. The president summarized his reasons for choosing the quarantine at a National Security Council meeting on October 22:

1) Air strikes could not guarantee the destruction of all of the missiles;
2) He did not know if any of the missiles had already been equipped with nuclear warheads or whether all of the missiles had been located;
3) He feared that an air strike without prior warning would be remembered like the Japanese attack on Pearl Harbor; and
4) An air strike could escalate the crisis towards a nuclear war.

He summarized that an air strike "would not insure the destruction of every strategic missile in Cuba, and would end up eventually in our having to

[75] Minutes of the 505th Meeting of the National Security Council, October 20, 1962, *FRUS, 1961-1963,* Volume XI: Cuban Missile Crisis and Aftermath, http://www.state.gov/www/about_state/history/*FRUS*XI/26_50.html, accessed on June 18, 2008.

[76] Notes on October 21, 1962 Meeting With The President, JFKL, Kennedy Papers, National Security Files, Meetings & Memoranda, Box 313, Folder – NSC Meetings, 1962, No. 506, 10/21/62.

invade."[77] Finally, he knew the quarantine allowed him to keep his options open by continuing to develop military contingencies while still looking for a peaceful solution to the crisis.

To this point, only Kennedy's inner circle knew of the crisis and of the decision-making process. Kennedy had to decide how to best inform the nation, its allies, and its enemies of his decisions. This was more difficult than it might appear since the president received word on the 21st that the *New York Times* was planning to run a story on the crisis. Kennedy personally called reporter James Reston and asked him to withhold the story, which he agreed to do. He then decided that he would go on television at 7:00 pm the next day and explain the situation and his plans to the American population. During the day on October 22, he met with Congressional leaders from both parties, consulted with his key overseas allies, and right before his speech, ordered U.S. military forces to go to Defense Condition Three (DEFCON-3).[78]

President Kennedy's last meeting before going on the television and radio to announce to the world the situation in Cuba was with congressional leaders. He and his key advisors met with Senators Everett Dirksen, William Fulbright, Bourke Hickenlooper, Hubert Humphrey, Thomas Kuchel, Mike Mansfield, Richard Russell, Leverett Saltonstall, and George Smathers, and Representatives Carl Albert, Leslie Arends, Hale Boggs, Ronald Chiperfield, Charles Halleck, John McCormack, Thomas Morgan, John Taber, and Carl Vinson to explain the background to the crisis and the administration's plans.[79] Senators Russell and Fulbright, in particular, expressed their opposition to the quarantine and spoke out in favor of more direct military action. Russell contended that "stronger steps" needed to be taken and questioned why Kennedy had not already launched an attack.[80] Fulbright supported an "all-out" invasion.[81] The president recognized that whatever choice he made was

[77] Minutes of the 507th Meeting of the National Security Council, October 20, 1962, *FRUS 1961-1963*, XI: Cuban Missile Crisis and Aftermath, http://www.state.gov/www/about_state/history/*FRUS*XI/26_50.html, accessed on June 18, 2008.

[78] Polmar and Gresham, *DEFCON-2*, pp. 126-27.

[79] See Memorandum of Conference with the President, October 22, 1963, JFKL, Kennedy Papers, National Security Files, Chester V. Clifton, Box 345, Folder – Confs. w/the President, Congressional Leaders, 1961-1962; and May and Zelikow, *The Kennedy Tapes*, p. 163.

[80] May and Zelikow, *The Kennedy Tapes*, pp. 172-73.

[81] Ibid., p. 180.

"one hell of a gamble."[82] While not fully satisfied, the congressmen and senators agreed "to support the President all the way."[83]

Kennedy went on air at 7:00 pm and for the next 17 minutes explained to the American population and the world what had occurred over the previous week and announced that the United States was instituting a quarantine around Cuba. He announced that "this urgent transformation of Cuba into an important strategic base—by the presence of these large, long-range, and clearly offensive weapons of sudden mass destruction—constitutes an explicit threat to the peace and security of all the Americas." He added "this secret, swift, and extraordinary buildup of Communist missiles … is a deliberately provocative and unjustified change in the status quo which cannot be accepted by this country, if our courage and our commitments are ever to be trusted again by either friend or foe." To meet this threat, he warned that "all ships of any kind bound for Cuba from whatever nation or port will, if found to contain cargoes of offensive weapons, be turned back."[84]

Kennedy's speech outraged both Khrushchev and Castro. The Cuban leader had ordered his military to begin mobilization when Kennedy announced plans for the speech and accelerated these preparations that evening. Khrushchev initially ordered the Soviet ships to proceed to their destinations in Cuba but on Tuesday he decided to keep the ships with offensive weapons onboard outside the quarantine zone. He also placed his own strategic forces on alert, and received word that 30 SS-4s in Cuba were now operational and could be fired with less than three hours notice. In many ways, it was now Khrushchev's turn to sweat and make the hard decisions. Stopping the ships was one thing, but as long as the missile sites were under construction, the United States did not seem willing to back down.[85] Khrushchev had to decide whether to call Kennedy's bluff and refuse to remove the missiles or to back down. If he refused, he knew he might be setting the stage for World War III.

As Kennedy and Khrushchev attempted to resolve the crisis, important elements to the eventual resolution of the crisis were taking place behind the scenes. President Kennedy asked his brother to meet with Soviet Ambassador

[82] Ibid., p. 176.

[83] Memorandum of Conference with the President, October 22, 1963, JFKL, Kennedy Papers, National Security Files, Chester V. Clifton, Box 345, Folder – Confs. w/the President, Congressional Leaders, 1961-1962.

[84] Radio and Television Report to the American People on the Soviet Arms Buildup in Cuba, October 22, 1962, *Public Papers of the Presidents, John F. Kennedy*, http://www.presidency.ucsb.edu/ws/?pid=8986, accessed on June 27, 2008.

[85] Polmar and Gresham, *DEFCON-2*, pp. 182-85.

Anatoly Dobrynin at the Soviet embassy on Tuesday night, October 23. While the meeting resulted in only more frustrations as Dobrynin had not been informed by Moscow about the missile deployment, it did set the stage for a later meeting with the attorney general to work out a settlement.[86]

Tensions continued to increase on October 24 and 25 as Kennedy and his advisers attempted to determine their course of action. With the quarantine in place, there was a real possibility of a confrontation at sea as ships approached Cuba. Kennedy was not sure whether the ships headed to Cuba would attempt to run the quarantine resulting in the U.S. navy having to decide whether to use force or let them proceed. Realizing the danger implicit with stopping a Soviet ship at sea, Robert Kennedy questioned "whether we might decide that it was better to knock out the missiles by air attack than to stop a Soviet ship on the high seas."[87] The Americans decided to let the first ships approaching the quarantine line to pass realizing that they were not carrying prohibited weapons or equipment, and ultimately decided to stop a Lebanese-based merchant ship destined for Cuba. They knew that the Russians would not have put illicit materials on a non-communist vessel, but decided to stop her anyway "to show that we could and would do it."[88]

As the Americans showed discretion in the Caribbean, the Soviet premier determined on October 25 to "take the initiative before events spiraled out of control."[89] Khrushchev described it as "a prudent move" to offer Kennedy a workable agreement and decided to seek a straight forward exchange, the removal of the missiles in return for a pledge from the United States not to invade Cuba.[90] Besides just sending a letter to Kennedy offering the exchange, Khrushchev or one of his advisers also decided to send a message through a back channel. On October 26, Alexander Feklisov, the Soviet embassy's public affairs officer and the KGB's Washington station chief, arranged a luncheon meeting with John Scali, ABC News' State Department correspondent. Feklisov knew that Scali had contacts with the Kennedys and was the neighbor of Kennedy aide, Kenneth O'Donnell. The KGB chief asked

[86] Memorandum From Attorney General Kennedy to President Kennedy, October 24, 1962, *FRUS, 1961-1963,* Volume XI: Cuban Missile Crisis and Aftermath, http://www.state.gov/www/about_state/history/*FRUS*XI/51_75.html, accessed on July 25, 2008. See also Fursenko and Naftali, *"One Hell of a Gamble,"* pp. 252-53.

[87] Summary Record of NSC Executive Committee Meeting, October 25, 1962, JFKL, Kennedy Papers, National Security Files, Meetings and Memoranda, Box 315, Folder – Ex. Com. Meetings, 1-5, p. 3.

[88] Quoted in Polmar and Gresham, *DEFCON-2*, p. 148.

[89] Quoted in Fursenko and Naftali, *Khrushchev's Cold War*, p. 483.

[90] Quoted in ibid., p. 484.

Scali whether the United States would be willing to negotiate a settlement based on the dismantling of the missiles in exchange for an American pledge that it would not invade Cuba. Scali passed along the "proposal," and it helped indicate to Kennedy that there was probably some room for a diplomatic solution.[91]

The evening of October 26 seemed to offer the climax to the crisis. Kennedy had received Scali's report and knew there was the possibility of a settlement but had not gotten Khrushchev's letter. Kennedy called British Prime Minister Macmillan to discuss the situation and the conversation indicated how dangerous the situation had become. Macmillan cautioned Kennedy that "any movement by you may produce a result in Berlin which would be very bad for us all." The president noted, "if in the end of 48 hours we are getting no place and the missile sites continue to be constructed, then we are going to be faced with some hard decisions." After Macmillan mentioned again the possible consequences of an American military action, Kennedy assured him "that is really why we have not done more than we have done, up till now."[92]

Soon after getting off the phone with MacMillan, Kennedy received a long telegram from Khrushchev. The Soviet leader deplored their strained relationship and challenged the American president concerning whether the missiles in Cuba were truly offensive weapons. However, he explained that he did not want war. Khrushchev noted, "if indeed war should break out, then it would not be in our power to contain or stop it, for such is the logic of war. I have participated in two wars and know that war ends when it has rolled through cities and villages, everywhere sowing death and destruction." He then proposed that if the president declared that the United States would not invade Cuba directly or support "any sort of forces which might intend to carry out an invasion of Cuba. Then the necessity for the presence of our military specialists in Cuba would disappear."[93] A solution to the crisis seemed at hand, but unfortunately, events the next day raised serious questions as to whether the crisis could be resolved peacefully.

---

[91] See Fursenko and Naftali, *Khrushchev's Cold War*, p. 485; Fursenko and Naftali, *"One Hell of a Gamble,"* pp. 264-65; and Polmar and Gresham, *DEFCON-2*, pp. 214-15.

[92] Quoted in May and Zelikow, *The Kennedy Tapes*, p. 295. See also Memorandum of Telephone Conversation Between President Kennedy and Prime Minister Macmillan, October 26, 1962, *FRUS, 1961-1963,* Volume XI: Cuban Missile Crisis and Aftermath, http://www.state.gov/www/about_state/history/*FRUS*XI/76_100.html, accessed on July 25, 2008.

[93] Telegram From the Embassy in the Soviet Union to the Department of State, October 26, 1962, *FRUS, 1961-1963,* Volume XI: Cuban Missile Crisis and Aftermath, http://www.state.gov/www/about_state/history/*FRUS*XI/76_100.html, accessed on December 16, 2008.

Three separate incidents occurred on October 27 that could have triggered a nuclear war. In the morning hours on October 27, U.S. Air Force Major Rudolf Anderson piloted his U-2 from his base in Florida on a reconnaissance mission over the length of Cuba from east to west. While Khrushchev had recently reasserted his control over decisions to launch the nuclear missiles, he had left decisions on how to respond to reconnaissance aircraft to General Issa Pliyev, the commander of Russian forces in Cuba. When Soviet radar operators detected the U-2 approaching Cuba from the east, they requested instructions from their superiors. General Pliyev was not at his headquarters and could not be reached by phone; so, his deputy commander and chief of staff decided it would be better to order the plane shot down than to let it proceed unmolested. A SA-2 missile battery fired two missiles at the U-2 and succeeded in destroying the plane and killing Major Anderson.[94]

At about the same time Kennedy and ExComm received the news of U-2 shoot down, they also were informed of another incident over Siberia. An American U-2 plane was flying a reconnaissance mission near the North Pole with the objective of collecting radioactive particles at high altitudes left over from Soviet nuclear tests. On his return to his base in Alaska, the U-2 pilot miscalculated his heading and strayed over Soviet territory. The Soviet Union sent two MIG-19s to confront the intruder. American radar operators, having already detected the American pilot's error and gotten him to make a course correction, scrambled two F-102 fighters to protect the U-2. The F-102s were armed with air-to-air missiles that carried a small nuclear warhead. Under the conditions of DEFCON-2, the pilots of these planes had the authority to use the nuclear weapons. The crisis was only averted because neither group of planes was able to get to the U-2 before it had to make a forced landing on a small Alaskan airfield out of fuel. Kennedy was exacerbated, "there's always [someone] who does not get the word."[95] In a message to President Kennedy the next day, Khrushchev asked, "How should we regard this? What is this: A provocation? One of your planes violates our frontier during this anxious time we are both experiencing, when everything has been put into combat readiness. Is it not a fact that an intruding American plane could be easily taken for a nuclear bomber, which might push us to a fateful step?"[96] Kennedy

[94] Polmar and Gresham, *DEFCON-2*, pp. 149-51.

[95] Robert S. McNamara, James C. Blight, and Robert K. Brigham, *Argument Without End: In Search of Answers to the Vietnam Tragedy* (New York: Public Affairs, 1999), pp. 149-50.

[96] Message From Chairman Khrushchev to President Kennedy, October 28, 1962, The National Security Archive, http://www.state.gov/www/about_state/history/*FRUS*XI/101_125.html, accessed on December 17, 2008.

ultimately apologized for the incident, and Khrushchev, seemingly recognizing that it was an error, did not make a big deal out of it.[97]

The third event was potentially even more dangerous as it involved a nuclear weapon with an even larger possible yield. In early October, the Soviet Union sent four Foxtrot diesel-electric submarines to join two other submarines already serving in the Atlantic. Each of these submarines carried one torpedo with a nuclear warhead that had the explosive potential of one-half the force unleashed on Hiroshima. The commanders of the Soviet submarines received orders after they were at sea to only use the torpedoes if attacked or if ordered by Moscow. Even without the knowledge of the Soviet nuclear-tipped torpedoes, Kennedy was probably more worried about an incident involving one of the submarines leading to the escalation of the crisis more than any other factor. At the October 24 ExComm meeting, Kennedy and his advisors discussed this possibility.[98] Deputy Under Secretary of State Alexis Johnson told ExComm that he had informed Soviet representatives the night before concerning the procedures the U.S. navy would follow if it encountered an unidentified submarine. Initially, the United States would use sonar signals to request the submarine to surface. Assuming this did not work, and this was the expectation, U.S. anti-submarine forces would use practice depth charges to force the Soviet submarine to surface. According to Robert Kennedy, "these few minutes were the time of greatest worry by the president. His hand went up to his face & covered his mouth and he closed his fist. His eyes were tense, almost gray."[99]

At this point in the discussion, Kenneth O'Donnell asked, "What if he doesn't surface, then it gets hot?" President Kennedy showed his own doubts if the submarine was not clearly preparing to attack by asking, "At what point are we going to attack him [the Soviet Submarine]?" The answers of both Army Chief of Staff Maxwell Taylor and Secretary of Defense McNamara indicated the difficulty of the situation. Taylor suggested that "Well, we won't get to that unless the submarine is really in a position to attack our ship." McNamara questioned whether the United States could wait to see what the

97 For accounts of the incident, see Polmar and Gresham, *DEFCON-2*, p. 151-52; and "Missing Over the Soviet Union," June 11, 2008, http://www.gwu.edu/~nsarchiv/nsa/cuba_mis_cri/dobbs/maultsby.htm, accessed on December 16, 2008.

98 Executive Committee Meeting of the National Security Council, October 27, 1962, reprinted in May and Zelikow, *The Kennedy Tapes*, pp. 227-29.

99 "The Submarines of October: U.S. and Soviet Naval Encounters During the Cuban Missile Crisis," in National Security Archive Electronic Briefing Book No. 75, The National Security Archive http://www.gwu.edu/~nsarchiv/NSAEBB/NSAEBB75/, accessed on December 17, 2008.

submarines exact intentions were because "We could easily lose an American ship by that means." By the end of the meeting, there really was no answer to the dilemma beyond the hope that the American and Soviet navy commanders on the scene would decide to not escalate the crisis.[100]

This was the setting on October 27 when the U.S. navy attempted to force the B-59 to the surface. Three U.S. destroyers detected a submerged submarine and initiated the procedures outlined in the ExComm meeting to force it to the surface. The destroyers used sonar signals and at least five practice depth charges each to force the submarine to the surface. While the Soviet commander ultimately decided to surface, the American captains did not know how close they had come to being involved with the first use of nuclear weapons since World War II. The Soviet intelligence officer on the B-59, Vadim Orlov, remembered the depth charges exploding "right next to the hull. It felt like you were sitting in a metal barrel, which somebody is constantly blasting with a sledgehammer." He added that the conditions on the submarine deteriorated during the American "attack" as carbon monoxide levels and the temperatures rose making it very difficult to make decisions. While Captain Savitsky threatened to fire his nuclear torpedo, he was eventually "able to rein in his wrath."[101] The crisis had obviously entered a truly crisis stage as a little provocation or miscalculation could have triggered a nuclear war.

Each of these incidents indicated just how little control Khrushchev and Kennedy actually had over the situation. Both men were doing their best to overt a nuclear war, but as these three incidents reveal, military officers on both sides had the authority to initiate a tactical nuclear confrontation that could have easily expanded to a full-fledged nuclear war. When Dino Brugioni, a photographic analyst in the CIA's National Photographic Interpretation Center, later described the Cuban Missile Crisis as 'Eyeball to Eyeball,' he effectively captured just how dangerous the situation was in 1962.[102] If any of the men described in these incidents had decided to act differently, then the outcome could have been much worse.

As the news of these events poured into the White House, Kennedy received a second letter from Khrushchev that made greater demands than the

---

[100] Excerpt from the Executive Committee (ExComm) of the National Security Council, October 24, 1962, The National Security Archive, http://www.gwu.edu/~nsarchiv/NSAEBB/NSAEBB75/asw-II-1.pdf, accessed on December 17, 2008.

[101] "Recollections of Vadim Orlov (USSR Submarine B-59) We Will Sink Them All, But We Will Not Disgrace Our Navy," ibid., http://www.gwu.edu/~nsarchiv/NSAEBB/NSAEBB75/asw-II-16.pdf, accessed on December 18, 2008.

[102] Dino A. Brugioni, *Eyeball to Eyeball: The Inside Story of the Cuban Missile Crisis* (New York: Random House, 1993).

ones the night before. Instead of proposing just a pledge from the United States to not invade Cuba in exchange for the removal of the Soviet missiles, the Soviet leader now added the demand that the United States withdraw its missiles from Turkey. It is unclear why he revised his offer, but it might have been because he was emboldened by a story written by Walter Lippmann claiming that President Kennedy was willing to make the trade.[103] The new letter triggered a great deal of alarm, even though Kennedy recognized that Khrushchev had made "a very good proposal."[104] However, the difficulty was how America's allies would perceive such a swap. Thomas Finletter, the U.S. representative to NATO's North Atlantic Council had reported that there was widespread opposition among the NATO countries to such a deal. In a telegraph to the secretary of state, he noted, "I think that we must be fully aware there is [a] real possibility that ... [the] whole alliance might be dismayed by such a deal."[105]

Ultimately Kennedy decided he could not justify a war over Cuba that could have been avoided by simply removing the already obsolete Jupiter missiles from Turkey. "We can't very well invade Cuba," Kennedy told ExComm, "with all this toil and blood it's going to be, when we could have gotten them [the Soviet missiles] out by making a deal of the same missiles in Turkey."[106] After much deliberation, he sent his brother to deliver a letter to Soviet Ambassador Dobrynin agreeing to the deal that Khrushchev had proposed the night before, while ignoring the Soviet premier's later proposal for a missile swap.[107] In addition, he gave his brother permission to tell Dobrynin that while the United States could not remove the missiles from Turkey as a quid pro pro, it would quietly do so four or five months later if the Russians had kept their end of the bargain in Cuba.[108] Khrushchev agreed to

[103] See May and Zelikow, *The Kennedy Tapes*, pp. 434-36; Fursenko and Naftali, *"One Hell of a Gamble"*, pp. 277-79; and Fursenko and Naftali, *Khrushchev's Cold War*, p. 488.

[104] Executive Committee Meeting of the National Security Council, October 27, 1962, reprinted in May and Zelikow, *The Kennedy Tapes*, p. 318.

[105] Finletter to Secretary of State, October 25, 1962, JFKL, Kennedy Papers, Presidential Office Files, Countries, Box 115, Folder – Cuba Security Missile Crisis Planning Subcommittee, 10/24/62-10/28/62. McGeorge Bundy shared Finletter's assessment in ExComm meeting on October 27. See Executive Committee Meeting of the National Security Council, October 27, 1962, reprinted in May and Zelikow, *The Kennedy Tapes*, p. 330.

[106] Executive Committee Meeting of the National Security Council, October 27, 1962, reprinted in May and Zelikow, *The Kennedy Tapes*, p. 386.

[107] See Sorensen, *Counselor*, pp. 2-8; and Fursenko and Naftali, *"One Hell of a Gamble,"* pp. 278-83.

[108] Memorandum for the Secretary of State from the Attorney General, October 30, 1962, JFKL, Kennedy's Papers, Presidential Office Files, Countries, Box 115, Folder – Cuba Security Missile Crisis Planning Subcommittee, 10/24/62-10/28/62.

this deal, and while it took several weeks for the crisis to truly die down, the Cuban Missile Crisis had been brought to a close.[109]

While tensions lingered for months after the difficult days of late October, both sides had been profoundly affected by the crisis and knew that this type of situation had to be avoided in the future. Neither Kennedy nor Khrushchev knew just how close their countries had come to at least a limited nuclear exchange, but they both did fully recognize that they had pushed the world to the brink. Over the remainder of Kennedy's life and while Khrushchev remained in power, they both sought ways to reduce tensions and to enter a new era of U.S.-Soviet relations.[110] While it was too much to expect real friendship or trust, they did believe a more positive relationship could be developed.

---

[109] See May and Zelikow, *The Kennedy Tapes*, p. 337-38; Polmar and Gresham, *DEFCON-2*, pp.264-77; Fursenko and Naftali, *Khrushchev's Cold War*, pp. 489-91; and Fursenko and Naftali, *"One Hell of a Gamble,"* pp. 283-89.

[110] Leffler, *For the Soul of Mankind*, pp. 158-90.

Chapter 8

1963 – PROGRESS AND TRAGEDY

Kennedy emerged from the Cuban Missile Crisis a changed leader. While some of Kennedy's policies and actions had helped lead to the crisis, he handled the trying times well and emerged with a greater recognition of the dangers of an escalating Cold War. As discussed in Chapter 6, he also knew that the country had entered a precarious time in the civil rights movement as the struggle over segregation and discrimination had seemingly come to a boiling point. Kennedy reached his stride as president in 1963 as he came to grips with the immensity of the problems that faced the nation while having to overcome the personal tragedy of Jackie and him losing a newborn son. He sought to strengthen the Atlantic Alliance by addressing key differences with his European allies, began to move forward on reducing tensions with the Soviet Union, and reluctantly increased American involvement in Vietnam. Unfortunately, on a warm, sunny day in late November, an assassin cut short John F. Kennedy's life and presidency.

America's relations with its key European allies faced new challenges in the months following the Cuban missile crisis. While there had been plenty of other issues, in particular the Berlin situation, which pointed to Europe's importance in the Cold War, the Cuban crisis brought it into new focus. The Kennedy administration had consulted with its key European allies—Harold Macmillan in Great Britain, Charles de Gaulle in France, and Konrad Adenauer in West Germany—during the crisis, but they had little say over U.S. policies. Since those policies could have a significant influence on Europe's future, its leaders sought more influence in the Kennedy decision making process.[1] Kennedy worked diligently in late 1962 and 1963 to improve U.S. relations with these leaders. While he had a great deal of success with Great Britain, U.S. relations with West Germany, and especially, France remained a challenge.[2]

During the 1950s, the United States had developed the Skybolt ballistic missile to be part of its nuclear delivery system, and Great Britain had decided to make it the basis of its nuclear deterrent. However, tests of the Skybolt had shown that it was not very reliable and too expensive. Furthermore, both Kennedy and Secretary of Defense McNamara came to see the Skybolt as unnecessary because of the success of the Polaris SLBM and the Minuteman ICBM and decided to cancel the program. Kennedy explained his decision in late 1962 "How many times," he asked, "do you have to hit a target with nuclear weapons? That is why when we are talking about spending this $2.5 billion [on the Skybolt], we don't think that we are going to get $2.5 billion worth of national security."[3] While cancelling the program made financial and military sense for the United States, it was a major blow to the British who had planned their nuclear deterrent around acquiring the missile.[4]

To soothe the British, Kennedy met with Prime Minister Macmillan in Bermuda on December 18 to discuss the rift between the two countries. After several days of meetings, they reached an agreement to scrap the Skybolt, but in return, the United States would help Great Britain build nuclear powered submarines that would be armed with Polaris missiles and British nuclear warheads.[5] In announcing the agreement, they claimed "this new plan will strengthen the nuclear defense of the Western Alliance."[6] With this crisis

---

[1] For example of the Europe's fears of being caught in the middle between the United States and the Soviet Union, see Waverley Root, "French, British Make Progress in Atom Talks," *The Washington Post, Times Herald*, December 19, 1962, p. A10.

[2] Marc A. Trachtenberg, *A Constructed Peace: The Making of the European Settlement, 1946-1963* (Princeton: Princeton University Press, 1999), pp. 330-398.

[3] Television and Radio Interview: "After Two Years – A Conversation with the President," December 17, 1962, *Public Papers of the Presidents, John F. Kennedy*, http://www.presidency.ucsb.edu/ws/?pid=9060, accessed on December 31, 2009.

[4] Last conversation with President before NATO meeting of December 1962, JFKL, Kennedy Papers, National Security Files, McGeorge Bundy Correspondence, Box 405, Folder – Memos to the President, 12/62. See also Arthur Veysey, "Britain to Press U. S. for Skybolt Missile: Pins A-Strength Hopes on Its Development," *Chicago Daily Tribune*, December 9, 1962, p. 37.

[5] Trachtenberg, *A Constructed Peace*, pp. 359-67.

[6] Joint Statement Following Discussions with Prime Minister Macmillan – The Nassau Agreement, December 21, 1963, *Public Papers of the Presidents, John F. Kennedy*, http://www.presidency.ucsb.edu/ws/?pid=9063, accessed on December 31, 2009. See also Richard E. Neustadt, *Report to JFK: The Skybolt Crisis in Perspective* (Ithaca, NY: Cornell

resolved, the United States and Great Britain would be able to work together closely on several issues in the coming year, including negotiating the nuclear test ban treaty.

While the agreement with Great Britain mended fences, it caused strains with French President de Gaulle who had determined that it was in the best interest of France to pursue policies distinct from either the Soviet Union or the United States. After his country successfully tested a nuclear bomb in early 1960, he fully intended for France to develop its own nuclear force that would make his country a force in the world. Kennedy did offer France the same Polaris deal that he had negotiated with the British, but de Gaulle refused.[7] He preferred to pursue an independent policy built on closer ties with West Germany. In January 1963 France rejected Great Britain's application for membership in the European Economic Community, and one month later it signed a mutual defense pact with West Germany. While still in NATO, de Gaulle actions threatened America's position in Europe and had the potential to undermine the Atlantic alliance's effectiveness.[8]

France's actions concerned Kennedy greatly, and in early 1963 he feared difficulties "with France may escalate."[9] He told some of his key advisers in late January that "our relations with de Gaulle during the next few months may be in for very heavy going." He explained that the United States normally had two ways of pressuring Europe, manipulating its financial assistance and military forces in Europe. However, the United States no longer provided financial assistance, and he feared the development of France's nuclear capabilities could neutralize U.S. military pressure. Finally, he actually believed there was a possibility of a Franco-Soviet treaty.[10] A week later, he stressed "our problem is to find out how we can continue to work with the

University Press, 1999); Freedman, *Kennedy's Wars*, p. 277; and Dallek, *An Unfinished Life*, p. 609.

[7] "NATO to Get U.S. Atomic Arms: Invited Role by De Gaulle in West Plan: Britain to Build Polaris Force," *Chicago Daily Tribune*, December 22, 1962, p. 1.

[8] See Jeffrey Glenn Giauque, *Grand Designs and Visions of Unity: The Atlantic Powers and the Reorganization of Western Europe, 1955-1963* (Chapel Hill: University of North Carolina Press, 2002), pp. 98-223; Erin R. Mahan, *Kennedy, De Gaulle, and Western Europe* (New York: Palgrave Macmillan, 2002); Leffler, *For the Soul of Mankind*, pp. 179-80; Dallek, *An Unfinished Life*, pp. 610-11; and Freedman, *Kennedy's Wars*, pp. 277-78.

[9] Memorandum for the Secretary of the Treasury, January 19, 1963, JFKL, Kennedy Papers, National Security Files, McGeorge Bundy Correspondence, Box 405, Folder –JFK Memos to Departments and Agencies, Treasury to VA, p. 1.

[10] Summary Record of NSC Executive Committee Meeting No. 38 (Part 11), January 25, 1963, ibid., Meetings & Memoranda, Box 316, Folder – Ex. Com. Meetings, Meetings 38-42, 1/25/63-3/29/63, p. 1.

Europeans. If the Europeans do not wish to continue with us, then, indeed, a turning point is here."[11]

While Kennedy was rightfully concerned with de Gaulle's independent actions, his fears were overblown.[12] Undersecretary of State George Ball reported on a meeting he attended in France in late March where he found little support for most of de Gaulle's policies. He concluded "Europeans are not prepared to have de Gaulle speak for them." He added "most Europeans did not want the U.S. to get out of Europe."[13] Kennedy gained a firsthand view of the situation in Europe when he visited there from June 23 to July 2. He spent almost half his trip in Germany and was met by cheering crowds wherever he went.[14] He reassured Europeans everywhere that while it was "a crucial time in the life of the Grand Alliance … we recognize a duty to defend and to develop the long Western tradition which we share, resting as it does on a common heritage."[15] While de Gaulle remained a wildcard in European relations, Kennedy came away from his trip confident that the turning point in U.S.-European relations that he had feared had not arrived.

As Kennedy worked to maintain a strong alliance with his allies in Europe, he also strove to take advantage of a thaw in U.S.-Soviet relations after the Cuban missile crisis.[16] Both sides came out of the crisis recognizing the need to reduce tensions and move towards what would later be called peaceful coexistence. Both Kennedy and Khrushchev also recognized the inherent danger of a nuclear war.[17] The Soviet leader wrote Kennedy in December 1962 explaining the need to reduce the chance of a nuclear war. He described how in a modern war "nuclear weapons will stride across seas and oceans within minutes. Thermonuclear catastrophe will bring enormous losses and sufferings to the American people as well as to other peoples on earth. We must," he stressed, "develop between ourselves peaceful relations and solve all

---

[11] Ibid., p. 8

[12] Freedman, *Kennedy's Wars*, p. 278.

[13] Summary Record of National Security Council Meeting, April 2, 1963, JFKL, Kennedy Papers, National Security Files, Meetings & Memoranda, Box 314, Folder – NSC Meetings, 1963 No. 510, 4/2/63, p. 2.

[14] Dallek, *An Unfinished Life*, pp. 623-25.

[15] Remarks upon Arrival in Germany, June 23, 1963, *Public Papers of the Presidents, John F. Kennedy*, http://www.presidency.ucsb.edu/ws/?pid=9289, accessed on December 31, 2009.

[16] Television and Radio Interview: "After Two Years – A Conversation with the President."

[17] Letter From Chairman Khrushchev to President Kennedy, October 30, 1962, *FRUS, 1961-1963*, Volume VI – Kennedy-Khrushchev Exchanges, http://www.state.gov/www/about_state/history/volume_vi/exchanges.html, accessed on January 1, 2010.

issues through negotiations and mutual concessions."[18] In a later critique of the Chinese who claimed that fighting a nuclear war would be better than giving in to the west, Khrushchev claimed that in the aftermath of such a war the survivors "would envy the dead."[19] President Kennedy told his National Security Council in January 1963 that "our big problem is to protect our interests and prevent a nuclear war." In describing the Cuban Missile Crisis, he noted "it was a very close thing whether we would engage in a quarantine or an air strike."[20]

A top secret report by the National Security Council's Net Evaluation Subcommittee (NESC) in the late summer of 1963 revealed just how devastating a nuclear war between the United States and the Soviet Union would have been. The NESC, at Kennedy's request, performed a study of a "series of general wars initiated yearly during the period 1963 through 1968."[21] It examined different scenarios ranging from either U.S. or Soviet pre-emptive attacks to retaliatory strikes. It concluded that a war initiated by the Soviet Union with nuclear weapons would result in between 93 and 134 million U.S. fatalities, while the Soviet Union would suffer around 140 million.[22] In a U.S. initiated attack, expected U.S. fatalities ranged from 64 to 120 million with the Soviet Union losing close to 150 million people.[23] It concluded that "in the years of this study, 1965-1968, neither the U.S. nor the USSR can emerge from a full nuclear exchange without suffering severe damage and high casualties" regardless which country initiated the attack.[24]

In a meeting to discuss the report, Kennedy asked his military advisors whether the level of damage the United States would suffer if it launched a preemptive nuclear war against the Soviet Union would be unacceptable, and they responded affirmatively. Secretary of Defense McNamara explained that he had authorized studies to determine if the United States increased its defense budget significantly for blast shelters and made increases in offensive

[18] Letter from Khrushchev to Kennedy, December 19, 1962, JFKL, Kennedy Papers, President's Office Files, Countries, Box 115, Folder – Cuba Security Missile Crisis, Khrushchev Correspondence, 10/23/62-12/19/62, pp. 1-2.

[19] "Let People Be Judge, Nikita Dares Chinese: Asks – Would Living in A-War Envy Dead?," *Chicago Tribune*, July 20, 1963, p. 2.

[20] Notes of Remarks by Kennedy before the National Security Council, January 22, 1963, JFKL, Kennedy Papers, National Security Files, Meetings & Memoranda, Box 314, Folder – NSC Meetings, 1963, No. 508, 1/22/63, p. 1.

[21] Report of the Net Evaluation Subcommittee of the National Security Council, August 27, 1963, http://www.gwu.edu/~nsarchiv/nukevault/special/doc08.pdf, accessed on December 28, 2009.

[22] Ibid., p. 8.

[23] Ibid., pp. 10-11.

[24] Ibid., p. 19.

and defensive weapons systems whether that would result in a significant reduction in U.S. casualties. All of the studies concluded that "the minimum number of fatalities was in excess of 30 million."[25] Under no scenario did the NESC or the president's advisors see a situation where the United States could survive a nuclear war without horrific casualties and the country being transformed in very negative ways. As one general exclaimed, "nuclear war is impossible if rational men control governments."[26]

Realizing that several of the scenarios could have unfolded in the Cuban missile crisis, Khrushchev and Kennedy both decided to find more common ground between their two countries. One of the first steps they took was to ensure easier communication in times of a crisis by agreeing to establish a direct link between the White House and the Kremlin. Kennedy wrote Khrushchev in November 1962 explaining "I believe it is vital that we should re-establish some degree of confidence in communication between the two of us. If the leaders of the two great nuclear powers cannot judge with some accuracy the intentions of each other, we shall find ourselves in a period of gravely increasing danger—not only for our two countries but for the whole world."[27] The next month he proposed a direct connection between the two governments so that they could reach other in times of crises.[28] He described how in the Cuban crisis there were long delays for both sides because of the time it took for transmitting and translating messages. He noted that in the nuclear age these delays could have significant consequences; therefore, he proposed the establishment of a direct link which would provide instantaneous or nearly instantaneous communication. Kennedy preferred a teletype line as it would provide quicker translations than a telephone.[29]

The two countries began to discuss establishing the hot line at the Geneva disarmament conference in April and after eighteen technical sessions reached an agreement.[30] They agreed to establish a teletype linking the two

[25] Resume of Discussion During NESC Briefing, September 12, 1963, JFKL, Kennedy Papers, National Security Files, Meetings & Memoranda, Box 314, Folder – NSC Meetings, 1963, No. 517, 9/12/63, p. 1.

[26] Summary Record of National Security Council Meeting, September 12, 1963, ibid., p. 4.

[27] Letter From President Kennedy to Chairman Khrushchev, November 6, 1962, *FRUS, 1961-1963*, Volume VI – Kennedy-Khrushchev Exchanges, http://www.state.gov/www/about_state/history/volume_vi/exchanges.html, accessed on January 1, 2010.

[28] Chalmers M. Roberts, "Kennedy Endorses Direct Teletype Between White House and Kremlin," *The Washington Post, Times Herald*, December 13, 1962, p. A1.

[29] The President's News Conference, December 12, 1962, *Public Papers of the Presidents, John F. Kennedy*, http://www.presidency.ucsb.edu/ws/?pid=9054, accessed on December 23, 2009.

[30] Max Frankel, "U.S.-Soviet 'Hot-Line' Pact Set for Signing in Geneva," *New York Times*, June 6, 1963, p. 1.

governments "for use in time of emergency." The telegraph circuit went from Washington to London to Copenhagen to Stockholm to Helsinki to Moscow, and both countries agreed to split the costs.[31] It went into operation on August 30, 1963 when both sides successfully sent test messages. The American message stated "the quick brown fox jumped over the lazy dog's back 1234567890."[32]

While establishing the hot line was not that significant by itself, it was the first agreement reached between the United States and the Soviet Union at the Geneva disarmament talks that had started several years before.[33] The Geneva talks had been occurring off and on since the Eisenhower administration, and their general objectives were to lead to agreements to limit nuclear weapons and eventually to disarmament. The United States had stopped nuclear tests in October 1958 and pledged to not renew them unless the Soviet Union resumed tests of its own. For the remainder of the Eisenhower administration, both countries refrained from conducting more tests.[34]

Kennedy hoped when he came into office that he would be able to negotiate a permanent test ban treaty with the Soviet Union.[35] Soon after his inauguration, he appointed John McCloy as his chief adviser for issues related to disarmament and arms control, giving those areas greater emphasis than Eisenhower had.[36] He began preparations for the renewal of talks with Soviet Union in March and was fairly optimistic that an agreement could be reached. Before his chief negotiator, Arthur Dean, left for the conference in Geneva,

---

31 Memorandum of Understanding Between the United States of America and the Union of Soviet Socialist Republics Regarding the Establishment of a Direct Communications Link, June 20, 1963, http://www.state.gov/t/isn/4785.htm, accessed on December 23, 2009.

32 "'Hot Line' Opened By U.S. and Soviet to Cut Attack Risk," *New York Times*, August 31, 1963, p. 1.

33 Glenn T. Seaborg, *Kennedy, Khrushchev, and the Test Ban* (Berkeley: University of California Press, 1981), p. 206.

34 "United States Nuclear Tests July 1945 Through September 1992," U.S. Department of Energy, December 2000, http://www.lanl.gov/history/hbombon/pdf/United%20States%20Nuclear%20Tests,%20July%201945%20through%20September%201992.pdf, accessed on December 28, 2009, p. vii. For background information on Eisenhower and the nuclear test ban debates, see Benjamin P. Greene, *Eisenhower, Science Advice, and the Nuclear Test-Ban Debate, 1945-1963* (Stanford, CA: Stanford University Press, 2007).

35 Seaborg, *Kennedy, Khrushchev, and the Test Ban*, p. 36.

36 Letter From President Kennedy to His Adviser on Disarmament, January 27, 1961, *FRUS, 1961-1963*, Volume VII – Arms Control and Disarmament (Washington, D.C.: U.S. Government Printing Office, 1995), http://www.state.gov/r/pa/ho/frus/kennedyjf/vii/50950.htm, accessed on December 28, 2009. For the importance Kennedy gave to arms control and the appointment of McCloy, see Andreas Wenger and Marcel Gerber, "John F. Kennedy and the Limited Test Ban Treaty: A Case Study of Presidential Leadership," *Presidential Studies Quarterly* 29:2 (June 1999), p. 463.

Kennedy instructed him: "The main obstacle heretofore has been the lack of agreement on the establishment of an effective control system. You should, therefore, seek to discover whether a reasonable basis for accord can be found which provides adequate controls and is consistent with the security of the United States."[37]

From the outset of the delegations' arrivals in Geneva, there was one basic roadblock to successfully concluding a ban on nuclear tests—verification. Both sides argued that it was in every country's best interest to ban nuclear tests, but they were never able to agree as to how to verify each other's compliance with any treaty agreements.[38] This problem was quickly apparent when talks opened on March 21, and the lead Soviet negotiator, Semyon Tsarapkin, proposed that the nuclear powers at that time—the United States, the Soviet Union, and Great Britain—create a three-man commission with one representative from the United States and Great Britain, one from the Soviet Union, and one from a neutral country. The commission would be responsible for verifying each country's compliance with treaty agreements, and each commissioner would have veto power over the commission's actions.[39] The Americans and British wanted a much more elaborate verification system including 180 manned detection stations and up to 20 on-site inspections annually in each territory if any violations were suspected. The two sides had staked out almost polar opposite positions from the beginning and discussions quickly stalled.[40] Although discouraged, Kennedy still held out some hope that an agreement could be reached, and he told reporters in April "if there is any chance at all of getting an agreement on a cessation of nuclear tests, regardless of what appear to be the obstacles, I think we should press on."[41]

Kennedy raised the issue with Khrushchev in June when they met in Vienna hoping personal diplomacy might offer the opportunity for a breakthrough but to no avail. The Soviet premier stated that he believed "three inspections a year would be sufficient" and argued "a larger number would be tantamount to intelligence, something the Soviet Union cannot accept." In response, Kennedy emphasized that being able to verify testing through on-site inspections was essential and tried to link the continuation of testing with

---

[37] Airgram from the Department of State to the Consulate General in Geneva, March 8, 1961, *FRUS, 1961-1963*, Volume VII – Arms Control and Disarmament, http://www.state.gov/r/pa/ho/frus/kennedyjf/vii/50950.htm, accessed on December 28, 2009.

[38] Freedman, *Kennedy's Wars*, pp. 262-63.

[39] Seaborg, *Kennedy, Khrushchev, and the Test Ban*, pp. 54-55.

[40] Ibid., p. 58.

[41] The President's News Conference, April 21, 1961, *Public Papers of the Presidents, John F. Kennedy*, http://www.presidency.ucsb.edu/ws/?pid=8077, accessed on December 29, 2009.

nuclear proliferation. He explained to the Soviet leader that "while a nuclear test ban would be no certain guarantee against the proliferation of nuclear weapons, it would certainly impede such proliferation."[42]

After Kennedy returned home, he expressed his frustrations. The president announced, "the Soviet Union's refusal to negotiate seriously on a nuclear test ban at Geneva is disheartening to all those who have held high hopes of stopping the spread of nuclear weapons and the pace of the arms race. It also raises a serious question about how long we can safely continue on a voluntary basis a refusal to undertake tests in this country without any assurance that the Russians are not now testing."[43] In a letter to British Prime Minister Macmillan, Kennedy elaborated on the dilemma they faced concerning possible secret Soviet nuclear tests. He pointed out that several studies had indicated that "we simply cannot be sure, without a control system, that the Soviets are not testing, and if they are testing, they can be learning important things. … We don't know—but for the long run it is just this simple fact that is disturbing--in this field what we don't know can hurt us." He concluded that if progress was not made soon, he would have to consider resuming testing. [44]

Debates concerning nuclear testing continued throughout the Kennedy administration. During the summer of 1961 when both the United States and Soviet Union continued to refrain from resuming nuclear tests, Kennedy's advisers offered conflicting advice as to whether the United States should resume testing. John Kenneth Galbraith, the American ambassador to India, encouraged Kennedy to consider the potential reaction of uncommitted and neutral countries before resuming nuclear tests. He stressed that "there is no question that a resumption of testing would cause us the gravest difficulties in Asia, Africa and elsewhere;" therefore, "a decision to resume testing must be weighed with the greatest care."[45] On the other hand, General Maxwell Taylor, the key military adviser to the president, cautioned that the Soviet Union had

---

42 Memorandum of Conversation, June 4, 1961, *FRUS, 1961-1963*, Volume VII – Arms Control and Disarmament, http://www.state.gov/r/pa/ho/frus/kennedyjf/vii/50950.htm, accessed on December 28, 2009.

43 The President's News Conference, June 28, 1961, *Public Papers of the Presidents, John F. Kennedy*, http://www.presidency.ucsb.edu/ws/?pid=8209, accessed on December 29, 2009.

44 Letter from President Kennedy to Prime Minister Macmillan, Aug. 3, 1961, *FRUS, 1961-1963*, Volume VII – Arms Control and Disarmament, http://www.state.gov/r/pa/ho/frus/kennedyjf/vii/50950.htm, accessed on December 28, 2009. For a view of Kennedy and Macmillan's relationship, see Kendrick Oliver, *Kennedy, Macmillan, and the Test-Ban Debate, 1961-1963* (New York: St. Martin's Press, 1998). On Kennedy's concerns about resuming testing, see Schlesinger, *Journals*, p. 106.

45 Memorandum for the President, June 12, 1961, JFKL, Kennedy Papers, President's Office Files, Special Correspondence, Box 29A, Folder – Galbraith, John Kenneth 3/6-10/61, p. 1.

several military advantages that the United States needed to counter. He then argued "a failure to resume testing seriously retards progress in developing both light strategic warheads and very small atomic weapons."[46] The fear that consistently arose in meetings where Kennedy and his advisers discussed nuclear testing was that the Soviet Union could carry out nuclear tests without the United States knowing—"the party which is engaged in concealment can always succeed if a sufficient effort is made."[47]

After the decision was ultimately made to do so, the debates moved to whether there should be tests in the atmosphere. Adlai Stevenson, the U.S. ambassador to the United Nations, was the chief voice of concern within the Kennedy administration about whether the United States should resume atmospheric testing. He told Kennedy that he doubted "whether we have weighed adequately the political and moral factors in the national power equation."[48] He also raised an intriguing question. He asked the president, "are we sure that additions to gross destructive power really increase our national security once power has reached its present level? If we already have the power to destroy the enemy X times over, does it necessarily follow that we become the stronger by acquiring the power to destroy the enemy X + 1 times?"[49]

The question of whether to resume nuclear testing became more pressing in late August when the Soviet Union announced it was going to begin a new series of nuclear tests.[50] Kennedy and Macmillan denounced the Soviet Union and called for it to join them in pledging to not conduct tests that would produce fallout in the atmosphere. They argued that the Soviet Union had no reason to not accept this limitation as it did not call for any new detection

---

46 Memorandum from the President's Military Representative (Taylor) to President Kennedy, August 7, 1961, *FRUS, 1961-1963*, Volume VII – Arms Control and Disarmament, http://www.state.gov/r/pa/ho/frus/kennedyjf/vii/50951.htm, accessed on December 28, 2009.

47 Memorandum of Minutes of the 490th Meeting of the National Security Council, August 8, 1961, ibid.

48 Memorandum for the President, February 27, 1962, JFKL, Kennedy Papers, President's Office Files, Special Correspondence, Box 33, Folder – Stevenson, Adlai E., 1/3/62-9/12/63.

49 Letter from Stevenson to the President, undated but attached to a memorandum dated February 27, 1962, ibid., p. 1.

50 Editorial Note #58, *FRUS, 1961-1963*, Volume VII – Arms Control and Disarmament, http://www.state.gov/r/pa/ho/frus/kennedyjf/vii/50951.htm, accessed on December 28, 2009. See also White House Statement on Soviet Resumption of Nuclear Weapons Tests, August 30, 1961, *Public Papers of the Presidents, John F. Kennedy*, http://www.presidency.ucsb.edu/ws/?pid=8295, accessed on December 29, 2009.

devices or inspections.[51] However, the Soviet Union refused and began its tests. On September 5, Kennedy announced that the United States would resume underground nuclear tests.[52] Kennedy told the British prime minister "the world is being subjected to threats and terror. We have to show both our friends and our own people that we are ready to meet our own needs in the face of these new Soviet acts." He added, "In my judgment, at this hour the gravest of our dangers is that we may seem less determined than Khrushchev."[53]

The United States conducted its first nuclear test in almost three years on September 15, and over the next two years, it carried out 155 nuclear tests as part of Operations Nougat, Storax, and Niblick.[54] During the same time period, the Soviet Union completed 138 nuclear tests.[55] When later asked about the resumption of nuclear testing, the president claimed the failure to successfully negotiate a test ban treaty was "the biggest disappointment of my first year in office."[56]

In February 1962, the president faced the question of whether the United States would resume conducting nuclear tests in the atmosphere. He noted his reluctance to do so, but feared the advantages the Russians may have gained through their recent tests. He told reporters "I wholly disagree with those who would put all their faith in an arms race and abandon their efforts for disarmament. But I equally disagree with those who would allow us to neglect our defensive needs in the absence of effective agreements for controlled disarmament."[57] At a NSC meeting later in the month, he "indicated his own

[51] Joint Statement With Prime Minister Macmillan Proposing a Three-Power Agreement To End Atmospheric Nuclear Tests, September 3, 1961, ibid., http://www.presidency.ucsb.edu/ws/?pid=8306, accessed on December 29, 2009.

[52] See Statement by the President on Ordering Resumption of Underground Nuclear Tests, September 5, 1961, ibid., http://www.presidency.ucsb.edu/ws/?pid=8310, accessed on December 30, 2009; National Security Action Memorandum No. 87, September 5, 1961, *FRUS, 1961-1963*, Volume VII – Arms Control and Disarmament, http://www.state.gov/r/pa/ho/frus/kennedyjf/vii/50951.htm, accessed on December 28, 2009.

[53] Telegram From the Department of State to the Embassy in the United Kingdom, September 5, 1961, ibid.

[54] "United States Nuclear Tests July 1945 Through September 1992," pp. xi and 16-34.

[55] Soviet Nuclear Test Summary, http://nuclearweaponarchive.org/Russia/Sovtestsum.html, accessed on December 28, 2009.

[56] The President's News Conference, January 31, 1962, *Public Papers of the Presidents, John F. Kennedy*, http://www.presidency.ucsb.edu/ws/?pid=8747, accessed on December 29, 2009.

[57] The President's News Conference, February 7, 1962, ibid., http://www.presidency.ucsb.edu/ws/?pid=8892, accessed on December 29, 2009.

judgment that we must be prepared to test [in the atmosphere] and indeed to test, unless we can make significant progress [in Geneva]."[58]

On March 2, 1962, Kennedy delivered a major address on nuclear testing and disarmament and announced that the United States would be conducting series of nuclear tests in the atmosphere over the Pacific Ocean. He rationalized his decision by noting that further Russian tests "could well provide the Soviet Union with a nuclear attack and defense capability so powerful as to encourage aggressive designs." He then stressed "were we to stand still while the Soviets surpassed us—or even appeared to surpass us—the free World's ability to deter, to survive and to respond to an all-out attack would be seriously weakened."[59] Even with the resumption of tests, however, Kennedy had not given up on reaching a test ban agreement. Not only was he concerned about the dangers posed by the radioactive fallout that resulted from the nuclear tests and the possibility of nuclear proliferation, he also feared that other countries might blame the United States for the failure to obtain an agreement on a test ban. He told Undersecretary of State Ball that he did not want history to record that "an agreement could have been reached, but we [botched] it up."[60]

The United States sent a delegation, headed by Arthur Dean, to the Eighteen Nation Disarmament Talks which opened in March in Geneva.[61] The United States actively participated in the talks throughout 1962 with Dean's instructions emphasizing that "whatever measures are agreed to must be subject to verification in order to determine whether the agreed measures are in fact being carried out."[62] The opening of the new talks resembled the ones from the previous spring as both sides made proposals that the other viewed as unacceptable.[63] By the end of March, Secretary of State Rusk reported that "on testing, it was utterly clear that the Soviets would accept no inspection in the

58 Memorandum of the National Security Council Meeting, February 27, 1962, *FRUS, 1961-1963*, Volume VII – Arms Control and Disarmament, http://www.state.gov/r/pa/ho/frus/kennedyjf/vii/50952.htm, accessed on December 28, 2009.

59 Radio and Television Address to the American People: "Nuclear Testing and Disarmament," March 2, 1962, *Public Papers of the Presidents, John F. Kennedy*, http://www.presidency.ucsb.edu/ws/?pid=9084, accessed on December 29, 2009.

60 Memorandum of Telephone Conversation Between President Kennedy and Acting Secretary of State Ball, March 20, 1962, *FRUS, 1961-1963*, Volume VII – Arms Control and Disarmament, http://www.state.gov/r/pa/ho/frus/kennedyjf/vii/50953.htm, accessed on December 28, 2009.

61 In reality only seventeen nations participated as France decided to not attend. Seaborg, *Kennedy, Khrushchev, and the Test Ban*, p. 142.

62 Memorandum from the Acting Director of the Arms Control and Disarmament Agency, March 14, 1962, *FRUS, 1961-1963*, Volume VII – Arms Control and Disarmament, http://www.state.gov/r/pa/ho/frus/kennedyjf/vii/50953.htm, accessed on December 28, 2009.

63 Seaborg, *Kennedy, Khrushchev, and the Test Ban*, pp. 143-44.

USSR, in any way, shape or form."[64] In defending the American position, the president announced "we know of no way to verify underground nuclear explosions without inspections, and we cannot at this time enter into a treaty without the ability and right of international verification. Hence we seem to be at a real impasse."[65]

While the rest of 1962 saw little movement in the Geneva talks, Kennedy did begin to consider more seriously a more limited test ban which would not require on-site inspectors. Secretary of State Rusk telegraphed the American negotiating team in Geneva explaining "if the Soviet Union continues to indicate unwillingness to accept obligatory on-site inspections on Soviet soil, the United States should be ready to discuss affirmatively an atmospheric-outer space-underwater test ban treaty."[66] To see if this type of limited test ban could be plausible, Kennedy asked Jerome Wiesner, his chief science adviser, whether the United States should consider a ban on tests in outer space. Wiesner concluded that such a "ban would not involve any real risks to this country from a military security point of view."[67] Reassured by this advice and other consultations, Kennedy and Macmillan issued a joint statement in late August offering a draft treaty to end all nuclear testing and an alternative one ending tests in the atmosphere, outer space, and underwater.[68] Although nothing came of this offer at the time, it laid the foundation for an agreement the following year.

While the foundation had been laid, there was still a ways to go before the countries could reach an agreement. Things seemed to look promising in late December when Khrushchev, after making reference to the recent crisis in Cuba, wrote Kennedy, "Can't we solve a far simpler question – that of

---

[64] Minutes of Meeting of the National Security Council, March 28, 1962, *FRUS, 1961-1963*, Volume VII – Arms Control and Disarmament, http://www.state.gov/r/pa/ho/frus/kennedyjf/vii/50953.htm, accessed on December 28, 2009.

[65] Statement by the President on Nuclear Test Inspection, March 29, 1962, *Public Papers of the Presidents, John F. Kennedy*, http://www.presidency.ucsb.edu/ws/?pid=8574, accessed on December 29, 2009.

[66] Telegram from the Department of State to the Delegation to the Eighteen-Nation Disarmament Committee, August 3, 1962, *FRUS, 1961-1963*, Volume VII – Arms Control and Disarmament, http://www.state.gov/r/pa/ho/frus/kennedyjf/vii/50954.htm, accessed on December 28, 2009.

[67] Memorandum for the President, August 9, 1962, JFKL, Kennedy Papers, President's Office Files, Staff Memos, Box 67, Folder – Wiesner, Jerome B., 1962, p. 1.

[68] Editorial Notes #224, *FRUS, 1961-1963*, Volume VII – Arms Control and Disarmament, *FRUS, 1961-1963*, Volume VII – Arms Control and Disarmament, http://www.state.gov/r/pa/ho/frus/kennedyjf/vii/50954.htm, accessed on December 28, 2009. See also Joint Statement with Prime Minister Macmillan on Nuclear Testing, August 27, 1962, *Public Papers of the Presidents, John F. Kennedy*, http://www.presidency.ucsb.edu/ws/?pid=8834, accessed on December 29, 2009.

cessation of experimental explosions of nuclear weapons in … peaceful conditions?"[69] In the spring of 1963, Kennedy sent a letter to Khrushchev trying to reassure him that there was no duplicity in the U.S. position on nuclear testing. He stressed, "these are difficult and dangerous times in which we live, and both you and I have grave responsibilities to our families and to all of mankind. The pressures from those who have a less patient and peaceful outlook are very great—but I assure you of my own determination to work at all times to strengthen world peace."[70] He insisted in a national security memorandum that despite the impasse in the Geneva talks he had not changed his mind concerning "the desirability of a test ban treaty or the value of our proposals on general and complete disarmament. Further," he explained, "the events of the last two years have increased my concern for the consequences of an un-checked continuation of the arms race between ourselves and the Soviet Bloc."[71]

Both sides continued to push for a comprehensive test ban based on their earlier proposals. Khrushchev wrote to Kennedy in May claiming that the United States really was not seeking an agreement to end nuclear tests, since it kept insisting on on-site inspections. From the Soviet leader's perspective these inspections were needless from a scientific and technical standpoint. He insisted that the Soviet Union was ready to reach an agreement "without spying inspections in foreign territories. This is the crux of the whole problem."[72] Kennedy responded to Khrushchev that "we most sincerely and categorically affirm that we have no such purpose [using inspections to spy on the Soviet Union]." However, he maintained the position that "we think that reasonable provisions for on-site inspections will make it possible for us to work out a treaty which will endure and not be liable to break down because of unfounded suspicions which could easily have been dispelled by reasonable provisions for verification."[73]

While the two countries had made little progress, both Kennedy and Khrushchev were moving towards an understanding. They both had sought a

[69] Letter from Khrushchev to Kennedy, December 19, 1962, JFKL, President's Office Files, Countries, Box 115, Folder – Cuba Security Missile Crisis, Khrushchev Correspondence, 10/23/62-12/19/62, p. 6

[70] Message from President Kennedy to Chairman Khrushchev, April 11, 1963, *FRUS, 1961-1963*, Volume VII – Arms Control and Disarmament, http://www.state.gov/r/pa/ho/frus/kennedyjf/vii/50955.htm, accessed on December 28, 2009.

[71] National Security Action Memorandum No. 239, May 6, 1963, ibid.

[72] Letter From Chairman Khrushchev to President Kennedy, May 8, 1963, ibid.

[73] Telegram From the Department of State to the Embassy in the Soviet Union, May 30, 1963, ibid.

comprehensive test ban treaty outlawing all nuclear testing, but they were coming to the realization that neither side was going to be able to accept the other's proposals. President Kennedy delivered a very influential speech on June 10 that stressed the importance of world peace. He noted "both the United States and its allies, and the Soviet Union and its allies, have a mutually deep interest in a just and genuine peace and in halting the arms race." He then pointed to the need for a treaty outlawing nuclear tests. He acknowledged that "a fresh start" was badly need, but then pointed to the virtues of such a treaty. It would "check the spiraling arms race", "place the nuclear powers in a position to deal more effectively with one of the greatest hazards which man faces in 1963, the further spread of nuclear arms", and "increase our security" by decreasing the chances of war.[74] The Russian reaction was positive with Khrushchev claiming it was "the best speech by any President since Roosevelt."[75]

In a speech in East Berlin on July 2, Khrushchev again called for a comprehensive agreement, but expressed his "readiness to include an agreement on the cessation of nuclear tests in the atmosphere, in outer space and under water."[76] This was the first time Khrushchev had indicated his willingness to accept such an agreement since Kennedy and Macmillan had proposed it the previous August. Kennedy responded to Khrushchev's suggestion by writing the Soviet premier telling him, "I share the view which you have put forward in your important statement in Berlin that it is sensible to reach agreement where agreement is now possible, in the area of testing in the atmosphere, under water, and in outer space."[77] Furthermore, he instructed Averell Harriman, his lead negotiator in upcoming talks in Moscow, to seek a treaty banning nuclear weapons tests in the atmosphere, outer space and under water and "to carry such negotiations as far as you can."[78]

Harriman's team engaged in intensive negotiations with their Soviet counterparts beginning on July 15 and ultimately reached an agreement

---

[74] Commencement Address at American University in Washington, June 10, 1963, *Public Papers of the Presidents, John F. Kennedy*, http://www.presidency.ucsb.edu/ws/?pid=9266, accessed on December 30, 2009.

[75] Quoted in Beschloss, *The Crisis Years*, p. 601. For further background on and importance of the speech, see Seaborg, *Kennedy, Khrushchev, and the Test Ban*, p. 218; Leffler, *For the Soul of Mankind*, pp. 182-86; and Fursenko and Naftali, *Khrushchev's Cold War*, pp. 523-525.

[76] Editorial Note #309, *FRUS, 1961-1963*, Volume VII – Arms Control and Disarmament, http://www.state.gov/r/pa/ho/frus/kennedyjf/vii/50956.htm, accessed on December 28, 2009.

[77] Telegram From the Department of State to the Embassy in the United Kingdom, July 12, 1963, ibid.

[78] Instructions for the Under Secretary of State for Political Affairs (Harriman), July 10, 1963, ibid.

prohibiting nuclear tests in the atmosphere, underwater, or in outer space.[79] Kennedy announced the agreement in a radio and television address on July 26. He explained "I speak to you tonight in a spirit of hope. ... Yesterday a shaft of light cut into the darkness. Negotiations were concluded in Moscow on a treaty to ban all nuclear tests in the atmosphere, in outer space, and under water. For the first time, an agreement has been reached on bringing the forces of nuclear destruction under international control." He acknowledged that the treaty would not stop nuclear tests conducted underground, but emphasized that "this limited treaty will radically reduce the nuclear testing which would otherwise be conducted on both sides; it will prohibit the United States, the United Kingdom, the Soviet Union, and all others who sign it, from engaging in the atmospheric tests which have so alarmed mankind; and it offers to all the world a welcome sign of hope." He concluded by saying, "My fellow Americans, let us take that first step. Let us, if we can, step back from the shadows of war and seek out the way of peace. And if that journey is a thousand miles, or even more, let history record that we, in this land, at this time, took the first step."[80]

Kennedy was unsure whether the Senate would ratify the treaty and also knew that neither France nor West Germany liked it. He personally consulted with de Gaulle from France and Adenaur from Germany to assuage their fears.[81] To mollify the Senate, especially Republicans, Kennedy insisted that a bipartisan group of senators travel to Moscow to mark the formal implementation of the treaty.[82] Kennedy and his advisers then carefully worked through the ratification process, and in late September the Senate voted 80 to 19 in favor of the treaty and the president signed it on October 7.[83] Ted Sorenson later wrote that "no other accomplishment in the White House ever gave Kennedy greater satisfaction."[84]

---

[79] For a discussion of these negotiations, see Seaborg, *Kennedy, Khrushchev, and the Test Ban*, pp. 235-53.

[80] Radio and Television Address to the American People on the Nuclear Test Ban Treaty, July 26, 1963, *Public Papers of the Presidents, John F. Kennedy*, http://www.presidency.ucsb.edu/ws/?pid=9360, accessed on December 29, 2009. See also Bundy, *Danger and Survival*, p. 460.

[81] See Letter from President Kennedy to President de Gaulle, July 25, 1963; and Telegram From the Department of State to the Embassy in Germany, August 6, 1963, *FRUS, 1961-1963*, Volume VII – Arms Control and Disarmament, http://www.state.gov/r/pa/ho/frus/kennedyjf/vii/50957.htm, accessed on December 30, 2009.

[82] Seaborg, *Kennedy, Khrushchev, and the Test Ban*, pp. 258-60.

[83] Ibid., 263-82. See also Beschloss, *The Crisis Years*, pp. 631-636.

[84] Quoted in Beschloss, *The Crisis Years*, p. 636.

While Kennedy's attention was drawn to the civil rights movement at home and negotiations with the Soviet Union for a nuclear test ban treaty, events in Southeast Asia began to take more of his time in 1963. As had been the situation in 1961, continuing troubles in Laos drew Kennedy's attention to Southeast Asia two years later. While the Soviet Union and the United States generally had kept to their 1962 promises to remove their military advisers from Laos and to encourage the development of a neutral government, the area's regional actors often failed to fulfill their roles.[85] In particular, the Pathet Lao within Laos and the North Vietnamese, through the use of infiltration routes through Laos to South Vietnam, challenged the peace in the region.[86] In April 1963 as concern about the situation in Laos grew, Kennedy "requested that a study be made for his consideration … of feasible military actions to be taken against the northern Vietnamese" who were using trails through Laos to send forces and supplies into South Vietnam.[87] Ultimately, however, Kennedy's main concern was to prevent the situation from mushrooming into something much larger than it really was as neither the Soviet Union nor the United States wanted a Cold War confrontation there. The crisis settled down after Undersecretary of State Harriman met with Soviet Foreign Minister Andrei Gromyko in Moscow in late April where they both pledged "to support an independent and neutral Laos."[88]

While the United States and Soviet Union renewed their agreement to follow a policy of neutrality regarding Laos, the flare up in the spring of 1963 brought new attention to the situation in Vietnam. Prior to 1963, Kennedy had recognized that the struggle between North and South Vietnam was important, but it had been overshadowed by many other issues in significance. His administration had been divided in 1961 over what policy to pursue, and Kennedy ultimately chose to increase U.S. involvement by sending more military advisers and increasing financial support. This expansion did lead to some U.S. forces being engaged in combat as Kennedy noted that if the American advisers were "fired upon they are, of course, to fire back, to protect

[85] For U.S. covert operations in Laos, see Memorandum, April 22, 1963, April 20, 1963, JFKL, Kennedy Papers, National Security Files, Meetings & Memoranda, Box 314, Folder – NSC Meetings, 1963 No. 513, 4/22/63, pp. 1-6.

[86] See Freedman, *Kennedy's Wars*, pp. 352-55; and Kaiser, *American Tragedy*, pp. 197-200.

[87] Summary Record of the National Security Council Meeting, April 20, 1963, JFKL, Kennedy Papers, National Security Files, Meetings & Memoranda, Box 314, Folder – NSC Meetings, 1963 No. 512, 4/20/63, p. 1.

[88] Memorandum of Conversation, April 26, 1963, ibid., Box 315, Folder – Standing Group Meeting, General, 4/30/63, p. 14. For the difficulties both the United States and Soviet Union faced in dealing with Laos and their decision to avoid a crisis there, see Kaiser, *American Tragedy*, pp. 352-55.

themselves."[89] However, their main role was as advisors and generally they avoided combat situations.

To assist the South Vietnamese, the Kennedy administration placed great stress on the importance of counterinsurgency efforts and developing a strategic hamlet program.[90] This program called for "grouping the peasant population in fortified, defensible settlements and undertaking various measures within these settlements to weed out Viet Cong sympathizers, improve the villager's lot, enhance the government's image, and give the peasant grounds for identifying himself with the government's fight against the Viet Cong."[91] By 1963, Kennedy was particularly pleased with the Army's Special Forces that focused on counterinsurgency warfare as he told his secretary of state "This program is proceeding well."[92] There were also reports that "The strategic hamlet program ... has acquired both momentum and balance. Its impact is most favorable."[93]

Kennedy's dilemma was that he knew that without U.S. aid, the South Vietnamese government would likely fail and another country in the world would have been lost to communism. However, he did not know whether expanding U.S. efforts would actually lead to victory.[94] While he had deliberately resisted calls by some in 1961 to expand the American role and commit American forces to combat operations, he had significantly increased the U.S. military presence. Between his inauguration and assassination, the United States increased its number of military advisors from 685 to 16,732. The increase had also come at a significant cost as 73 American military personnel died during that time while serving in their advisory roles.[95] Events in 1963 raised further questions as to whether American policies were succeeding or even had a chance of success. Ultimately, Kennedy made

---

[89] Max Frankel, "Calls Situation Sensitive," *New York Times*, February 12, 1962, p. 1.

[90] Kaiser, *American Tragedy*, p. 171. Kaiser documents that there were divisions within the Kennedy administration over how to fight the insurgency.

[91] National Intelligence Estimate 53-63, April 17, 1963 in *Estimative Products on Vietnam, 1948-1975*, p. 194.

[92] Memorandum for Secretary of State, July 24, 1963, JFKL, Kennedy Papers, National Security Files, Chester V. Clifton Papers, Box 345, Folder – Confs. w/the Pres., JCS, 2/63-11/63 & undated, p. 1. See also Freedman, *Kennedy's Wars*, p. 356.

[93] Report by the Joint Chiefs of Staff's Special Assistant for Counterinsurgency and Special Activities, undated [early July 1963], *FRUS, 1961-1963*, Volume III – Vietnam, January-August 1963 (Washington, D.C.: U.S. Government Printing Office, 1991), http://www.state.gov/r/pa/ho/frus/kennedyjf/iii/8168.htm, accessed on December 22, 2009.

[94] Freedman, *Kennedy's Wars*, p. 339.

[95] Ibid., p. xii.

difficult decisions that increased the chances of greater U.S. military involvement in Vietnam in the future.[96]

One of Kennedy's problems was that he received conflicting information as to the exact conditions in South Vietnam.[97] An intelligence estimate in April 1963 painted a cautiously optimistic picture of the situation in South Vietnam. It noted that "Communist progress had been blunted and the situation is improving" and "further progress can be made in expanding the area of government control in creating greater security in the country side." It cautioned, however, that "despite South Vietnamese progress, the situation remains fragile," and the South Vietnamese "government's capacity to embark upon the broader measures required to translate military success into lasting political stability is questionable."[98] An undersecretary in the State Department captured it aptly, "the Viet Nam story is one of great complexity and with infinite shadings and nuances. There is considerably more gray than there is black or white."[99]

In a new intelligence estimate in July, there was much less optimism. It explained "the Buddhist crisis in South Vietnam has highlighted and intensified a widespread and longstanding dissatisfaction with South Vietnam's leader Ngo Dinh Diem and his style of government. If, as is likely, Diem fails to carry out truly and promptly the commitments he has made to the Buddhists, disorders will probably flare again and the chances of a coup or assassination attempts against him will become better than even."[100] It did not predict a coup and noted that the communists might not even want one. However, it did note that the removal of the Diem might not be all bad. It concluded, "a non-Communist successor regime might be initially less effective against the Viet Cong, but, given continued support from the U.S., could provide reasonably effective leadership for the government and the war effort."[101]

The Buddhist crisis mentioned in the intelligence estimate developed from Diem's propensity to give preferential treatment to Catholics in both the

---

96 Leffler, *For the Soul of Mankind*, p. 177.

97 Kaiser emphasizes the problem of conflicting information in *American Tragedy*.

98 National Intelligence Estimate 53-63, April 17, 1963 in *Estimative Products on Vietnam, 1948-1975*, pp. 186-87.

99 Memorandum From the Under Secretary of State for Political Affairs' Special Assistant (Jorden) to the Assistant Secretary of State for Far Eastern Affairs, March 21, 1963, *FRUS, 1961-1963*, Volume III – Vietnam, January-August 1963, http://www.state.gov/r/pa/ho/frus/kennedyjf/iii/8160.htm, accessed on December 22, 2009.

100 SNIE 53-2-63 – The Situation in South Vietnam, July 10, 1963 on CD in *Estimative Products on Vietnam, 1948-1975*, p. 1.

101 Ibid.

government and military. The South Vietnamese leader's policies favoring Catholics over the majority Buddhist population were not new, but in the spring of 1963, things changed. The Buddhists had remained primarily passive during the decade that Diem had been in power, but in May 1963, the government began enforcing a policy right before the celebration of Buddha's birthday that prohibited the flying of religious flags.[102] While the enforcement of this regulation would have angered the Buddhists anyway, the government had made the situation worse by recently encouraging the flying of Papal flags in honor of the archbishop of Hue. Buddhists in Hue began protesting the restrictions on celebrating Buddha's life, and during one of their marches, a government force fired on and killed several protestors.[103] The government's "stiff-necked handling" of the situation caused widespread disenchantment within the lower and middle levels of the South Vietnamese military and government bureaucracy wherein most were Buddhists. Also, many members of the South Vietnamese security forces realized that "promotions tended to be based upon presumed loyalty to Diem rather than upon professional competence."[104] The CIA concluded that "inept government handling has permitted a localized incident in Hue to grow into a potential political crisis. Unless Diem is able to reach a quick reconciliation with the Buddhists, the issue could have serious repercussions on governmental stability."[105]

Under growing U.S. pressure, Diem belatedly and with little conviction tried to reach an accord with the Buddhist opposition.[106] The crisis took a new

---

[102] David Halberstam, "Buddhists Defy Regime in Saigon: Religious Flags Are Flown--More Protests Planned," *New York Times*, June 13, 1963, p. 5. See also Kaiser, *American Tragedy*, p. 213

[103] SNIE 53-2-63, pp. 2-3. See also Telegram from the Consulate at Hue to the Department of State, May 9, 1963, *FRUS, 1961-1963*, Volume III – Vietnam, January-August 1963, http://www.state.gov/r/pa/ho/frus/kennedyjf/iii/8163.htm, accessed on December 22, 2009.

[104] NIE 53-63, April 17, 1963 in *Estimative Products on Vietnam, 1948-1975*, p. 193

[105] Current Intelligence Memorandum Prepared in the Office of Current Intelligence, Central Intelligence Agency, June 3, *FRUS, 1961-1963*, Volume III – Vietnam, January-August 1963, http://www.state.gov/r/pa/ho/frus/kennedyjf/iii/8165.htm, accessed on December 22, 2009.

[106] See Memorandum of Conversation, July 4, 1963, ibid., http://www.state.gov /r/pa/ho/frus/kennedyjf/iii/8168.htm. accessed on December 22, 2009; Telegram From the Department of State to the Embassy in Vietnam, June 1, 1963 ibid., http://www. state.gov/r/pa/ho/frus/kennedyjf/iii/8165.htm, accessed on December 22, 2009; Telegram From the Embassy in Vietnam to the Department of State, June 9, 1963, ibid., http://www.state.gov/r/pa/ho/frus/kennedyjf/iii/8166.htm, accessed on December 22, 2009; Telegram From the Embassy in Vietnam to the Department of State, June 11, 1963, ibid., Max Frankel, "U.S. Warns South Vietnam On Demands of Buddhists: Diem Is Told He Faces Censure if He Fails to Satisfy Religious Grievances, Many of Which Are Called Just," *New York Times*, June 14, 1963, p. 1; and David Halberstam, "Saigon Concedes 2 Buddhist Points: Is Reported Yielding on Flag and Restriction Issues," ibid., June 15, 1963, p. 1.

direction in early June when a Buddhist monk committed suicide by self-immolation in front of hundreds of onlookers in the middle of an intersection in Saigon.[107] Over the course of the summer several other monks and one nun took their lives the same way.[108] These very graphic and public displays of protests drew American attention to the situation in Vietnam in ways not seen before. When Kennedy saw a picture of the burning monk, he told his new ambassador to Vietnam Henry Cabot Lodge, "This sort of thing has got to stop."[109] In early August, Diem's sister, Madame Nhu, only made the situation worse when she described one of the monks who killed himself a "barbeque".[110] In the ultimate of understatements, Kennedy told reporters in early September that the Diem regime had clearly "gotten out of touch with the people."[111]

The crisis reached its peak in the late summer and early fall when the Kennedy administration reluctantly came to the conclusion that the Diem regime was no longer viable and military leaders in Vietnam began to plot a coup.[112] The final straw was when the South Vietnamese government launched a series of raids on Buddhists pagodas to disrupt the growing opposition.[113] In

---

107 "Burns Self to Death in Viet Protest: Monk a Human Torch Before Thousands," *Chicago Tribune*, June 11, 1963, p. 3. Malcolm Browne was the only Western correspondent to witness the death. He took numerous pictures. See Reporting America at War – The Reporters: Malcolm W. Browne: The Buddhist Protests of 1963, http://www.pbs.org/weta/reportingamericaatwar/reporters/browne/protests.html, accessed on December 22, 2009.

108 See "Another Suicide Arouses Vietnam: Young Priest Burns Himself to Death in Coastal Town in Protest Against Diem: Troops Take Away Body," *New York Times*, August 5, 1963, p. 1; and "2 More Buddhists Suicides by Burning In Vietnam Protest," ibid., August 16, 1963, p. 1.

109 Reporting America at War – The Reporters: Malcolm W. Browne, http://www.pbs.org/weta/reportingamericaatwar/reporters/browne/protests.html, accessed on December 22, 2009.

110 Telegram 190, quoted in Footnote 6 of Memorandum From Michael V. Forrestal of the National Security Council Staff to the President, August 9, 1963, *FRUS, 1961-1963*, Volume III – Vietnam, January-August 1963, http://www.state.gov/r/pa/ho/frus/kennedyjf/iii/8170.htm, accessed on December 21, 2009.

111 Transcript of Broadcast With Walter Cronkite Inaugurating a CBS Television News Program, September 2, 1963, *Public Papers of the Presidents, John F. Kennedy*, http://www.presidency.ucsb.edu/ws/?pid=9388, accessed on December 23, 2009.

112 See Memorandum Prepared by the Office of Current Intelligence, Central Intelligence Agency, August 21, 1963, *FRUS, 1961-1963*, Volume III – Vietnam, January-August 1963, http://www.state.gov/r/pa/ho/frus/kennedyjf/iii/8177.htm, accessed on December 22, 2009; and Telegram From the Central Intelligence Agency Station in Saigon to the Agency, August 27, 1963, ibid., http://www.state.gov/r/pa/ho/frus/kennedyjf/iii/8178.htm, accessed on December 22, 2009. See also Kaiser, *American Tragedy*, pp. 230-32; and Seth Jacobs, *Cold War Mandarin: Ngo Dinh Diem and the Origins of America's War in Vietnam, 1950-1963* (Lanham, MD: Rowman & Littlefield Publishers, Inc., 2006), pp. 157-62.

113 "Buddhists Seized: Police Hurl Tear Gas and Grenades During Saigon Attacks," *New York Times*, August 21, 1963, p. 1.

a series of meetings in the last week of August, Kennedy and his advisers discussed how to proceed. There were great divisions over what to do.[114] According to Ted Sorensen, "the division within the Kennedy administration over whether to defend Diem against his own army, or to permit a coup to install a new leader, became the deepest division over any issue during Kennedy's years in the White House."[115] On August 24, the president authorized Ambassador Lodge to "urgently examine all possible alternative leadership and make detailed plans as to how we might bring about Diem's replacement if this should become necessary."[116] Kennedy did not openly advocate a change as "he saw no point in trying a coup unless there was a chance of its success."[117] However, his telegram to Lodge set in motion actions that were soon going to be outside U.S. control.

August 29 proved to be a pivotal day as after a lengthy meeting with his advisors, Kennedy decided to throw his support, at least tentatively, behind a coup being planned by several South Vietnamese generals.[118] The president authorized General Paul Harkins, the U.S. military commander in Vietnam, to support the CIA approaches to the Vietnamese generals and gave Ambassador Lodge "authority over all overt and covert operations."[119] The president sent a separate personal memoranda to Lodge reiterating that these decisions had his "full support" and his administration would "do all that we can to help you conclude this operation successfully." However, he did reserve the right "to change course and reverse previous instructions." He explained to the ambassador, "When we go, we must go to win, but it will be better to change

[114] Students can now listen to some of the Kennedy administration's deliberations in the last week of August and see select documents made available by the National Security Archive. See Kennedy Considered Supporting Coup in South Vietnam, August 1963: Newly Declassified Audio Tapes Reveal JFK Saw Only Negative Choices, National Security Archive Electronic Briefing Book No. 302, http://www.gwu.edu/~nsarchiv/NSAEBB/NSAEBB302/index.htm#item12, accessed on December 30, 2009.

[115] Sorensen, *Counselor*, p. 354. See also Kaiser, *American Tragedy*, p. 277; Giglio, *The Presidency of John F. Kennedy*, p. 248; and Dallek, *An Unfinished Life*, p. 674.

[116] Telegram from the Department of State to the Embassy in Vietnam, August 24, 1963, *FRUS, 1961-1963*, Volume III – Vietnam, January-August 1963, http://www.state.gov/r/pa/ho/frus/kennedyjf/iii/8177.htm, accessed on December 23, 2009. On Lodge's role in Vietnam, see Anne E. Blair, *Lodge in Vietnam: A Patriot Abroad* (New Haven, CT: Yale University Press, 1995), pp. 1-70.

[117] Memorandum of Conference with the President, August 27, 1963, JFKL, Kennedy Papers, National Security Files, Meetings & Memoranda, Box 316, Folder – Meetings on Vietnam, 8/29/63-8/31/63, p. 4.

[118] Memorandum of Conference with the President, August 29, 1963, *FRUS, 1961-1963*, Volume IV – Vietnam, August-December 1963, http://www.state.gov/r/pa/ho/frus/kennedyjf/iv/8202.htm, accessed on December 22, 2009.

[119] Ibid.

our minds than fail." Lodge responded that he understood that the president reserved that right, but noted that "to be successful, this operation must be essentially a Vietnamese affair. … Should this happen you may not be able to control it."[120]

Kennedy's decision on August 29 set in motion the more formal planning for a coup attempt by Vietnamese generals. This was not a U.S. planned coup, and prior to November, there were continued efforts to persuade Diem to change, although generally without a lot of optimism. The real dilemma for Kennedy was not whether Diem would ever truly support democracy, but whether he could reform his government sufficiently to win the support of the people and defeat the communist insurgency.[121] There was widespread disagreement whether Diem could win the war. Secretary of State Rusk did not believe Diem could.[122] However, the Deputy Director of Intelligence could not "rule out all possibility of winning the war under a Ngo administration." He asserted "that it took the British nine years of intensive effort to best … the Communist rebellion in Malaya, where the problems were less than those in Vietnam."[123] From Kennedy's perspective, the biggest problems were Diem's brother, Nhu, and sister-in-law, Madame Nhu. He thought it might be possible to salvage Diem's regime if the Vietnamese leader would remove the former from power and muzzle the latter.[124] Unfortunately, neither seemed like a good possibility.[125]

Until late October, the United States held out some hope that regime change in South Vietnam might not be necessary.[126] However, during the last week of the month, reports of an imminent coup, led by General Duong Van

---

[120] Eyes Only for General Clifton, August 30, 1963, JFKL, Kennedy Papers, President's Office Files, Staff Memos, Box 62A, Folder –Bundy, McGeorge 7/63-12/63. The title page of the memo stated, "The Enclosed envelope should be opened by the President only, and when he has read the messages it contains you should destroy them." See also Memorandum, 30 August 1963, http://www.jfklibrary.org/Asset+Tree/Asset+Viewers/Image+Asset+Viewer.htm?guid={E5AAE0BC-CD87-4BB2-91FF-9272DB571E98}&type=Image, accessed on December 31, 2009.

[121] Freedman, *American Tragedy*, p. 386.

[122] Memorandum of Conversation with the President, September 6, 1963, JFKL, Kennedy Papers, National Security Files, Meetings & Memoranda, Box 316, Folder – Meetings on Vietnam, 9/1/63-10/31/63, p. 2.

[123] Memo – South Vietnam's Leaders, September 4, 1963 on CD in *Estimative Products on Vietnam, 1948-1975*, p. 3.

[124] Editorial Note #67, *FRUS, 1961-1963*, Volume IV – Vietnam, August-December 1963, http://www.state.gov/r/pa/ho/frus/kennedyjf/iv/12646.htm, accessed on December 22, 2009.

[125] Memorandum of Conversation, September 29, 1963, ibid., http://www.state.gov/r/pa/ho/frus/kennedyjf/iv/12650.htm, accessed on December 22, 2009. See also Freedman, *Kennedy's Wars*, p. 371.

[126] Kaiser, *American Tragedy*, p. 257.

Minh, became widespread.[127] On October 29, Kennedy met with his key advisers to discuss the purported coup. Even at this point, the president was reluctant to give his final approval. He explained to his advisors, "it appears that the pro- and anti-Diem military forces are about equal. If this is so, any attempt to engineer a coup is silly."[128] At a meeting later that afternoon, the president again cautioned that if the chances of a successful coup were not great, then it should be called off because if it failed, "we could lose our entire position in Southeast Asia overnight."[129]

As Lodge had predicted two months earlier the United States really had little influence over the timing of the coup. While there was widespread knowledge of the planned coup, the speed of its initiation was a surprise. General Harkins reported to General Maxwell Taylor, "Instead of getting four hours or two days notice, we got approximately four minutes."[130] Throughout the day on November 1, the Kennedy administration received reports of the progress of the coup and discussed how to react to it. Their discussions resolved around the coup's potential of success, the implications for the struggle against the Viet Cong, whether Diem would continue to resist, and how to "square recognition of the Vietnamese rebel government which had overthrown a constitutional government." The most prominent of these concerns was to determine "how we can get everyone behind the effort to expedite the winning of the war against the Viet Cong."[131]

By the next morning, it was clear that the coup had succeeded. There was relatively little fighting in Saigon or elsewhere between Diem's supporters and the coup's forces, and Diem had been captured.[132] Secretary of State Rusk now

---

127 Telegram From the Central Intelligence Agency Station in Saigon to the Agency, October 24, *FRUS, 1961-1963*, Volume IV – Vietnam, August-December 1963, http://www.state.gov/r/pa/ho/frus/kennedyjf/iv/12652.htm, accessed on December 22, 2009. For background information on Duong Van Minh, see "Leader of Uprising Duong Van Minh: Called New Strong Man Known as 'Big Minh'," *New York Times*, November 2, 1963, p. 2.

128 Memorandum of Conference with President Kennedy, October 29, 1963, 4:20 p.m., *FRUS, 1961-1963*, Volume IV – Vietnam, August-December 1963, http://www.state.gov/r/pa/ho/frus/kennedyjf/iv/12652.htm, accessed on December 22, 2009.

129 Memorandum of Conference with President Kennedy, October 29, 1963, 6:00 p.m., ibid.

130 Telegram from the Commander, Military Assistance Command, Vietnam (Harkins) to the Chairman of the Joint Chiefs of Staff, November 1, 1963, ibid., http://www.state.gov/r/pa/ho/frus/kennedyjf/iv/12653.htm, accessed on December 22, 2009.

131 Memorandum of Conference with the President, November 1, 1963, JFKL, Kennedy Papers, National Security Files, Meetings & Memoranda, Box 317, Folder – Meetings on Vietnam, 11/1/63-11/2/63, p. 1.

132 Telegram From the Commander, Military Assistance Command, Vietnam (Harkins) to the Joint Chiefs of Staff, November 2, 1963, 6:00 a.m., *FRUS, 1961-1963*, Volume IV – Vietnam, August-December 1963, http://www.state.gov/r/pa/ho/frus/kennedyjf/iv/12653.htm, accessed on December 23, 2009. See also Jacobs, *Cold War Mandarin*, pp. 175-80; and William J.

saw the most important question as "how to get on with the war in Vietnam against the Viet Cong."[133] General Taylor hoped that a strong government would emerge from the coup "to prosecute the war with improved effectiveness."[134] While discussions of the prosecution of the war predominated, Diem's fate did concern Kennedy. During the night, reports came in that the South Vietnamese leader and his brother had committed suicide after they were captured. However, the president had serious doubts that as "Catholics the two would have committed suicide" and feared the repercussions that their deaths "would have here and abroad."[135] Photographs soon emerged of Diem and his brother's "bloodstained bodies lying with hands tied behind their backs on the floor of an armored personnel carrier."[136] When the president heard that Diem had been assassinated, he "leaped to his feet and rushed from the room with a look of shock and dismay on his face."[137] He evidently believed that the worst thing that would happen to Diem is that he would have been forced into exile.

The administration moved over the next few weeks to work with the new regime to stabilize the situation and move forward with the war effort. By the evening of November 2, the United States was prepared to continue and expand economic aid to South Vietnam "in order prevent disruption of war effort and economy and avoid hardships on population."[138] The leader of the coup, Duong Van Minh, assumed the presidency, and the CIA reported that "the Vietnamese … are groping around the organizational, bureaucratic and political jungles, trying to turn their convictions and their popular support into

Rust, *Kennedy in Vietnam: American Vietnam Policy, 1960-63* (New York: Scribner, 1985), pp. 161-75.

133 Memorandum of Conference with the President, November 2, 1963, 9:15 a.m., JFKL, Kennedy Papers, National Security Files, Meetings & Memoranda, Box 317, Folder – Meetings on Vietnam, 11/1/63-11/2/63, p. 1.

134 Telegram From the Chairman of the Joint Chiefs of Staff (Taylor) to the Commander, Military Assistance Command, Vietnam, November 2, 1963, 12:25 pm, ibid.

135 Memorandum of Conference with the President, November 2, 1963, 9:15 a.m., p. 2.

136 Thomas L. Alhern, Jr. "CIA and the House of Ngo: Covert Operations in South Vietnam, 1954-1963," Center for the Study of Intelligence, p. 213, http://www.foia.cia.gov/vietnam/ 2_CIA_AND_THE_HOUSE_OF_NGO.pdf, accessed on December 30, 2009. Spacing Issue at the beginning of this line.

137 Maxwell Taylor, *Swords and Plowshares* (New York: W.W. Norton, 1972), p. 301 quoted in Editorial Note #274, *FRUS, 1961-1963*, Volume IV – Vietnam, August-December 1963, http://www.state.gov/r/pa/ho/frus/kennedyjf/iv/12653.htm, accessed on December 22, 2009. See also Dallek, *An Unfinished Life*, p. 684.

138 Telegram From the Department of State to the Embassy in Vietnam, November 2, 1963, *FRUS, 1961-1963*, Volume IV – Vietnam, August-December 1963, http://www.state.gov/ r/pa/ho/frus/kennedyjf/iv/12671.htm, accessed on December 23, 2009.

specific ways of strengthening the country."[139] Van Minh had little success and was forced out of office in late January 1964 by another coup.[140]

The Kennedy administration's efforts in South Vietnam reflected its commitment to resist communist expansion wherever it occurred. He had inherited a difficult situation and struggled for three years to develop policies that would support the Diem regime, while successfully defeating the communist insurgency. Unfortunately, the president and his advisors were unable to do this. They raised the American commitment to Diem's regime by sending thousands more military advisers and increasing economic aid. Neither effort produced the results they wanted, and by the fall of 1963, they were ready to move in a different direction by supporting Van Minh. Little did they know, however, that the new government would last only three months. One of Kennedy's deepest admirers later noted that Vietnam "was the only foreign policy problem handed off by JFK to his successor in no better, and possibly worse, shape than it was when he inherited it."[141] While exaggerating Kennedy's accomplishments, this assessment accurately reflects the limitations of Kennedy's policies in Southeast Asia.[142]

While it is easy to forget that Kennedy the president was also Kennedy the husband and Kennedy the father, the last half of 1963 brought these latter roles to the forefront. In the midst of the Vietnam crisis and the negotiations over the Limited Test Ban Treaty, Kennedy and his wife had to deal with a personal tragedy. On August 7, 1963, Jackie Kennedy gave birth five and half weeks early to the Kennedy's third child, Patrick Bouvier Kennedy. Their young son developed hyaline membrane disease, better known today as respiratory distress syndrome, and died two days later.[143] Understandably, the family was devastated, and President Kennedy never recovered from the loss.

Little did the family know that little Patrick's death would not be the only death they would have deal with in 1963. Just weeks after coup plotters assassinated Diem in Saigon, Kennedy embarked on a two-day campaign trip to Texas which would involve visits to five cities. The trip was part of series of

---

139 Telegram From the Central Intelligence Agency Station in Saigon to the Agency, November 16, 1963, ibid., http://www.state.gov/r/pa/ho/frus/kennedyjf/iv/12672.htm, accessed on December 23, 2009.

140 Memorandum from Michael V. Forrestal of the National Security Council Staff to the President, January 30, 1964, *FRUS, 1964-1968*, Volume I – Vietnam, 1964, http://www.state.gov/www/about_state/history/vol_i/1_27.html, accessed on December 23, 2009.

141 Sorensen, *Counselor*, p. 359.

142 Giglio, *The Presidency of John F. Kennedy*, p. 254. See also Freedman, *American Tragedy*, p. 379.

143 William M. Blair, "Kennedys Mourning Baby Son: Funeral Today Will Be Private," *New York Times*, August 10, 1963, p. 1.

campaign excursions during the fall that were designed to highlight the president's achievements and set the stage for his run for re-election in 1964. Kennedy viewed Texas with its 24 electoral votes as one of several pivotal states.[144] Even with Lyndon Johnson on the ticket in the 1960 election, Kennedy had only defeated Nixon by two percentage points.[145] By the fall of 1963, Texas Democrats were deeply divided, and Kennedy was not popular with everyone. In the *Dallas Morning News* on November 22, a group called the American Fact-Finding Committee ran an advertisement accusing the president of being soft on communism.[146] After seeing the ad, Kennedy supposedly told his wife that "We're heading into nut country today. But, Jackie, if somebody wants to shoot me from a window with a rifle, nobody can stop it, so why worry about it?"[147] Kennedy believed the risk was worth it as he and his advisers feared that Texas might vote for the Republican candidate in the coming election. The loss of such a large state could have been devastating to Kennedy's re-election chances.

Accompanied by his wife, Kennedy flew from Washington to San Antonio on November 21 and then traveled to Houston before finally stopping in Ft. Worth for the night. The next morning the president delivered two speeches in Ft. Worth before taking a short flight to Dallas. After greetings at the airport, President Kennedy and Jackie joined Texas Governor John Connally and his wife in a convertible limousine. The Connallys sat in the front seat with the driver, while the Kennedys sat in the back. The presidential motorcade traveled ten miles from the airport to downtown Dallas where the president was scheduled to deliver a speech at the Trade Mart. As the Kennedys waved to enthusiastic crowds, the president's limousine turned into Dealey Plaza and passed the Texas School Book Depository. At 12:30 pm (CDT) the sound of guns shots reverberated throughout the plaza and both President Kennedy and Governor Connally slumped over in the car. While Connally was injured in his chest, wrist, and thigh, the president's wounds were much worse.[148]

---

144 "November 22, 1963: Death of the President," John F. Kennedy Presidential Library & Museum, Historical Documents, http://history-matters.com/archive/contents/church/contents_church_reports_rockcomm.htm, accessed on December 31, 2009.

145 W. J. Rorabaugh, *The Real Making of the President: Kennedy, Nixon, and the 1960 Election* (Lawrence, KS: University Press of Kansas, 2009), p. 210.

146 For the full page advertisement in the *Dallas Morning News*, see http://mcadams.posc.mu.edu/ad1.gif, accessed on December 31, 2009.

147 O'Donnell and Power, *"Johnny, We Hardly Knew Ye"*, p. 26.

148 "November 22, 1963: Death of the President." See all national newspapers.

The driver of the limousine immediately sped from the plaza to Parkland Memorial Hospital, which was only a few minutes away. Kennedy had been hit in the head and neck, and the wounds were mortal. Witnesses reported seeing "pieces of bone and brain tissue and bits of reddish hair flying through the air."[149] While the doctors made every effort to save his life at the hospital, there was nothing that could be done. A Catholic priest gave the president his last rites, and thirty minutes after the shots were fired, Kennedy was dead. Barely two hours later, Kennedy's body had been taken to Air Force One for transport back to Washington, and Lyndon Johnson had been sworn in as the thirty-sixth president of the United States.[150]

Since that tragic day in November 1963, numerous efforts have been made to explain how and why Kennedy was assassinated. Within roughly an hour of the shots being fired, Dallas police arrested Lee Harvey Oswald for Kennedy's assassination as well as for the fatal shooting of police officer J.D. Triplett. The police accused Oswald of firing three shots from a rifle that killed the president and using a revolver to later kill the patrolman. Oswald was a 24-year old former Marine who had a history of erratic behavior. He had attempted to defect to the Soviet Union in 1959 and lived there until 1962. He was also sympathetic to Castro. Besides favoring communism and not liking the president, his motives for shooting Kennedy are unclear. Unfortunately, he was shot and killed on November 24 by nightclub owner and Kennedy admirer Jack Ruby while being transferred from the police headquarters to the county jail. His true motives died with him.[151]

A week after the assassination, Lyndon Johnson established a commission headed by Supreme Court Justice Earl Warren to investigate Kennedy's death. It delivered its report to Johnson in September 1964 concluding that only one gunman, Lee Harvey Oswald, was responsible for shooting President Kennedy.[152] Several government studies since then including a panel created by Attorney General Ramsey Clark in 1968, the 1975 U.S. President's Commission on CIA activities within the United States headed by Vice President Nelson Rockefeller, and the 1978 U.S. House of Representatives Select Committee on Assassinations all concluded that Oswald killed the president, but they did challenge several of the findings from the Warren

---

[149] Ibid., pp. 27-28. See also Stossel, *Sarge*, p. 306; and witness accounts at http://mcadams.posc.mu.edu/dpwound.htm, accessed on December 31, 2009.

[150] "November 22, 1963: Death of the President."

[151] David Burner, *John F. Kennedy and a New Generation*, 2nd ed. (New York: Pearson-Longman, 2005), pp. 168-70.

[152] *A Presidential Legacy and the Warren Commission* (Nashville, TN: Flatsigned Press, 2007), pp. xi-xiv.

Commission investigation and questioned its failure to thoroughly investigate leads that might have led to different conclusions. The House Select Committee, in particular, raised the possibility of a second shooter that was in front of the president's car on a grassy knoll in Dallas.[153]

In the over four decades since his death, a cottage industry of conspiracy theorists have proposed ideas as to who killed Kennedy and why they did it. In fact, a Gallup Poll in 2003 indicated that 75 percent of Americans believe that Oswald did not act on his own.[154] The supposed killers range from those angry over Diem's death to mobsters like Sam Giancana and Jimmy Hoffa to Castro or one of his supporters to anti-Castro forces who did not think Kennedy was doing enough to remove the Cuban leader to elements of the CIA and U.S. military who opposed Kennedy's policies to supporters of Lyndon Johnson. While many of the theories are intriguing, most have only a limited basis of evidence and rely on a great deal of conjecture.[155]

After being returned to Washington, Kennedy's body lay in state first in the East Room of the White House and then in the Capitol Rotunda. In the one day that Kennedy's casket was in the Rotunda, 250,000 visitors came to pay their respects. At 11 am on November 25 the funeral procession left the capitol and walked to St. Matthew's Church for Mass. After the church service, Kennedy was taken to Arlington National Cemetery where he was laid to rest.[156]

1963 had started with great promise for President Kennedy. He had shown strong leadership during the Cuban missile crisis and was confident that the coming year would provide opportunities to improve relations with America's allies as well as the Soviet Union. In November he could look back with pride

---

153 The Warren Commission Report and House Select Committee report can be viewed at http://www.archives.gov/research/jfk/ and in *A Presidential Legacy and the Warren Commission*. The report of the Ramsey Clark panel can be found at http://www.jfklancer.com/ClarkPanel.html. The Rockefeller Commission Report can be found at http://history-matters.com/archive/contents/church/contents_church_reports_rockcomm.htm.

154 Lydia Saad, "Americans: Kennedy Assassination a Conspiracy: No Consensus About Who Was Involved," November 21, 2003, http://www.gallup.com/poll/9751/Americans-Kennedy-Assassination-Conspiracy.aspx, accessed on January 9, 2010.

155 John C. McAdams, a political science professor at Marquette University, has put together a masterful website, "The Kennedy Assassination," at http://mcadams.posc.mu.edu/home.htm, which explores the Kennedy assassination and the various conspiracy theories. You should also see Gerald L. Posner, *Case Closed: Lee Harvey Oswald and the Assassination of JFK* (New York: Random House, 1993); *A Presidential Legacy and the Warren Commission*, pp. xv-xxix; Giglio, *The Presidency of John F. Kennedy*, pp. 279-81; and Dallek, *An Unfinished Life*, pp. 698-99.

156 For descriptions of the funeral, see "November 22, 1963: Death of the President;" and Stossel, *Sarge*, pp. 302-22.

at the signing of the Limited Test Ban Treaty and the overall thawing of tensions with the Soviet Union. However, he also would have seen the continued strains in the America's relationships with its allies, especially France, and the deteriorating situation in South Vietnam. He would have recognized that there was still much work to be done, but he would have been optimistic about the future. Unfortunately, that optimism came to crashing halt on November 22 when a bullet from Oswald's rifle snuffed out the young president's life.

CONCLUSION

In February 2005, over 40 years after Kennedy's assassination, Sotheby's held a three-day sale of Kennedy family memorabilia. Thousands of people made bids on the close to 700 items in their efforts to own part of the Kennedy legacy. A rocking chair that Kennedy once used sold for $96,000; a painting of Kennedy's children brought in $51,000; and a red wool blanket with Kennedy's initials monogrammed on the back sold for $18,000.[1] What drove people to spend so much on relatively trivial items is impossible to explain, but it does reveal the enduring legacy of John F. Kennedy and his family. Kennedy's life still captivates many Americans, and he has been judged as a very successful president. A Gallup Poll in 2003 found that Americans ranked Kennedy and Lincoln as the two greatest U.S. presidents.[2] In a 2009 survey, over 60 historians ranked Kennedy as the sixth best president in American history.[3] Why do so many people, including academic scholars, rank him so high? This study shows Kennedy to be a very charismatic leader who handled many situations well, but also one who at times relied heavily on rhetoric and less so on actions. While Kennedy was clearly a pretty good president, his lofty rankings are a bit exaggerated.

Kennedy had to deal with numerous Cold War issues and crises during his presidency. He came into office believing that the United States had to do

---

[1] Carol Vogel, "Another Kennedy Auction Brings Out Nostalgia and Wallets," *New York Times*, February 16, 2005, http://query.nytimes.com/gst/fullpage.html?res=9F07E3DE133AF935A25751C0A9639C8B63&sec=&spon=&pagewanted=1, accessed on January 9, 2010.

[2] Frank Newport, Jeffrey M. Jones, and Lydia Saad, "Ronald Reagan from the People's Perspective: A Gallup Poll Review: Reagan's Image Improved Substantially in the Years after He Left Office," http://www.gallup.com/poll/11887/Ronald-Reagan-From-Peoples-Perspective-Gallup-Poll-Review.aspx, accessed on January 9, 2010.

more to combat the Soviet Union and the spread of communism. As a result, he increased U.S. defense spending dramatically and expanded American involvement overseas. His efforts produced mixed results. He was ultimately able to reduce tensions with the Soviet Union by maintaining a dialogue with Nikita Khrushchev and pushing for a nuclear test ban treaty. He did not receive the total ban on nuclear testing that he desired, but his leadership did lead to the limited test ban treaty—the first such agreement in the Cold War. By the time of his assassination, U.S. relations with the Soviet Union were improved and there was considerable optimism they could get even better.

His handling of other Cold War issues highlights his efforts to meet the threat of communism while avoiding a nuclear war. In Cuba, Berlin, Laos, and Vietnam, he waged a struggle against communism. He deserves high marks for his handling of the Cuban missile crisis and using its aftermath to push for better relations with the Soviet Union. However, he should be justifiably criticized for the Bay of Pigs debacle and his efforts to overthrow Castro in the years that followed. The Bay of Pigs invasion revealed an unsure leader who vacillated over what to do, and his efforts to remove Castro show a vindictive leader who allowed his pride to interfere with him making sound decisions. Berlin and Laos had less clear outcomes. During the height of the Berlin crisis in the summer of 1961, he exaggerated the threat and raised American fears beyond what was necessary. However, by realizing that the communists' construction of the Berlin Wall actually mollified the situation, he rightly pledged to defend West Berlin but refrained from taking more assertive actions. In Laos, he inherited a very difficult situation and made the best of it by agreeing to accept a neutral government. He recognized the reality that neither the United States nor the Soviet Union had much influence there and it was not worth producing a crisis.

Kennedy took a different approach in Vietnam. Eisenhower had committed the United States to helping South Vietnam emerge as an independent, non-communist state by providing significant financial aid and almost 600 military advisers. Kennedy believed the United States needed to do more but struggled throughout his presidency to develop an effective strategy. He resisted early efforts by some to involve American military forces in combat operations, but he did decide to expand the U.S. role substantially. By the time of his assassination, the United States had over 16,000 military advisers in South Vietnam, and Kennedy had supported the overthrow of the

[3] C-SPAN 2009 Historians Presidential Leadership Survey, http://www.c-span.org/Presidential Survey/Overall-Ranking.aspx, accessed on January 9, 2010.

South Vietnamese government. While some have suggested that Kennedy would have withdrawn American forces from Vietnam after the 1964 election, there is little in the evidence to support this assertion. Kennedy typically did not make decisions without careful deliberations and before he had to. Neither one of the situations had occurred in November 1963.[4] What is certain is that the situation in Vietnam in November 1963 was much worse than what Kennedy inherited two and a half years earlier.

Kennedy implemented other policies related to the Cold War that made a lasting impact. Kennedy, more so than his predecessors and many of his successors, recognized that the appeal of communism was greatest in areas where people lived in poverty. He instituted the Alliance for Progress and the Peace Corps to help peoples from around the world improve their standard of living and resist the temptations of communism. The Peace Corps has become one of Kennedy's most enduring legacies. Since its inception, thousands of Americans have volunteered their time to serve in impoverished regions of the world to help the people who lived there. Whether it influenced the outcome of the Cold War is doubtful, but the program improved America's images in many nations. The Alliance for Progress was less successful. Kennedy devoted only a limited amount of attention to the program after launching it with great fanfare and, in the end, it only produced minimal results in Latin America.

His record at home is also mixed but generally favorable. Kennedy did not push his domestic agenda has heavily as his national security policies. As with the Alliance for Progress, it was not unusual for him to initiate programs with great rhetorical flourish and then leave it to others to push for their approval and implementation. He failed in his efforts to create government programs that would have provided hospital coverage for the elderly and more federal aid for education. In the neither case, despite large Democratic majorities in both the House of Representatives and the Senate, was he able to marshal the necessary votes for Congressional action. While he did have to deal with a significant number of conservative Democrats who resisted many of his policies, with more forceful leadership he could have accomplished more. Despite having average favorably ratings of over 70 percent throughout his presidency, he never put his full political weight behind these issues.[5]

---

[4] Sorensen, *Counselor*, p. 357.

[5] Jeffrey M. Jones, "Despite Recent Lows, Bush Approval Average Is Midrange: Extreme High and Low Ratings Characterize Bush Presidency," January 5, 2009, http://www.gallup.com/poll/113641/Despite-Recent-Lows-Bush-Approval-Average-Midrange.aspx, accessed on January 9, 2010.

Kennedy had more success on other domestic issues, including increasing the minimum wage, expanding federal aid for underdeveloped regions of the country, and making it easier for American families to buy a home. He also deserves credit for leading the country out of the recession he inherited and fighting for an economic program that benefited the United States greatly in the mid-1960s. While he did not obtain all he wanted in any of these programs, they were significant nevertheless. He was able to persuade Congress to expand the minimum wage by 25% and to expand the number of workers eligible to receive it. His programs to help Americans by a new home or escape poverty marked a positive step for many. Finally, his economic policies, especially the tax cut program that he had initiated by the time of his death, helped the economy prosper and bring down unemployment during the early years of the Johnson administration.

The most difficult domestic issue during the Kennedy administration to evaluate is civil rights. Kennedy spoke loudly and often during the 1960 campaign in support of expanding civil rights for black Americans. Yet, before the summer of 1963, he seldom took any sort of strong position for black Americans. While he did issue a series of executive orders that brought some progress, he did not make civil rights legislation a priority. He only reluctantly involved his administration in crises over the Freedom Rides in Alabama and the University of Mississippi's resistance to desegregation in 1961 and 1962. It was only after the outbreak of violence in Birmingham in the spring of 1963 that he began to take a more personal interest in the plight of black Americans. Beginning in June 1963, he became a stronger advocate and proposed significant civil rights legislation. However, he had accomplished relatively little for a group to whom he had promised so much. He deserves credit for laying the foundation of the 1964 Civil Rights Act, but that praise needs to be tempered by his lack of action throughout most of his presidency.

No evaluation of Kennedy can be complete without accounting for several serious character flaws. No man or woman is perfect, but the Camelot myth surrounding Kennedy made it seem like he was.[6] Almost all pictures show him looking like he was in the prime of health. Prior to his presidency he experienced several health crises, but Kennedy and his family were able to hide their seriousness. During the campaign, they repeatedly denied charges he had Addison's disease or any other illness that would have impaired his ability

[6] Theodore White first used the term Camelot to describe the Kennedy family and White House in an article published in *Life* magazine a few weeks after Kennedy's death. For background on the article and excerpts from it, see http://www.jfklancer.com/pdf/Camelot.pdf, accessed on January 9, 2010.

to be president. While it is debatable whether Kennedy's illnesses or injuries affected him as president, his blanket denials about any health problems point to a lack honesty and trust. Further, and more seriously, to cope with his Addison's disease and the discomfort from his back injury, he resorted to taking numerous medications. During his time in office, the president typically took seven prescription medicines daily and was treated by several different doctors often without the others' knowledge. One of the doctors, Dr. Max Jacobson, was nicknamed "Dr. Feelgood" because of his various prescription cocktails that almost always included doses of amphetamines.[7] While it is impossible to know how Kennedy's drug use influenced his actions and decision-making, it is very scary to know that the only American with the ability to start a nuclear war on his own may have been under the influence of medication or other drugs while making life and death decisions.

The pictures of the Kennedy family always showed smiling children and a thriving home life. While there is little question that Kennedy loved his children, he was unfaithful to his wife, as since his teenage years, Kennedy had always enjoyed the company of women, and this behavior did not stop when he got married.[8] His reckless behavior cannot be justified. When Kennedy's personal life is included in the discussion of his overall effectiveness as president, it makes the evaluation more difficult. It is almost impossible to determine to what degree Kennedy's health issues, drug use, and philandering affected his presidency, but they do raise legitimate questions.

How effective was Kennedy as president? Without question, the country benefited from his leadership in many ways. The New Frontier was inspirational. His economic policies led to unprecedented growth, and he skillfully led the country through the Cuban missile crisis. Additionally, while he was not always as assertive as he should have been, his final commitment to civil rights led to legislation that was long overdue. However, these benefits have to be balanced with his ineffective leadership (and Congress's reluctance) on issues like hospital care for the elderly and federal aid for public education. Furthermore, his personal missteps cannot be ignored. Finally, any evaluation has to take into count that Kennedy served less than three years in office. His assassination devastated the country and prevented him from completing what

---

[7] James Giglio, "The Medical Afflictions of President John F. Kennedy." *White House Studies* 6:4 (Fall 2006), pp. 343-55. See also Dallek, *An Unfinished Life*, pp. 398-99, 408, 471-72, and 581-82.

[8] See Mark J. White, "Behind Closed Doors: The Private Life of a Public Man," in Mark J. White, ed., *Kennedy: The New Frontier* (Washington Square, NY: New York University Press, 1998), pp. 258 and 270-72; Giglio, *The Presidency of John F. Kennedy*, pp. 267-69; and Dallek, *An Unfinished Life*, pp. 475-80.

he had started. In the end, Kennedy should be remembered as a fairly effective president who potentially could have done much more if not for his own character flaws and his unwillingness to fight for some programs that his rhetoric indicated were important to him and to his nation.

BIBLIOGRAPHY

MAJOR COLLECTIONS OF PRIMARY SOURCES

John F. Kennedy Library and Museum, Boston, MA
- Archive and Manuscript Collections
- National Security Files
- Papers of Individuals and Organizations
- Pre-Presidential Papers
- President's Office Files
- White House Staff Files

Newspapers

Chicago Tribune
Christian Science Monitor
Los Angeles Times
New York Times
Wall Street Journal
Washington Post and Times Herald

Published Primary Sources

A Presidential Legacy and the Warren Commission. Nashville, TN: Flatsigned Press, 2007.

Brugioni, Dino A. *Eyeball to Eyeball: The Inside Story of the Cuban Missile Crisis*. New York: Random House, 1991.

Bundy, McGeorge. *Danger and Survival: Choices about the Bomb in the First Fifty Years*. New York: Random House, 1988.

Dallek, Robert, and Terry Golway, eds. *Let Every Nation Know: John F. Kennedy in His Own Words*. Naperville, IL: Sourcebooks Media Fusion, 2006.

Donald, Aïda DiPace, ed. *John F. Kennedy and the New Frontier*. New York: Hill and Wang, 1966.

Eisenhower, Dwight D. *Waging Peace: The White House Years, 1956-1961*. Garden City, NY: Doubleday & Company, Inc., 1965.

Estimative Products on Vietnam, 1948-1975. Pittsburgh, PA: National Intelligence Council and the Government Printing Office, 2005.

Executive Orders of President John F. Kennedy, www.lib.umich.edu/govdocs/jfkeo.html.

Ferrell, Robert H., ed. *Off the Record: The Private Papers of Harry S. Truman*. New York: Penguin Books, 1980.

Foreign Relations of the United States, 1961-1963. Multiple Volumes. Washington, D.C.: U.S. Government Printing Office, multiple dates. http://www.state.gov/r/pa/ho/frus/kennedyjf/index.htm

Gavin, James M. *War and Peace in the Space Age*. New York: Harper, 1958.

Goodwin, Richard N. *Remembering America: A Voice from the Sixties*. Boston: Little, Brown and Company, 1988.

Harris, Seymour E. *Economics of the Kennedy Years and a Look Ahead*. New York: Harper & Row, Publishers, 1964.

Kennedy, John F. *Profiles in Courage*. New York: Harper & Row, 1956.

_____. *While England Slept*. New York: Wilfred Funk, Inc., 1940.

Kennedy, Joseph P. *Hostage to Fortune: The Letters of Joseph P. Kennedy*. Edited by Amanda Smith. New York: Viking, 2001.

Logsdon, John M. Logsdon, ed. *Exploring the Unknown: Selected Documents in the History of the U.S. Civil Space Program*, Volume 1: *Organizing for Exploration*. Washington, D.C.: National Aeronautical and Space Administration, 1995.

Martin, Edwin McCammon. *Kennedy and Latin America*. New York: University Press of America, 1994.

May, Ernest R., and Philip D. Zelikow, eds. *The Kennedy Tapes: Inside the White House During the Cuban Missile Crisis*. New York: W. W. Norton & Company, 2002.

McNamara, Robert S., James C. Blight, and Robert K. Brigham. *Argument Without End: In Search of Answers to the Vietnam Tragedy*. New York: Public Affairs, 1999.

Neustadt, Richard E. *Report to JFK: The Skybolt Crisis in Perspective*. Ithaca, NY: Cornell University Press, 1999.

New Frontiers of the Kennedy Administration: The Texts of the Task Force Reports Prepared for the President. Washington, D.C.: Public Affairs Press, 1961.

1960 Campaign Speeches of Senator John F. Kennedy and Vice President Richard M. Nixon, http://www.jfklink.com/html/speeches.html.

Nixon, Richard M. *Six Crises*. Garden City, NY: Doubleday & Company, Inc., 1962.

O'Donnell, Kenneth P. and David F. Power. *"Johnny, We Hardly Knew Ye": Memories of John Fitzgerald Kennedy*. Boston, MA: Little, Brown and Company, 1970.

Public Papers of the Presidents, Dwight D. Eisenhower, http://www.presidency.ucsb.edu/ws/.

Public Papers of the Presidents, John F. Kennedy, http://www.presidency.ucsb.edu/ws/.

Salinger, Pierre. *With Kennedy*. Garden City, NY: Doubleday & Company, Inc., 1966.

Schlesinger, Arthur M. *Journals: 1952-2000*. Edited by Andrew and Stephen Schlesinger. New York: Penguin Press, 2007.

Seaborg, Glenn T. *Kennedy, Khrushchev, and the Test Ban*. Berkeley, CA: University of California Press, 1981.

Shriver, Sargent. *Point of the Lance*. New York: Harper & Row, Publishers, 1963.

Sorenson, Ted. *Counselor: A Life at the Edge of History*. New York: Harper, 2008.

Summary of the Three Year Kennedy Record (Legislation), www.jfklibrary.org/jfk_leg_record.html.

Swanson, Glen E., ed. *"Before This Decade Is Out..": Personal Reflections on the Apollo Program*. Washington, D.C.: National Aeronautics and Space Administration, NASA History Office, Office of Policy and Plans, 1999.

Tayler, Maxwell D. *The Uncertain Trumpet*. New York: Harper, 1960.

The National Security Archive, The George Washington University, Washington, D.C., http://www.gwu.edu/~nsarchiv/.

The Statistical History of the United States: From Colonial Times to the Present. New York: Basic Books, 1976.

Wofford, Harris. *Of Kennedys & Kings: Making Sense of the Sixties.* Pittsburgh, PA: University of Pittsburgh Press, 1992.

Secondary Sources

Adams, Velma. *The Peace Corps in Action.* Chicago, IL: Follett Publishing Company, 1968.

Ambrose, Stephen E. *Eisenhower*, Volume 2: *The President.* New York: Simon and Schuster, 1984.

_____. *Nixon: The Education of a Politician, 1913-1962.* New York: Simon and Schuster, 1987.

Anderson, Christopher. *Jack and Jackie: Portrait of An American Marriage.* New York: William Morrow and Company, Inc., 1996.

Balmer, Randall. *God in the White House: How Faith Shaped the Presidency from John F. Kennedy to George W. Bush.* New York: HarperOne, 2008.

Benson, Thomas W. *Writing JFK: Presidential Rhetoric and the Press in the Bay of Pigs Crisis.* College Station, TX: Texas A&M University Press, 2004.

Berg, Manfred, and Andreas Etges, eds. *John F. Kennedy and the 'Thousand Days': New Perspectives on the Foreign and Domestic Policies of the Kennedy Administration.* Heidelberg, Germany: Universitätsverlag, 2007.

Berkowitz, Edward D. "The Politics of Mental Retardation During the Kennedy Administration." *Social Science Quarterly* 61:1 (June 1980): 128-143.

Bernstein, Irving. *Promises Kept: John F. Kennedy's New Frontier.* New York: Oxford University Press, 1991.

Beschloss, Michael R. *The Crisis Years: Kennedy and Khrushchev, 1960-1963.* New York: Edward Burlingham Books, 1991.

Blair, Anne E. *Lodge in Vietnam: A Patriot Abroad.* New Haven, CT: Yale University Press, 1995.

Bly, Nellie. *The Kennedy Men: Three Generations of Sex, Scandal and Secrets.* New York: Kensington Books, 1996.

Bohning, Don. *The Castro Obsession: U.S. Covert Operations Against Cuba, 1959-1965.* Washington, D.C.: Potomac Books, Inc., 2005.

Borstelmanm, Thomas. "'Hedging Our Bets and Buying Time': John Kennedy and Racial Revolutions in the American South and Southern Africa." *Diplomatic History* 24:3 (Summer 2000): 435-463.

Bostdorff, Denise M., and Daniel J. O'Rourke. "The Presidency and the Promotion of Domestic Crisis: John Kennedy's Management of the 1962 Steel Crisis." *Presidential Studies Quarterly* 27:2 (Spring 1997): 343-362.

Brauer, Carl M. "Kennedy, Johnson, and the War on Poverty." *Journal of American History*. 69:1 (June 1982): 98-119.

Bryant, Nick. *The Bystander: John F. Kennedy and the Struggle for Black Equality*. New York: Basic Books, 2006.

Burner, David. *John F. Kennedy and a New Generation*, 2nd ed. New York: Pearson-Longman, 2005.

Canterbery, E. Ray. *Economics on a New Frontier*. Belmont, CA: Wadsworth Publishing Company, Inc., 1968.

Caro, Robert A. *Master of the Senate: The Years of Lyndon Johnson*. New York: Alfred A. Knopf, 2002.

Carty, Thomas J. *A Catholic in the White House? Religion, Politics, and John F. Kennedy's Presidential Campaign*. New York: Palgrave Macmillan, 2008.

Chalmers, David. *And the Crooked Places Made Straight: The Struggle for Social Change in the 1960s*. 2nd Ed. Baltimore, MD: Johns Hopkins University Press, 1996.

Cohen, Warren I. *The Cambridge History of American Foreign Relations*, Volume IV: *America in the Age of Soviet Power, 1945-1991*. New York: Cambridge University Press, 1993.

Dallek, Robert. *An Unfinished Life: John F. Kennedy, 1917-1963*. Boston, MA: Little, Brown, and Company, 2004.

DeWitt, John. "The Alliance for Progress: Economic Warfare in Brazil (1962-1964)." *Journal of Third World Studies* 26:1 (Spring 2009): 57-76.

Divine, Robert A. *Foreign Policy and U.S. Presidential Election: 1952 1960*. New York: New Viewpoints, 1974.

Dobbs, Michael. *One Minute to Midnight: Kennedy, Khrushchev, and Castro on the Brink of Nuclear War*. New York: Knopf, 2008.

Donaldson, Gary A. *The First Modern Campaign: Kennedy, Nixon, and the Election of 1960*. Lanham, MD: Rowman & Littlefield Publishers, Inc., 2007.

Donovan, Robert J. *PT 109: John F. Kennedy in World War II*. New York: McGraw-Hill, 1961.

Dudziak, Mary L. *Cold War Civil Rights: Race and the Image of American Democracy*. Princeton, NJ: Princeton University Press, 2000.

Erskine, Hazel Gaudet. "The Polls: Kennedy as President." *The Public Opinion Quarterly* 28:2 (Summer 1964): 334-42.

Fairlie, Henry. *The Kennedy Promise: The Politics of Expectation*. New York: Doubleday & Company, Inc., 1973.

Freedman, Lawrence. *Kennedy's Wars: Berlin, Cuba, Laos, and Vietnam*. New York: Oxford University Press, 2000.

Fursenko, Aleksandr, and Timothy Naftali. *Khrushchev's Cold War: The Inside Story of an American Adversary*. New York: W. W. Norton & Company, 2006.

_____. *"One Hell of a Gamble": Khrushchev, Castro, and Kennedy, 1958-1964*. New York: W. W. Norton & Company, 1997.

Giauque, Jeffrey Glenn. *Grand Designs and Visions of Unity: The Atlantic Powers and the Reorganization of Western Europe, 1955-1963*. Chapel Hill, NC: University of North Carolina Press, 2002.

Gibbs, Nancy, and Michael Duffy. *The Preacher and the President: Billy Graham in the White House*. New York: Center Street, 2007.

Giglio, James N. *The Presidency of John F. Kennedy*. Lawrence, KS: University Press of Kansas, 1991.

_____. *The Presidency of John F. Kennedy*, 2nd Ed. Lawrence, KS: University Press of Kansas, 2006.

_____. "The Medical Afflictions of President John F. Kennedy." *White House Studies* 6:4 (Fall 2006): 343-358.

Gil, Federico G. *Latin American-United States Relations*. New York: Harcourt Brace Jovanovich, Inc., 1971.

Graham, Hugh Davis. *The Uncertain Triumph: Federal Education Policy in the Kennedy and Johnson Years*. Chapel Hill, NC: University of North Carolina Press, 1984.

Greene, Benjamin P. *Eisenhower, Science Advice, and the Nuclear Test-Ban Debate, 1945-1963*. Stanford, CA: Stanford University Press, 2007.

Grow, Michael. *U.S. Presidents and Latin American Interventions: Pursuing Regime Change in the Cold War*. Lawrence, KS: University Press of Kansas, 2008.

Halberstam, David. *The Making of a Quagmire: America and Vietnam during the Kennedy Era*. Revised edition. Lanham, MD: Rowman & Littlefield Publishers, Inc., 2008.

Harper, Paul, and Joann P. Krieg, eds. *John F. Kennedy: The Promise Revisited*. New York: Greenwood Press, 1988.

Harrison, Cynthia E. "A 'New Frontier' for Women: The Public Policy of the Kennedy Administration." *The Journal of American History* 67:3 (December 1980): 630-646.

Hart, Robert A. "Failed Spine Surgery Syndrome in the Life and Career of John Fitzgerald Kennedy." *The Journal of Bone and Joint Surgery* 88A:5 (May 2006): 1141-1148.

Heath, Jim F. *Decade of Disillusionment: The Kennedy-Johnson Years*. Bloomington, IN: Indiana University Press, 1975.

_____. *John F. Kennedy and the Business Community*. Chicago, IL: The University of Chicago Press, 1969.

Herring, George C. *America's Longest War: The United States and Vietnam, 1950-1975*, 3rd Ed. New York: McGraw-Hill, Inc., 1996.

Heymann, C. David. *R.F.K.: A Candid Biography of Robert F. Kennedy*. London, England: Heinemann, 1998.

Hoffman, Elizabeth Cobbs. *All You Need Is Love: The Peace Corps and the Spirit of the 1960s*. Cambridge, MA: Harvard University Press, 1998.

Hoopes, Roy, ed. *The Peace Corps Experience*. New York: Clarkson N. Potter, Inc., Publisher, 1968.

_____. *The Complete Peace Corps Guide*. New York: The Dial Press, 1966.

Howard-Pitney, David. *Martin Luther King, Jr., Malcolm X, and the Civil Rights Struggles of the 1950s and 1960s: A Brief History with Documents*. Boston, MA: Bedford/St. Martin's, 2004.

Immerman, Richard H., and Robert R. Bowie. *Waging Peace: How Eisenhower Shaped an Enduring Cold War Strategy*. New York: Oxford University Press, 1998.

Jacobs, Seth. *Cold War Mandarin: Ngo Dinh Diem and the Origins of America's War in Vietnam, 1950-1963*. Lanham, MD: Rowman & Littlefield Publishers, Inc., 2006.

Jones, Howard. *The Bay of Pigs*. New York: Oxford University Press, 2008.

Kaiser, David. *American Tragedy: Kennedy, Johnson, and the Origins of the Vietnam War*. Cambridge, MA: The Belknap Press of Harvard University Press, 2000.

_____. *The Road to Dallas: The Assassination of John F. Kennedy*. Cambridge, MA: The Belknap Press of Harvard University Press, 2009.

Kaufman, Burton I. "John F. Kennedy as World Leader: A Perspective on the Literature." *Diplomatic History* 17:3 (Summer 1993): 447-469.

Kaufmann, James L. *Selling Outer Space: Kennedy, the Media, and Funding for Project Apollo, 1961-1963*. Tuscaloosa, AL: The University of Alabama Press, 1994.

Kenen, Peter B. "Measuring the United States Balance of Payments." *The Review of Economics and Statistics* 46:2 (May 1964): 39-44.

Kessler, Ronald. *The Sins of the Father: Joseph P. Kennedy and the Dynasty He Founded.* New York: Warner Books, 1996.

Kilpatrick, Carroll. "The Kennedy Style and Congress." *The Virginia Quarterly Review* 39:1 (Winter 1963): 1-11.

Kochavi, Noam. *A Conflict Perpetuated: China Policy During the Kennedy Years.* Westport, CT: Praeger, 2002.

LaFeber, Walter. *The American Age: United States Foreign Policy at Home and Abroad Since 1750.* New York: W. W. Norton & Company, 1989.

Lambright, W. Henry. *Powering Apollo: James Webb of NASA.* Baltimore, MD: The Johns Hopkins University Press, 1995.

Lasky, Victor. *J.F.K.: The Man & The Myth.* New York: The MacMillan Company, 1963.

Latham, Michael E. *Modernization as Ideology: American Social Science and "Nation Building" in the Kennedy Era.* Chapel Hill, NC: University of North Carolina Press, 2000.

Launius, Roger D., and Howard E. McCurdy, eds. *Spaceflight and the Myth of Presidential Leadership.* Urbana, IL: University of Illinois Press, 1997.

Launius, Roger D. "Kennedy's Space Policy Reconsidered: A Post-Cold War Perspective." *Air Power History* 50:4 (Winter 2003): 16-29.

Leamer, Laurence. *The Kennedy Men: 1901-1963.* New York: William Morrow, 2001.

Leffler, Melvyn P. *For the Soul of Mankind: The United States, the Soviet Union, and the Cold War.* New York: Hill and Wang, 2007.

_____. *A Preponderance of Power: National Security, the Truman Administration, and the Cold War.* Stanford, CA: Stanford University Press, 1992.

Logsdon, John M. *The Decision to Go to the Moon: Project Apollo and the National Interest.* Cambridge, MA: The MIT Press, 1970.

Mahan, Erin R. *Kennedy, De Gaulle, and Western Europe.* New York: Palgrave Macmillan, 2002.

Maier, Thomas. *The Kennedys: America's Emerald Kings.* New York: Basic Books, 2003.

Matthews, Christopher J. *Kennedy & Nixon: The Rivalry that Shaped Postwar America.* New York: Simon & Schuster, 1996.

McDougall, Walter A. *...the Heavens and the Earth: A Political History of the Space Age.* New York: Basic Books, Inc., Publishers, 1985.

McQuaid, Kim. *Big Business and Presidential Power: From FDR to Reagan.* New York: William Morrow and Company, Inc., 1982.

Miroff, Bruce. *Icons of Democracy: American Leaders as Heroes, Aristocrats, Dissenters, and Democrats*. New York: Basic Books, 1993.

_____ . *Pragmatic Illusions: The Presidential Politics of John F. Kennedy.* New York: David McKay Company, Inc., 1976.

Munton, Don, and David A. Welch. *The Cuban Missile Crisis: A Concise History*. New York: Oxford University Press, 2007.

Nash, Philip. *The Other Missiles of October: Eisenhower, Kennedy, and the Jupiters, 1957-1963*. Chapel Hill, NC: University of North Carolina Press, 1997.

_____. "Nuclear Weapons in Kennedy's Foreign Policy." *Historian* 56:2 (Winter 1994): 285-300.

Neustadt, Richard E. "Kennedy in the Presidency: A Premature Appraisal." *Political Science Quarterly*, 79:3 (September 1964): 321-334.

Nichols, David A. *A Matter of Justice: Eisenhower and the Beginning of the Civil Rights Revolution*. New York: Simon & Schuster, 2008.

Niven, David. *The Politics of Injustice: The Kennedys, the Freedom Rides, and the Electoral Consequences of a Moral Compromise*. Knoxville, TN: The University of Tennessee Press, 2003.

Oliver, Kendrick, *Kennedy, Macmillan, and the Test-Ban Debate, 1961-1963.* New York: St. Martin's Press, 1998.

Olsen, James C. *Stuart Symington: A Life*. Columbia, MO: University of Missouri Press, 2003.

Paper, Lawrence J. *The Promise and the Performance: The Leadership of John F. Kennedy*. New York: Crown Publishers, Inc., 1975.

Parmet, Herbert S. *JFK: The Presidency of John F. Kennedy*. New York: The Dial Press, 1983.

Pauley, Garth E. *The Modern Presidency and Civil Rights: Rhetoric on Race from Roosevelt to Nixon*. College Station, TX: Texas A&M University Press, 2001.

Pearce, Kimber Charles. *Rostow, Kennedy, and the Rhetoric of Foreign Aid.* East Lansing, MI: Michigan State University Press, 2001.

Pechman, Joseph A. "Individual Income Tax Provisions of the Revenue act of 1964." *The Journal of Finance*. 20:2 (May 1965): 247-72.

Pietrusza, David. *1960--LBJ vs. JFK vs. Nixon: The Epic Campaign That Forged Three Presidencies*. New York: Union Square Press, 2008.

Plotkin, Stephen. "Sixty Years Later, the Story of PT-109 Still Captivates." *Prologue,* 35:2 (Summer 2003), http://www.archives.gov/publications/prologue/2003/summer/pt109.html.

Polmar, Norman, and John D. Gresham. *DEFCON-2: Standing on the Brink of Nuclear War During the Cuban Missile Crisis*. New York: John Wiley & Sons, 2006.

Posner, Gerald L. *Case Closed: Lee Harvey Oswald and the Assassination of JFK*. New York: Random House, 1993.

Prachowny, Martin F. J. *The Kennedy-Johnson Tax Cut: A Revisionist History*. Northhampton, MA: Edward Elgar, 2000.

Preble, Christopher A. *John F. Kennedy and the Missile Gap*. DeKalb, IL: Northern Illinois University Press, 2004.

Rabe, Stephen G. *Eisenhower and Latin America: The Foreign Policy of Anticommunism*. Chapel Hill, NC: The University of North Carolina Press, 1988.

_____. *The Most Dangerous Area in the World: John F. Kennedy Confronts Communist Revolution in Latin America*. Chapel Hill, NC: The University of North Carolina Press, 1999.

_____. "After the Missiles of October: John F. Kennedy and Cuba, November 1962 to November 1963." *Presidential Studies Quarterly* 30:4 (December 2000): 714-726.

Reeves, Richard. *President Kennedy: Profile of Power*. New York: Simon & Schuster, 1993.

Reeves, Thomas C. *A Question of Character: A Life of John F. Kennedy*. New York: The Free Press, 1991.

Rice, Gerard T. *The Bold Experiment JFK's Peace Corps*. Notre Dame, IN: University of Notre Dame Press, 1985.

Rorabaugh, W. J. *Kennedy and the Promise of the Sixties*. New York: Cambridge University Press, 2002.

_____. *The Real Making of the President: Kennedy, Nixon, and the 1960 Election*. Lawrence, KS: University Press of Kansas, 2009.

Rosenberg, David Allen. "The Origins of Overkill: Nuclear Weapons and American Strategy, 1945-1960." *International Security* 7:4 (Spring 1983): 3-71.

Rosenberg, Jonathan and Zachary Karabell. *Kennedy, Johnson, and the Quest for Justice: The Civil Rights Tapes*. New York: W. W. Norton & Company, 2003.

Rust, William J. *Kennedy in Vietnam: American Vietnam Policy, 1960-63*. New York: Scribner, 1985.

Scheman, L. Ronald, ed. *The Alliance for Progress: A Retrospective*. New York: Praeger, 1988.

Schlesinger, Arthur M., Jr. *Robert Kennedy and His Times*. New York: Ballantine Books, 1978.

Schlesinger, Arthur M., Jr., ed. *History of American Presidential Elections, 1789-1968*, Volume IV. New York: Chelsea House Publishers, 1971.

Shank, Alan. *Presidential Policy Leadership: Kennedy and Social Welfare*. Lanham, MD: University Press of America, 1980.

Sitkoff, Harvard. *The Struggle for Black Equality*. Revised Edition. New York: Hill and Wang, 1993.

Sloan, John W. *Eisenhower and the Management of Prosperity*. Lawrence, KS: The University Press of Kansas, 1991.

Smith, Peter H. *Talons of the Eagle: Dynamics of U.S. Latin American Relations*. New York: Oxford University Press, 1996.

Smyser, W.R. *Kennedy and the Berlin Wall: "A Hell of a Lot Better than a War"*. Lanham, MD: Rowman & Littlefield Publishers, 2009.

Snead, David L. *The Gaither Committee, Eisenhower, and the Cold War*. Columbus, OH: Ohio State University Press, 1999.

Spector, Ronald H. *Advice and Support: The Early Years of the U.S. Army in Vietnam, 1941-1960*. New York: The Free Press, 1985.

Stern, Mark. *Calculating Visions: Kennedy, Johnson, and Civil Rights*. New Brunswick, NJ: Rutgers University Press, 1992.

_____. "Eisenhower and Kennedy: A Comparison of Confrontations at Little Rock and Ole Miss." *Policy Studies Journal* 21:3 (Autumn 1993): 575-588.

Stern, Sheldon M. *Averting 'The Final Failure': John F. Kennedy and the Secret Cuban Missile Crisis Meetings*. Stanford, CA: Stanford University Press, 2003.

Stossel, Scott. *Sarge: The Life and Times of Sargent Shriver*. Washington, D.C.: Smithsonian Books, 2004.

Strober, Deborah Hart, and Gerald S. Strober. *The Kennedy Presidency: An Oral History of the Era*. Revised Edition. Washington, D.C.: Brassey's, Inc., 2003.

Taffet, Jeffrey F. *Foreign Aid as Foreign Policy: The Alliance for Progress in Latin America*. New York: Routledge, 2007.

Talbot, David. *Brothers: The Hidden History of the Kennedy Years*. New York: Free Press, 2007.

Trachtenberg, Marc A. *A Constructed Peace: The Making of the European Settlement, 1946-1963*. Princeton, NJ: Princeton University Press, 1999.

Tucker, Spencer C., ed. *The Encyclopedia of the Vietnam War: A Political, Social, and Military History*. New York: Oxford University Press, 1998.

Unger, Irwin. *The Best of Intentions: The Triumph and Failure of the Great Society Under Kennedy, Johnson, and Nixon*. New York: Doubleday, 1996.

Wenger, Andreas, and Marcel Gerber. "John F. Kennedy and the Limited Test Ban Treaty: A Case Study of Presidential Leadership." *Presidential Studies Quarterly* 29:2 (June 1999): 460-487.

Whalen, Richard J. *Founding Father: The Story of Joseph P. Kennedy*. New York: New American Library, 1964.

White, Mark J., ed. *Kennedy: The New Frontier Revisited*. New York: New York University Press, 1998.

Williams, Robert J., and David A. Kershaw. "Kennedy and Congress: The Struggle for the New Frontier." *Political Studies* 27:3 (September 1979): 390-404.

Zelman, Patricia G. *Women, Work, and Policy: The Kennedy-Johnson Years*. Ann Arbor, MI: UMI Research Press, 1982.

INDEX

A

B

C

D

G

H

I

J

K

L

M

N

O

P

Q

R

S

T